THE CRAFT OF RELIGIOUS STUDIES

The Craft of Religious Studies

Edited by

Jon R. Stone
University of California, Berkeley

palgrave

THE CRAFT OF RELIGIOUS STUDIES
Copyright © Jon R. Stone, 2000.
All rights reserved. Printed in the United States of America. No part
of this book may be used or reproduced in any manner whatsoever
without written permission except in the case of brief quotations
embodied in critical articles or reviews.

First published in hardcover in Great Britain 1998 by
MACMILLAN PRESS LTD

First published in hardcover in the United States of America 1998
by ST. MARTIN'S PRESS, INC.

First paperback edition published 2000 by
PALGRAVE™
175 Fifth Avenue, New York, N.Y. 10010 and
Houndmills, Basingstoke, Hampshire, England RG21 6XS
Companies and representatives throughout the world.

PALGRAVE™ is the new global publishing imprint of
St. Martin's Press LLC Scholarly and Reference Division
and Palgrave Publishers Ltd (formerly Macmillan Press Ltd).

ISBN 0-312-23887-8 (paperback)

Library of Congress Cataloging-in-Publication Data
available upon request from the Library of Congress.

Transferred to digital printing 2006

First paperback edition: December, 2000
10 9 8 7 6 5 4 3

In honor of my grandparents

Irene Timme

and

Curtis and Lois Stone

whose lives exemplify all that is true, beautiful, lovely,
and good

Contents

Preface

The idea for a collection of autobiographical essays on methodological issues in the academic study of religion had its origins in 1988 when, in preparation for my doctoral exams, I was reading Phillip E. Hammond's classic edited volume, *Sociologists at Work*. While, I must confess, most of the chapters in that book bored me, the thought of gathering together a set of essays by senior scholars whose work in religious studies had defined the field had fired my imagination. It was not until 1992, however, while I was teaching at the University of Northern Iowa, that this present volume began to take definite shape.

Late that autumn, Martin E. Marty had been in town for a series of public lectures and it had fallen to me, the most junior member of my department, to take Marty to the nearest airport very early the next morning – well before roosters yawn. While we waited for his flight and sipped lukewarm vending machine tea, I shared my book idea with this sleepy Chicago historian. To my surprise, Marty liked the concept and volunteered to be its first contributor. That next afternoon, I wrote to over 20 other senior scholars asking if they might be likewise interested. Most declined my invitation but, by that next spring, I had added Ninian Smart, Rodney Stark, Jacob Neusner, and Edith Wyschogrod to my list of potential essayists.

In November 1993, after taking up residence as a research fellow at UC Santa Barbara's Center for the Study of Religion, I received a small 'seed' grant from the Lilly Endowment to commission four pilot essays with the promise that if this sampling attracted a publisher, then Lilly would generously fund the remaining 11 to 12 projected essays. After a few false starts and a number of rejections from university publishing houses ('we like the idea but we don't think it will sell'), Macmillan UK/St. Martin's Press kindly awarded a publishing contract. Then, after Lilly provided the promised funding, the remaining 11 essays were quickly commissioned. While most of the contributors finished their first drafts and (multiple) revisions in an amazingly brief time, unfortunate illnesses and an avalanche of other commitments forced the withdrawal of Charles Long and Jonathan Z. Smith.

From the outset, I decided that this would not be a 'Who's Who in Religious Studies' volume but that the contributors would be representative of the methodological diversity of the field, that they would favor interdisciplinary conversation, and, most importantly, that they would have something interesting to teach us about the academic study of religion. Happily, the essays have been as enlightening and methodologically instructive as they have been delightful to read. And while the contributions in this volume are by no means definitive – the last word on how to approach the study of religion – at the very least, it is hoped, this collection of autobiographical essays should initiate fruitful and continuing discussion on methodological issues within the field more generally.

Among the many friends and colleagues who provided encouragement and (sometimes) helpful advice along the way, I would especially like to thank Edward Amend, Katherine Baker, Eileen Barker, John and Carrie Birmingham, Michael A. Burdick, Walter H. Capps, Jonathan Cordero, Phillip E. Hammond, Helen Harrington, Benton Johnson, Jacob Neusner, Casey and Kathy Roberts, Wade Clark Roof, Bryan R. Wilson, and the original pilot essayists: Martin E. Marty, Ninian Smart, Rodney Stark, and Edith Wyschogrod. I would also like to thank Craig Dykstra of the Lilly Endowment for his generous support, Tim Farmiloe, Annabelle Buckley and Charmian Hearne at Macmillan UK for shepherding this project 'through the valley of the shadow of death', Maura Burnett at St. Martin's Press for her keen and invaluable advice, Sara Duke at the Center for her tireless efforts on my behalf, Jeanie Cornet and Jan Jacobson at UCSB's CORI office for saving me from bureaucratic pitfalls, and Richard Callahan for compiling the index.

In addition to those mentioned above, I must acknowledge the unfailing support of my parents, Robert and Bobbie Jean Stone, and of my brothers and their wives, Richard and Dawn Stone and David and Mary Stone, along with my nieces and nephews, Lauren, Shawna, Christopher, Brenton, Zachary, and Bethany. While I may give pretense to being an ivory tower scholar, the boys and girls on Santa Barbara High School's junior varsity water polo and swimming teams, whom I coached from 1994 to 1997, knew better. I want to thank them for alleviating the frustration of one task by adding the joyful frustration of another. As always, my dedications go to those whom I love most in this world; thus, in the case of this book, I would like to honor my grandparents: Irene Timme and Curtis and Lois Stone.

Servata Fides Cineri.

JON R. STONE
University of California, Berkeley

Notes on the Contributors

Wendy Doniger is the Mircea Eliade Distinguished Service Professor of the History of Religions at the University of Chicago. She has been elected President of both the American Academy of Religion and the Association of Asian Studies, and is the author of over a dozen books and 150 articles.

Andrew M. Greeley is Professor of Social Science at the University of Chicago and a Visiting Professor of Sociology at the University of Arizona and at the University of Cologne. He is also an honorary senior fellow at University College Dublin. He is a priest of the Archdiocese of Chicago, and has written mysteries, science fiction and full-scale novels.

Giles Gunn, currently Professor of English at the University of California, Santa Barbara, is the author and editor of a variety of books which include, most recently, *Thinking Across the American Grain: Ideology, Intellect, and the New Pragmatism* and the anthologies *Redrawing the Boundaries: the Transformation of English and American Literary Studies* and *Early American Writing*.

Phillip E. Hammond is the D. Mackenzie Brown Professor of Religious Studies and Sociology at the University of California, Santa Barbara. He received a Ph.D. in Sociology from Columbia University in 1960 and taught at Yale, Wisconsin, and Arizona before going to Santa Barbara in 1978. His latest book is entitled *From Toleration to Liberty: an Essay on Religion and Conscience*.

John Hick was educated at Edinburgh and Oxford Universities, and has taught the philosophy of religion in both Britain and the United States. He is the author of a number of books, various of which have been translated into 11 languages. His Gifford Lectures, 'An Interpretation of Religion', received the Grawemeyer Award in Religion for 1991.

Martin E. Marty is the Fairfax M. Cone Distinguished Service Professor at the University of Chicago, Director of the Public

Religion Project, Senior Editor of *The Christian Century*, and the George B. Caldwell Senior Scholar in Residence at the Park Ridge Center for the Study of Health, Faith and Ethics. The most recent of his 50 books are *The One and the Many: America's Struggle for the Common Good* (Harvard) and *Under God, Indivisible*, Volume III in his *Modern American Religion* (University of Chicago).

Jacob Neusner, Distinguished Research Professor of Religious Studies at the University of South Florida and Professor of Religion at Bard College has published more than 675 books and is the most published humanities scholar in the world. He has received six US and European honorary doctorates, from the University of Chicago, the University of Rochester, Bologna University, Cologne University, Tulane University, and St. Louis University, and he holds 14 academic medals and prizes, including The University Medal of Excellence, Columbia University, the Medal of Collège de France, the University of Tübingen Medal commemorating that University's 500th anniversary, the Queen Christina of Sweden Medal of Åbo Akademi (Finland), and the Abraham Berliner Prize in Jewish History of the Jewish Theological Seminary of America.

James M. Robinson is Professor of Religion at Claremont Graduate University, and Director of the Institute for Antiquity and Christianity. He is Secretary of UNESCO's International Committee for the Nag Hammadi Codices and Editor of its *Facsimile Edition of the Nag Hammadi Codices*; of *The Nag Hammadi Library in English*; and of *The Coptic Gnostic Library* (the critical edition in 12 volumes). He founded the International Q Project and is co-editor of *Documenta Q* (its Database in 31 volumes, 1996 ff) and its *Critical Edition of Q* (in preparation).

Ninian Smart taught for 20 years at Lancaster University, where he founded Britain's first major department of Religious Studies. He has taught also at the University of California, Santa Barbara. He has written books on cross-cultural philosophy of religion, Indian philosophy, Buddhism and Christianity, Hindu religion, religious education, politics and the methods and shape of the study of religion.

Frits Staal is Professor Emeritus of Philosophy and of South Asian Studies at the University of California, Berkeley. His books in

English include: *AGNI: The Vedic Ritual of the Fire Altar* (1983), *Universals: Studies in Indian Logic and Linguistics* (1988), *Rules without Meaning* (1990, 1993) and *The Language Animal* (forthcoming).

Rodney Stark is Professor of Sociology and of Comparative Religion at the University of Washington. He is the author or co-author of 20 books, the most recent being *The Rise of Christianity* (Princeton, 1996).

Jon R. Stone currently holds a faculty appointment in the Division of Undergraduate and Interdisciplinary Studies at the University of California, Berkeley, where he teaches courses in the Religious Studies Program. From 1993 to 1997, he served as a Post-Doctoral Research Fellow in the Center for the Study of Religion and sometime Lecturer in the Religious Studies Department and the English Writing Program at the University of California, Santa Barbara. From 1990 to 1993 he was Assistant Professor in Philosophy & Religion at the University of Northern Iowa. He is the author of *A Guide to the End of the World: Popular Eschatology in America* (1993), the award-winning *Latin for the Illiterati* (1996), *Prime-Time Religion* (with J. Gordon Melton and Phillip Lucas, 1997), *On the Boundaries of American Evangelicalism* (1997), and editor of *Expecting Armageddon* (2000), among others.

Ivan Strenski is Holstein Family Community Professor of Religious Studies at the University of California, Riverside. Beginning with his *Four Theories of Myth in Twentieth-Century History* (1987), he has authored numerous historical and social studies of major figures in religious studies, most recently *Durkheim and the Jews of France* (Chicago, 1997).

Mark C. Taylor is the Preston S. Parish Professor of Humanities and Director of the Center for Technology in the Arts and Humanities at Williams College. He is also the Director of the Peter B. Lewis Critical Issues Forum at the Guggenheim Museum.

Edith Wyschogrod is Distinguished Professor of Religious Studies at Rice University. A former president of the American Academy of Religion, she is the author of several groundbreaking studies in postmodern ethical reflection, including *Emmanuel Levinas: the Problem of Ethical Metaphysics, Spirit in Ashes: Hegel, Heidegger, and*

Man-Made Mass Death, and *Saints and Postmodernism: Revisioning Moral Philosophy.*

1

Introduction

JON R. STONE

Anthropologist Clifford Geertz recounts a story from his field work in Java in which a large, oddly shaped, toadstool sprouted up in the home of a carpenter and his wife in the surprising space of only a few days. So strange was this event that people from the surrounding region traveled to the carpenter's home to see it, each pilgrim offering his or her own explanation for this uncanny occurrence. Whether discussion centered on the size, peculiar shape, color, height, or perceptible changes in appearance over the following days, one thing was certain, an account of its intrusion into the ordinary experience of the community had to be given. As Geertz relates: 'One does not shrug off a toadstool which grows five times as fast as a toadstool has any right to grow' (1973:101). As one might expect, explanations for its sprouting multiplied as each visitor came to inspect the carpenter's fungal phenomenon, some perhaps comparing this experience to similar events in the community's collective memory. Could this mysterious occurrence mean something? As Geertz writes further: 'In the broadest sense, the "strange" toadstool did have implications, and critical ones, for those who heard about it. It threatened their most general ability to understand the world, raised the uncomfortable question of whether the beliefs which they held about nature were workable, the standards of truth they used valid' (1973:101).

For this community, the toadstool episode was unsettling because it defied traditionally reliable explanations and cast doubt on an accepted interpretive system. How then does a people respond adequately to a phenomenon beyond normal human experience and which requires interpretive solutions that go well beyond a culture's received wisdom? Since experience creates knowledge and knowledge, in turn, shapes one's interpretation of subsequent experiences, the introduction of an experience that is 'wholly other' challenges, and even changes, fixed epistemic groundings,

1

sometimes subtly, sometimes radically. Put more directly, when experience calls into question established beliefs about the nature of things, groups, as well as the individuals belonging to them, are compelled to refine or even redefine their assumptions about the world, how it works, and their place within it.

The presence of religion in human experience is very much like this Javanese toadstool and the study of religion is not unlike the carpenter's curious neighbors who offered speculations – some fascinating, others facile – on why the toadstool appeared and what it meant for the carpenter and for the community. Religion is a phenomenon within the dimensions of human experience. Religious studies is an attempt to understand and account for that phenomenon. As with the strange toadstool, with each generation of observers, speculation about religion has multiplied as have disagreements over which observations have been the more accurate and useful. Indeed, over the past century, a great number of theories have been offered and rejected and scores of new methods and approaches have been adopted and abandoned. As decades have passed, the catalog of knowledge about religion has grown, becoming a body of scholarship far too vast, complex, and contradictory for even the most aspiring and erudite student of religion to command. Yet, as great and detailed as that knowledge has become, much of it has remained largely descriptive, a description of a phenomenon that most would agree has been nearly impossible to define with satisfactory precision. Similar, then, to Winston Churchill's oft-quoted description of Soviet Russia, religion is likewise 'a riddle wrapped in a mystery inside an enigma'. Perhaps the reason a century of scholarship has failed to move human knowledge beyond the mere description of religious phenomena – however 'thick' – lies less with how one studies religion than it does with the nature of religion itself.

EXPLAINING THE INEXPLICABLE

The problem of definition – and hence explanation – arises from the complexity of phenomena typically gathered under the heading 'religion'. Unlike other humanistic disciplines, the study of religion must wrestle with a phenomenon that touches every dimension of human experience and human existence, be it social, psychological, philosophical, artistic, literary, architectural, historical, political, judicial, economic, gastronomic, or other. Religion is at once deeply personal as well as inherently communal and familial. It is the simplicity of the Zen master's great empty circle and the beautifully intricate geometric detail of Muslim aniconography. It is a gesture, a smile, an upturned hand. It is the human body, sacrificial blood, spirits of the dead, an empty tomb. Religion is sound and it is silence. It is love and it is hate. It is colored sand paintings and majestic marble statues. It is a mask, a gate, a spire. It is a rattle, a bell, the burning of incense, a flower. Religion is also fire and water, air and ether. It is the sun and the moon, planetary movements and extraterrestrial forces. It is gold and silver, a jeweled net, potter's clay and even filth. Religion is a mother and her child, a father and his son. It is a word, a chant, a riddle, a story. It is a drop of ink on a sheet of paper and a drop of water in a vast ocean. Religion is all things ordinary and extraordinary, logical and paradoxical, visible and invisible, intelligible and ineffable. It is the simplicity of one and the unity of three. It is good and evil – and something in between. Religion is all these things and it is none of them.

To say this about religion is not to say anything particularly profound. Religion is everywhere around us. But, while its ubiquitous presence in humanity's past and present cannot be overlooked, its meaning is not as apparent as the vast variety of phenomena that testify to its existence. We talk about religion ceaselessly and write about it voluminously, filling conference halls and library shelves with insights into the mysteries surrounding human existence. Though it is perhaps the one aspect of human culture most familiar to us, religion appears ever beyond humanity's abilities to comprehend fully. Scholarship only approximates, it never fully apprehends what it studies. Herein lies the problem: how does one describe and explain a phenomenon that is at once all things within human experience and all things beyond it?; what method does one use to achieve such an end?

Over a generation ago, Wilfred Cantwell Smith pointed to this fundamental problem in the academic study of religion, that is, the problem of separating the essence of religion from its myriad of manifestations. While 'the externals of religion – symbols, institutions, doctrines, practices – can be examined separately', he asserted, 'these things are not in themselves religion, which lies rather in the area of what these mean to those that are involved'

(1959:35). Religion, Smith might well have added, is not merely thought or perception, but it is a community, an activity, a symbolic object, a feeling, a belief, a connection between past and present, and all other aspects of human culture and of human existence. Religion is not a 'thing', but the meaning of a 'thing' to those who observe and venerate it. But, beyond defining the 'what' of religion, religious studies has occupied itself with the search for a method – a way – by which religion can be properly and effectively studied. If such a method exists, one might ask, does it differ from those of other disciplines in the academy?

THE SEARCH FOR A 'METHOD'

The search for a method that distinguishes religious studies as a legitimate field of inquiry standing alongside other academic disciplines has been long-standing. Traditionally, the 'discipline' of religious studies traces its birth to 1873, when the German linguist, Max Müller, coined the term 'Religionswissenschaft' (science of religion). His method, though a decided break from theology, was primarily philological, examining linguistic developments in preliterate societies in order to discover the essence of religion, which, he believed, was the personification of natural phenomena. Though its methods were modestly comparative, adding insights from the anthropological findings of its day and even adopting theoretical terminology from the newer disciplines of sociology and psychology, the science of religion remained well within the wider disciplinary orbit of philosophy.

In time, this new field of inquiry branched out into several related areas and became known as 'die Religionsgeschichteschule' or the 'history of religions'. Since its disciplinary base was primarily history and literature, and its typical approach phenomenological, much of the earlier discussion on methodology in the history of religions tended toward more or less textual and linguistic problems. The major methodological concerns in the early decades of this century centered around the issue of personal religious faith and its potentially deleterious affect on a scholar's own objectivity. As the history of religions became established in American universities, most especially in Chicago, debate over the problems of developing objective approaches to the study of religion became all the more pronounced. In time, a relatively objective methodology would come to define the history of religions, but not without serious disagreement and debate.

Among the many studies published during the heyday of the methodological debates arising out of Chicago was the now classic volume, *The History of Religions: Essays in Methodology*, edited by Mircea Eliade and Joseph Kitagawa (1959). This collection of essays is representative of the earlier generation's search for a methodology, especially one that would distinguish the history of religions from other disciplines within the academy.

In this collection, the essayists argued that, as a discipline, the one common focus of the history of religions is the desire to understand 'the phenomenon of man as a religious being' (1959: viii). First and foremost, wrote Jerald Brauer in the Preface, those who approach the study of religion properly, must do so in 'an attitude of respect and openness toward the religious reality itself' (1959:viii). Besides approaching the study of religion from an empathetic, if not sympathetic, perspective, the essayists in this volume believed that the most pressing issue toward this goal was that of a methodology 'appropriate to the discipline' (1959:ix). As Brauer put it:

> In spite of the favorable circumstances, it will not be easy for the history of religions to establish itself as one of the leading scholarly activities in the modern university. In fact, the great danger is that it will be completely absorbed by certain other fields. The history of religions deals with materials handled also by philosophy of religion, psychology, sociology, anthropology, history and theology. Its problem is to demonstrate that it is not merely ancillary to these other studies but is a discipline in its own right, drawing upon, yet making unique additions to, these areas of knowledge.
>
> (1959:ix)

Indeed, continued Brauer, 'Unless a satisfactory answer can be found concerning the content and method adapted to the history of religions, it will not be able to fulfil its potential role' (1959:ix).

The assumption these essayists made was that, because there is something unique or *sui generis* about religion, those who study it must do so without reducing its essence to something other than itself, as sociologists and psychologists tended to do. In his own contribution to this volume, Eliade argued that the essence of religion is a 'sacred event' (hierophany) and that the study of religion is properly, if not exclusively, the province of the history of religions. As Eliade himself put it: 'The greatest claim to merit of the history of religions is precisely its effort to decipher in a "fact", conditioned as it is by the historical moment and the cultural style of the epoch, the existential situation that made [religion] possible' (1959:89). According to Eliade, the study of religion assumes that the sacred event occurred *in illo tempore* and that religion represents the human ability to apprehend and humanity's attempts to give expression and meaning to it, what Eliade referred to as *homo religiosus*, the human person's innate ability to apprehend the sacred. Whether right or wrong, this theoretical view lent urgency to the search for a methodology, a theoretical approach, by which religion scholars could clearly distinguish the history of religions from other disciplines in the human sciences, all of which tended to regard religion as an incidental aspect of human culture.

Though Eliade and the Chicago School were largely unsuccessful in setting forth a theoretical approach to the study of religion that was both unique and unifying, the question they raised still begs an answer: Is there a methodology – a way to study religion – that is unique to the history of religions or to the field we now call Religious Studies?

AN APPROACH APPROPRIATE TO THE 'DISCIPLINE'

When speaking about method and methodology, however, confusion arises when scholars use these terms uncritically, mistaking one with the other. This confounding of 'method' with 'methodology' presents a number of problems that can be avoided by a proper understanding of these terms. By definition, method is the way one collects data, the means or process of selecting information for analysis. By contrast, methodology is properly defined as the assumptions and preconceptions that influence one's analysis and interpretation of data, that is, the theoretical and analytical framework, even personal feelings, one brings to the task of organizing and analyzing facts. While methodologies may differ, there is no real distinction between the methods of science and those of the academic study of religion. For, as Wilfred Cantwell Smith has reminded us, 'Academic method is what all scholars have in common, not what differentiates them' (1975:3). Put another way, the search for a methodology to distinguish the study of religion from other humanistic disciplines is not a search for a way of collecting data as much as it is a search for a unique way of understanding and interpreting those data.

We might say, then, that the differences between religious studies and other humanistic disciplines have more to do with its concern over proper methodology than with method proper. And even then, disciplinary approaches tend to vary more by their subjects of study than by type. To some degree, all humanistic disciplines are concerned about the problem of subjectivity. But few disciplines are as self-critical about it as religious studies, which talks in terms of 'insiders' and 'outsiders', sensitive to every nuance that might validate the perceptions and interpretations of one scholar or invalidate those of another (see Rudolph 1994:358–60 and Capps 1995:*in passim*).

Religious studies is not altogether unique in this regard. Other disciplines, such as history, sociology, anthropology, and philosophy, have likewise been vexed by theological and other ideological dogmatisms and have had to contend with persistent charges of Western cultural bias. In the case of religious studies, however, the awareness has been more keenly felt and more difficult to escape. By its very nature, 'religion' is fraught with human emotion. Unlike English literature, where one's research, say, into the authorship of Beowulf may not severely disturb a person's religious faith – of even the researcher – as deeply as would a discussion of the authorship of Genesis. For this reason, the language of 'epoché' – the suspension of personal value judgments – that religion scholars imported from philosophy, has, for better or for worse, become a major defining methodology of the study of religion. It is a methodology that has helped scholars contend with the problem of unexamined subjectivity.

While the human dimension of research scholarship can sometimes undermine attempts toward academic objectivity, the 'subject' does play a role in the way research questions are framed that should not be overlooked. The methodological approaches that determine the direction of one's research oftentimes reflect the human questions and personal concerns with which scholars themselves wrestle. Rather than condemn the human dimension of humanistic research as altogether biased, we might gain some useful insights into how research questions develop and how scholarship proceeds by examining such dynamics through the lives of a representative number of thoughtful and reflective scholars who study religion.

REFLECTIONS AND CONVERSATIONS

The main focus, therefore, of this present collection of essays in the academic study of religion centers on methodological issues as seen through the lives of 14 scholars of religion, all with national or international reputations in their particular fields of inquiry. These essays represent the variety of research and analytical methods scholars employ when examining religious phenomena, religious actions, religious groups, religious ideas. In some cases, while their methodologies have generally been shaped by the assumptions of their respective disciplines, their methods have been largely dictated by the questions they have asked and the issues they have sought to explore. As their autobiographical musings reveal, because religious phenomena cut across the spectrum of human culture and experience, of necessity, the approaches they have taken and methods they have employed cut across disciplinary lines. To this point, Ninian Smart, in the lead essay, writes that, as an 'enterprise', religious studies is necessarily 'aspectual', 'plural', 'non-finite', or, in a word, 'multidisciplinary'. Consequently, the common ground among scholars of religion becomes their efforts to describe and explain religious phenomena as an aspect of human culture and experience and not the paths they undertake to reach that end. Thus, despite the elusive and sometimes enigmatic nature of religious phenomena and the interdisciplinary character of religious studies, to their credit, differences in method and approach have actually added strength and vitality to the academic study of religion. Indeed, much of this vitality is seen in the autobiographical cast of the essays in this volume.

Autobiography involves self-awareness (reflection) and self-criticism (analysis) – and a great deal of self-censorship and self-control. Through self-reflection, the patterns of one's life become retrospectively self-evident. The selection of important episodes and the interpretation of what they mean as related to the whole of one's life involve a blending of proximity and distance, or rather, the subjective made objective (see Burr 1909). One reason I have chosen this particular genre as the framework of this volume on methodology in the study of religion lies in what it can teach us about a person's intellectual journey. Most scholars' lives represent a quest, a quest in which each new question and each new discovery provides the next passage toward the search for understanding. Books are milestones that mark that passage in that a person's body of published works tells us something about his or her intellectual odyssey. In this way, an intellectual autobiography can teach us something not only about the person writing it, but more importantly about his or her methods and approaches to the study of religion – and even something about religion itself.

Similar to an interview session, then, each author was asked to ponder a series of general questions: How did you first come to the study of religion?; What are some of the major questions you have tried to address in your scholarship?; What methods or trends have you followed?; What have you discovered?; What surprises have you found along the way?; and How have your views changed or remained the same? As before, rather than answer these questions from a professional or traditionally objective frame of reference, it seemed to me that we might gain greater insight into the workings of the field if each author considered these questions from his or her own life experience. Thus, an obvious result is that these essays are reflective, conversational, and interesting as well as methodologically instructive.

A BRIEF PROFILE OF THE ESSAYS

To wit, in the first essay, Ninian Smart discusses the creation of Religious Studies in Britain and the United States as a sub-field separate from theology, tracing his own movement away from the reigning theological approaches of his time to the development of his own polymethodological and cross-cultural schema. His six-dimensional model (now seven), through which he examines traditional and non-traditional religions in terms of their experiential, mythic, doctrinal, ethical, ritual, social (and later, material) aspects, typifies his creative attempts to cut across disciplinary lines.

The essay by Wendy Doniger presents a non-harmonic counterpoint to that of Smart in that while Smart has methodological issues well in mind, Doniger finds herself somewhat the outsider to such discussions. In her piece, Doniger, who has made her reputation making the inaccessible accessible through her translations of classical Hindu texts, discusses her passion not for methodological concerns but for the telling and interpreting of myths and stories. At the heart of myth, she writes, 'is an always doomed attempt to solve an insoluble contradiction'. Paradoxically, 'the inevitable failure of that enterprise is what drives a culture to tell the same story over and over again, finding ever new ways to show how the square peg does *not* fit into the round hole'.

The ambulant life of Vedic scholar, Frits Staal, provides yet another glimpse at the diverse approaches to the study of religion. In a fairly provocative essay, Staal repudiates scholars' uncritical use of the term 'religion', a Western invention – what he calls the 'Protestant paradigm' – that does not fit what his 40 years of field experience in the Indian subcontinent and elsewhere in Asia have taught him. Rather than trust the work of library scholars, Staal urges students to 'immerse themselves in the life of a people', leaving behind their presuppositions and prejudices. Indeed, sometimes the assumptions researchers bring with them about what is and what is not 'religion' or 'religious' may not help them make logical sense of the materials before them. What may seem 'religious' may not be and what one assumes to be 'religion' may be something other. In short, there may be no religion there. As Staal writes: 'If I had not been able to at least imagine and then ponder on such unexpected consequences, I could not have arrived at the conclusion that Vedic ritual is a ritual-without-religion.'

John Hick approaches his work in the philosophy of religion through the avenue of experience and perception. He tells us that because the human world is primarily an environment of 'interpreted awareness', one must understand religion not as simply a set of propositions to which persons give assent and to which they adhere but a dimension of greater awareness about the world in which they live. As a *comparative* philosopher of religion, the questions that Hick seeks to answer are generally those that religious people have asked and will continue to ask, including those questions whose answers the religious could never in good conscience accept. His approach, then, is essentially 'problem-driven': the concerns of the religious frame the questions which the philosopher should appropriately address.

In mild contrast to Hick's comparative approach, Jacob Neusner asks one simply worded, well-focused, but ever-evolving, question: How did Judaism, as we know it, come into being? In solving this mystery, Neusner has had to traverse across disciplinary lines, moving progressively from history, literature, and the history of religions, to theology. In his attempts to explain 'the relationship between the religious ideas that people hold and the social world that they create for themselves', Neusner has demonstrated creative energy and intellectual imagination that few can rival (indeed, who would have thought that such an innocent question as 'What exactly do you mean by Judaism?' would take over 40 years and 675 published volumes to answer!).

The study of religion assumes, therefore, the existence of records – written accounts – in which experiences and ideas are preserved. Those who study texts comprise perhaps the largest segment of scholars of religion, especially of ancient and pre-modern times. Among those included in this volume who translate and interpret textual materials, the reconstructive work of James M. Robinson stands out as unique, if not for the problems he encountered in his attempts to secure open access to the Nag Hammadi library of esoteric Coptic texts. Less an essay in methodology than one documenting the dark and unseemly side of antiquarian scholarship, Robinson's intriguing story about his own relentless efforts – even at great personal risk – to reconstruct, transcribe, and publish these remarkable texts from the early Christian era gives the reader a much fuller picture of the divine drudgery of textual work. Texts, he reminds us, do not fall from the heavens and into air-conditioned archives. Nor are they always available to whomever comes calling. Politics and personal advancement sometimes intervene. Indeed, Robinson's work as archaeologist, coptologist, papyrologist, codicologist, and spy attests to the difficulties one might experience while doing otherwise painstaking and uneventful text work. Though less exciting than his Nag Hammadi adventure, Robinson's detective work reconstructing Q, the sayings source of the Gospels of Matthew and Luke, is no less significant to our understanding of early Christian literature, and no less praiseworthy.

The essays in this volume then turn from discussion of essentially textual to contextual approaches, with a focus primarily on religion and American culture. Martin E. Marty, who wryly observes that most approaches to the study of religion are 'idiosyncratic' and that most self-made methodologies tend toward the 'idiopathic', has made his career as an historian interpreting the shape of American religion both in the public and private spheres. Since those who study religion are not usually inclined to build on previous work, he observes, little work has progressed beyond definitional questions and foundational issues. This observation does not seem to bother him. For Marty, who advocates and embodies a 'public mission for the humanities', the point of religious studies is to clarify the meaning and import of religion within human culture, that is, to inform the public about itself. This mission requires comparative and interdisciplinary approaches from scholars not easily flustered by what Marty calls 'messiness at the boundaries of the discipline' or, what others might tag, methodological drifting. One can hardly build a disciplinary edifice upon such shifting foundations.

In the essay by sociologist Rodney Stark, the main direction of his comments centers on the framing of research questions and on the proper use of method, a feature of the scholar's craft that far too many, in their search for a defining methodology, overlook. Stark's career as a tireless student of the theoretical dynamics of religious organizations has taken him from an examination of 1960s counter-culture religion to the expansion of the early Christian Church. His offering in this volume illustrates the one simple guiding principle for his scholarship and his critique of the work of others: 'that research questions must determine what method or methods are suitable – *how* to find out depends on *what* you want to know'. As Stark notes further, 'When one's primary commitment is to a particular methodology, one's ability to pursue important questions is severely limited'. Accordingly, Stark's essay provides examples of how one can focus his or her field of inquiry and use a number of creative and unorthodox methods for arriving at some interesting, if not controversial, results. One thing Stark does stress is that the necessary data is not always there waiting to be analyzed. For him, such work in the sociology of religious movements 'took imagination, some luck, and reasonably sophisticated statistical methods to reconstruct our primary data'.

While Stark's work focuses on the broader question of the conditions under which religious groups form and the reasons for their success or failure, Andrew M. Greeley centers his research on religious experience within one tradition: American Catholicism. Although his initial studies as a Catholic priest laid stress on the theoretical writings of notable French Catholic theologians, Greeley's experience as a parish priest in the years directly before and after Vatican II and the Church's controversial pronouncements on family life gave him a different view of Catholic faith. Intrigued by its inexplicably tenacious loyalty to the Church, Greeley set out to profile this 'renegade' segment of Catholicism using quantitative methods as the basis upon which his narrative accounts would rest. What he has found since that time is that despite the Church's conservative social agenda and antiquated ecclesiology, people are drawn to it by the enduring magic of stories. 'Religion is story', Greeley tells us, thus providing the anchor for his theory that, above all else and after everything else, religion is grounded in experience, story, and imagination. In this sense, religion becomes communal, the social experience sacramental.

As a further example of how research questions direct the methods one employs, Phillip E. Hammond gives an account of how one line of inquiry can sometimes unwittingly lead the scholar not only to disciplinary approaches that are to him foreign but to the reframing of older questions long ignored. Though Hammond's essay can be read as a practical guide to the craft of academic scholarship, one thematic lesson which his reflections draw is how the pattern of one's research program comes into clearer focus retrospectively. A child and grandchild of the manse with a deeply rooted sense of the moral mission of the mainline Protestant establishment, Hammond's long career chronicling issues of religion and conscience in America coincides the declining fortunes of the Protestant mainline and the concomitant emergence of sacred experience through structural channels not traditionally associated with the sacred. The sacred, however defined, resides beyond church walls and within the midst of even the most secularly circumscribed society. The advent of legitimate religious experiences outside traditional and state-sanctioned settings can create tensions within a society that sometimes find their way to courts of law. Hammond's own work in this area provides a glimpse of the complexity of such social tensions and the implications legal solutions present in shaping religion and public life.

The final turning of the wheel takes the reader from contextual studies to a return to textual and philosophical approaches but as seen through the lens of so-called postmodern critical analysis. Edith Wyschogrod, who, like Doniger, closely connects her intellectual pilgrimage to her early childhood experiences, discusses her lifelong quest to comprehend and conquer the 'twin nots of ignorance and injury to the other'. The point of departure for Wyschogrod begins with the fundamental ethical pronouncement, couched in negation, that we all learned as children: 'Thou shalt not'. As a moral philosopher, Wyschogrod, reflecting on the horror of the genocides that have come to characterize the barbarity of the twentieth century, attempts to adumbrate what she calls 'an ethic for my own dark times'. By examining the ethical conception of 'consideration of the Other' – an individual's openness to being 'morally alterable by the proximity of the Other' – Wyschogrod seeks 'a new context for ethics that would have a direct bearing upon seemingly insoluble social ills'.

If the logic of negation provides one necessary ground for ethical (non) action toward the Other, then the non logic of affirming negation as the ground for (non) action – as Mark Taylor might phrase it – provides still another. In his essay, Taylor, a self-professed deconstructive constructive a/theologian who was prodded by the student movements of the 1960s, reflects on the problem of political action and social engagement through the writings of Kierkegaard and Hegel as mediated by Nietzsche and Derrida. To state the problem simply, since a transcendent model of God places legitimacy for action beyond reach (Kierkegaard) and an immanent model makes God indistinguishable from this-worldly processes (Hegel), could there be a third way between the two that would neither affirm nor negate affirmation or negation of action? 'While transcendence leads to a "No" that allows no "Yes"', Taylor observes, 'radical immanence issues in a "Yes" that cannot say "No".' Taylor's own work points toward an exploration and explication of a third way between this polarity by asking: 'might it be possible to refigure God by thinking a "reality" that is *neither* transcendent *nor* immanent?' and 'might such a concept or, more precisely, "nonconcept" of the real create the possibility of critical engagement instead of hopeless resignation?' The trajectory of his work, as highlighted in his essay, illustrates his attempts to find options that move beyond the binary negations of either/or and the binary affirmations of both/and.

At this point the reader may begin to wonder, where, in this newer direction in religious studies, is religion? Has it disappeared through the clever devices of philosophical and deconstructive *legerdemain*? Indeed, postmodern critical analysis seems less concerned with religion than it is with that which lies behind religion, behind texts, rituals, myths, and so on. Religion becomes, as Taylor would say, nothing more – and certainly nothing less – than a sign pointing to a sign. In this interpretive frame religion is the way people treat others and how people make existence bearable and daily actions and life events meaningful. It is humanly constructed, imbued with human significance, and reflective of human aspirations and existential yearnings. Its postmodern (re)formulation is primarily ethical, examining the 'oughts' of human social life.

But religion is not merely ethical reflex(ion) and it cannot be rendered in simple I-Thou/I-it correlates. While it may be 'human, all-too-human', religion can also be regarded as 'not human, not-at-all-human'. This is not to suggest that postmodern critical theory does not provide a helpful corrective to traditional approaches, only that we should not be so quick to replace one grand theory of religion with another. Accordingly, the essay offered by Giles Gunn reminds the reader that traditional approaches need not be abandoned altogether as they do provide insights that can complement more recent critical perspectives. Returning the focus once more to broader methodological concerns, then, Gunn reminds us that it has been the work on the boundaries of the disciplines – its 'interdisciplinarity' – that has given religious studies its creative vitality. Such a broad critique, as with Marty's methodological messiness, requires the 'surveying of disciplinary borders'. As Gunn notes, 'disciplinary crossings can sometimes produce not only a new configuration of methodological practices but a new refiguration of the material on which they are directed. Change the paradigm by which one discipline makes sense of itself to itself by forcing it to look through the eyes of another and you can sometimes alter the way disciplines represent their own knowledge to themselves.' The aim, Gunn might add, is not a dissolving of the disciplines but interdisciplinary interlinking achieved through dialogue, especially dialogue that fosters conversation among scholars whose disciplinary affiliations and methodological assumptions might otherwise separate them.

The final essay, by Ivan Strenski, brings this collection full circle, as it were, with a critique of the methodology of the reputed fathers of religious studies. As an historian of ideas, Strenski seeks to set accepted theoretical models within their historical contexts so as to understand the social, personal, and political circumstances that gave rise to their reputedly innocent formations. As Strenski writes, 'theories are not simply propositions, ideas or arguments to be applauded or dismissed. They are also cultural creations or "social facts". As such they can best be understood by linking them to the actual situations in which they emerged.' By applying this methodological assumption to the thought of Eliade, Heidegger, and others, Strenski provides a necessary critique of the 'received' theories through which many scholars have viewed religious phenomena and through which they have then framed their own research questions. As he demonstrates, history and biography can teach us something about how circumstances and life experiences can shape theoretical assumptions. This approach can also yield fascinating, and sometimes very disturbing, revelations about an author's seemingly benign, objective, and innocent theorizing. What is more, while deconstruction need not be negative or destructive, Strenski does show us that a certain hermeneutical suspicion can sometimes benefit the field by generating new questions about accepted theories and thereby open new avenues of investigation, explication, and further understanding.

References and Sources

Burr, Anna Robeson. 1909. *The Autobiography: A Critical and Comparative Study*. Boston & New York: Houghton Mifflin Company.
Capps, Walter H. 1995. *Religious Studies: The Making of a Discipline*. Minneapolis, MN: Fortress Press.
Eliade, Mircea. 1959. 'Methodological Remarks on the Study of Religious Symbolism'. pp. 86–107 in *The History of Religions: Essays in Methodology*, edited by Mircea Eliade and Joseph Kitagawa. Chicago: The University of Chicago Press.
Eliade, Mircea and Joseph Kitagawa (eds). 1959. *The History of Religions: Essays in Methodology*. Chicago: The University of Chicago Press.
Geertz, Clifford. 1973. *The Interpretation of Cultures*. New York: Basic Books.
Kitagawa, Joseph. 1959. 'The History of Religions in America'. pp. 1–30 in *The History of Religions: Essays in Methodology*, edited by Mircea Eliade and Joseph Kitagawa. Chicago: The University of Chicago Press.
Rudolph, Kurt. 1994. 'We Learn What Religion Is From History: On the Relation between the Study of History and the Study of Religion'. *Historical Reflection/Reflexions Historiques* 20:357–76.
Sharpe, Eric J. 1983. *Understanding Religion*. London: Duckworth.
——.1986. *Comparative Religion: A History* (2nd edn). La Salle, IL: Open Court.
Smart, Ninian. 1983. *Worldviews: Crosscultural Explorations of Human Beliefs*. New York: Charles Scribner's Sons.

Smith, Wilfred Cantwell. 1959. 'Comparative Religion: Whither – and Why?' pp. 31–58 in *The History of Religions: Essays in Methodology*, edited by Mircea Eliade and Joseph Kitagawa. Chicago: The University of Chicago Press.

———.1975. 'Methodology and the Study of Religion: Some Misgivings'. pp. 1–30 in Robert D. Baird (ed.), *Methodological Issues in Religious Studies*. Chico, CA: New Horizons Press.

2

Methods in My Life

NINIAN SMART

The invention of Religious Studies was a personal thing to me. When I say 'Religious Studies' I mean the study of religion as an aspect of human existence in a cross-cultural way and from a polymethodic or multidisciplinary perspective. Though there had been the comparative study of religion in my youth, it was not yet really combined with the social or human sciences. It was only with the combination of the study of the histories of religions with the social sciences that you get what I call the modern 'Religious Studies'. Any tradition has its roots and its formation: these are two differing periods. For example, the roots of Hinduism lie in many places – in the Vedic hymns, in early Brahmanism, in sramanic movements, in folk mythology, in temples, images, pilgrimages, caste. So though Hinduism has ancient roots it does not really gel together till the first to third centuries CE. Similarly though Religious Studies has its roots in the nineteenth century it scarcely is formed until the 1960s.

This was surely so in Britain. There, between the two world wars, even the comparative study of religions barely existed. It was kept alive by two farseeing Anglican clergymen named A. C. Bouquet and E. O. James. In the late 1930s and the postwar period, when the Swiss theologian Karl Barth dominated – noble, creative, benighted Barth – James's Chair in Leeds was converted to the narrowest form of Christian theology. The study of religions lived at the periphery of Anglican and other divinity schools and University Departments of Theology in State schools, all of which were dominated by Anglican thought, as they still greatly are today.

This point is worthy of further amplification. Religious Studies as a university enterprise did not exist in Australia, New Zealand, South Africa or other English-speaking countries. As a discipline or sub-discipline or even as a focus of study separate from Theology, it scarcely existed in European countries other than Britain. In the United States, while something like it occurred in Princeton and in a form devised by Joachim Wach in Chicago, it was really with the advent of the subject in public institutions that Religious Studies came into full being in North America. Since I was involved in the setting up of Lancaster's Department of Religious Studies, which pioneered the subject in its full form in Britain and was to be influential in other Commonwealth countries, I was much involved in the creation of its modern form. I was fortunate to be able to work in a new expanding university which was committed to a Religious Studies Department and to be helped by various younger scholars, among them Adrian Cunningham, Robert Morgan, Michael Pye and Stuart Mews. This is what I mean by saying that the invention of Religious Studies was a personal thing for me.

The roots of my concern with the study of religion I shall come to anon. But the formation of Religious Studies as a discipline began when I was H. G. Wood Professor of Theology at Birmingham University, a Chair I occupied when I was but 34 years old. Though I entered into the world of philosophical theology with verve, I had a wider vision. One day in the middle 1960s a colleague who lived nearby, the noted Egyptologist Rundle Clark, came to see me. He came before dinner time and I brought him into my study for a glass of sherry. He wanted to discuss some university politics. Inadvertently he left behind a copy of the *Universities Quarterly*. In it was an article called 'Theology as a Discipline', dealing with the possibility of establishing Theology in the then coming New Universities. It was a new age in British higher education, with great optimism about what these new-style universities were going to do. One or two had already been started, notably Sussex. I sat down that evening and wrote a reply to this article. Because there was a post box down the street with a pickup time of ten p.m., I went out and mailed it to the journal that very evening. For me, it was a seminal article. When Lancaster University, attracted by my article, invited me to advise them about a new Department a year later, they only had one thing in mind: they did not want the old Theology. In the process of the consultation, I was cajoled into transferring from being adviser to being candidate. Many of my friends thought me insane. I was in the swim as it happened, being invited to seven posts in the USA, including the chairs of the Columbia and Pennsylvania departments, and was invited to apply for the philosophy of religion job at Oxford. Lancaster was a wonderful opportunity, however, a *tabula rasa*, a new field. The ideas I formulated were expressed in my inaugural lecture there, delivered on St Valentine's Day in 1968, and reprinted in *Concept and Empathy* (1986). In it I declared that Religious Studies, as an enterprise, is necessarily

> **aspectual,** that is it deals with an aspect of human existence, experience, institutions, ideas and so on;
>
> **plural,** both because there are many religions, and because cross-cultural work is often equivalent to experimentation in the sciences and for other reasons necessary in the field: she who knows but one religion knows none (to exaggerate a cliché);
>
> **non-finite,** because traditions and the like often classified as not being religions (such as communism, rationalisms and so forth) have some great resemblance to traditional religions and cannot be excluded from our study – the family may include some 'illegitimate children' outside, and family resemblance is the correct mode of definition of religion; polymethodic or multi-disciplinary, for obvious reasons: history, philology, archaeology, sociology, anthropology, philosophy and so on are obviously relevant to the study of religion and religions.

The department in Lancaster also started a graduate program straight away. Because of our innovative curriculum and Commonwealth connections, about 60 of our graduates presently teach worldwide in institutions of higher education. Several of these are in North America, including Ivan Strenski and Donald Wiebe, both noted for their critical acumen.

Perhaps I can outline a few of the roots of that formative period in which I came both to formulate and practice what I preached. Part of it was that after a fine education at the Glasgow Academy, I went into the military in early 1945. After sundry forms of infantry training, I was set to learn Chinese for the Intelligence Corps, mainly at the School of Oriental and African Studies, part of London University. After a year and a half of immersion in the language, my colleagues and I dreamt in Chinese. Then as officers we went East, to Singapore, then Sri Lanka (at that time Ceylon). I was roused from my Western slumber with the call of diverse and noble cultures. I had had a fine education in the Classics among other things. I had a scholarship to Oxford. When I came back from the Army to Oxford, I pursued my original avocation (Chinese and Oriental Studies had pathetic curricula) of Classics, Ancient

History and Philosophy, but at graduate level I did philosophy of religion, then a highly unfashionable thing, especially when combined with comparative religion. My main mentor was J. L. Austin of performative fame; but I also consorted with Robert Zaehner. I wrote the first dissertation in Oxford on philosophy of religion after World War II. It was also the first comparative study and likewise the first to give a performative analysis of religious language. I was too early for the times. My book *Reasons and Faiths* (1958) flowed from this work. Though original, it was not yet 'Religious Studies' in orientation. Rather, it showed what I had learned from my military 'orientalization', a work in the philosophy of religion approaching cross-cultural study but not yet arriving. In those days, when you had to go to Asia from Europe by ship, the East was still a vague notion in the European and American imaginations. My early work reflected this Western vagueness.

The philosophy which I had been involved with in Oxford was so-called 'linguistic philosophy'. This had certain merits and certain defects. Because it tried to look at philosophical questions through the lens of language, it began to encounter many of the issues which have since become fashionable, such as problems of essentialism (hence Wittgenstein's theory of family resemblance alluded to above), interpretation, contextualism and so on. On the other hand, it tended to be too much bound up with 'our' language, which therefore uncritically built in various assumptions of our own culture, that is, largely of Western culture. I found that my experience with learning Chinese, my service in the East and various other factors made me critical of restrictions in regard to common sense language philosophy as then understood. It also seemed to me important that just as the philosophy of science was beginning to take the history of science seriously, so the philosophy of religion should take the history of religions seriously as well. It is still obvious that the philosophy of religion is only very partially interested in these wider cross-cultural issues, even in the 1990s. My *Reasons and Faiths* was an early venture in this cross-cultural and linguistic philosophy of religion.

In this book I incorporated also a theory of religious experience, distinguishing roughly between numinous and mystical strands of religion and language (that is, taking Rudolf Otto in one direction and William Stace and others in another). I was much influenced however by reading in the Pali canon, and by the apparent fact that

Buddhism was a kind of 'mysticism without God'. I was thus critical of Otto's assumption that there was one central core of religious experience. I consider that the notion of two or more main types does much more to explain the variety of religions, a point I will return to below. But before that, I would like to outline some of the main themes in my own thinking as a scholar and crusader of Religious Studies from a comparative perspective.

One of the themes of my thinking is that Religious Studies scholars need to be phenomenological in the descriptive, historical task. I came to this partly from my admiration for Popper, but partly out of my reflection upon how to study religion. On the Popper side, we need clean and yet dense descriptions of the meaning of religion in people's lives. The reason is simple: if we build theories into our descriptive stance (say Marxian theory) we already cannot test the theory, for it has already infected the data. It is a simple but vital point. Second, to bring out meaning we need informed empathy. I mean empathy: a critical perspective that is sliding tragically towards meaning 'sympathy'. But neither sympathy nor antipathy is needed. Empathy is. And this subtle but powerful difference implies 'epoché', a bracketing out of one's feelings and assumptions about the phenomenon at hand. For me personally, this perspective came as a result of the influence of one of the few British values which I retain – no doubt caught from long years of playing beloved cricket, namely, the sense of fair play: the sense that our description of Buddhist or Hindu or other non-Western values has to be 'fair'. All this I characterized as 'warm neutralism'. Some of my critics say you cannot do it, that empathy without sympathy is a fraud. I, however, hold that while this is difficult to achieve in a pure sense, you can at least aim at it, aim at an approach to religions which is much better than aiming at unfairness, lack of empathy, and ignorance.

Thus, to return to my own intellectual biography, in the late 1960s I was thinking of Religious Studies as plural, polymethodic, non-finite and aspectual, and involving the phenomenological or warm neutralist method. But there was another important theme emerging in my thinking, a way of studying religions in their totality by analyzing their various common dimensions, dimensions often disregarded by practitioners.

The way this insight emerged as an important aspect of my work was somewhat unintentional on my part. I was asked by Scribners to write a book to be called *The Religious Experience of Mankind* (later in its fourth edition called *The Religious Experience*) and luckily for me the copy editor turned out to be a wise person named Dorothy Duffy. I had written an introductory chapter for this projected text which she did not much like. In 1967 I read a paper outlining a theory of the dimensions of religion at Columbia and she came along. After hearing the lecture, she urged me to make this paper the introduction to the book. The idea fit perfectly. The thesis of the paper pointed out that religion has various dimensions, of which I identified six: experiential, ethical, doctrinal, mythological, institutional and ritual. My aim in this paper was a simple one, namely, to try to ensure that scholarly descriptions of religion be balanced. At that time, and even today, there were so many treatments of religion that were not balanced, from those such as Mircea Eliade's which ignore the sociological and institutional side, to those such as Wendy Doniger's which overplay the mythological (beguilingly I do not deny), to those such as Paul Johnson's work on Christianity which overemphasize the doctrinal, and so on. By this I am not saying that each dimension is equally important in each religion. But the schema of six dimensions (later seven, the material, in a later book *The World's Religions*) created the possibility of a balance, a balance which is vital and reflects the multidisciplinary view of our subject. To deal with myth without looking at society, or with ethics without dealing with ritual, or with doctrine without contemplating experience, is to present an incomplete and unintegrated picture of religious phenomena.

So then, my view of the study of religions was that it should be conducted on a base of informed empathy, but with dimensional outreach, and with a recognition of its plural, aspectual, multidisciplinary, and nonfinite character. In the early 1970s I wrote two books to that effect. One of those, *The Science of Religion and the Sociology of Knowledge*, which included a critique of Peter Berger (of his methodological atheism, assuming the non-existence of God, rather than the more appropriate methodological agnosticism), was in line with my neutralist program. That is, I did not suppose that 'reflections' about religion had to be neutral, but simply open and pluralist. My critique of Berger is important, for it deals with the whole problem of reductionism, the tendency to speak of a religious phenomenon as if it were the result of something other than religion itself, and hence not genuine. From this perspective of empirical analysis, it is not important to us to opt for affirming either that God exists or that She does not. The question is what effects does a religious stance or institution have. If its development is more heavily affected by outside factors, then that is perhaps what people mean by reductionism. But if the other way round, then religion as a causative factor is important, at least for the period and place in question. Thus, in critiquing Berger, I worked out a theory of the focus of a religion which leaves its status as existing or not undecided. What is vital is whether it is 'real' in the minds and lives of those who participate in the religion in question. Much discussion about reductionism is confused if it does not take methodological agnosticism as the framework for empirical research.

With the creation of Religious Studies as more or less a new discipline in the 1960s and early 1970s, life for me was heaven on earth. It was made even more delightful by 1977 when I began dividing my time between Lancaster and the University of California, Santa Barbara – the two liveliest outfits in the field. Although I had taught in Harvard in the days of John Carman at the Center, in Princeton much earlier, and in Cape Town – all with fine programs – some of the places I had taught, and others elsewhere, were somewhat deficient in the breadth that I believe Religious Studies requires. For instance, comparative religion or history of religions was the norm in graduate studies in Harvard and Chicago, with hardly any emphasis on reflective, philosophical or social-scientific work. Eliade, who was highly influential, used his history of religions materials as the clothing for a religious worldview which he wished to promote. There is in my view nothing wrong with promoting a worldview either by worldview construction or worldview promotion (rather than the more descriptive higher-order activity of worldview analysis) but it is best if scholars are both aware of what they are doing and announce it. This applies both to people like Eliade and to Marxists and so on. However, the point I really wished to make that under Eliade's influence the history of religions was a kind of theology. The practice of 'epoché' becomes important in a kind of Buddhist sense, then, in otherwise being self-aware of the status of one's utterances: as intentionally descriptive and analytic, or as being loaded with one's personal agenda, and so on. The danger to Religious Studies is when some monolithic position takes over, whether Christian theology, Marxism, deconstructive theories, or whatever. It may be worth remarking at this point that while I have come in for a lot of fire from Christians, I am in fact an Episcopalian. But both in Britain and America the fact that I assault establishmentarian tendencies in the name of education leads to erroneous conclusions about my personal (as opposed to my professional) position.

At any rate, the 1970s were the most creative years in Religious Studies. The field was getting institutionalized in Canada and the United States, especially in public universities, in South Africa, Australia, New Zealand (an early leader in the field) and elsewhere in the Anglophone world. It had weaknesses, however: its professional emplacement could be peculiar. For example, the Society for the Scientific Study of Religion in the US did not coordinate with the American Academy of Religion. Much of the sociology of religion was tribal, dealing with the West but not venturing much across cultural traditions. The philosophy of religion was overwhelmingly Westernized. Colonialism still abounded in the academy. But as we are approaching the next century, it appears that these deficiencies are only slowly being remedied.

A major motif of my thinking since early days has been the impact of Theravadin studies on religious history and theory. Because of a great deal of ignorance about the actual history of religions among otherwise sophisticated scholars and even among people who regard themselves as experts in religion, various theories which appear to be called into question by Buddhism and by Theravada Buddhism in particular can survive unmodified long after they should have been altered or abandoned. The main point about Theravada is that because it does not involve belief in an Absolute or God, various concepts do not work, such as the notion of a *unio mystica* (mystical union), the importance of sacrifice, the image of a Father figure, theophanies and kratophanies, a single ultimate focus of religions, the centrality of the concept of faith, and various Western stereotypes of religion. Other traditions than Theravada might have an equally alarming affect on received opinion. But for me my early experience in Ceylon and subsequent Pali studies opened my eyes. My teacher at Yale, a wonderful linguist called Paul Tedesco, rescued from a German death camp at the end of World War II and brought to the US by Franklin Edgerton, never discussed the content of the texts beyond their immediate meanings. This focus enabled me to come to my own conclusions without being dominated by earlier, often distorted, interpretations of Buddhism. In general, I feel that scholars are much too respectful of dead people's theories (I used to say 'Who do these dead men think they are?', though I shall later make a plea for respect for ancestors). Anyway, Theravada deeply challenges various theories, chief among them the many views of mysticism, including those of Stace and Aldous Huxley, Girard's account of sacrifice and the origins of religion, Freudian analysis, Eliade's metaphysics, John Hick's Copernican revolution, Wilfred C. Smith's general account of faith, and various definitions of religion. Also though many anthropological ideas have seemed fruitful to scholarship, they seem singularly thinly grounded in major traditions, including Theravada. I am thinking of the ideas of Victor Turner particularly, but the framework of relatively enclosed societies makes some ideas plausible which would need severe modification in a wider context. In this instance, I am thinking of Durkheim and Lévi-Strauss.

Theravada also deeply challenges the assumptions of Rudolf Otto. His delineation of the numinous experience is masterly, but it does not apply to contemplative or mystical experience. I made the dialectic between these two main forms of religious experience central to my first book, *Reasons and Faiths*. In it, I evolved a theory of the ramification of language in order to deal with the problem of built-in interpretations. I published this first in an article 'Mystical Experience and Interpretation' which appeared in the first issue of the well-known journal *Religious Studies*, and more recently published a paper in Steven Katz's *Mysticism and Language* (1992) entitled 'What would Buddhaghosa have made of The Cloud of Unknowing?', involving a dense comparison of texts, Theravadin and Christian. If you asked me which of the many articles I have published were the most important I would point to these two. I was proud, by the way, that I wrote the first in 17 days aboard the liner *Canberra* between Colombo and Southampton. With 2000 Australians onboard ship and rum selling at ten cents a glass, this was surely no small feat!

An important thought among scholars during these years was that there is a vital distinction between two quite different senses of phenomenology. The sense in which I favor it methodologically is as the practice of empathy. Now it is sometimes used in quite a differing sense as meaning morphology, as in the magisterial work by G. Van der Leeuw, *Religion in Essence and Manifestation*, and as to some extent in the work of Eliade (though I am critical of his ideological slant which underlies his morphology). The morphological enterprise is designed to pick out differing and important themes among religions and worldviews more generally. This is of course a tricky task, since it is important also to make subtle allowance for context. Still, I believe that it is a possible and illuminating exercise (and I have just completed a large-scale enterprise to follow in the footsteps of van der Leeuw).

So far then my theorizing had to do with the complex nature of Religious Studies (plural, polymethodic, non-finite and so forth), the need for informed empathy or phenomenology in one sense of the term, and the need for good methods in examining the nature of religious experience. In addition, I was concerned with balance, as encouraged through my theory of the dimensions of religion. Another concern involved the teaching of religion in public schools. During the 1970s I was involved in two projects concerned with religious education in public schools in England and Northern Ireland. These projects aimed at working with teachers in introducing world religions into the curriculum, and our views came to be highly influential in the English schools system. I was also involved in a dynamic group known as the Shap Working Party in World Religions in Education, started in the late 1960s at the Shap Wells Hotel in Northern England, which has done a tremendous amount to create materials and facilities to assist the better teaching of religion and religions in schools at all levels. I believe that Religious Studies ideals are best for all ages. Even if a (say Catholic) school believes in a special regimen for inculcating values, this does not exempt it from sensitively informing all children of the history and nature of the world's religions. I was also involved in the early 1970s as editorial consultant for the BBC series *The Long Search*, widely used still in education. I learned that documentary television has already much the same values as those of Religious Studies phenomenology or informed empathy. Making the films was amazingly interesting. It added an extra dimension to my understanding of how to understand religions and how to communicate that understanding to students and the public at large.

The next main methodological lesson I would like to introduce relates to what I in 1968 had called the 'non-finite' character of the field in which I held that there is no serious distinction between secular and religious worldviews. This is a most vital point, from a number of angles. It is important from a theoretical point of view. It happens that modern life tries to make a big distinction between religious and secular worldviews. Tax and other laws give certain privileges (wrongly in my view) to religious organizations, often on some assumption that religions are good, and somehow worthy of tax concessions and the like. Religions are both good and bad, and it is scarcely the business of the State to adjudicate. But beyond that point lies the perception that often religions and secular worldviews blend. Take, for instance, religion and nationalism. There is in some countries, notably the United States, a separation between Church and State. In my view there should be a separation between worldview-affirming organizations and the State. This would also alter educational guidelines. But whether this angle of vision commends itself, there are many areas where secular ideologies need to be brought into the discussion of religions. So, I have been increasingly preoccupied with the analysis of nationalism in particular through my schema of dimensions. My University of California colleague Peter Merkl, a noted analyst of modern German history and institutions, and I ran a conference at the end of the 1970s on religion and politics. But because the political world at that time was not quite ready for a set of essays on politics and religion, we had great difficulty in selling the book that followed from our conference thereafter. Yet thanks to the Ayatollah Khomeini, the topic soon became fashionable and the book did rather well.

What all this means is that in general Religious Studies would cover the whole aspect of human life summed up in the holding, expression and institutionalization of ultimate or higher values. While we may begin from the base of more traditional systems to which we in the West and elsewhere tend to assign the name 'religions', our field should include the study of ideologies and philosophies. There was always something unfortunate about the segregation and, indeed, protection therefore of the category of religion. Thus, the philosophy of religion became an alleged specialism rather than the philosophy of worldviews (which would be a better title, stretching beyond God-talk and the like). But perhaps the time has not come to make this move boldly. But it seems obvious to me that a person can analyze nationalism, for instance, through the application of the theory of dimensions of religion. In the old days Paul Tillich called on scholars and others to see religions in terms of ultimate concern. But he hesitated before Nazism and Communism, which he called 'quasi-religions' rather than religions. But men and women died for these causes. Nazism was a kind of hyper-nationalism, which has reaped a wondrous crop of the heroic dead. Every village war memorial in Europe testifies to this. What could be more ultimate than the willingness to die? Presbyterianism is by contrast genteel, even pusillanimous. How many die or would die for it today? Thus, when I compare nationalism and traditional religions I make use of my dimensional analysis. A nation has its myth or myths (history as taught in high school and the like, loaded history, of course, underlining heroes and national values); its rituals of various kinds, from inaugurations to memorials to the dead, even its sports and its language; its emotions of patriotism and pride, and so on; its institutions; its ethics (how to be a good citizen); its material and artistic dimension (from its land, to its monuments and music, and so on); and its doctrines (democratic ideals, ideology, religious tradition, and so on).

In the 1980s I also got interested in the analysis of modern religions – not so much the new religious movements as the trans-formation of old traditions. Here I saw the key as being colon-ialism. Again there is a strong methodological content to my interest because the new movements among major faiths have to do with something which is beyond, but of the same order, as nationalism (in fact, some cases cannot strictly be distinguished from it). The key to all this is colonialism or imperialism, which was a kind of nationalist hubris. The religions, helping to shape civilizations, needed to remake themselves in the face of the challenge of the West, which came not just imperially, but came as nations superior in science, military power, organization, to some degree culturally, and brimming with democratic modernity, not to mention a condescending breed of religion. I wrote up a lot of my conclusions in what in the USA was treated as a textbook, though by Cambridge University Press in Britain as a work of reference, my *The World's Religions* (1989). The first half of the book deals with ancient and medieval history of religions. The second half deals with the colonial period and its aftermath. This second half provides a kind of general theory of religious responses to the challenge of the West. The two main forces to emerge were types of modernism (Islamic, Hindu, Buddhist, Japanese, and so on) and forms of 'fundamentalism', returning to supposed traditional values but also in their own way modernizing. These trends were also manifest in the colonizing religions, mainly Christianity, which also experienced the pressures of the new post-Enlightenment, industrial, democratic, socially transformed modern world.

How I came to write the book was amusing. A company called John Calmann and King, very skilled and enterprising, was commissioned by Cambridge and Prentice-Hall to produce the book. Their offices are over the way from the British Museum. They called me and asked me to drop in one day. I went to see them. Larry King and an assistant talked to me, he being the boss. They wanted me to do the book but, because I already had my *Religious Experience* on the market, I said, 'Look, this new book would only be a rival to my old book.' In reply, King said: 'But you wouldn't want some other bastard to do it, would you?' I succumbed. I wrote the book with fervor and on a wholly different plan from my old one. I treated regions rather than traditions and sliced history at the colonial period. It was much more sociological (or should I say macrosociological) than the old book which was more oriented to my theory of types of religious experience. I started on July 1st of that year at my wife's place in Italy and, with only a week off for a trip down the Po valley, finished 240 000 words later on September 30th. I was near dead, but happy. I was happy because I had made an important statement. But because it was classified in America as a textbook, it has been slow in receiving recognition, though I find that texts creep into professors' theoretical consciousness slowly but surely. I do not mind if eggheads read Foucault but teach Smart! Anyway, all of my efforts in the 1980s were more oriented to the whole idea of worldview analysis as a larger category than simply the history and phenomenology of religions.

Though it will no doubt be obvious that in a broad sense I believe in comparative methods and ambitions, it is not quite true that she who knows only one tradition knows none. Consider bhakti religion. It occurs in Christianity, pretty obviously. Does the fact that it is rife in Indian theism not make a difference to our account of it in the West? Because of the high importance I assign to it (but equally recognizing the vitality of contextual analysis too), I am disturbed by two tendencies in the past 20 years or so. One is the trend to the particularization of cultures – even to the suggestion that cultures are incommensurable. This is eminent nonsense which I need not remark on except to say that it is like saying that because we are all individuals we do not have noses. It is a kind of racism, dividing humanity into subspecies. The specialists often despise comparativists, but comparative methods are common sense responses to obvious challenges posed by both similarities between traditions and differences. The second worry about Religious Studies is a product of its very successes in the past 30 years. We hire someone in Taoism, let us say, and take a powerful candidate from Sinology. But she may not really be interested in Religious Studies or the logic of our enterprise. Such already exists in both Judaism and Christian studies. In Christian studies, worse, you often get scholars who refuse to teach across the board. In my view, the pseudo-specialization of traditional Christian scholars is frequently a disgrace, but I shall refrain from going on. The net result of 'specialist' tendencies could be the fragmentation and disintegration of Religious Studies. I am deeply worried by this trend, since there are so many pressures in academic life in this direction. I know that often earlier comparativists and Religious Studies scholars could be shallow. Nowadays, monographs are deeper, and it is a great pleasure to see how many good scholars there are in the academy.

This brings me to a vital methodological point, which is increasingly influential in my thought now that we are in the mid-1990s. I was myself fortunate in having been immersed in philosophy in my early days, and having taught it in the Universities of Wales, Yale, Wisconsin-Madison, Hong Kong and elsewhere from time to time. I chose to move into Religious Studies, it is true, but philosophy gave me a sense for conceptual clarity. I have carried that over into the study of religion. I often think that some of my colleagues in the field lack it. They do not always make much effort to bring new conceptual order into their thinking. Often, they think it is enough for a person to know Sanskrit or Hebrew or Chinese. Far be it from me to decry language skills! I have spent a lot of my life learning Latin, Greek, French, Chinese, Sanskrit, Pali and so forth. But linguistic skill is often rated above conceptual insight, and wrongly so. I know a senior Indologist who is a conceptual idiot, and conversely one of the best books written on Confucius was by a relatively non-linguistic philosophy colleague, Herbert Fingarette. Often the assumptions of scholars channel their activities in unfortunate ways. I consider the critical and fresh look at categories always to be vital. Sometimes newly fashionable writers, such as Foucault in the 1980s, can loosen up and change perspectives, but not if they are turned into dogmas. It is difficult to know quite what the right word is for such conceptual freshness and clarity. I have regarded it as an important part of my contribution to Religious Studies. It is no doubt true that sometimes I stick too much to clear ideas (and perhaps they can be shallow), but I do regard it as important in a new field that people should know what they are doing, beset as they are by the Scylla of faith and commitment on the one shore and the Charybdis of unempirical and fashionable theories on the other.

Since the notion of conceptual analysis has already been pre-empted by philosophers and the application of concepts in religion needs to apply to comparative data, I shall use the phrase conceptual synthesis to stand for the intellectual tasks which I have in mind. Let me give two examples for the kind of thing I mean. First, I think it is important to distinguish between the roots and the formation of a tradition. Thus the period of the formation of classical Christianity, with its doctrines, narratives, liturgical life, and organization, could be said to be the fourth century CE, even though it has its roots in the life of Christ and the memory of ancient Israel, and so on. It is fallacious to see roots as somehow the whole of origins. This has afflicted modern attempts to see Hinduism already there *in nuce* in the Vedic hymns and the Upa-nishadic corpus. Again, sorting out the notion of syncretism is important: why do we count a blend between a tradition and a secular worldview as not being syncretism? Maybe, moreover, a less loaded term, such as blend, is needed. Another variety of conceptual synthesis lies in the introduction of a genuinely cross-cultural vocabulary into our field, using notions such as bhakti, li (correct performative behavior), dhyana, and so on just as in the past we have coopted totem, tabu, and so on. I carried out a bit of this program of globalization in my Gifford lectures, *Beyond Ideology* (1981).

Much earlier I adverted to my theory of dimensions of religion. This can give us entrée to a number of comparative and theoretical questions. After the monographs are written, after the texts and archaeology are published, it is surely necessary to try to make sense of human worldviews and religiosity, to piece together a general theory of worldviews. For instance, we may contemplate the relations between the doctrinal and experiential dimensions. If it be the case that mystical consciousness frequently culminates in a sense of non-dual experience, then this helps to make sense of certain doctrinal or philosophical trends: the expression in theistic religions of a close communion or union with the Divine; the notion of the non-dual experience in Hindu Advaita and related doctrines; the advaya consciousness in Mahayana absolutism; the realization of nirvana (there being no Other to be united with) in the Theravada, and so on. There appear in short to be correlations between the dimensions. Certain organizations, such as monasticism, obviously favor the contemplative life and, with it, experience. Rituals of worship and devotional prostration favor and are favored by personal theism and a sense of divine Otherness. The concept of substance in philosophy is often correlated with the use of sacramental and magical rituals. I found myself returning to this broader vision of our field's speculative power in the book I referred to earlier when speaking of van der Leeuw, entitled *The Dimensions of the Sacred: an Anatomy of the World's Beliefs* (1996).

I consider it is part of our task as intellectuals not only to theorize about the configurations of religions and worldviews, but to reflect more philosophically about the relations between religions. I addressed the idea of dialogue in a number of works, including *A Dialogue of Religions* (1960), written very early in my career, and again in *The Yogi and the Devotee* (1968). I returned somewhat to these themes in *Buddhism and Christianity: Rivals and Allies* (1993). I do not think Religious Studies should remain so purist that it eschews all philosophical and critical questions about religion. It will also be seen from my account that I prefer a road vision of what we might do. We do not want to be trapped in simply descriptive and historical researches, admirable as these are for much of what else we engage it. There is a reflective side to our field, and we should be suitably speculative, and taken notice of more by our colleagues in adjacent fields. Philosophical reflection can do much to enhance students' excitement about our field. While empirical, social-scientific, and historical studies necessarily aim at impartiality and 'objectivity', after we have surveyed the religious scene there remain some vital questions. In the long run, these questions affect educational practice. While I remain very critical of those who secretly sell a metaphysics while claiming to be empirical, there is no reason why we cannot distinguish between our various activities in the field.

But comparisons are still vital if we are to move towards theory in Religious Studies. Moreover, morphology should be dynamic, that is we should compare types of changes as well as types of more static phenomena. I consider this of some importance in my concern with the modern and colonial period. We can see differing kinds of reactive changes to the challenges of the West. Different cultures have tried to absorb differing lessons from the rampant West, and attempt to stave off domination in diverse ways. This is adapting some general approaches of Max Weber to dealing with our better knowledge of the history of modern religions. There is an analogy with recent similar work on the genesis of so-called fundamentalism.

The years since I entered the field – a little over 40 – have been a great success story, though littered too with threats and confusions. The coexistence of Christian and other theological enterprises with Religious Studies confuses outsiders. The drive to specialization may fragment the field. New theories, such as deconstructionism, do not herald well for research; too many of our fellow practitioners may have ideological or spiritual axes to grind. It is difficult to combine one's commitments and professionalism. But all in all, the story of Religious Studies, especially in English-speaking countries, has been spectacular. Moreover, the whole former Soviet empire is opening up to the field. Though the days of older scholars seem far away – men like E. O. James, A. C. Bouquet, and Sydney Brandon in Britain, and George Foot Moore, Erwin Goodenough, and Joachim Wach in America – we must be grateful to these our ancestors. Some of them kept the ideal of cross-cultural studies of religion alive in hard days. In some ways they were naive when compared with more fashionable trends today. But our intellectual forebears should be entitled to their cult of ancestors. They are the living dead. Perhaps the chief difference between those days and now is the great advance of social science and more generally cultural studies in our field. Another good change – especially in Britain – is that increasing attention is paid to Religious Studies in high schools. Our field has always held high the banner of cross-cultural studies and the repudiation of older colonial attitudes in education.

To sum up, then: from the perspective of my fairly lengthy career of scholarship and from my long-time personal and professional interest and involvement in the idea of 'Religious Studies', I see our field as aspectual, plural, non-finite and multidisciplinary. I consider the dimensional analysis of religions and worldviews is necessary to balanced accounts of religions. I advocate strongly the extension of our field to non-traditionally religious worldviews. I consider that, in addition to the expansion of monographic knowledge, we need new theories of religion and worldviews. I do not wish us in a fit of purist empiricism to cut out reflective work in our field: it is just that we need to know when we are doing what. I believe moreover that we should strive to achieve a more cross-cultural and global vocabulary for dealing with traditions both ancient and modern. The net result of such precepts is to bring religion, politics, and human life in general closer together. I think Religious Studies, provided it does not choke on specialisms or commit methodological suicide, has a marvelous future.

3

From Great Neck to Swift Hall: Confessions of a Reluctant Historian of Religions

WENDY DONIGER

Though I have lived a rather bookish life, all that I ever learned I learned for the love of some person, so I must tell the story of my intellectual odyssey in terms of the people who changed my life. I was born in 1940 in New York and raised in Great Neck by Jewish parents who had come to America (my father from Russia/Poland, in 1918, my mother from Vienna/Marienbad, in the 1920s) searching, like modern pilgrims, for freedom *from* religion. My mother was a devout Communist; it was not until I went to school that I learned that there was such a thing as paper white on both sides; I had done my early drawings on the backs of flyers for Henry Wallace (in high school, I was vice-president of the Great Neck chapter of the World Communist Youth organization). My father was a New Dealer and later a Stevenson man. Both of them regarded themselves as ethnically Jewish; they sent money to Israel and to the local temple, fought for the Rosenbergs and against anti-Semitism, and always managed to get some more pious relatives to invite us to a Passover seder. But neither of them would be caught dead in a synagogue.

My mother felt that the world would not be fit to live in until the last rabbi was strangled with the entrails of the last priest. My father, Lester Doniger, was a much more moderate man, in his religious sentiments as in his politics.[1] His father had been a Talmudic scholar, but my father's bible was Frazer's *The Golden Bough*, much of which he knew by heart and shared with me. He had learnt it at New York University, where he had worked his way through school as a stringer for *The New York Times*, going around to all the major churches in Manhattan every Sunday and summarizing the sermons; he was paid by the inch. Eventually it dawned on him that it might be profitable to serve as a kind of matchmaker between those ministers who yearned to see their sermons in print and those ministers who were eager to have at their disposal every week the sermons of the first sort of ministers. Thus he founded in the late 1940s and published throughout his life two magazines for the Protestant clergy, *Pulpit Digest* and *Pastoral Psychology*. Soon he attracted the leaders in the field; the very first issue of *Pastoral Psychology*, in 1950, included articles by Lawrence S. Kubie and Rollo May. But from time to time, when he was short of copy, he wrote, under various pseudonyms, sermons that were preached all over America by Protestant clergymen who little dreamed that their homilies had been composed by an Eastern European Jew. When I was four or five years old, a picture of me in pigtails, sitting in the sun in my mother's daisy patch, graced the cover of a Spring issue of *Pulpit Digest*, over a stanza from the Song of Songs: 'For, lo! The winter is past, the rain is over and gone...'.

So my father found himself active in inter-faith movements. I cherish a photograph I have always thought of as 'Daddy and the Archbishop': there he is, looking so young, with a rather strained smile on his face, accepting from some stunningly ecclesiastical-looking WASP a plaque on behalf of *Pulpit Digest*. I didn't know the phrase 'token Jew' in those days, or even the concept of what Sir [sic] Isaiah Berlin called the 'court Jew'. My father was more than that, but I think, in retrospect, that he probably was that too. He was close friends for many years with Samuel McCrea Cavert, long a driving force in the World Council of Churches; my father also worked closely, and affectionately, with the pastors of the local Episcopal and Roman Catholic churches. I met these men at his office from time to time, and he frequently lunched with them, in Great Neck or New York. But he knew better than to bring them home to my mother.

It was in this atmosphere that I developed, in my very early teens, a passionate interest in religion; it was one way I could rebel against my mother, who had already, herself, rebelled against all the things that children usually rebel against. My announcement that I wanted to start going to Temple Bethel was met with a horror greater than if I had confessed that I was pregnant or a heroin addict. But my religious calling was not merely reactive; I had been, from very early childhood, enchanted by stories about other

worlds, fairies and gods, a fact that is corroborated by a large
portrait of me painted (badly) by my uncle, Harvey Haines, when
I was just five years old: I'm holding a fairy-tale castle, Disney-
turretted and covered with swirls of oil paint patterned like end-
papers, and I'm reading a book that begins, 'Once upon a time...'.

Having been denied access to the religion that was officially
mine, I began poaching. I hung out with the very few Catholic kids
in my overwhelmingly Jewish town. I read the King James Bible
and began writing parables and fables in King James English. I
aspired to become a nun; an ex-nun friend of mine, to whom I
confessed this longing a few years ago, remarked drily, 'Well,
you'd make an excellent Mother Superior, but you'd never be able
to work your way up through the ranks.' When I lived in Oxford,
from 1965–75, my gang consisted primarily of Anglo-Catholic
converts to whom I was introduced by Penelope Betjeman; I had
met her in a convent in Kathmandu, a meeting preserved in a
photograph she took of me with a nun, whom I am eyeing with
speculative envy. The rest of my Oxford world was peopled by
scholars that colleagues referred to as 'brilliant but erratic' – homosexual, alcoholic Catholics like R. C. Zaehner, who directed my
Oxford dissertation. To this day I am far more at home in a
Catholic mass than a Yom Kippur service. I married an Irishman,
but when I was in a bad automobile accident in 1964, I surprised
myself by writing 'Jewish' on the check-in form; as a result, a
Jewish chaplain kept visiting me and annoying me. When I went
back to the hospital for further surgery, I decided to head the rabbis
off at the pass by writing 'Hindu' on the form; scarcely was I out of
the recovery room than a nun came to visit me, asking, 'Tell me,
Mrs O'Flaherty, when did you first embrace the Hindu faith?'

But I am getting ahead of my story. Back in Great Neck, my
mother nourished my passion for myth and fantasy by giving me
her Bible, *Alice in Wonderland*. She carried a copy in her purse at all
times, and pulled it out to read in traffic jams and doctors' offices; I
still know it just about by heart, along with *Through The Looking
Glass*, and I draw from it, like the *sortes Virgilianae*, appropriate
quotations for almost every occasion. She also gave me E. M.
Forster's *A Passage to India*, which persuaded me that India was a
country where everyone was extremely religious. My mother also
cherished a copy of the great four-volume work on the temple of
Angkor Vat published in 1930 by the École Française de l'Extrème
Orient; all her life she wanted to visit Angkor, and she finally did,

on her way home after visiting me in India in 1964. That book remained a kind of icon to me throughout my youth; when she died in 1991 it came to me, and I have passed it on (together with my mother's politics and my own counteracting brand of humanism and eclecticism) to my son, Michael O'Flaherty, who began his graduate study in the history of Southeast Asia at Cornell in 1995.

In high school I fled from what I had come to regard as the excessive reality of the real world by studying Latin and, in unofficial sessions with my devoted Latin teacher, ancient Greek. She taught me that Sanskrit was the language of ancient India, which meant to me the language of *A Passage to India* (and, by extension, Angkor Vat). I was hooked, and I chose to go to Radcliffe, rather than Swarthmore, largely because I could learn Sanskrit at Harvard. And so I did, as a 17-year-old freshman. But I never studied religion at Radcliffe; what would my parents have said? I did take one course in comparative religion, with the great Arthur Darby Nock, who often came to class staggeringly drunk and inspired many anecdotes about his nudity, but was not otherwise, as far as I knew, what I would later call 'brilliant but erratic'. I also took several classes with Albert Lord, who taught me most of what I know about oral epics and folklore.

I recognized even then my mother's influence in this flight from religion, but oddly enough I did not until quite recently acknowledge her equally great influence in what I fled *to*. For surely the long shadow of Angkor Vat fell over me as I sat in the dusty little room in the top of Widener library, studying Sanskrit with Daniel H. H. Ingalls. A charistmatic teacher and old-fashioned gentleman, who owned and ran the 'restricted' (i.e. anti-Semitic) Homestead, in West Virginia, in his spare time. He was the formative intellectual influence of my university years. He taught me not only Sanskrit but Indian literature, Indian history, Indian religion, and something else, harder to define, something about the pleasure of scholarship, the elegance of the written word, the luxury of the world of the mind. I also, in the manner of old-fashioned Sanskritists and 'Orientalists', studied Greek with Zeph Stewart, Sterling Dow, John Finley, and Adam Parry, and English literature with Reuben Brower, William Alfred, and Harry Levin.

So I was trained not as an historian of religions but as a Sanskritist. But I was not a *real* Sanskritist; *real* Sanskritists (Ingalls was not at all typical) are 'anal-retentive' pedants interested only in verbs and nouns, and I was a hot-blooded ex-ballet dancer still interested primarily in stories. *Real* Sanskritists, on two continents, have been known to turn and leave a room when I entered it. I looked elsewhere for my intellectual nourishment. I roomed with an anthropologist, Alice Kasakoff, who had been assigned to me by the Radcliffe authorities; in those days of unspoken quotas, Jewish girls somehow just seemed to end up with Jewish roommates. Alice introduced me to her colleagues (Vogt, the Whitings, Beidelman, Mayberry-Lewis) and instilled in me an enduring admiration for anthropologists. Later, at Oxford, Evans-Pritchard and Rodney Needham supplied most of my intellectual nourishment; like Blanche Du Bois, I have always depended upon the kindness of strangers, and who more strange than anthropologists? In 1968, when Christoph von Fürer-Haimendorf (an anthropologist) wanted to hire me to teach in the School of Oriental and African Studies, where he was acting as Director, he found it impossible to sell me to the Sanskritists, and instead winkled me into the History Department, where Bernard Lewis welcomed me and protected me until I left England in 1975.

Back at Harvard, my husband, the Irishman, studied Judaism with Ben-Sasson, but I did not dare. I did, however, wish that I could learn Hebrew, to read the Bible in the original; this I regarded as a legitimate desire, philological rather than theological. In my junior year, when I was 20 and my brother Tony was ten, I came home for Thanksgiving and saw that, after dinner, my father was reading something with Tony; it transpired that he was teaching him Hebrew, in preparation for his Bar Mitzvah. I was astonished, and the questions burst out: 'Daddy, do you know Hebrew?' ('Of course I know Hebrew'); 'Why is Tony having a Bar Mitzvah?' ('He wanted it; all his friends are having them, and getting presents'); 'Why didn't you teach me Hebrew?' ('You're a girl'). The last was the hardest to swallow, of course, and the most paradoxical: my father was so anti-orthodox that he never ever intimated to me that he could read Hebrew – the subject simply never came up – but some conservative Jewish strain in him compounded that reticence with the instinctive feeling that it was not right for a girl to learn Hebrew. I finally learned a bit of Hebrew three or four years ago, sitting in on a class in Swift Hall taught by a student who was studying Judaism with Michael Fishbane and the history of religions with me; when he came to my office, we would take turns: he would play teacher, answering my questions about Hebrew verbal forms, and then I would play teacher, answering his questions about Eliade.

Eliade had been the turning point for me. When I finished my Harvard dissertation in 1968 and sent it, all 950 pages of it, to Ingalls, he read it and asked Mircea Eliade to serve as reader, since my dissertation was about *yoga* and the mythology of Siva, and Eliade was the world's greatest mythologist and had published, in 1958, a definitive work on *yoga*. (Ingalls believed in having the best of everything.) Eliade liked the dissertation well enough ('Il y a des longeurs', is one phrase from his long, hand-written French evaluation that still makes me wince as I recall it) and published two parts of it in two issues of the journal, *History of Religions*, that he had founded just two years previously; this was my first publication. Eliade and I began to correspond, and he published another article of mine, the seed of my 1973 Oxford dissertation, in 1971. But we never met in person until 1978, when I moved to Chicago to take up my post as professor of the history of religions and as an editor of the journal that had first published my work. But again, I am getting ahead of my story.

By the time I started teaching at SOAS in 1968 I had begun to write books, based on Sanskrit texts, all right, but books about myths. When I was in Moscow, in 1970–1, with nothing to do but plot with Jewish dissidents, ride horses, and conceive my child, I turned my Harvard dissertation into a book. The major challenge was to find a way to refer to all the different versions of the central myths without retelling each one in its entirety as I had done in the 950-page dissertation with its 'longeurs'. The works of Claude Lévi-Strauss gave me the key I needed, the principle of the *mytheme*, a unit of symbolic meaning that could be identified in several different versions. This meant that I did not have to discuss each version in detail, but could begin to make statements that applied not only to the structures but to the meanings of a whole corpus of variants. A related, but less mechanical and more philosophical, tool that Lévi-Strauss gave me was the idea of the paradox at the heart of myth, certainly at the heart of the erotic/ascetic conflict that was the subject of my dissertation. Lévi-Strauss taught me that a myth is an always doomed attempt to solve an insoluble contradiction, and that the inevitable failure of that enterprise is what drives a culture to tell the same story over and over again, finding ever new ways to show how the square peg does *not* fit into the round hole. I published the book, *Asceticism and Eroticism in the*

Mythology of Siva (1973) and was quickly, and not entirely justifiably, welcomed into the cadre of structuralists; the structuralist anthropologist Edmund Leach reviewed my book in the *Times Literary Supplement* of January 18th, 1974, my very first review. Lévi-Strauss himself expressed his pleasure in finding that his method worked as well for written texts as it did for the oral traditions for which he had devised it. This was the first in a series of works in which I attempted to forge a new kind of link between Sanskrit and Western letters.

Then I published the first of three Penguin Classics, *Hindu Myths: A Sourcebook, translated from the Sanskrit* (1975). The editor of the Penguin Classics at that time was a wonderful woman named Betty Radice, who taught me a great deal about writing and translating[2] and rescued me from the Groucho Marx paradox ('I don't want to be a member of any club that would have me for a member') as applied to translation: 'I don't want to write a translation for anyone stupid/lazy/uneducated enough to make use of a translation.' It was she who provided, *in her own person*, the ideal audience for a translation from the Sanskrit: an intelligent, educated, intellectually curious person who did not claim to know very much about Indian literature. And it was she who, in her optimism and modesty, taught me that there were thousands of people like her who would buy such translations. My father, the publisher, had also been such a person, but he had died in 1971, before I published my first book. Betty Radice also replaced my father in another essential role, one that I have always tried to play for my students: that of a presumed or implied reader who is *on your side*, who has both the intelligence and the good will to give you the benefit of the doubt when you dare to take a chance, to stretch your knowledge and your intelligence beyond what you have done before. Years later, Morris Philipson, Director of the University of Chicago Press, took over that role when he became, as he remains, a stimulating and courageous companion in my writing, emboldening me to undertake projects, such as the English edition of Yves Bonnefoy's daunting *Dictionnaire des Mythologies* (1991), that would have made other publishers run and hide behind their balance sheets. More than that, Morris has understood all that I have written, from early drafts, even before I understood it myself, and opened up new possibilities in projects that were just beginning to take shape in my mind. He is the last in the line of publishers who have been, along with anthropologists, my essential intellectual companions.

I continued to learn from Betty Radice when I worked on *The Rig Veda* (1981), and though she had died by the time I did the last Penguin, *The Laws of Manu* (with Brian K. Smith, 1991), her friendly ghost still hovered over the work, as it continues to hover over my subsequent translations, such as *Textual Sources for the Study of Hinduism* (1990) and the final books of the *Mahabharata*, which I am translating for the Chicago project begun by the late Hans van Buitenen (who was brilliant and in certain ways erratic). For me, the translations balance the more interpretive books, filling me up with a world of knowledge gleaned from an intimate and detailed response to a particular author, in contrast with the more diffuse and more self-generated conversation that drives me when I write the other sort of book. It troubles me that many departments do not regard translations as 'real' works, that they will not count them toward tenure; for I have learned as much from my works of translation, and certainly contributed something that will be more useful to other scholars for longer, than from my 'original' works of scholarship.

While I was working on the first Penguin, I was also working with Zaehner on my Oxford dissertation, about heresy, which I then turned, with the encouragement of yet another great publisher, Philip Lilienthal, into a much broader and more theological book about evil: *The Origins of Evil in Hindu Mythology* (1976). Zaehner was working at that time on his wild book about Charles Manson (*Our Savage God*), and I benefited enormously from long, boozy dinners with him at the Elizabethan restaurant, next door to the Sheep's Shop immortalized by Lewis Carroll; we talked about Manson and the Pope and Aristotle and cabbages and kings. I also realized, years later, that writing this book, which is in large part about the evil of death, was a way of trying to make sense of my father's death, my first major experience of inexplicable and unjust evil. I had failed to draw any comfort from Jewish or Christian approaches to the problem, and found a more compatible meaning in the Hindu mythology of evil. The Hindu solutions (or, rather, non-solutions: Lévi-Strauss was right) encompassed many of those proposed by Judaism and Christianity, such as the idea of plenitude (that God wants the universe to include everything, including injustice and suffering), while it eliminated others, such as the conflict between the goodness and omnipotence of God, on the one hand, and the existence of evil, on the other (most Hindu gods are neither good nor omnipotent). But the comparability of these non-solutions, the very fact that many of them were tried by both Hindus and Jews, began to lay the foundation for a comparative method that I was only to recognize explicitly some years later.

In 1975 I gave up tenure in London and followed my husband to Berkeley, where I hovered uneasily on the margins of the Department of South and Southeast Asian Languages. Here the Sanskritist syndrome raised its ugly head in earnest, and for the first (and, I am happy to say, the last) time in my academic life I found myself *persona non grata* in an academic institution. Not only was I not the right sort of Sanskritist, but I was writing books about sex (a subject that made Sanskritists nervous) and I was a woman (ditto). Berkeley, like most Sanskrit departments at that time, divided the world into two groups: white men, who taught courses about Ideas and were tenured, and women of color, sometimes married to the white men in the first group and informally referred to as 'pillow dictionaries', who taught Languages and were untenured. As a white woman with Ideas, I was what my friend Mary Douglas (another anthropological good fairy in my life) has taught us to call a category error, matter out of place, dirt. My colleagues wanted me to go away, and though friends like Alan Dundes (an anthropologist) and Phil Lilienthal sustained me with their sympathy and anger at my treatment, I went.

I went to Chicago, accepting an invitation that Joseph Kitagawa, Dean of the Divinity School, had been extending to me, on and off, for some years, and one that I had long resisted on grounds both official (I had absolutely no training as a historian of religions, which seemed to me a very good reason not to take a job teaching it) and unofficial (as a New Yorker, I scorned and despised the Midwest and didn't want to live that far away from the Atlantic ocean; I had visited Chicago only once, on a visit to my Radcliffe anthropologist roommate, Alice, and remembered nothing but people fishing for smelts at night with lights, which I regarded as barbaric). So I went, kicking and screaming, simply because I was broke and my marriage, to a man who had dug his toes into the sands of California and refused to leave, was broken and I needed a job.

I would not have had the courage, or the hubris/chutzpah, to take the job in the Divinity School, were it not for the fact that I was to have a joint appointment in the Department of South Asian Languages and Civilizations (SALC), the field in which I had been spawned, if not nourished, and one in which I already had several supportive colleagues in Chicago. I had lived with Edward Cameron Dimock and his family during my year in Calcutta, in 1963–4 (Ronald Inden, also at Chicago, had also been a member of the extended Dimock family that year); I had worked happily in Berkeley with A. K. Ramanujan and McKim Marriott on a Social Sciences Research Council project on karma, which resulted in an edited book, *Karma and Rebirth in Classical Indian Traditions* (1980); I had met Milton Singer in Madras in 1964, and I had not forgotten his gracious kindness to my mother there; and I had admired Susanne Rudolph from afar at Harvard in the early 1960s. These were not Sanskritists but *Indologists*, a mellower and more exciting group, quasi-anthropological; they liked me and had kept my ego alive during the dark Berkeley days by inviting me to Chicago and listening with interest to my reports of works in progress. I figured, if I bombed as an historian of religions, I could always earn my keep as an Indologist. I was also told that I had an appointment on the Committee on Social Thought, but I had never heard of it and therefore did not realize what a difference it was going to make to my life.

My willingness to rush in where historians of religions feared to tread was also sustained by conversations with several card-carrying historians of religions, chiefly David Knipe and Frank Reynolds, who persuaded me that I was, in fact, very much a self-made Historian of Religions, that my long-standing and enduring interest in myths, in other peoples' religions, in *religion*, a current flowing even deeper and longer than my interest in India and Sanskrit, gave me precisely the mind-set that was wanted at Chicago. Once a year, I would run to Frank Reynolds and announce that I was going to resign from the Divinity School, that the imposter syndrome was getting me down and I was tired of being asked about my methodology; and he would patiently explain to me why I belonged there and urge me to face the fact that I did, in fact, have a method. And from the other side, card-carrying Indologists like Ed Dimock (an ordained Unitarian minister) and A. K. Ramanujan (a trained comparative folklorist, and an old friend of Alan Dundes) persuaded me that I was not the only Indologist who had failed to sleep easily on the Procrustean bed of the Sanskritists, that there were – at Chicago – other misfits like me. I began to understand that I had found my true home at last. I would soon learn that the Committee on Social Thought often characterized itself, with inverted arrogance, as a *salon des refusés*; the SALC department, despite the fame and success of its members, seemed to me very much the same sort of place, my sort of place. After years of feeling myself an ugly duckling, a Sanskritist *manqué*, at last I realized that I had always been a young swan, an historian of religions in Sanskritist's clothing. And only years later did I realize that most historians of religions are created, like mules, by intellectual hybrid breeding, a cross between, say, a Sanskritist and an anthropologist (I leave the reader to decide which is the horse, which the donkey), or a theologian and an African historian; they do not usually breed directly from mule to mule, one historian of religions cloning another.

So I came to Chicago and began my religious education by teamteaching, with Mircea Eliade, a course entitled 'Classical Problems in the History of Religions'. It met once a week in the evening and was divided into two halves which I came to regard as hell and heaven: for the first hour or so, a student would present a paper, often a very bad and boring paper, and I would have to fight hard to keep from nodding off (a life-long problem: I am an early morning riser and evening nodder-offer). Then we would break for coffee, and Eliade and I would respond to the paper. He went first, and with infinite kindness would fish out the one interesting point the student had made, or, failing that, the one interesting point that the student *should* have made about the subject, and he would then present, under the guise of an expansion of the student's insight, his own ideas on the subject. He was wonderful, infinitely learned, raising difficult questions, suggesting problematic solutions, and dropping precise bibliographic references like the pieces of gold that fell from the mouth of the good daughter in the fairy tale. He was equally kind to me when I ventured my own, at first largely Indological, comparative insights. At the end of the two quarters of that course, I felt that I was beginning to understand what the history of religions was all about, though I was still afraid to go it on my own.

That Spring, I continued to play it safe with Indological courses (Mythology in the Brahmanas, and The Translation of Religious Texts: (*The Rig Veda*)), but I also branched out in another new direction, albeit timidly and again not alone: I taught a course on the *Bacchae* of Euripides and the *Frogs* of Aristophanes, but I taught it with James Redfield, of the Committee on Social Thought. It was on the Committee that I learned that, though not a certified classicist, I had enough Greek from the old Harvard days not, perhaps, to teach Greek, but to hold my head up in a discussion of Greek literature and religion. James Redfield once remarked, accurately if ungenerously, that I had Loeb Greek: I was only confident in my Greek if the English was there on the opposite page. Dr Jonson might also have damned me, along with Shakespeare, with the accusation that I got the Greek from the meaning, not the meaning from the Greek.

It was there that I learned, from David Grene, that, as an Indologist, I could see things in Greek texts that classicists might not see, and might be glad to be shown. It was there that I learned, again from David Grene, that my own view of a primary text, indeed my own view of the real world, was a legitimate source of my scholarship and my academic vision, something that I must put into my teaching and my writing. This was probably the single most transformative thing that I learned at Chicago. David Grene has remained the dominant intellectual influence in my life; we have taught many courses together (often with David Tracy making up the troika), courses on the *Odyssey*, the *Iliad*, Greek tragedies, Herodotus, Hesiod, and Plato. And together we translated *Antigone* (in 1983) and the *Oresteia* (1986) for performances by the Court Theatre. David Grene did for my understanding of Greek literature what Eliade did for my understanding of the history of religions. Even now, every time I dash off a sentence that is merely clever or glib, or sounds as if it is saying more than it is really saying, the voice of David Grene sounds in my ear, like Jiminy Cricket, 'Now, now, ducky, say what you really mean.'

The books that I wrote after that were different. I had always chosen topics that moved me, and I had always informed my philology with my own tastes and opinions; indeed, this was one of the factors that the Sanskrists had held against me. I had written the book about evil in order to understand my father's death. But now I began, from the start of each project, to wrestle with problems that had come to me not only from India but from my own world, the world of Communism and Freud and, later, feminism, the world of ballet and opera and Russian novels. These books were written not out of a desire to put in print what I understood, but, rather, in order to find out what I understood. A woman once said to Abraham Lincoln, 'How do I know what I think until I hear what I say?'; I have only known what I thought about many major issues by reading what I have written. Even more, I have found out what I thought by teaching each of my books, in its embryonic stages, to my students, whose sharp challenges ('That's not at all clear') and generous contributions ('I just came across a Chinese text on that theme') have inspired me and kept me more or less honest.

It was in Chicago during this period that I also began to think about religious issues in a new way, largely under the stimulus of my friendship with David Tracy, who sustained not only my love for Catholicism and my fascination with enduring religious questions such as evil, death, and the purpose of human life, but my newly growing interest in contemporary approaches to these issues. And so, with a little help from these friends, I began to write about what I cared about, to write truly comparative works integrating my academic training in the study of India with my broader education in Western literature and religion. I also began to supplement my basic approach, which remained a combination of old-fashioned philology and a modified Lévi-Straussian structuralism, with other approaches, some of which I had long known but felt unqualified to use in print, some of which I picked up from my colleagues – and, more often, from my students – in Chicago.

For instance, *Women, Androgynes, and Other Mythical Beasts* (1980) examines the problems of powerful women in a world of frightened men, and draws on some basic Freudian approaches to human sexuality. Some people decided then and there that I was a Freudian, and the label has stuck. Writing that book taught me a lot about my own complex relationship with feminism; I also began to see connections between the Hindu myths and aspects of popular American culture, such as Superman comics. Putting together my Sanskrit, always the basis of any mythological project, with the Greek texts that I had now been teaching for some years, I ventured into the tenuous world of Indo-European studies, a kind of halfway house between the mono-cultural discipline of Indology and the kind of Eliadean or Jungian universalism that I was still unwilling to tackle. Drawing parallels between Indian, Greek, and Irish mythologies of the horse, and trying to make sense of them in the light of what I had actually learned from the horses I had owned and known ever since Penelope Betjeman taught me to ride, I ventured on a comparative model of the meaning of stallions and cows, bulls and mares. Though I have since learned to distrust the Dumézilian and historical aspects of this paradigm, I still have confidence in its cross-cultural symbolic patterns. And I would now state in more boldly feminist terms the formulations about relationships between men and women and texts that are sketched rather tentatively in the sections of the book that deal with sexual fluids and with the power struggles between gods and goddesses. *Tales of Sex and Violence* (1985), another work from this period, also makes use of Freudian approaches to the imagination; it made me see the psychological connections between the apparently disparate worlds of ancient Indian Brahminical sacrifice and folklore. But it challenges certain implications of the Freudian symbolic system by raising the question of symbols that seem to stand for themselves, or that, at least, do not seem to stand for the things that Freudians say they stand for. Thus, if a cigar may sometimes symbolize not a phallus but a cigar, so the Siva-lingam, the phallus of the god Siva, may symbolize either itself or something else, like death.

Dreams, Illusion, and Other Realities (1984) continues this challenge to Freudian paradigms as well as to Western scientific paradigms, contrasting them with the 'softer' approaches of Indian idealism and Jungian idealism. It was this book that got me labeled as a Jungian in some circles. I had started Radcliffe as a math major, as well as a Sanskrit major, and my first teaching job was as a T. A. in the History of Science, with Leonard Nash at Harvard; that training suddenly came back to me for this book, persuading me, incidentally, that nothing in life is ever really wasted. But *Dreams* owes less to psychology than to philosophy; reading Michael Polanyi and medieval Indian Vedantic texts taught me to take far more seriously than I had ever done before the philosophical levels of myths that I had hitherto interpreted largely on the structural, theological, and psychological levels.

The books I am working on now are even more personal. One, *The Mythology of Horses in India*, is based on the 1986 Radhakrishnan Lectures that I gave at All Souls College, Oxford; it is in part a celebration of my life with horses, and is dedicated to Penelope Betjeman, who taught me to ride, and to David Grene, my riding partner in Chicago and Ireland. *The Bed Trick: Sex, Text, and Masquerade* is a monstrous, megalomaniacally cross-cultural study of the basic theme that has snaked its way through all of my books, the relationship between sexuality, identity, and narrative representation. *Illusory Women and Double Goddesses*, the 1996 Jordan Lectures at the University of London, compares the Hindu and ancient Greek myths of the phantom Sita and the phantom Helen, Ahalya and Alkmene, Renuka and Scylla/Charybdis,

Damayanti and Penelope. And *Horses for Lovers, Dogs for Husbands* is a novel about my relationship with my parents and with the creatures in the title.

Over the years, people kept asking me why I did what I did, but I resolutely resisted all the requests to lay out my 'method', for the very good reason that I didn't think I had one – several, maybe, but not one. I finally succumbed and wrote *Other Peoples' Myths: The Cave of Echoes*, a kind of a cross between an argument for the study of other religions and an *apologia pro vita mea*. In this work, I attempted to provide an answer to Allan Bloom and other scholars' critiques of contemporary attitudes toward cultural pluralism, and to open up new avenues for conversation between cultures in an age increasingly anxious about cultural contact. Another work in progress, *The Implied Spider: Myths as Political and Theological Micro-scopes and Telescopes*, the 1996–7 ACLS/AAR Lectures, is a defense of the comparative method in a politically correct climate. These works together are a long-delayed repayment to Frank Reynolds for his early faith in the existence of my invisible methodology and for his encouragement of my fledgling persona as an historian of religions. So, I guess, is this present essay.

The lives of many women are, I think, inspired by their desire to be unlike their mothers; but so often, like Alice in Looking-Glass Land, the farther we try to run away from that house of mirrors, the quicker we find ourselves walking back in at the door. In my case the pattern was enhanced by my desire to be like my father, a desire acknowledged by Freudians but frowned upon in the pre-feminist society of my youth. And, finally, the accidents of marriage and professional opportunities landed me in a role that I had never dreamt of, indeed had never known the existence of, before I accepted it – the role of a professor of the History of Religions at the University widely regarded as the *axis mundi* of that discipline. Indeed, the discipline itself is now changing in new directions that render rather *vieux jeux* the approaches that were regarded as radical when I first tried them out. Somehow, like a Kafka character, I went to bed one night an *enfant terrible* and woke up the next morning an old fuddy duddy. But I don't regret missing my 15-minute allotment of, if not fame, at least trendiness. Non, je ne regrette rien.

Notes

1. Some of the material in this paragraph is reproduced from pp. 13–14 of *Other Peoples' Myths: The Cave of Echoes*. New York: Macmillan, 1988; Chicago: The University of Chicago Press, 1995.
2. Part of this paragraph is taken from my essay, 'On translating Sanskrit myths'. pp. 121–8 of *The Translator's Art: Essays in Honor of Betty Radice* Harmondsworth: Penguin Classics, 1987.

4

There Is No Religion There

FRITS STAAL

I was born in 1930 in Amsterdam which was then – and still is – a flourishing center of culture. My serious education began at the Barlaeus Gymnasium, one of those almost legendary continental European 'gymnasia' where we were not naked (γυμνός) – gymnastics being kept firmly on the periphery – but where the concentration was on learning. The foundation for my knowledge was laid there and I have continued to draw upon it throughout my life. My family background was in the arts. I was the only child of an architect father with children from other marriages and a mother whose occupation was *haute couture*; there were not only drawing-boards but a small *atelier* where girls were sewing clothes. My mother had played the piano, but that was before me. I took to the violin at five and played almost daily for the next 19 years – first because I wanted it, then because my mother made me do it, finally doggedly and despite the obvious fact that I was never going to be good at it. My teacher was a violinist in the Concertgebouw Orchestra and took me along during rehearsals where I was allowed to sit on a podium chair. Before my legs could reach the floor I had heard and seen all the great conductors of Europe.

The Barlaeus Gymnasium was a few miles' walk, passing within a stone's throw of the Concertgebouw and through the large passage gateway underneath the Rijksmuseum. At the Barlaeus, I became what I have always remained: a scholar. I like giving lectures but have never looked upon myself as a teacher, let alone an 'educator'. I like to think of myself as a writer of non-fiction or, if need be, 'an unsuccessful writer', as my first tax consultant (in London) had declared. The term 'scholar' refers in American English to a person who has a scholarship or someone who is concerned with the 'humanities' which is not what I am interested in; I believe in *human sciences*. The English language separates 'the two cultures of arts and sciences', a separation derived from the

52

distinction between *Naturwissenschaften* and *Geisteswissenschaften* introduced by nineteenth-century German philosophers. This distinction, paradoxically, is not reflected in German or any other European language: in Dutch, German, French or Russian, 'scholar' is the same as 'scientist'. The term refers to anyone who studies such subjects as we were taught at the gymnasium: in addition to geography and history, not just of the Netherlands but of the world, mathematics, physics, chemistry and biology, and many languages along with elements of their classical literatures. In addition to Dutch, we had six years of Latin and German; five of Greek and French; four of English; and two of Italian and Hebrew, optional but included by a good-sized minority. I was especially interested in Greek, perhaps because it was the most exotic or best taught, but all our teachers were learned, lively and eccentric men and women with a great interest in developing the minds of their pupils. At the final oral examination, in 1948, my best subject was contemporary Dutch poetry. The questions must have been wide-ranging for the outside examiner, a Professor of Theology from the University of Amsterdam, asked me what year Nietzsche died. I did not know but have always remembered the correct answer: 1900.

Readers will have noticed that the Second World War occurred during the years I have described without mentioning it. Naturally, all our preoccupation with learning does not signify that I did not, like every other Dutchman who was not a moron or deserter, hate the Germans who were marching in our streets. Nor had the German occupation failed to affect me personally. My father had died in 1940, a few days before the outbreak of that war. My mother was Jewish and was murdered by the Nazis in a concentration camp in Poland in 1943. I escaped and was taken in, along with their three children, by a Dutch aristocratic family to whom I dedicated my book *AGNI* 40 years later. It is they who regarded it as obvious that I should attend the University of Amsterdam and enabled me to do so. The only question was: to study *what*?

Before I was 20, at the middle of the century, all subjects seemed to hang together though not equally closely; the human and natural sciences did not differ in method but in development because the human animal was being neglected; the 'humanities' stressed education and culture more than science or knowledge. I did not know that the humanities were to become more trendy and that human sciences would grow out of linguistics and the biological sciences which in depth, breadth and complexity were going to make as much progress during the second half of the century as physics had made during its first.

Being a scholar means that I have always been, and still am, more interested in principles than recent events. I have always disliked the worldview that the media try to force upon us and that concentrates, to the virtual exclusion of almost everything else, on politics, wars and catastrophes – the more, longer and bigger they are, the better. The world is infinitely more beautiful and interesting than the mess most of our leaders are making of it. I don't think we should forget the holocaust (as some Europeans who preach human rights to Asians or Africans seem to do), but I have always disliked its continuing discussion, now for more than half a century – as if nothing more monstrous or of greater significance happened elsewhere at any time. Freudians will be quick to call it denial but I feel we should be trying to forge ahead. Most young adults growing into maturity do not grow up in political history, especially not in the Netherlands, a small country without a strong sentiment of national identity. Our identity is living in the cosmos, probably our first and only chance. I consider myself lucky in that I adopted some such perspective early and have never been lured away from it by thinkers, theologians or politicians pontificating on historicity, ethnicity and the like.

Unimpressed by power (though there are people who have told me that I am quite good at wielding it) and always more interested in the universe in which we live than in who wins an election, I stumbled along, trying to find my place. That led me to mathematics and physics, biology and the study of humans, not only those about whom I had been taught but also non-Europeans and especially Asians. I collected fossils, insects, stamps, looked through a microscope, gazed at exotic maps and drew Chinese characters. My first girlfriend's mother was half Chinese and half Indonesian and her Dutch father was a professor of anthropology. I learned that anthropology is quite different from geography and that there were important subjects we had not been taught. I thought, at first, that the social sciences could contribute something really different but when I examined some of them a little more closely, I found that my earlier conclusions should be extended: there is no principle or methodological difference between those sciences and the natural or human sciences but only that they lag even further behind. In 1948, I could not have explained what those common principles or methods were, though I might have declared: 'facts and logic'. Before this essay is over I shall try to have a better go at it.

On entering the university I had to make a decision. I wanted to do mathematics and philosophy but that combination did not exist and so I was advised to begin with the more serious – and difficult – of the two. Thus I started upon a program of mathematics and physics, with a minor in astronomy; and was allowed to do logic which was, in mathematics, the closest equivalent to philosophy. Amsterdam was not only a center of culture but its university was a center of what our Berkeley Chancellor now likes to call 'academic excellence'. As it happened, the Tenth International Congress for Philosophy was held in Amsterdam in 1948, the year I became an undergraduate. I knew nothing of the subject but listened with awe to some of the world's great philosophers. I remember only a few lectures: one by the topologist and founder of intuitionistic mathematics L. E. J. Brouwer who included in his talk a long quotation from the *Bhagavad Gita*, torn out of its natural context and placed in a new and totally unintelligible environment; one by I. M. Bochenski, a Dominican logician, on the history of logic; and two by Indian philosophers, T. M. P. Mahadevan on 'The Place of Reason and Revelation in the Philosophy of an Early Advaitin', and another who taught me that Indian philosophers are also capable of producing absurdities.

LOGIC

At Amsterdam University I became a pupil of the first of four great scholars who influenced me: Evert Beth, Professor of Mathematical Logic and the Methodology of Science, a formidable worker and writer. I was first his student, then his assistant and later became his colleague. Beth disliked people who had the reputation of immense learning but never wrote anything. He taught me to start publishing on a topic before I knew everything about it: not only because the fastest way to make progress is by writing and no one is ever going to know everything about anything; but also because it is the most efficient method to disseminate knowledge and involve others. Beth was a redoubtable organizer. When he received a form from an academic administrator, he wrote diagonally across it 'I have no time for this' and everyone accepted it. He organized and later involved me in the 'Division of Logic, Methodology and Philosophy of Science' of the 'International Union of History and Philosophy of Science' of UNESCO.

But I am running ahead. Students of philosophy had to do all the usual subjects and in addition were required to select two special fields. I had piled the philosophy program on top of my courses in the 'exact' sciences and my specials were predictable: logic and Greek philosophy. At the Barlaeus, two ambitious young teachers had already read some bits of Platonic dialogues with us; my little knowledge of philosophic Greek came in useful. At the University, the chief diet in Greek philosophy consisted naturally of Plato and Aristotle. When I needed a topic for an undergraduate thesis, I shied away from the two giants about whom so much had already been written, and took up Plotinus who also seemed to provide a link with Asia (Plotinus was born in Egypt and went eastward with the army of Roman Emperor Gordian hoping to study philosophy in Persia and India, but the army was defeated and Plotinus settled in Rome). During my first years at Amsterdam University I also took Arabic. The professor, who came once a week from Leiden to teach a handful of students, was a specialist in Arabic geography (a Dutch tradition) and insisted on reading al-Khwarizmi with me: 'The other students are afraid of it but you are a mathematician.'

With one student friend I read Heidegger's *Sein und Zeit* and Kleene's *Introduction to Metamathematics*, a 550-page volume that combined much logic with some intuitionistic mathematics. L. E. J. Brouwer, already mentioned, was a legend but those of us who wanted to put our eyes on his person could feign a headache and visit a pharmacy on the outskirts of the city where he assisted his wife dispensing drugs. My foster parents suggested that I join a fraternity and though it did not appeal to me I followed their advice and made very good friends. During the summers we went on long tours to Southern Europe hitch-hiking, then a favorite student pastime. Our best bet was to catch an American tourist in a large automobile that would take us many hundreds of kilometers, say, from outside Paris all the way to the Cote d'Azur. Italy was my favorite and I was fluent in Italian at that time. The furthest south we reached was the Greek temple at Paestum. In Amalfi, south of the Bay of Naples, we were allowed to camp in the garden of a Dutch count who was interested in Hinduism. He was a follower of René Guénon and I began to frequent the bookshop of that coterie in Paris and the *Etudes traditionelles* – my first brush with one of many Western distortions of 'Oriental mysticism'.

Guénon hated mysticism, anthroposophy and religion, the things in which he was most deeply embroiled. What was my own religious upbringing? I ask that question only because I am writing this 'Essay in the Academic Study of Religion' and some readers may consider it relevant. Outside the Netherlands, the Dutch are famous or notorious for Calvinism but when I grew up there, I could not have explained what it was about. I mentioned Hebrew: we read the beginning of *Genesis* but though it was my first exposure to the Bible, it was not a religious class. None of my parents, foster parents or friends seem to have been 'religious'. It is not that they were atheists, agnostics or humanists. There was no religion there. On my wanderings through Amsterdam, where the synagogues had already been closed or vanished altogether, I passed many churches but they were mainly used for nonreligious purposes. Once a year, Bach's *Matthaeus Passion* was performed in a church in the small township of Naarden with its hexagonal townplan and that was probably the first time I entered such a building. It was draughty, the wooden benches were uncomfortable and we looked with undisguised curiosity upon the locals who had come, apparently, to listen to the words. University ceremonies were also held in a church and when I gave my inaugural lecture there many years later, I had to climb a pulpit and put my manuscript on top of a large Bible. The 'secular' uses of churches, now widespread in the Euro-Americas, continue as I noted in May 1996, when Professor Wang Gungwu from Singapore lectured on Chinese nationalism in another magnificent Amsterdam specimen. What did strike me this time was its almost Vermeerian luster and cleanliness, allegedly Dutch qualities but rare in academic surroundings even there.

In 1950, two years after the Congress of Philosophy, the Seventh Congress for the History of Religions was held in Amsterdam and was, on that occasion, turned into an 'International' congress. Though the subject was once again one about which I knew nothing, I listened to some of its best proponents and scholars. President of the congress was Gerardus van der Leeuw. No one knew that he was to die two months later but he was an impressive personality, not only the founder of the phenomenology of religion but also Minister of Education, Arts and Sciences in the then Socialist Dutch cabinet. The congress was not held in a church but in the 'Colonial Museum' that later took note of changing times and changed its name to 'Institute for the Tropics'. I knew the museum and its Indonesian treasures well and it was a congenial atmosphere in which to listen to Dutch scholars such as my then-hoped-for future father-in-law who spoke on the Batak of Sumatra; J. van Baal on 'The function of reason in primitive religious systems' (he had been Governor-General of Irian Jaya, then called New Guinea, where, working as an anthropologist, he had discovered homosexual initiation rites); and Sinologist Duyvendak on 'The mythico-ritual pattern in Chinese civilization' (the same Duyvendak who accepted as genuine a fake diary of a Chinese official at the court of the Empress Dowager and was referred to as 'the Dutch oracle' by British historian Hugh Trevor-Roper who had himself vouched earlier for the authenticity of Hitler's 'memoirs'). Mircea Eliade was there but I don't remember him. I was intrigued by Karl Kerenyi, a Jungian classicist now forgotten. The people who impressed me were Henri-Charles Puech on 'Temps, histoire et mythe dans le Christianisme des premiers siècles', A. D. Nock, Raffaele Pettazzoni, and especially Louis Massignon, the great authority on al-Halladj and Islamic mysticism.

It took four years before the germs of that congress produced what might be regarded as my first effort in comparative religion: 'On the circular and rectilinear concept of time'. First published in a Dutch literary journal and reprinted in 1986, it starts with two mottos, in Latin and Greek: Augustine's 'in circuitu impii ambulant' and Heraclitus' 'αιων παις εστι παιζων, πεσσευων' ('life's time is a child playing, playing dice'). The four world periods of the Indian Puranas are similarly called after the throws of dice. The essay went on to paint a familiar contrast heavily indebted to Puech, Erich Auerbach (who contrasted the literary styles of Homer and the Old Testament) and Oscar Cullmann (*Christus und die Zeit*), further inspired by Nietzsche's 'eternal recurrence' and Eliade's 'myth of eternal return'. By roughly that time, I had became convinced that the three monotheisms of 'the West' and the so-called religions of 'the East' are not the same kind of thing though I would not have been able to make clear what the differences were apart from the contrast between rectilinear and circular time.

INDIA

I had just finished what corresponds, roughly, to a BSc and was getting ready for a lengthy program in philosophy and mathematics when something happened more or less by chance which seems to be typical of much of my life. I have always and until the present day avoided reading newspapers or paying attention to the media – an archaic standpoint, I admit, but who can quarrel about taste? A friend handed me a newspaper advertisement: 'Something for you!' The Government of India offered a one-year scholarship to a Netherlands student. I applied and was awarded the scholarship, much to my surprise, until I discovered that the Indians preferred to a professed India expert a student who might know something else and have an open mind. I now had to decide on numerous things about which I knew virtually nothing. I was informed I should forthwith select an Indian university. I had played with Sanskrit but my only half-way serious study of an Asian language had been of Arabic. I did not feel I should go to India to study an Islamic civilization. I had read somewhere that Hinduism was more alive in South India than in the North. Then I found out that Mahadevan, who had talked about early Advaita at the Congress of Philosophy, was Head of the Department of Philosophy at the University of Madras. Madras sounded like hot beaches lined with palm trees and tropical jungles in the *hinterland*. My choice was made and it was a fortunate one.

At that time we went by boat – I have done it since on many occasions – and, after crossing through the Strait of Gibraltar, the Suez Canal and over the Indian Ocean with its flying fish and dolphins, one is ready for something different and new. That something new was Queen Victoria's Gateway of India in the Bombay harbor – a touch of Naples heated to the boiling point – where I started a two-day train journey across the subcontinent and saw for the first time the faces, lit with curiosity, of what seemed to be about a million Indians. Thus did I embark, in 1954, upon the best period of my life.

Mahadevan suggested that I write a PhD thesis. The subject became, predictably, *Advaita and Neoplatonism: A Critical Study in Comparative Philosophy*. It was subsequently published by the Madras University but is now, alas, outdated. My first draft started with a phrase about the 'notorious Sankara'. Why 'notorious?' asked Mahadevan and proceeded to explain that, in English, that word has a pejorative sense and I better replace it by something else. Mahadevan was a very gentle person; he would mainly comment on my grammar and on matters of philosophy only if I had written something outrageous. But I knew all the time that one cannot study Indian philosophy without Sanskrit. In Indian universities, Indian philosophy was taught in departments of philosophy through the medium of English; a British leftover, convenient for me but only temporarily. Mahadevan referred me to his colleague, V. Raghavan, one of the world's greatest Sanskrit scholars. He was rumored to be a difficult man and when I went to call on him my knees almost gave away. He turned out to be efficient and helpful but it was obvious that I could not study Sanskrit at an Indian university where Imperial pressure had not been able to prevent that incoming first year students already read that language with some measure of ease. Raghavan introduced me to an old pandit at the Madras Sanskrit College who knew English and taught Sanskrit to little children using Panini's method. His name was Sankarasubrahmanya Aiyar – by then, Indian names no longer posed a problem for me. I walked daily a few miles under a large black umbrella, like every Indian who can afford one, and started upon a course of studies which familiarized me with Panini's system of grammar before I knew Sanskrit.

I stayed for three years in India. Until I lived in other parts of Asia, I never met so many genuinely friendly people or made greater friends. I lived for two years in a room in Victoria Student Hostel, Triplicane, Madras, which now seems (when I visited it again in March 1996) like a small cell: a heavy door, a barred window, a stone floor and no furniture. If we except a Tamil Hindu from Sri Lanka (then called Ceylon) and a Buddhist boy from Ladakh, I was the only foreigner. There was one other research student, Ramachandran, a brahman mathematician interested in topology. He became my first Indian friend and introduced me to life in India. My training began with the purchase of a mat, soon followed by a pillow and very thin mattress because of my fervent pleading with Ramachandran who said: 'You people are soft!' He would also declare: 'Indians are lazy', but walk for miles to save a few annas, not unlike my Barlaeus teacher who taught us that mathematicians are lazy and then took any amount of trouble to find a shorter proof. Not that saving annas was not important to me: my 200-rupee monthly stipend from the Government of India often arrived late and Mahadevan advanced the money from his own pocket (one rupee consisted of 16 annas; at present, 200 rupees pays a one-way taxi ride from Delhi airport to New Delhi).

It was as if I could not get enough of the people of India. I understood why Nehru wrote that his greatest inspiration came from their large numbers and exuberant vitality. I did not address four million people as he did on the beach of Madras, rows of loudspeakers extending for miles and miles. I talked to philosophers about Heidegger and to mathematicians about Gödel's theorem. I strolled with my fellow students on the beach in the evening, when the heat of the day was over. I participated in large temple festivals, surrounded by Chola art and architecture and startled by the sound of enormous bells. The main sculptures of the gods were regaled like kings with foods and oblations and bathed in liquids while their representatives, 'travel' images cast in bronze by the 'lost wax' technique, were carried around and outside into the streets and sometimes to river banks or the sea. In Kanchipuram, on one of those memorable occasions, the leaders of the two main Vaishnava sects arrived on elephant back and argued with each other surrounded by throngs of followers. The name of one was Prativadam Bhayankaram, 'Terrible Refutation'. Logic and religion combined in one fantastic spectacle. Later, in the North, I heard the bhajan songs of bhakti devotionalism which most Indian philosophers look down upon as 'childishness'. I preferred the vigorous structures of Veda recitation, resembling the counterpoint of classical European music but without the harmony and heard in brahmin homes more than temples. It started as a hobby in Chidambaram outside the temple of the Dancing Shiva and progressed to Kerala, southwest India, where the Nambudiri brahmin community was reputed to be the most inaccessible, traditional and orthodox in all of India. I found that their style of recitation and chant was very different from the prevailing style of Veda recitation in southeast India. Later I discovered that there are regional differences throughout the subcontinent which tell us something about the Vedic schools. I slowly began to understand that the Vedas are not 'holy books' but the repositories from which mantras originate by a curious process of taking bits and pieces and transforming them into something fit for ritual use. In this process, attention is not given to meaning but to form.

I did not know that some recitations I heard were intended to accompany ritual performances. A member of the Amsterdam intelligentsia would never give ritual a thought and I discovered only later that the appropriate concept in India is not *orthodox*, 'of right opinion', but *orthoprax*, 'of right activity', that is, *ritual* activity. That the Nambudiris performed Vedic ritual could not have occurred to me because I started without any knowledge of the Vedas or Vedic ritual even though I was a student of Vedanta which means: 'end of the Veda'. Why did my Nambudiri friends not tell me about it? Because I did not ask.

My second great teacher after Beth became T. R. V. Murti of Banaras Hindu University, a South Indian brahman who had walked from Madras to Banaras and stayed there, eventually becoming Sayaji Rao Gaekwad Professor of Indian Civilisation and Culture (and later, replacing Radhakrishnan temporarily, Spalding Professor of Eastern Religions and Ethics at Oxford). Murti held a series of traditional and modern degrees and his Sanskrit was as strong as any pandit or professor of Sanskrit. He knew everything by heart, all the sutra texts, the Upanisads and other philosophical classics, Panini's grammar, of course, and long passages from Patanjali, author of its 'Great Commentary'; but all of that was only the core of his knowledge. Upon that foundation, he would argue, distinguish truth from falsehood and evaluate doctrines and ideas. He was famous for *The Central Philosophy of Buddhism: A Study of the Madhyamika System*, a philosophic book based on the Sanskrit sources – an unusual topic for a Professor at BHU, or any Indian professor.

Since I wanted to study with him but had no money, he procured me an appointment as a Temporary Lecturer of German. I had to teach chemistry students how to read a textbook and was a little embarrassed when the German ambassador paid a visit. It was more interesting to meet German Sanskrit scholars such as von Glasenapp whom I rowed across the Ganges (I was a member of the BHU Swimming and Boating Club). I witnessed his struggle with the billboards on the river banks in the Hindi script which is the same as Sanskrit Devanagari, spelling it out with increasing alarm: KO – KA – KO – LA! I am not implying that von Glasenapp did not know Sanskrit; I don't know how much he knew but he certainly was accustomed to it only in Roman transliteration. At that time Hajime Nakamura also visited Banaras; he knew the script well. I got to know him better at the Buddha Jayanti in New Delhi in 1956 where he spoke along with Nehru, the Dalai and Panchen Lamas and a plethora of Buddhist leaders and scholars from all over the world. I studied under Murti together with a Japanese Sanskritist and met students from Bali in the 'College of Indology'. I worked separately with a Bengali pandit in the old city on a text of 'navya nyaya' or 'modern logic'.

Murti was an Indian philosopher of the classical type, like the ancient Greeks and Chinese: he paid serious attention to argument. After his classes we walked with him, missing our hostel's dinners, and he would stop at each cross-road, raise his arms and put his hands behind his head, holding forth while bicycles, bullock-carts and rickshaws passed by. Few would dare to interrupt him but many became his friends. He owned a house in the city and when he was Vice-Chancellor of the Sanskrit University, he let me stay at the Chancellor's Lodge with one servant who prepared large dinners for anyone I invited. On the last occasion I met him in India, Murti introduced me to the audience as abhinava-kautsa, 'a new Kautsa' after the ritualist Kautsa whose thesis had been, two-and-a-half millennia ago, that mantras have no meaning. Murti did not agree with that thesis but he was eager to discuss it, unlike the Western monotheisms which he regarded as unworthy of serious discussion because they paid no attention to logic anyway. Buddhism was another matter; he knew it not only from the texts but had taught Buddhist students in Buddhist surroundings in Sri Lanka, then still called Ceylon. I had been there first in 1954, when the Indian Philosophical Congress met at Peradeniya. A Bengali scholar of Buddhist logic and I were lucky in making friends with a young monk who took us around to some of the lesser known temples and monuments. Though monks have nothing to do with the world, our guide belonged to an influential family which opened all doors. That is not inconsistent with Murti's memorable statement made during a Berkeley discussion with Edward Conze many years later: 'Buddhism is Hinduism for export.'

During long university vacations, I began to travel through the subcontinent, mainly by bus and train, later on motorbike or by car. India is replete with natural beauty and ancient monuments. You might come across a semi-ruined temple in a forest not mentioned in any guidebook or marked on any map. There were few tourists but India abounds in interesting personalities, traditional and modern. Student friends took me to the Srngeri Sankaracarya, one of four (or five) 'pontiffs' of the Advaita Vedanta philosophy which is also a sect. He spoke Sanskrit and I could answer him only many years later. Srngeri was on the banks of a river surrounded by the jungle I had been dreaming about. Another friend took me to his fishing community on the West coast; he became a theoretical physicist who lectured at Oxford and Harvard. Indians with a modern education know more about the world than Euro-Americans and so do many Asians. They are, like others, not free from prejudice, but they know contemporary civilization in addition to some part of their own tradition. In Europe or the Americas, the few people who know India are 'specialists' who try to distinguish what they know from everything they do not know.

In my third Indian year, I reached the foothills of the Himalayas. I do not remember homesickness at any time, but I must have had a touch of it for I read Proust and Thomas Mann in a place referred to by English-speaking villagers as 'Crank's Ridge'. It was inhabited by a collection of foreigners gone spiritual, including a Danish Swami who called himself *Sunyata* ('emptiness'), two Australian women carrying Suzuki's 'Doctrine of No Mind' (which elicited other local comments), the Argentinian lama Anagarika Govinda with his Parsi wife Li Gotami and, temporarily, me.

Determined to ascend later up to the real Himalayas, I returned to South India, completed my dissertation and my collection of recordings of Vedic recitation, representative of different styles, some of them very rare and never heard by outsiders since they were intended for brahman ears only. On the boat-trip back to Europe, I prepared an annotated list of these recordings and wrote a small book entitled *Nambudiri Veda Recitation* which explains the different styles, methods of learning and oral transmission and what uses are made of them. The list was sent to the few people I thought might be interested, including another Dutchman, Arnold Bake, Reader in Indian Music at the School of Oriental and African Studies, London. By return mail a letter arrived inviting me to come to London and play my recordings for a SOAS audience. Afterwards the head of the department, John Brough, asked me to come to his office where he then offered me the Lectureship in Vedic. I had not heard of it and explained, in my Indian accent, that I was a logician who knew some Panini, little Sanskrit, and practically no Vedic. Brough may have thought that I was not only a scholar but also a gentleman. He was interested in logic (he explained Indian logic on the BBC to British philosopher A. J. Ayer whom some Indians mistook for an Aiyar brahmin) and offered me an Assistant Lectureship in Sanskrit as a compromise. Back in Amsterdam, I asked the advice of Beth. He said: 'I cannot offer you anything like that soon, but I must warn you that you will be labeled a logician, a Sanskritist or something else and that label will stick. Even Bertrand Russell was labeled a mathematician by people who did not share his philosophy. You better make up your own mind.' That remark about 'labeling' has stayed with me throughout my life.

SANSKRIT AND ASIAN STUDIES

I went to London and found in Brough my third teacher though he was a colleague and not a teacher – should we say preceptor? He was a genius with a liking for difficult problems and texts and a dislike of idle chatter. Never sermonizing on samadhi or meditation like many loquacious mediocrities, Brough possessed an extraordinary power of concentration. I once saw him reading a Sanskrit text and making notes. It reminded me of Russell and his friend Crompton Davies who stood 'at a distance of no more than a yard' in front of Whitehead who was writing mathematics and watched him cover page after page with symbols. 'He never saw us, and after a time we went away with a feeling of awe.'

Brough's most well known contribution is the edition and translation of the Gandhari *Dharmapada*, a Buddhist Dhammapada text in a language that did not have a name. The text had to be put together from manuscript fragments, originally found in Khotan, Central Asia, and now preserved in Paris and St Petersburg. The Introduction pays due attention to history, geography, the language of the text, and then turns to religion. Brough could write but he also knew what he was writing about: 'The resulting vast accumulation of insipid mediocrity which piety preserves is by no means peculiar to Buddhism. It is even probable that religions in general have an inherent tendency to conserve indiscriminately the dreary and the insufferable, which, because of the virtuous intentions of their authors, are accorded no less reverence than great religious art and literature.'

SOAS had been established in 1917 by a Royal Charter which specified that it should 'give instruction in the Languages of Eastern and African peoples, Ancient and Modern, and in the Literature, History, Religion, and Customs of those peoples'. For an extended period of time, the salaries of the instructors were extremely low and when the School made an urgent appeal for help to the Treasury, the then Financial Secretary, Lord Baldwin, replied: 'The opportunities of earning an income from the teaching of Oriental languages must be so limited that it does not appear to me that you ought to have any difficulty in retaining your existing lecturers or acquiring new ones on existing terms.'

At SOAS, there was plenty of opportunity to go overseas on extended periods of fieldwork and not much discussion of students or requirements, least of all the busy-body interference of administrators with trivia which is now so endemic to American academia. Instruction was provided on demand and no one paid attention if there were no students in any particular subject. David Snellgrove, one of the best-known scholars of Tibetan Buddhism, was often without students and left for Nepal, trekking through unknown Tibetan areas close to the main Himalayan range and collecting materials. We once discussed the idea of me accompanying him to Dolpo and spending the winter there. I would have learned Tibetan but I was just getting engaged to an Indian girl and perhaps the fear of freezing temperatures had also something to do with it; the fact is, I did not go. David went, returned and published two volumes on *Four Lamas of Dolpo*, one of his least-known and most impressive books. About Chris Hooykaas, Reader in Old-Javanese, we did not know whether he did or did not have students at any particular time. He wrote in his office volume after volume on Balinese ritual, always promptly published by the Royal Netherlands Academy of Sciences. Without his work we would possess no reliable information on Balinese ritual and be left with the untutored opinions of the Geertzes and their likes.

How and why was it possible for such opportunities for free and unhampered research to be tolerated and even encouraged? Because SOAS had been set up by the government for the benefit of the India Office, the Foreign Office, and other representatives 'of Government, commerce or missions' – precisely the reasons Edward Said is fretting about in his book *Orientalism*. As a matter of fact, governments never ask for or profit from experts' advice. They set up their own teams of 'experts' who tell the politicians what they want to hear. Said wrote down what people, who know as little about Asia as he did himself, wanted to read. Not surprisingly, his book became fashionable among dilettantes and outsiders. Orientalists no longer dare to call themselves Orientalists for fear of being out of date though the label 'Oriental' is no worse than 'Western' and a great deal better than 'non-Western'.

Presently, everyone yearns for 'Integration', but few realize that the strength of Orientalism is that it puts together what other disciplines cut up into pieces: 'Languages, Ancient and Modern, Literature, History, Religion and Customs'. SOAS provided tools for handling some of what I had learned in India and plenty of opportunity to learn more. It was precisely what I needed.

What *had* I learned in India? Scientific publications tell more than autobiographic musings but there are a few generalities that I may be excused for ventilating here even though they stand in need of qualification. In India, I learned that, from the Indian viewpoint, Judaism, Christianity and Islam are the same and that India offers something quite different that could hardly be characterized by the same concept – 'religion', for example. I found that the most seriously misleading mistakes in the study of the so-called religions of India have been made by scholars who adhered to the idea that the Christian, especially Protestant, idea of religion is universally valid. That prejudice is not confined to missionaries; it is part of Euro-American civilization and modern culture. It is found in many early students of religion and in cult figures such as René Guénon where the Christian roots are further disfigured by elitist and even fascist overtones that also occur in related writings such as those of Eliade.

A particular Christian-Protestant ethnocentricity is to look everywhere for creator gods, creation myths and sacred books. Such entities are either absent from or very rare in South, Southeast and East Asia. Deconstructionists have still much work to do in these domains where theologians have reigned too long. In these same areas, no words for 'theology' or 'religion' existed prior to the nineteenth century. The case of Indonesia is particularly instructive because the Dutch missions bequeathed to the government the notion that every Indonesian adheres, or should adhere, to a religion with a belief in 'One Almighty God' and a holy book. Not applicable to Balinese, Dayaks, Chinese and many others, it was wielded once as a weapon against communism (or personal enemies) and led to dreadful scholarship.

Studying the bhakti movements is not impossible from a missionary or Christian point of view because there are similarities; but other features of Asian religion hardly fit the Protestant paradigm. I began to discover that in India and it is now getting more widely known. Gregory Schopen wrote about it with reference to the study of Indian Buddhism in *History of Religions* in 1991. It does not follow that Protestant or even missionaries' work is always wrong. Among the world's best-known funeral rites are the tiwah rites of the Dayaks of Kalimantan, described by Hans Scharer, a member of the Basel Mission. The methodological vicissitudes of his work are of particular interest. Scharer lived for seven years in Kalimantan making copious notes (in some 800 notebooks) based upon what he was told by informants, especially ritual experts. Subsequently he went to Leiden, studied anthropology with J. P. B. de Josselin de Jong, and wrote a dissertation in German which was published in English translation as *Ngaju Religion. The Conception of God among a South Borneo People* in 1963.

In the Preface to this book, de Josselin de Jong is surprisingly ambiguous about the contribution of anthropology to Scharer's work. On the one hand, 'It was never granted to Scharer, with his self-acquired insight, to pursue his studies on religion in Borneo as a trained anthropologist; it is likely the result would have been work of inestimable value.' On the other hand, he acknowledges 'a remarkable thing', that is, 'that much of Scharer's interpretation of Ngaju religion was not due to his anthropological training but had already developed during the years of close and continued contact with the Ngaju, before he made the acquaintance of academic anthropology'.

Parts of Scharer's 1963 book were based upon his original note-books, but these themselves were published later, in particular *Der Totenkult der Ngadju Dajak in Sud Borneo* of 1966. The two books are often inconsistent with each other. Which of the following is true:

> The conception of God is the focal point of Dayak culture, by which everything is defined and to which everything is referred ... the social and economic aspects of this sacred contest must also be seen and interpreted in relation to it (1963);

> We learned that if we wished to get to know the Dayak religion better, we must first of all know the funeral cult which is one of the most important features of the religious, economical and social life of the Dayaks (1966)–?

The first statement, written later but published earlier, is a straight-forward expression of the missionary faith, apparently unchecked by anthropology. 'Social and economic aspects' are mentioned but interpreted in terms of a 'sacred contest', that is, in theological terms. The ethnocentricity of Scharer's views may have been elicited by the influential opinion of the nineteenth-century linguist A. Hardeland, author of a Dayak grammar and dictionary, that 'the highest divinity of the Dayaks is a shadowy being devoid of significance' – a view consistent with much of Scharer's own materials as was sagaciously remarked by J. van Baal (referred to above). What happened, apparently, is that Scharer, when writing his dissertation, was pressed to conform to 'academic anthropology' and 'methodology' and speculated accordingly along the lines of his missionary background and education with results that were predictable and uninformative insofar as they were not also misleading. The resulting *credo* was quite different from the original statements published in 1966 which ring more true, in particular to someone familiar with oral civilizations of Asia.

We learn here how reliable descriptions by a missionary may be distorted because of the methodological requirements of 'scientific anthropology' – a curious result! (For further detail and connections with Balinese 'Hinduism', see my recent book, *Mantras between Fire and Water: Reflections on a Balinese Rite*, 1995.)

LINGUISTICS

I cannot follow my peregrinations in detail but there are a few points of interest in the present context. On leave from London, I taught Indian Philosophy at the University of Pennsylvania, where I also married the Indian student of anthropology I had met in London. My stay in Philadelphia enabled me to participate in 1960 in the International Congress for Logic, Methodology and Philosophy of Science at Stanford where I heard and met Noam Chomsky. Not all linguists welcomed or understood his linguistics but I was not a linguist and to me it seemed the natural synthesis of logic and Panini. Chomsky knew logic well but had not been directly exposed to Panini until much later (I discuss the details in my forthcoming book, *The Language Animal*). I concluded that linguistics is a universal science like mathematics or the 'natural' sciences. Chomsky became my fourth preceptor, at first mainly through his writings through which he was already the preceptor of an entire generation of scholars and scientists. Through Morris Halle, Chomsky's right hand whom I also came to know there, the Stanford congress led to my first publication in linguistics ('A

Method of Linguistic Description: The Order of Consonants according to Panini', *Language* 38 1962:1–10).

Late in 1960, back in Philadelphia, I received a call from Amsterdam sounding me about a prestiguous chair in philosophy that had been lying vacant for seven years. Frantic consultations followed. Norman Brown, the Pennsylvania Sanskritist, was looking for a successor: 'philosophy is a non-subject; Asian studies is where the future of humanity lies'. Brough was sympathetic: he was interested in logic and not in the future of personkind. In Continental Europe, philosophers are regarded as Thinkers with Profound Wisdom. By accepting the Amsterdam chair, referred to by my friends as the 'golden cage', I became a center of public attention. I set up an Institute of Philosophy, wrote in the newspapers, gave interviews and did a little research. I had no opportunities to do fieldwork and could not even get a sabbatical leave to accept Chomsky's invitation to visit MIT for one year, teach the Sanskrit grammarians and see what was going on there in linguistics and related disciplines.

In 1967, after five years, I decided to resign from my Amsterdam chair and leave for the United States. Chomsky regarded it, for political reasons, as the wrong decision but I have never regretted it although I would not now recommend such a risky move to any academic with a family (ours then counted two children in addition to ourselves). Chomsky's department at MIT was not unlike Plato's *Academy* and transformed not only linguistics, philosophy and psychology but gave birth to the cognitive sciences and other new disciplines. The idea was born there that domain-specific rather than domain-general mechanisms characterize the human mind as they do the organs of other animals. It is not often that one gets a chance to witness from nearby the birth of a science. When I arrived, it had already happened; the baby was crawling and beginning to talk. Gone were the concerns with methodology that had hovered so heavily over earlier linguistics and other immature sciences. While new discoveries were made almost daily, Chomsky made it crystal clear why there was no 'discovery procedure' as positivist and behaviorist philosophies of science had proclaimed. Whatever method there was conformed to Bertrand Russell's statement I quoted in my book *Rules without Meaning*: 'Instinct, intuition, or insight is what first leads to beliefs which subsequent reason confirms or confutes.' Scientific knowledge springs from intuitions steeped in facts, sharpened by logic and continuously tested by both.

BERKELEY AND ASIA

The second half of my life began in 1968 when I joined the University of California at Berkeley. It has been at least as interesting and rewarding as the first but I shall not write about it in any detail. My assignment was to set up a Department of South Asian Studies, later South and Southeast Asian Studies. I tried to create something like SOAS but was more successfully recently in the Netherlands where there is now, at Leiden, a post-doctoral International Institute for Asian Studies. At Berkeley I was half-time in the Department of Philosophy, teaching Indian philosophy and, through 'philosophy of language', a bit of linguistics. A paradox about philosophy, professedly the most general of all subjects, is that philosophers, especially good philosophers, are with few exceptions extraordinarily provincial. The bad ones may be interested in 'Oriental philosophy'. The good ones at Berkeley wanted me to teach Indian philosophy not because they were interested in it but because it met a fashionable demand, soon also in the eyes of the administration. I have never liked teaching Indian philosophy to people who do not know Sanskrit. It is showbusiness more than serious training or scholarship and good students know it.

A typical Berkeley product was my book *Exploring Mysticism: A Methodological Essay* (1975, 1988; also a Penguin Book and translated into Italian, Dutch, Japanese and Swedish). I argue there that mysticism can and should be studied rationally and that it is difficult or impossible to distinguish between the effects of mantra recitation, meditation, breathing exercises and hallucinogenic drugs. Mystics and others have tried to make sense of mystical experience by constructing 'superstructures', and my book is such an interpretative superstructure. I have never had a full-blown mystical experience but have tasted the fruits of meditation, which are not any more illusory than dreams. At Berkeley, I had other good opportunities to do research. I worked on Indian logic and linguistics with special attention to the question of the universality of these disciplines. Some of my essays and articles were published together in book form under the title *Universals: Studies in Indian Logic and Linguistics* (1988).

The philosophy department had a course on the books called 'Philosophy of Religion' which had mostly been taught by professors who had little difficulty in exposing flaws in the well-known

Christian proofs of the existence of God. When they retired or got
tired of it, the department asked whether I was willing to teach that
course. I thought it would be easy and require little preparation. The
textbooks and readers offered little about the so-called religions of
Asia and I applied 'terrible refutation' to them in areas or topics they
professed to clarify by making them more obscure. Most of these
books spent much time on the ontological argument and I explained
why it cannot be translated into Chinese – or most languages, for that
matter.

Berkeley never prevented me from doing fieldwork in India. A
decade of work in California and India was devoted to the study of
the almost 3000-year-old Vedic Agnicayana ritual which had been
considered extinct for about a thousand years but was performed
in a small village in Kerala in 1975. We were able to document this
event fully which resulted in two large volumes prepared in colla-
boration with the two chief Nambudiri ritualists, C. V.
Somayajipad and M. Itti Ravi Nambudiri. Luxuriously produced
in 1983 as *AGNI: The Vedic Ritual of the Fire Altar*, these volumes are
now expensive and rare (though a less expensive Indian edition is
in preparation). This is unfortunate because they provide the
empirical foundation in terms of which any theory of religion
ascribed to me must be tested first. Luckily there have been other
spin-offs. Harvard anthropological film-maker Robert Gardner
produced the film *Altar of Fire* and there were other publications,
such as on the spread of Vedic mantras and ritual to other parts of
Asia, mudras, 'hand gestures', ritual syntax, and ritual geometry
which, as in ancient Greece, is related to altar construction. I continued these studies within the perspective of the history of science.

An unexpected bonus of working in California is not only the
increasing Asian student population but also the choice I have
between two itineraries to India: Calcutta is slightly nearer
across the Pacific, Bombay across the Atlantic. For many years, I
preferred the Pacific which was virgin territory to me as it was *terra
incognita* on early maps. Instead of stopping in Europe, I stopped in
Japan, Hong Kong and Thailand which were all on the way. At that
time, the American dollar was powerful even in Japan. I began to
make contacts, give lectures, and started doing a little fieldwork
here and there. I did not know the languages but, in Asia, Sanskrit
opens many doors. Sanskrit studies in Japan are an offshoot of the
study of Indian Buddhism but their excellence is due at least in
part to the fact that they are kept distinct from Buddhist studies

carried out by Buddhist missionaries with their own agenda. That is related to a methodological puzzle: all over the world, Buddhist studies have come into their own as a flourishing branch of higher studies, but they are so totally divorced from Indian studies that some students now believe that Buddha was born in China. By the same token, Indologists avoid Buddha who was either India's greatest son or one of two – the other being Panini. Panini, incidentally, is a key figure in Indian civilization, in some respects the counterpart of Euclid. The methodology of the Sanskrit grammarians was influenced by that of the *science of ritual* of the early ritualists. In 1982, I delivered a series of lectures in Poona which were published there under that title.

In addition to places in or on the way to India, I visited others on what was about to be named the Pacific Rim. I stayed in southern Taiwan where there flourishes a tradition of Taoist ritual (also rediscovered in southern China), journeyed via Beijing and Lhasa to Mount Kailas in Western Tibet, traveled in Indonesia and attended most recently, in Bangkok in March 1996, the cremation of the Princess Mother which was as spectacular a ritual ceremony as I have witnessed anywhere. Having had an opportunity to look at the Himalayas from both sides has been an extraordinary privilege but all these experiences, valuable in their own right, have been richly instructive and that applies, last but not least, to living in California with male lovers from Asia.

What methodological lessons may be extracted from such an ambulant life? I am not sure, but one thing I learned is that Asia is, to a surprising extent, *one*, although, by definition, that unity is invisible to area specialists. The contrasts drawn between India and China, for example, are generally misleading and when anthropologists or other field-workers return from their area or village with extraordinary reports or stories of something 'existing only here', I often know that it is pan-Asian. My first advice to students of religion would be to forget about books and methodology and totally immerse themselves in the life of a people, for as long as universities, grants and other practical considerations permit. What are 'a people'? Well, I suppose, a student of religious studies would want to study a group of people who are held together, or held to be held together, by a religion. I would select a manageable group, avoiding the Scylla and Charybdis of what biologists call too much lumping (such as putting snakes and camels together) or splitting (such as separating right-handed and left-handed ringtailed lemurs). Learn the language and concentrate on a set of data or phenomena that can be demarcated and distinguished relatively clearly from others, for example, rituals and mantras (as I tried to do). Try to eradicate all presuppositions and prejudices. That may be easier said than done but attempting it is more fruitful than discussing whether it can, or why it cannot be done. Here is an example. We should never assume that people 'adhere to' the religion that may have figured prominently in our grant application. The names of many religions, after all, are labels attached by outsiders and perhaps there is no religion there. If I had not been able to at least imagine and then ponder on such unexpected consequences, I could not have arrived at the conclusion that Vedic ritual is a 'ritual-without-religion'. That was not the presupposition I set out with when I started to study Vedic ritual. It dawned upon me in the course of writing the first volume of *AGNI*. It was formulated, for the first time and not very clearly, in the Preface to the second.

Two simple objections must be answered before I put a definite stop to these meanderings. The first is that studying religion or anything similarly confined to human beings is different from studying the universe and therefore requires a different methodology: after all, as so many thinkers have told us, we are in these cases studying *ourselves*, and we cannot study ourselves objectively. The answer is that studying ourselves is studying the universe because we belong to the universe. We cannot study the universe *unobjectively* because we cannot study anything *unobjectively*. Studying attempts objectivity or else it would not be studying. I, for one, am not of the opinion that study is the best thing one can do in life. But *if* you do it, it makes no sense to claim that it also cannot be done objectively, that is, that it cannot be done.

The second objection is that studying religion requires a religious sense. That objection was partly answered by a comment once made by Harvard linguist Roman Jakobson, an expert on Slavic languages and also Russian. When it was proposed to appoint Vladimir Nabokov to the chair of Russian literature at Harvard, everyone expected Jakobson to warmly support it. But he explained that he was against it because he was also against appointing an elephant as a Professor of Zoology. Jakobson's quip demonstrates that a special sense is no special qualification but it suggests more than we want. An elephant cannot teach zoology to humans but a literary or religious sense does not disqualify anyone from studying literature or religion. The upshot is that special senses or intuitions are fine, provided they are (as we have already noted) steeped in facts, sharpened by logic, and continuously tested by both.

I have never been a 'student of religion' but have, from my early days with Evert Beth, been interested in the methodology of science. That discipline may throw light on the status of 'The Academic Study of Religion'. I do not question the existence of a 'Science of Ritual' but hesitate about 'Science of Religion', an expression that other practitioners also seem to avoid, unlike Max Müller and others in the nineteenth century. My hesitation is due to the fact that *religion* does not seem to constitute a meaningful, let alone a universal category that may be studied profitably by itself (like *language*, for example). I hasten to add that such a situation occurs elsewhere.

Reality increasingly appears to be one which implies that all names and classifications of sciences are ephemeral and that all and sundry methodological implications are open to discussion. My own work in 'religion', whatever its merit, can only be understood when it is placed in a much wider context. I examine several such contexts in *Rules Without Meaning: Ritual, Mantras and the Human Sciences* (1989, paper 1993) and the perspective is wider in my forthcoming book, *The Language Animal: Wandering with Science in Eurasia*. That book, in which I use the term 'religion' sparingly, inquires into the origin of language and the evolution from natural to artificial languages with animal communication, ritual, mantras, philosophy and science all playing their part. Naturally, I may be wrong in my approach; it is too early to tell, if only because rites and mantras have been insufficiently studied. At any rate, I am uttering this self-indulgent autobiographic grumble in the hope that it may convey or at least illustrate some of the lessons learned from my ambulant life of scholarship and some of the reasons for what I have done.

5

Climbing the Foothills of Understanding

JOHN HICK

The particular sub-division of the wide field of religious studies in which I have worked is the philosophy of religion. During the past 40 years the subject has changed considerably in both its scope and its internal variety. I have been conscious of this particularly in producing revised editions of my small students' text on the philosophy of religion in Prentice-Hall's Foundations of Philosophy series, the first edition appearing in 1963 and the fourth in 1990.

My own books, reflecting these same developments, are of three kinds. First, there are those, coming at roughly ten-year intervals, in which I have made my own contribution, such as it is, to religious thought: *Faith and Knowledge* (1957, 1966), *Evil and the God of Love* (1966, 1977), *Death and Eternal Life* (1976), and *An Interpretation of Religion* (1989), together with smaller books applying some of these themes to Christian theology. Second, there are collections of mostly previously published articles in which I have repeated, anticipated, elaborated, or defended aspects of that contribution, and also some edited and co-edited works dealing with the same issues. And third, there are students' texts and books of readings.

I shall refer here only to the first group. These have all been problem-driven, in the sense of being attempts to contribute to the solution of acutely felt problems facing religious persons. The facing of each has led on to the next, like climbing a mountain range and finding that as soon as you reach a summit another higher mountain comes into view – but with the compensation that each stage of the climb opens up a wider view of the territory, and yet also with the awareness that only the foothills of truth have been reached.

THE MEDIATED CHARACTER OF OUR AWARENESS OF REALITY

The climb began at Edinburgh University, where as part of preparation for the Presbyterian ministry I took the four-year honours course in philosophy. This was under the guidance of Norman Kemp Smith and then, after a wartime gap in the Friends' Ambulance Unity from 1942–5, under his successor A. D. Ritchie, and John Macmurray in ethics. (John Macmurray's writings are now being read and appreciated again after a period of relative neglect. In addition to philosophers, his social thought has influenced the newly elected Prime Minister of Britain, Tony Blair. My impression, attending his lectures and seminars as an undergraduate, was that he had some very important insights – principally that personality is essentially inter-personality – which we, his students, gladly absorbed, but that there were also considerable vaguenesses and lacunae in his larger metaphysical system.) Of these three teachers, much the most influential, so far as I was concerned, was Kemp Smith. He was not primarily an original thinker, but he was a major historian of philosophy, and had a massive, coherent mind formed at the end of the idealist period in British philosophy. While Smith was an important interpreter of Kant (his translation of the *Critique of Pure Reason* is still widely used), his book on Hume revolutionized Humean studies and his work on Descartes was also quite original. However, what I chiefly received from Kemp Smith was the basic Kantian insight that the mind is not passive in perception but continuously active in selecting and grouping, extrapolating, organizing and relating; so that the world as we are aware of it is partly a human construction. In Kantian terms, the diverse impacts upon us of our environment come to consciousness in terms of the system of concepts that are necessary for those impacts to be unified within a single finite consciousness. The central point that took hold in me is that all awareness of our environment is an interpreted awareness. Already at Edinburgh it occurred to me that this could have an application to the epistemology of religion; and in a notebook filled during a slack period in Italy in 1944 I sketched out the basic idea of what was later to be my doctoral dissertation at Oxford.

That there was such a dissertation was due to one of those unpredictable accidents which account for so much of the shape of our lives. During my final year at Edinburgh someone died, triggering the endowment of the Campbell-Fraser scholarship to enable an Edinburgh graduate in philosophy or classics to go to Oriel College, Oxford for two years of research, and I had the good fortune to be the first recipient. My Oxford supervisor – in the British system a graduate student has a single supervisor rather than a committee of three, as in the States – was H. H. Price, the author of major books on epistemology.

Price was independent of the Oxford school of linguistic philosophy then headed by Gilbert Ryle, although of course fully *au fait* with it. His independence from that movement suited me very well, for the kind of linguistic analysis then dominant in Oxford would have had no place for my project. Though Price had a much broader outlook, in his own work he set the highest standard of conceptual clarity and precision of expression. I later (after three years of theological study) turned the dissertation, on 'The relation between faith and belief', into a book while serving as a Presbyterian minister with a rural congregation in northern England, and took it with me to my first teaching post, in the philosophy department at Cornell University, where it was published by the Cornell University Press, and has been in print ever since, currently from Macmillan in London. (It may be encouraging to some graduate students to know that before being accepted by the Cornell U. P. the book was rejected by several British publishers, and that there were seven years between the completion of the Oxford dissertation and its eventual appearance as *Faith and Knowledge*.)

The Kantian distinction between the noumenal thing in itself, and its phenomenal appearance(s) to consciousness, the latter depending upon the cognitive equipment and conceptual resources of the observer, later connected in my mind with Wittgenstein's (1953) concept of 'seeing-as'. Wittgenstein illustrated this with Jastrow's duck-rabbit picture, which we can see *as* the picture of a rabbit's head facing right or *as* the picture of a duck's head facing left; and, as he said, 'we see it as we interpret it' (1953:198). Wittgenstein himself thought that seeing-as is peculiar to puzzle pictures and other manifestly ambiguous phenomena, rather than pervading all visual experience, so that, as he said, ' "seeing as.." is not part of perception' (1953:197). He pointed out that it would not be natural to say of the knife and fork on the table 'Now I am seeing it as a knife and fork.' This is certainly correct. But I think that he was mistaken in his conclusion. The reason why this would not for us be a natural way of speaking is that knives and forks are part of the familiar furniture of our culture, so that we automatically identify them as such. But a Stone-Age person suddenly transported here in a time machine might see the items on the table as small weapons, or as shining ornaments, or as sacred objects full of *mana* and not to be touched. What they are seen *as*, and how they are therefore responded to, depends upon the concepts in terms of which the observer identifies them.

I expanded the notion of seeing-as into that of experiencing-as, involving several or all of our senses together. In experiencing an object as having a certain character (for example being a knife) we are identifying it as having a specific meaning or significance. This is not semantic meaning, the meaning of words and sentences, but the pragmatic meaning in terms of which we live all the time. For to see what is there as a knife and fork includes being in a dispositional state to behave in relation to them in ways appropriate to their being a knife and fork, namely by using them as implements with which to eat. However, the world of meaning within which we live most of the time is composed of *situations*, which are more complex than individual objects and which have a pragmatic meaning over and above that of their constituent objects. The multi-layered sphere of overlapping meanings within which we live is jointly created by the impacts of our environment upon us and by the conceptual system formed within us by our own cognitive choices within a given cultural and linguistic world.

RELIGIOUS FAITH AS 'EXPERIENCING-AS'

The correlative notions of experiencing-as, and of the forms of meaning which it half discovers and half creates, can, I believe, be applied to the analysis of religious experience. The religious mind experiences both objects (the bread and wine in the eucharist, statues of saints, of the Virgin Mary, of Hindu gods, the sacred icons in an Orthodox church, Buddhist stupas, the tombs of Sufi saints, and so on) and situations (from life as a whole to particular occasions – the birth of a new life, the closure of a life in death, the experience of worship, of human goodness, 'miraculous' recoveries and escapes from injury, viewing the starry heavens above and being conscious of the moral law within, being struck by the beauty of nature – as mediating the presence of God or the enlightenment of the dharma or the requirements of heaven or awareness of the Tao...). In experiencing in this way the religious person is making an (often unconscious) cognitive choice. For the situation itself is always objectively ambiguous, capable of being experienced either in purely naturalistic terms or in religious terms (presupposing but going beyond its purely natural character). To take an ancient biblical example, the prophet Jeremiah's experience of the Chaldean army's attack on Jerusalem as Jahweh's punishment of faithless Israel did not cancel, but added a further dimension to, his awareness of the mundane political and economic significance of the event. And at the other end of the religious spectrum, when an 'awakened' person within the Mahayana Buddhist tradition comes to experience *samsara* (the process of ordinary life, with all its anxieties and suffering) selflessly, as *nirvana* (the blessed state of joyful serenity), the ordinary world is not obliterated but on the contrary is more intensely experienced, but in a new light.

In such cases the religious and non-religious minds are experiencing the same situation, but experiencing it differently because at a pre-conscious level they are interpreting in fundamentally different ways. And I identify this voluntary interpretive element within our conscious experience as faith. It follows that the purely naturalistic experience of the world is as much a matter of faith as the religious; for *all* our conscious experience is experiencing-as. This conception of faith does not replace but should be added to the traditional ideas of faith (*fides*) as believing propositions with a strength that exceeds that of the evidence for them, and also of faith (*fiducia*) as trust in someone or something.

In *Faith and Knowledge* this understanding of religious faith as an uncompelled interpretative choice led to the notion of 'epistemic distance', the idea that in order to preserve our human cognitive freedom in relation to the divine we exist at a distance from God – not however a spatial distance, but a distance in the dimension of knowledge. And that in turn is related to the idea that the universe is, from our present point of view within it, religiously ambiguous – that is, capable of being comprehensively understood both religiously and naturalistically – so that both options are objectively possible and both alike incur the risk of being profoundly mistaken.

ESCHATOLOGICAL VERIFICATION

This conception of faith has to face the dilemma of verifiability versus factual meaningfulness that was being so powerfully posed by Logical Positivism. This movement, launched into the English-speaking world by A. J. Ayer in the 1930s and 1940s, was rapidly fading out in Britain in the 1950s. But whereas many philosophers of religion thought that it could now simply be ignored, it seemed to me that the fundamental positivist insight, that to exist is to make an in principle experienceable difference, posed a challenge to religious belief that had never been satisfactorily answered. This challenge was renewed by, for example, Antony Flew in *New Essays in Philosophical Theology*, published in 1955. Flew and others said in effect: You believe that God exists; but how would the world be different if God did not exist? If there is no observable difference, even in principle, then the statement that God exists is empty or, as the Positivists put it, meaningless. It was not good enough to say that the *belief* that God exists makes a difference to us, for that difference could be made even if the belief is false. The correct religious response to the challenge seemed to me to lie in what I called eschatological verification. The basic idea is that although the human situation is religiously ambiguous from our present standpoint within it, the religions teach that its total structure is such that there will be continued human experience beyond this life and that this will be either instantly or, more likely, progressively incompatible with a naturalistic understanding of the universe. Thus the basic religious claim is, if true, experientially confirmable to the point of excluding rational doubt – although not of course falsifiable if false, since if it is false no one will ever be in a position to note this fact. In illustration I offered the parable of two travelers on the same road, one believing that it leads in the end to the Celestial City while the other believes that it only leads to a precipice and then nothingness. Neither can predict what will happen round each next corner except the last; but in the end it will be evident that one has been right and the other mistaken throughout. It follows that the difference between their beliefs was all the time a genuine and not a merely empty or meaningless difference.

RELIGIOUS EXPERIENCE AS THE BASIS FOR RELIGIOUS BELIEF

Given the religious ambiguity of the universe from our present position within it, and the ultimate post-mortem resolution of this ambiguity, together with the fact that many people now experience life, or some element or moment within it, religiously, the next question is whether they are rationally justified in living on the basis of the understanding of it prompted by their religious experience. I have argued that the basic principle that it is rational to base beliefs on our experience, except when we have positive reasons not to,[1] applies impartially to all forms of putatively cognitive experience, including religious experience. The debate about the rationality or otherwise of religious belief thus hinges upon possible reasons to distrust religious experience. There are a number of possible reasons – particularly the obvious differences between sense experience and religious experience – but these can, I believe, be dissolved. I developed this argument within the context of Christian belief, and was thus working on parallel lines to William Alston in his many articles over the years leading up to his definitive statement in *Perceiving God* (1991).[2] I particularly value being in the same camp as Bill Alston, so far as the epistemology of religion is concerned, because I regard him as the most important and successful contemporary thinker in this area. He has worked out the argument for the possibility of veridical experience of God much more fully and rigorously than I; though I also think that he has faced less fully the further implications of this position arising from the fact that the people of other religions are equally justified in basing beliefs on their own religious experience, and that many of the beliefs thus justified are mutually incompatible. This is the epistemological problem of religious plurality to which I shall come presently.

There are two other main recent developments in the epistemology of religion which all of us working in the field have had to take note of. One is the 'Reformed epistemology' of Alvin Plantinga (see his essay in Plantiga and Wolterstorff 1983) and a number of others. This holds that there are 'properly basic beliefs', which are foundational and thus not in need of external justification, and that belief in God is of this kind. This is open to two different interpretations. On one interpretation properly basic religious beliefs are 'free-standing', not grounded in religious experience; and this position does not seem to me to be defensible. But on the other interpretation – which is, I feel sure, the intended one – what makes a belief *properly* basic is its occurrence in appropriate circumstances. Thus 'I see a tree before me' is properly basic if I am having the experience of seeing a tree before me. And 'I am in God's presence' is properly basic if I am experiencing God's presence. This is very close to Alston's position, and seems to me to be basically sound.

The other recent development has been Richard Swinburne's attempt to show by means of Bayes' theorem that the probability of divine existence is more than half; and more broadly to show that the entire scheme of basic Christian theology constitutes the most probable picture of reality. This program seems to me not only to be anachronistic, a throwback to medieval scholastician and unrelated to the needs of the modern mind, but also not to succeed even in its own terms, as I have argued elsewhere (1989 and my essay in Padgett 1994).

Both of these developments, which are technically superb and which constitute impressive philosophical exercises, are seriously limited, in my opinion, by very conservative theological presuppositions. They belong to philosophy of religion in the now old-fashioned sense in which this is understood to be the philosophy of the Christian (or at most the Judaeo-Christian) tradition, and thus do not face the problems created by the fact that Christianity is one major world religion among others. Indeed Alston, Plantinga, Swinburne, and the many others who are working within the confines of their own tradition, are for the most part really doing philosophical theology rather than philosophy of religion. But if one claims to have established the epistemic propriety of believing, on the basis of religious experience, in the reality of the Christian deity, one should face the fact that there are others who believe, likewise on the basis of their own religious experience, in the reality of what are phenomenologically different deities, and also of even more different non-personal religious ultimates.

THE IRENAEAN THEODICY

But before coming to that, the next problem to hit me – not through any one particular event but just by being part of the human race – was the ancient and unavoidable problem of evil. This surely constitutes the biggest obstacle that there is to religious belief. I had begun to address it in my lectures at Cornell, and then at the Princeton Theological Seminary, and seized the opportunity of a year's sabbatical leave (helped out by a Guggenheim fellowship) to confront it more fully. With the two summers before and after the academic year I had almost 18 months available, which were spent with the family at Cambridge, England, where I was made a Bye-Fellow at Caius College. The result was *Evil and the God of Love,* in which I contrast the traditional Augustinian type of theodicy with what I call the Irenaean type. The Augustinian scheme hinges upon a catastrophic rebellion against God, first by Satan and his angels, and then by humanity. This has resulted both in the fallen and sinful state of human life and also in a disordering of the entire physical world, producing 'natural' evil – life preying upon life, diseases, earthquakes, droughts, famines, and so on. (There are of course other important themes in Augustine, particularly his privative conception of evil as a lack of good, which I also discussed at some length.) This traditional Augustinian and Calvinist picture, which is still held by many very conservative Christians, is open to obvious serious criticisms. There is no evidence for, and much against, the idea that there was once an 'unfallen' human race living in a right relationship with God and with one another. And the notion that natural evils are a result of the Fall is ruled out by the fact that they existed long before there was any human life. But more basically, the idea that God initially created a perfect universe – in the sense of a dependent universe that was as God wanted it to be – which then went radically wrong through the choice of free beings within it, is self-contradictory. Finitely perfect beings in a finitely perfect environment may be free to sin, but will not do so. If they do, they were not perfect after all. And so if God is the creator *ex nihilo* of everything other than God, then God cannot escape the ultimate responsibility for the entire history of the universe, including the 'fall' of the free creatures who are part of it. We remain of course individually and corporately responsible, in varying degrees, for what we freely do. But on a different level, which does not clash with our own human responsibility, God must have the final responsibility for having created such beings as us: this is where the buck stops!

In the writings of some of the early Greek-speaking Fathers of the church, particularly Irenaeus and Clement of Alexandria, but others as well, writing long before Augustine, there is the beginning of a different Christian theodicy. Instead of presenting Adam's fall as a crime of cosmic proportions which has ruined human life and its environment, Irenaeus saw it as more like an understandable slip.[3] Adam and Eve were immature creatures (pictured at one point as children), created only at the begining of a long process of growth and development. And human history is a phase of this second stage of creation in which beings made in the 'image' of God, that is, as rational and ethical animals, move freely towards the finite 'likeness' of God. Humanity was created, through the evolutionary process, as a 'fallen' creature, programmed for survival, and thus with the basic self-centeredness from which all that we call sin ultimately derives.

If the purpose of human life is that we may grow through our own free choices towards our perfection, what kind of world would provide a suitable environment for this? Not an earthly paradise devoid of any pain or suffering, without problems, difficulties, uncertainties, setbacks, disasters of any kind. For moral and spiritual growth always comes through challenge and response; and our world is a challenging environment. This does not of course mean that God has planned the particular challenges and hardships that we each face. It means that God has created a world-process that is, from our present point of view, very imperfect in that it is not designed for our comfort but includes unpredictable elements both of natural contingency and of the inputs of human freewill.

But the final responsibility, both for our human sinfulness and for the harsh and challenging world in which we live, has to be God's. The 'freewill defense' is valid on the human level but does not extend to God's *ultimate* responsibility. We have to accept that the divine love is a 'tough love' whose goodness, from our human point of view, lies in its eventual success in bringing us through what Keats called this 'vale of soul-making' to the infinite, because eternal, good of perfected existence.

Clearly, this type of theodicy has an inescapable eschatological dimension. For it is evident that the person-making process is not completed in this life, so that if it is ever to be completed there must be a continuation of existence beyond bodily death. I do not think that any religious response to the problem of evil can avoid this conclusion: 'No Theodicy without Eschatology'.

DEATH AND ETERNAL LIFE

The whole subject of death and the idea of life after death has been systematically neglected by most twentieth-century theologians, though not by the philosophers of religion. This is perhaps because the latter can discuss it as a purely intellectual issue whereas theologians must treat it with existential seriousness if they treat it at all – and so many prefer not to treat it. But Ludwig Feuerbach (1957) was right in noting that the idea of immortality is essentially involved in the idea of a loving God (see 174–5). For human nature includes immense potentialities which we see realized in varying degrees in remarkable men and women whom we regard, in our customary Western term, as saints, or in one of the Eastern terms as *mahatmas*, great souls. It follows that if our existence ceases at death the full human potential is only realized by those few who are able to do so in this present life, and in the great majority of men and women the higher potentialities must remain for ever unfulfilled. Such a situation is clearly incompatible, not only with a Christian belief in the limitless love of God, but equally with Jewish or Muslim belief in the divine love and mercy, and with an advaitic Hindu or a Buddhist belief in a universal destiny in union with Brahman or in the attainment of Buddhahood. There can be no loving God, and more generally no ultimate reality that is benign from our human point of view, if there is no continuation of human spiritual growth beyond the point reached at the time of bodily death.

But what kind of eschatology? This large, even though unanswerable, question was the subject of my next book, *Death and Eternal Life* (1976). Here for the first time, benefiting from extended study visits to India and Sri Lanka, I tried to take account of Eastern as well as Western thought. I distinguished between eschatologies (conceptions of an ultimate state) and pareschatologies (conceptions of that which occurs between bodily death and that final state). The world religions differ greatly in their pareschatologies – purgatory or some kind of intermediate state, reincarnation of the personality, rebirth of a karmic structure, or a nil pareschatology through an immediate translation to heaven or hell. Concerning eschatology there is the major divide between the broadly Western religious belief (in Judaism, Christianity and Islam) that individual personality, having attained or received its perfecting, continues eternally, and the broadly Eastern belief (in advaitic Hinduism and in Buddhism) that individual personality is ultimately transcended in the eternal consciousness of Brahman or in the presently unconceivable *parinirvana*.

These different conceptions are however only 'broadly' Eastern and Western, because 'Hinduism' includes the large stream of thought classically expressed by Ramanuja (11th–12th centuries CE), according to which individual *jivas* continue eternally within the life of Brahman, who is conceived of as personal. And Western mysticism, Jewish, Christian and Muslim, includes the thought that personal individuality is ultimately transcended as the soul, empty of self, is filled with the divine presence.

In this book I made more extended and sympathetic use of the Hindu conceptions of reincarnation and the Buddhist conceptions of rebirth than most other – or perhaps even any other – Western philosophers so far. The speculation – and it can of course only be speculation – offered in the last part of the book is based upon the thought that our human moral and spiritual growth can only take place under the pressure of the ever-approaching boundary of death and that therefore, if it continues beyond our present earthly existence, it must do so in a series of such bounded lives. These might occur by reincarnation in this world. But there are difficulties in that idea, and another and perhaps preferable speculation involves further lives in other worlds or indeed (as some contemporary scientific cosmologies permit) in other sub-universes. However I am now inclined, 20 years later, to stress more strongly the distinction between, on the one hand, the ego (that is, the now consciously thinking and acting personality) and, on the other hand, an underlying dispositional (or karmic) structure, which both affects and is affected by the former. One can then speculate that it is the latter that continues through a number of lives, being expressed in a new conscious personality each time – as much Hindu and Buddhist thought suggests. It could however also be, as is fairly strongly suggested by some of the parapsychological research, as well as by such religious sources as the Tibetan *Bardo Thodol*, that consciousness persists for a limited time between the embodiments of the continuing dispositional, or karmic, structure. According to this picture, I have to learn to accept that my present conscious self, or ego, will not live forever (even if it survives bodily death for a while), but that the deeper self of which I am a temporary expression is being modified all the time by the ways in which I am responding to my present options. I am thus continuously affecting my own future self or selves, whose nature will benefit from or be harmed by my present thoughts, emotions and actions. And all this within the continuum of mutual influences, mental and emotional, within which we are continuously (unconsciously) affecting one another for good and ill.

If we now ask to what end, if any, the whole process is moving, we do well, I think, to heed the agnosticism recommended long ago by the Buddha. Buddhism speaks of many rebirths of the karmic structure, leading towards an eventual universal nirvanic liberation or awakening. But when the Buddha, Gotama, was asked by a monk, Vaccha, in what kind of world or state the Tathagata (a fully enlightened being) arises after death, he rejected the question as having no answer because formed in terms of categories which do not apply (Horner 1957:101):

'Arise', Vaccha, does not apply.
Well then, good Gotama, does he not arise?
'Does not arise', Vaccha, does not apply.
Well then, good Gotama, does he both arise and not arise?
'Both arises and does not arise', Vaccha, does not apply.
Well then, good Gotama, does he neither arise nor not arise?
'Neither arises nor does not arise', Vaccha, does not apply.
                                        (*Majjhima Nikaya*, II, 431)

In other words, *parinirvana*, or *nirvana* beyond the round of rebirths, cannot be encompassed by our present set of concepts, which involve entities of some kind being in various states, or substances having various attributes. Rather, '*Freed from denotation by consciousness* is the Tathagata, Vaccha, he is deep, immeasurable, unfathomable as is the great ocean' (Horner 1957:166, emphasis added). Such talk of realities that lie beyond our present conceptual systems and powers of imagination seems to me to be realistic. We must free ourselves from the assumption that our human capacities are adequate to the nature of reality beyond its present impingements upon us (for a fuller discussion see Hick 1993).

As this reference to the Pali scriptures of Buddhism may suggest, I had become intensely interested in the other great world religions in addition to Christianity. Apart from a good deal of reading, I encountered Islam in Birmingham, England, where about 10 per cent of the population are Muslim, and also in Los Angeles; and Judaism in Britain and in the Los Angeles area, which has the third largest Jewish population in the world, and also briefly in Israel; and Hinduism and Sikhsm in India, as also in Birmingham and in California; and Theravada Buddhism in Sri Lanka, and the

Mahayana (mainly Zen and Tibetan) in the USA and in Japan. It seems clear to me that the philosophy of religion is not properly just the philosophy of the Christian (or Judeo-Christian) tradition, but in principle of religion throughout history and throughout the world. For the philosophy of religion, on analogy with the philosophy of science, philosophy of law, philosophy of art, philosophy of education, philosophy of mind, and so on, is properly the philosophy of *religion*, and not just of one particular form of it. Of course the philosopher of religion cannot hope to have a detailed first-hand knowledge of all the major, let alone minor, religious traditions, any more than the philosopher of science can hope to have a detailed first-hand knowledge of all the natural sciences. But he or she should have a general knowledge of the major religious traditions and should know how to acquire more detailed knowledge of particular aspects of any of them when necessary. This need is met to a reasonable extent today by most US graduate programs in Religion, though not by most of their European equivalents, which are still often confined to (Christian) Theology, still treated in religious, even if no longer in sociological, isolation.

RELIGIOUS PLURALISM

As I indicated earlier, the fact of religious plurality creates a fundamental problem for any religious apologetic hinging upon the rationality of basing beliefs on religious experience. A Christian philosopher can respond to this situation positively or negatively. The negative response is to feel threatened by the existence of other streams of religious experience, producing as they do belief-systems which are at many points incompatible with the Christian belief-system. This has been Alston's (1991) reaction. He accepts that the other world religions are as experientially well-based as his own; and he sees this as 'the most difficult problem for my position' (255), which is conceived as a defense of specifically Christian theism. His response to the problem of religious diversity is determined by the assumption that there can be at most one 'true religion', in the sense of a religion teaching the truth. Given this assumption, he has to justify privileging the Christian stream of religious experience, in which he participates, over all others. And his justification is that, in the absence of any way of establishing objectively that one stream is epistemically more reliable than another, it is rational to stay with the one in which one already participates. This seems to me to be a counsel of philosophical despair in face of the challenge of religious plurality. It seeks to justify one's belief that doctrines based on Christian religious experience are true whilst those based on non-Christian religious experience, at least in so far as they are incompatible with Christian beliefs, are false. But this makes one's own belief-system the sole exception to a general rule that beliefs based on religious experience are false! Thus the carefully defended principle that religious experience generally produces true beliefs is converted into the arbitrary principle that religious experience generally produces false beliefs – except in the case of Christianity! This does not seem to me to be a position in which a rational person can comfortably rest.

Already in my inaugural lecture as H. G. Wood Professor at Birmingham, England, in 1967 (see Hick 1973) I had identified the relation between the world religions as one of the four main problems facing Christian thought today. It was also the one that I had not yet then begun to address. Hence the period, mentioned above, of learning about the world religions – in particular Judaism, Islam, Hinduism, Sikhism, and Buddhism – and of reflecting on what can be called the philosophy of religions and the theology of religions.

This gave rise to successive publications, culminating in my Gifford Lectures, *An Interpretation of Religion* (1989). I was seeking a *religious* (as distinguished from a naturalistic) interpretation of religion in its various forms. By this I mean one based on the faith that human religious experience is not purely an imaginative projection (though this is certainly an element within it) but is also a response to a transcendent reality. The generic term that I have preferred for the ultimate religious referent is the Real – rather than such equally suitable alternatives as Ultimate Reality, the Transcendent, the Divine – mainly because the English term 'the Real' is not only acceptable within Christianity but also corresponds sufficiently to both the Sanskrit *sat* and the Arabic *al Haqq*.

Each of the great post-axial religions exhibits a soteriological structure, being concerned with the radical transformation of human existence from its state of 'fallenness', or of the spiritual blindness of *avidya*, or of subjection to *dukkha*, to a limitlessly better state in right relationship to, or identity with, or consciousness of, the ultimately real. And each seems, so far as we can tell from their spiritual and moral fruits in human life, to be more or less equally successful (and also equally unsuccessful) as contexts of this salvific transformation of individuals and, through them, of societies. Again, each has its own unique belief-system, arising from the immensely powerful religious experience of its founder(s) and their successors in the developing tradition.

In order to do justice to these data, it seems to me necessary to appeal to a distinction, found in some form within each of the great traditions, between the Real as it is in itself and the Real as humanly thought and experienced. This is supported by Aquinas's epistemological principle that 'Things known are in the knower according to the mode of the knower' (*Summa Theologica*, II/II, Q. 1, art 2), which implies a distinction between God *a se* and God as conceived and experienced in accordance with the mode of the human knowers. It is also supported by the Kantian distinction between a thing *an sich*, the noumenal reality as it is in itself, and that reality as a phenomenon of human experience. It seems to me that we should distinguish between the Real in itself, beyond the scope of our human conceptual systems, and the Real as variously humanly thought and experienced. In religion the 'mode of the knower' is differently formed within the different traditions, producing a corresponding range of ways in which the Real is humanly thought, and therefore experienced, and therefore responded to in life.

THE HUMANLY EXPERIENCED *PERSONAE* AND *IMPERSONAE* OF THE REAL

The two main concepts in terms of which religious experience is structured are the concept of deity, or of the Real as personal, and the concept of the absolute, or of the Real as non-personal. But we are never conscious of deity or of the absolute in general. Each becomes concretely experienceable or in Kantian language schematized in terms, not (as in Kant's system) of abstract time, but of the filled time of history and culture. Thus in one stream of thought and experience deity has become the figure of Jahweh who, developing through history, chose the Jewish people, entered into a covenant with them, rescued them from slavery in Egypt, led them into a new land, and who has through the centuries punished them when they strayed from his allegiance and blest them when they have been faithful to him. The Jahweh phenomenon exists in relation to the Jewish people and cannot be extracted from that relationship; he is part of their history, and they are part of his; and in the biblical accounts he shows no awareness of, for example, the peoples of China or India or the Americas. In quite a different strand of history deity became concretized as the Vishnu of India, God of a thousand names who has become incarnate on earth in times of human crisis (but always in India), for example as Rama and as Krishna. Vishnu, as pictured in the Hindu scriptures, shows no awareness of the Jews, or of the peoples of China or of Europe or the Americas. Again, the Holy Trinity of Christian faith, and the strictly unitary Allah of Islamic faith, are yet other phenomenologically different historical concretizations of deity. In each case, awareness of the Real as personal has taken a specific form provided by the human imagination as formed within a particular religious culture. Other religious cultures again have experienced the Real in non-personal terms, which have become specific as the Tao, or as the Brahman of advaitic Hinduism, or as the Dharmakaya, or Sunyata, or Nirvana of Buddhism. All these various *personae* and *impersonae* of the Real have formed at the interface between the Real and different realms of human consciousness. Each is the joint product of the universal presence of the Real and of a particular religious tradition with its own specific conceptuality together with its associated spiritual practices, exemplars, scriptures, history, culture and form of life.

On this hypothesis the Real in itself is, in Western terms, ineffable, or in Eastern terms, formless in that it is outside the scope of our human conceptual systems. We cannot apply to it any of the attributes of its manifestations as the God-figures and the non-personal absolutes. It cannot be said to be personal or impersonal, good or evil, purposive or non-purposive, substance or process, even one or many – though it can of course be said to have such purely formal, linguistically generated, attributes as 'being able to be referred to' and 'being ineffable'. The main argument for the ineffability of the Real is that it would be impossible to attribute to it the qualities of its *personae* and *impersonae*, because taken together these are at many points mutually incompatible. There is however a sense in which the Real can be said, from our human point of view, to be good or gracious, namely as the necessary condition of our highest good, which the great religious traditions variously speak of as eternal life, *moksha, nirvana,* union with the divine. And there is a sense, pointed out by Maimonides, in which the Real can be said to be one rather than many: 'In our endeavour to show that God does not include a plurality, we can only say "He is one", although "one" and "many" are both terms which serve to distinguish quantity' (1904:81; the Upanishads meet the same problem by speaking paradoxically of 'The One without a second', *Chandogya Upanishad,* VI, 2. 4). And if we ask why, from a religious point of view, we should suppose there to be a transcendent reality about which we can say so little, the answer is that the Real is the necessary postulate of the religious life. The difference between affirming and denying the Real is the difference between a religious and a naturalistic interpretation of religion.

On this view, the function of religion is to be an enabling context of salvation/liberation, which is the transformation of human existence from self-centeredness to a new orientation centered in the Real as variously manifested through the different religious traditions. And because the great world faiths seem to have proved over the centuries to be more or less equally salvific (and also more or less equally infected by human greed, cruelty, pride and selfishness), it seems to me proper to hold that they constitute, so far as we humans can tell, equally valid even though very different responses to the Real.

IMPLICATIONS FOR CHRISTIAN THEOLOGY

If so, the pluralistic hypothesis inevitably reflects back into the religious traditions, and those who accept a view of this kind will want to de-emphasize, and eventually filter out, that aspect of their own tradition which implies its unique superiority over all others. In the case of Christianity, this is the idea that Jesus of Nazareth was God (that is, the second person of a divine Trinity) incarnate. For it follows from this that Christianity alone, among the religions of the world, was founded by God in person and is thus God's own religion in a way in which no other can be. I have accordingly tried, in my capacity as a theologian, to contribute to the new self-understanding of Christianity as one 'true' religion among others.

This has involved a critique of the three basic interrelated doctrines of incarnation, trinity, and atonement. The traditional doctrine of the Incarnation holds that Jesus of Nazareth was the

second Person of a divine Trinity living a human life. The Council
of Chalcedon, which definitively formulated the official doctrine,
supported it by affirming that it is 'as the Lord Jesus Christ taught
us'. And until within the past hundred years or so virtually all
instructed (as well as uninstructed) Christians believed that Jesus
himself had taught his own deity in such statements as 'I and the
Father are one' (John 10:30), 'He who has seen me has seen the
Father' (John 13:9). However, today almost all New Testament
scholars are agreed that these are not words of the historical Jesus,
but words put into his mouth some 60 or 70 years after his death by
a Christian writer expressing the theology that had by then
developed in much of the church. Jesus probably thought of
himself as the final prophet, proclaiming the imminent coming of
God's kingdom on earth, and would have regarded as blas-
phemous the idea that he was himself God in either a unitarian
or a trinitarian sense. He is reported to have said at one point, 'Why
do you call me good? No one is good but God alone' (Mark 10:18).
And long before the Gospels were written in the period between
about 70 and 100 AD, the early church thought of Jesus as, in the
words attributed to St Peter in the Acts of the Apostles, 'a man
attested to you by God with mighty works and wonders and signs
which God did through him in your midst' (Acts 2:22).

Jesus himself spoke of God as his *abba*, father, and taught his
followers to pray to God as their heavenly father. But it has only
been widely known in modern times that it was common in the
ancient world to speak of outstanding individuals as sons of God.
In the wider Mediterranean world great rulers – Egyptian pharaohs
and, in Jesus's time, Roman emperors – and great philosophers (for
example, Pythagoras and Plato), and great holy men were spoken
of as divine or as a son of God; and within Judaism Adam, and
Israel as a whole, and angels, and indeed any outstandingly pious
Jew was often called a son of God. Within Judaism the phrase was
clearly intended metaphorically: 'son of' meant 'in the spirit of' or
'true servant of'. But when the gospel went out beyond Israel into
the Gentile world, where the term was often used much less clearly
metaphorically, and when the gospel had to be expressed in philosophical terms to appeal to the sophisticated classes of the
Empire, Jesus the metaphorical son of God was transformed into
the metaphysical God the Son, second Person of a divine Trinity,
having two complete natures, one human and the other divine.
However, the relationship between these two natures has never

been satisfactorily explained. Did Jesus have two consciousnesses? Did he have two wills? Was he, as genuinely human, able to sin? Was he, as genuinely divine, unable to sin? If so, does not the latter annul the former? If he was divinely omnipotent and omniscient, how was he also humanly weak and limited in knowledge? Such questions have never been given agreed answers, and for most Christians the doctrine is accepted as a holy mystery which we must believe but must not expect to understand.

The traditional doctrine takes the idea of divine incarnation literally. It holds that Jesus was literally (not metaphorically) human and literally (not metaphorically) divine. But this literally understood idea has not only proved to be inexplicable, but has also proved to be readily exploited to validate great human evils. The ancient charge of deicide presupposes a literal doctrine of Jesus's deity, and was used throughout medieval Christendom to justify the persecution and slaughter of Jews, thereby forming the continuing mind-set in which the secular anti-Semitism of the nineteenth and twentieth centuries could flourish and in which the Nazi holocaust of the 1940s could take place. The doctrine of the deity of Christ was also used to inspire the European colonists who conquered and then exploited so much of what today we call the Third World. And the idea that God became a man (not a woman) has been used to justify the ecclesiastical suppression of women down to our own day. None of this shows that the doctrine, thus literally understood, is false, but it does induce a certain 'hermeneutic of suspicion', and prompts us to ask whether this is the only way to understand the idea of divine incarnation.

It is evident that it is not the only way. Incarnation, or embodiment, is a familiar metaphor. 'Great men', it has been said, 'incarnate' the spirit of their age. Hitler was evil 'incarnate'. Winston Churchill, in 1940, 'incarnated' the British will to resist Hitler. And so on. And in this metaphorical sense God was incarnate in the life of Jesus in several interrelated respects. In so far as Jesus was doing God's will, God was acting through him and was thus 'incarnate' in Jesus's life. Again, in so far as Jesus was doing God's will he 'incarnated' the ideal of human life lived in openness and response to God. And again, in so far as Jesus lived a life of self-giving love, or *agape*, he 'incarnated' a love that is a finite reflection of the infinite divine love. Indeed, in this metaphorical sense whenever a man or a woman freely does the divine will, God becomes incarnate on earth in that action; and among these Jesus is the one who has captured the imagination of the millions who call themselves Christians.

Given a metaphorical understanding of divine incarnation, the traditional doctrine of the Trinity ceases to have any point. For its purpose was to safeguard a literal doctrine of Jesus's deity. And again, the various transactional understandings of atonement – as a ransom to the devil, or a satisfaction to God for the sins of the world, or a substitute bearing on our behalf the just punishment for human sin, likewise lose their point, for they all presuppose the literal divinity of Jesus. One can then return to the teachings of Jesus himself, who taught (for example in the parable of the prodigal son and in the words of the Lord's Prayer) that whenever there is genuine penitence for sin there is genuine and free divine forgiveness without any need for an atoning death.

And so as well as working as a philosopher of religion I have also functioned as a theologian, taking part along with many others in the modern re-understanding of Christianity as one valid context of human salvation among others. A parallel task exists within each of the other world religions, a task that is easier for some than for others and that can in each case only be undertaken from within the tradition itself.

This theological contribution, which has not surprisingly proved to be highly controversial, is presented most fully in my *The Metaphor of God Incarnate* (1993).

The broader hypothesis, within which this is a sub-theme, is developed in *An Interpretation of Religion* and defended from a variety of criticisms in (in the USA) *A Christian Theology of Religions* (1995) or (in the UK) *The Rainbow of Faiths* (1995). It exemplifies one, but of course by no means the only, way in which the philosophy of religion can respond to the epistemological problems created by the fact of religious diversity.

More generally, it seems to me that the philosopher of religion should be willing to embrace and reflect upon the great perennial human experiences of joy and suffering, life and death, and the sense of transcendence that is mediated through them and in many other ways, as well as the basic epistemological questions which determine one's response to the mysterious universe of which we are part.

Notes

1. Richard Swinburne has named this the 'principle of credulity', *The Existence of God* (Oxford: Clarendon Press, 1979, pp. 254f); but I prefer to call it the 'principle of rational credulity'.
2. Indeed in *Perceiving God* (Ithaca and London: Cornell University Press, 1991) Alston says (p. xi) that his thinking was 'strongly influenced' by *Faith and Knowledge*, and he has written elsewhere that 'From the first edition the book made a profound impression on me' ('John Hick: *Faith and Knowledge*' in Arvind Sharma (ed.), *God, Truth and Reality: Essays in Honour of John Hick*, London: Macmillan, and New York: St. Martin's Press, 1993, p. 25).
3. This idea also occurs in the fourteenth-century English mystic, Julian of Norwich, in the longer text of her *Showings*, chapters 47 and 55.

References

Alston, William. 1991. *Perceiving God*. Ithaca and London: Cornell University Press.

Feuerbach, Ludwig. 1957. *The Essence of Christianity* (trans. George Eliot). New York: Harper Torchbooks.

Hick, John. 1973. *God and the Universe of Faiths*. London: Macmillan.

———. 1989. *An Interpretation of Religion*. London: Macmillan and New Haven: Yale University Press.

———. 1993. *Disputed Questions in Theology and the Philosophy of Religion*. London: Macmillan and New Haven: Yale University Press.

Horner, I. B. (trans.). 1957. *The Collection of the Middle Length Sayings*. London: Luzac.

Maimonides. 1904. *The Guide for the Perplexed* (trans. M. Friedlander). London: Routledge & Kegan Paul.

Padgett, Alan (ed.). 1994. *Reason and the Christian Religion: Essays in Honour of Richard Swinburne*. Oxford: Clarendon Press.

Plantinga, Alvin and Nicholas Wolterstorff (eds). 1983. *Faith and Rationality*. South Bend, IN and London: University of Notre Dame Press.

Wittgenstein, Ludwig. 1953. *Philosophical Investigations* (trans. G. E. M. Anscombe and R. Rhees). Oxford: Blackwell.

6

From History to Religion

JACOB NEUSNER

My work for the past four decades has pursued a single problem, which is, to explain how Judaism as we know that religion came into being. I have wanted to account for its success, when and where it succeeded in its social goals, and to explain the conditions of its failure, when it did not. While a field-theory of the history of Judaism has emerged, my principal interest, beginning to present, has been in the formative age, the first seven centuries AD. Then the books came to closure that together with Scripture ('the Old Testament') form the definitive canon of Judaism as we know it. The canon set forth in written form the Judaic way of life, worldview, and theory of the social entity that it called 'Israel', this last a theological theory of the social order corresponding to Christianity's 'mystical body of Christ'. The work of description, analysis, and interpretation has carried me across four academic disciplines within the study of religion, in an overlapping sequence of approximately a decade each, history, literature, history of religions, and theology. I conceive religion to be accessible to this-worldly study when it is viewed as an account of the social order and the statement of a cultural system, and the problem of studying religion in my view is to explain the relationship between the religious ideas that people hold and the social world that they create for themselves.

To do this work I have translated Judaism's canonical books into English, many for the first time, some for the second: the Mishnah, Tosefta, Talmud of the Land of Israel, Talmud of Babylonia, and all of the score of compilations of scriptural exegesis called Midrashim that came to closure in late antiquity, down to the advent of Islam in the seventh century AD. My translations have provided all of the documents with their first reference system (equivalent to Scripture's chapter and verse), so that form-analytical studies of the way in which the documents make their statement could get under way. I have further read each document as a coherent statement of a theory of (its) Israel's social order (I called it 'system') and asked about the worldview, way of life, and theory of the social entity, that each writing set forth. Finally, I have provided a systematic account of the formative history of Judaism as a problem in the history of religions, specifically, the problem of how the religion that people practice together relates to the world in which they live.

Four periods over these 40 years mark the divisions of this single project of mine. In the first, 1954–64, I completed my formal education and post-doctoral studies in cognate subjects, besides the Judaic ones, in ancient history (Roman and Iranian, earliest Christianity, Zoroastrianism, Syriac, Armenian, and the like). In the second, overlapping period, 1960–70, I thought of myself as an historian and wrote mainly history. During that time I called into question the validity of the utilization of the Judaic religious sources for answering the kind of questions historians asked and further came to the realization that the Judaic system behind the writings I studied answered different questions from historical ones. Trying to find out precisely what questions the sources addressed, I moved from the study of history to the literary analysis of the forms and structure of documents. The period in which I invented and carried out in my translations the form-analysis of rabbinic literature, 1970–80, produced the first of my explanations of those writings. The third, also overlapping period, 1975–90, marked the transition from historical and literary study to the study of the history of the religion, inclusive of its ideas. As I grasped the literary structure and conceptual system of documents and began to see how one document related to others for the history of this religion, I formed a theory of the character of the Judaism that the documents, each in its way, addressed or represented in context. My work in the history of religions, with special emphasis upon formative Judaism, required that I set Judaic systems within the context of Jewish history over time – besides the Rabbinic one that has predominated. That effort did yield the field-theory of the history of Judaism that I had hoped to formulate.

But, by now predictably, the third period also contained within itself the beginnings of a fourth, the period devoted to hermeneutics and likely shading over, in due course, into theology, in which I am now engaged. From the later 1980s to 1996 I shaped a set of inquiries into the hermeneutics of the two Talmuds in particular. I furthermore kept in view a broader, now systematic theological interest; but concrete work is not yet under way or contemplated beyond what is already done. What I show in my commentaries to the two Talmuds through the detailed examination of problems of structure and system – hermeneutics of a concrete order – is how the framers of the Talmuds made connections and drew conclusions, what theory of mind told them what they wished to know and how to find it out. In this quest for an explanation of the principles of self-evidence that govern in Judaism, I finished a commentary to both Talmuds, along the way also revising my prior translations. For a religious system works out, in vast detail, a few simple ideas. In the principles of selection and exegesis – the making of connections and drawing of conclusions that, in the case of Judaism, embody the faith's applied logic and practical reason – God lives.

But I have gotten well ahead of my story, so let me start with beginnings.

ORIGINS

My mother once told me, 'You were a pest until you learned how to read. Then we never heard from you again.' From reading books I made the move to writing them as well. The particular subject – Judaism – also hardly surprises. I was born a fourth-generation American on my mother's side, third on my father's, and life's challenge came from the other direction, the Jewish one. That is what set me apart, identified for me the friends I would have (and not have), the careers for which I might prepare (or not prepare). A bitterly self-hating Jew, my mother despised everything Jewish and wanted to be only American; my father lived and breathed Jewishness – the ethnic formation of identity – and also took for granted the practice of Judaism. In 1929, after a brief career in journalism in the Jewish community, he founded the *Connecticut Jewish Ledger*, which my family published for nearly 30 years. There I grew up, moving from one office to the next and learning each job in sequence, from errand boy to reporter, editorial writer, book reviewer, layout designer, and the rest (though always errand boy) from age 13 to age 18. He also helped found the Connecticut Zionist Region and pretty much every other Jewish organization imaginable.

A self-hating Jew and a Zionist did not make for a great marriage; my mother's meanest curse of me was, 'You're just like your father.' It echoes in my ears every day. He suffered a near-fatal heart attack a month after I celebrated my becoming a bar mitzvah, at age 13, in 1945, and was a near-invalid until he finally died 15 years later of Parkinson's and its complications. She outlived him by 30 years and from his death rarely spoke of him. Of the two parents, she was the more successful. All of her grandchildren – except for my children – have married gentiles and have cut off any ties to the world of Judaism.

The resolution of such a textbook conflict took a predictable form: I thought I was closer to my mother but in fact I identified with my father. So my natural rebellion meant two things: for the sake of my father I would never go into journalism (so my son became a reporter and a co-author of books with me!); and for the sake of my mother I would become a rabbi. Each parent got an appropriate comeuppance. I went off to Harvard (my father would have settled for Trinity College), which my mother wanted; and I determined to read every Jewish book ever written and go to Hebrew Union College to become a rabbi, which my father found slightly awesome. From the publication of my first book, in 1962, to my mother's death, in 1994, over 32 years, to my knowledge my mother never read or even opened a book of mine; she certainly never discussed one of them with me.

EDUCATION

One obstacle to my ambition stood in my way: I'd never gotten a Jewish education and knew no Hebrew and nothing of the texts or practice of Judaism, except as filtered through the Reform Temple to which we belonged. At Harvard (1950–3) I took some elementary Hebrew; my adviser was Harry A. Wolfson, a beautiful soul, who offered everything and from whom, in my ignorance, I learned nothing. He was certainly the finest scholar of Judaism in the twentieth century, and one of the greats of the ages. Then at Oxford (1953–4) I encountered a vital, intellectual (if British and frigid) Orthodoxy and realized that Judaism the religion (which I could not have distinguished from Jewishness, the ethnic identification) meant something more specific and concrete than I'd known. Advised that I would get a better education at the Jewish Theological Seminary than at Hebrew Union College, I applied, signing a pledge to observe the laws of Judaism that mattered there.

The years at Jewish Theological Seminary (1954–60) – including one at the Hebrew University and at Mir Yeshiva in Jerusalem (1957–8) and two at Columbia-Union's doctoral program (1958–60) – brought me into what must be the most mean-spirited academic communities in the world, full of people who knew everything about Judaism except its main point, which (in the judgment of the Talmud) was and is, to purify the heart. But I went to accomplish a goal, which was, to get a first-rate education, and I did. When I left, I never went back, tore up their pledge, and chose my own path in the world.

It was not the path I expected. I always assumed I would become a rabbi in a pulpit, not a scholar and professor in a university. That is because, when I started at Harvard, few careers in learning in Judaism existed outside of Judaic theological or Jewish ethnic auspices. University positions were so rare that no one could take a degree in the anticipation of finding employment. Learning was truly for its own sake. I knew, also, that I should not want to teach at JTSA; after one week there, I saw what it was. But in the course of my years there, I heard about the National Council on Religion in Higher Education and its Kent Fellowships. Not sure why, I applied. At the Kent Fellows' 'Week of Work' I met three generations of scholars of religion, divinity school, university, and college professors of a field I did not know existed. The founders of the field as we know it, George Thomas at Princeton, for instance, the middle-age leaders of the day, Fred Berthold at Dartmouth and John A. Hutchison at Columbia, among many, and the younger generation – too many to name, and anyhow, my crowd, then and always! – got together and talked for a glorious week. They called each other by their first names, they clearly liked and respected one another, and they listened to, and argued with, one another – something I'd not seen in Harvard, Oxford, the Hebrew University, the Mir Yeshiva, or the Jewish Theological Seminary. And they said interesting, illuminating things. I never knew that life could be like that. But it was.

ENTRY INTO THE FIELD OF THE STUDY OF RELIGION

There I met Jack Hutchison, who asked whether I might like to study for a PhD at Columbia. With the Kent Fellowship, I enrolled. I started courses in the summer of 1958 (taking a course in sociology of religion with Sam Klausner, in the company of a young Haverford student who struck me then and thereafter as the most interesting person I'd ever met, named Jonathan Z. Smith). I found myself in a world of generalization, comparison and contrast, that opened possibilities also for what I might do. In the seminars of the coming year and in preparing for my doctoral examinations thereafter, I devoured the reading. Everything was new. Nothing was routine. I recall my first encounter with the writings of Mircea Eliade, just before the Days of Awe in 1958. It was *The Myth of the Eternal Return*, and I wondered how he could have known so much about Rosh Hashanah and Yom Kippur, which were then coming. But the scholar who to me wrote like an angel was Max Weber, in English translation. He set my agenda then and thereafter: the relationship between religious ideas and the social order of the people who hold them. For religion – Judaism – was lived in community; it was something that a 'we' did together. It defined the framework and parameters of family, home, and community. It was not limited to a set of beliefs or doctrines or localized rites but encompassed every inch of social existence. And Weber in general helped me to see the dimensions and proportions of Judaism in particular. At JTSA I studied texts. At Columbia I found a program of learning that I might bring to the texts, that might turn learning into more than collecting, arranging, and paraphrasing what was before me.

But if the books illuminated, the faculty did not. Neither at Columbia nor at JTSA did I find much scholarly – or human – greatness. One JTSA professor was the exception, Abraham Heschel. He both knew a great deal and found much to say. He was the worst class room teacher, but the best mentor, I ever knew. He was invariably interesting; he remembered everything he ever read; and he pursued questions of pure, religious interest. He was one of the handful of genuinely, authentically religious Jews at the Jewish Theological Seminary, and also the best mind of the lot of them. When I began my own work, he read and understood it, and he talked with me about my problems and the entire academic literature on them, which he knew well. While I did not admire much of his writing, which I thought mannered and out of control, I found his thinking ambitious, and his success in his one true masterpiece, *Passion for Truth*, beyond any imagining, surely the most elevated work of the theology of Judaism of this century. Here he combined his gifts of learning, intellectual rigor, ambition for the right word and phrase, and deep insight into the realities of the religious life. But I did not take him for my model; he was a theologian, and I then thought of myself as an historian.

Nothing in doctoral studies suggested any other identification; 'history of religions' was a field I'd not heard of, even while reading everything of Eliade's I could find. For nearly 20 years, I conceived my task to solve essentially historical questions, beginning with what happened, working outward from there. It was only in the late 1970s that I reached the twin conclusions that history is intellectually bankrupt, and that the history of religions really set tasks of surpassing interest, yielding the possibility of insight into the character of religion, through the case of Judaism, that mere history prevented. But neither then nor afterward did I identify with the organizations or faculties of the history of religions, none of which struck me as doing what they said they were doing. That is, they claimed to compare religions but studied only one (or none); they entertained few generalizations that might illumine real problems of learning and interpretation; and they tended to focus on narrowly construed intellectual questions, as if they were the very theologians they condemned so violently. Perhaps they found the social study of religion too concrete for their ruminations on myth and ritual, origins and structures. But I have never found an intellectual home in history of religions, though that is what I do, and I should not really want one there.

It was as an historian that I undertook my first book, *A Life of Yohanan ben Zakkai*, and the next major projects, *A History of the Jews in Babylonia, Development of a Legend: Studies on the Traditions Concerning Yohanan ben Zakkai, The Rabbinic Traditions about the Pharisees before 70*, and *Eliezer ben Hyrcanus: The Tradition and the Man*. (These were mainly multi-volumed works; I have laid out my program on a large scale, systematically representing the sources of my subject, and for any given inquiry that I undertake, I follow a program that leads me through literary, historical, and religious questions, sequentially. I find I can't clear my throat in less than eight volumes.) My principal interest focused upon what really happened, out of the mass of traditions and stories that the Judaic sources recorded. But very quickly, I found unsatisfactory the interpretive framework I assumed for myself out of the models at hand. To understand what follows, the reader must know that I have never found myself entirely pleased with anything I have done, and each large-scale work of mine not only answers questions of method and substance left open by its predecessor, but constitutes a scathing review – of both method and substance – of that predecessor. To verify that statement, readers need merely compare one major project with the next. I have not stood still, and I have not done the same thing twice. In general I work in three layers at once: the work I am doing, the work I am contemplating, and the work of which I am merely speculating and daydreaming. When I set to work, I have already thought through what I am about to undertake, not just in general but in vast detail. That makes the execution more focused and imparts to the work its own dynamic.

The Life of Yohanan ben Zakkai marks the movement outward from studying to taking charge of my own learning. The choice of the subject will surprise no one of my generation. I celebrated becoming a bar mitzvah, at age 13, in September of 1945. At that very season the concentration camps and death factories were just cooling down. While the Jewish world at that time had not yet transformed the catastrophe into a mythopoeic event and formulated its identification around it, I found myself profoundly changed by my initial intellectual encounter, which took place when I found at Blackwell's in Oxford Gerald Reitlinger's *The Final Solution*. That was in my first weeks there; at that age I would read anything Jewish, and here was something about a subject of interest. Here I was in Europe. I spent the next week reading the book, and for weeks afterward I found it difficult to speak to any gentiles. I went off, as soon as I could, to see Germany and meet people who had done such things. Now, six years later, I saw the world as before and after, and myself as one who had survived. I wanted to know, what do people do when the world ends? And I chose Yohanan ben Zakkai, because he was (universally represented as) the man who in the summer of 70 CE had led the Jews out of Jerusalem on the very eve of its destruction and had formed for Judaism the foundations of its long and vital life thereafter. Here was my model for the new age. But what did I want to know about him? Max Weber helped but Hegel and Marx supplied me with the answer: the dialectic of the routine and the charismatic in the synthesis of Yohanan's life and teaching. It struck me as an interesting way in which to read his life, and so I forced all the stories about him into a narrative, based on the uncriticized tales and sayings told about or attributed to him, of a tale I would tell Max Weber if I might meet him (I should confess, I never read a book of any consequence without writing the author, alive or dead, a letter in response to the book; I only occasionally send the result, sometimes because for some, such as Maimonides, I have no serviceable address).

It was conventional, uncritical, jerry-built, mechanical, paraphrastic, excessively erudite, and it won a huge prize from JTSA, $1,000, when my salary as an instructor at Columbia University was $5,000! But I found no challenge in more biographies. I moved on to another topic that concerned me because of my situation as a Jewish American. The other principal source of intellectual vitality in Judaism, beside the Holocaust (as it came to be called), was Zionism and the creation of the State of Israel. Like the Holocaust, which challenged our American Jewish trust in gentiles, Zionism raised those very questions that we Jewish Americans did not choose to answer. It maintained that life in the 'exile' (Golah) promised nothing; golah-Jews could accomplish nothing; all learning, for example, would take place in the State of Israel. Not only did we have no intellectual future, but we also had no hope of building a stable community. We would assimilate and cease to be Jews. We were doomed; the gentiles would stuff us into gas chambers, where we would die singing 'Silent Night'. So was the vision that the Israelis offered us for ourselves, a part of Zionist doctrine called 'the negation of the exile'. As a proud son of the Exile – I never found life in the State of Israel appealing on a variety of grounds and I never conceded one could be a Jew only there, or could be a better Jew if there not here – I wondered why exilic life promised so little.

After all, the most important and authoritative documents of Judaism after Scripture came from the Exile, and not from the Holy Land. If, as many maintain, the Exile bears responsibility for the Pentateuch, everyone concedes that the single authoritative document thereafter was, and is, the Talmud of Babylonia. Being an historian and little more than that, I determined to find out what in fact had happened in Babylonia in what they then called 'the period of the Mishnah and the Talmud'. I produced my *History of the Jews in Babylonia*, covering Parthian and Sassanian times. These earliest works, then, represented my turning my deepest human concerns as a Jew and an American into the definition of what, out of the classical past, I should wish to investigate: what it meant to survive catastrophe, and what it meant to build anew. I found metaphors for our situation in America, as Jews, after the

Holocaust, and I determined to investigate them in their own terms. And that is what I started out to do. Only much later did my work take on its own momentum and follow its own inner logic.

In the course of the years, 1962–9, in which I was doing the work, I became ever less certain that the way I was working led anywhere. For several reasons I found the work unsatisfying. First, I realized that an entire critical program, deriving from biblical studies and known to me especially in New Testament Gospels' work, played no role in my use of sources. Second, I found myself less and less sanguine that I brought to the sources a very interesting intellectual program. True, it was a standard and reasonably successful historical program: political setting, internal institutions, rabbinic authorities and their jurisdiction, religious ideas and the like. But even if my methods were critical (and no one's were), so that I dealt with hard facts, I wondered whether the program I produced had brought me closer to the point of the sources on which I was working. And that brings me to a third point of concern. I was at that time teaching at Dartmouth College; a year after I came, we appointed Hans Penner, who, along with Jonathan Smith, would form my model of what history of religions as a theoretical episteme ought to set forth. Penner paid attention to colleagues' work and reading mine asked, 'Why are you in a department of religion and not in a department of history?' It was a fair, tough question, and I had no suitable answer then, or for a while thereafter. The answer I gave was monumentally stupid: I am an historian working on essentially religious materials. He could see that and did not say it was an evasion. But I certainly huffed and puffed. Penner and Smith, in their courteous way, did not let up, and I thought of little else for years to come. I owe them.

At that very season I came across Clifford Geertz's 'Religion as a Cultural System', and he seemed to have written that wonderful essay as a personal letter to me. I commented on it in the Preface of Volume III of my *History*, where I identified it as the source for my scholarly paradigm. Later in this essay I shall spell out just what I mean. For he made me realize that I was dealing with the artifacts of a social order of a profoundly religious character, and that I should begin to formulate categories of organization and inquiry that would illuminate the characteristics – traits, components and their dimensions – of that social system. In time I would come to recognize that what I really had in hand constituted not reports of the social order but utopian designs for a social order, that is to say, a religious vision of the world formulated in concrete and this-worldly terms.

In thinking about Geertz's design of study of religion in its social aspect (and in later encounters with the wonderful writings of Peter Berger on the same subject), I began also to reflect on the main results of a great scholar I had known and much valued, Erwin R. Goodenough. When I read his *Jewish Symbols in the Graeco-Roman Period* (initially, volumes I–VIII in 1963, then the rest shortly thereafter), I faced for the first time a problem that would strike me as critical, and the solution of which, as liberating. Goodenough insisted that antiquity knew more than a single Judaism, the one we know from written evidence, particularly the writings of the ancient rabbis. When I read his Volume IV, on Method, I realized that once I turned to the question of Judaism and the social order, I should have to ask, which social order? Along with his insistence that there was then no single Judaism (he thought there were two, the one documented by the rabbis, the other by synagogue art), I realized, I should have to identify the social order that a given body of evidence described. That was the beginning of my notion that a given document must be read in the setting of the community that produced, valued, preserved, and meant to embody it. That is not to say a book is a Judaism, only that a book, as much as an artifact, has to be permitted to contribute to our account of the Judaism that said book means to state.

And to Smith and Penner I owe, also, my recognition of the fourth problem awaiting attention. Penner would put it simply, time and again: what exactly do you mean by 'Judaism'? He insisted that the task of the study of religion was to define Religion, and the task of the study of Judaism was to define Judaism. I would spend the rest of my career working on that problem.

At that point I decided to leave Dartmouth, much as I valued the intellectual challenge, because I did not want to raise my children in Hanover, New Hampshire. I wanted them to grow up regarding 'being Jewish' as normal, and the Jews of Hanover at that time offered no hope of doing so. I cannot refer to a 'Jewish community' when I speak of radically isolated individuals, most of them wishing to be ex-Jews and acting as though they were; these were mostly Marranos; the rest were self-haters, with perhaps three exceptions. One other professor, the brilliant philosopher, Bernard Gert, kept a kosher home. My children would not only grow up as the only Jews in their class room and isolated from all ordinary Jewish education and social life, they also would know only, or mainly, ex-Jews and anti-Semitic Jews and Jews full of contempt for Judaism. It took me years to realize that that was, and remains, the condition of American Jewry, whether in small-town New Hampshire or in big-city New York.

CAREER CATASTROPHE: 20 YEARS IN PURGATORY

Nothing ever mattered more than, or as much as, my wife, home, and children. I placed my highest priority upon finding a university in a Jewish community where my wife and I could raise our children to be normal and happy Jews. In those now-unimaginable years, the mid-1960s, positions came my way from day to day; I turned down Princeton's tentative inquiry without even a visit, since Princeton struck me as only a snobbier, richer, and more prestige-driven Hanover; Duke and Stanford because I did not want to raise my children there; and Columbia (twice), because I wanted to see the children a great deal and commuting would make that difficult. As it happens, I worked at home (when I taught at Brown, the Department of Religion gave me no office I could use), so I had three meals a day with the children until they went off to school. When Brown made its offer – start a graduate program immediately, take a full professorship at age 35! – I accepted on the spot. It was a catastrophic error, one I regretted nearly from the outset, except for one consideration, which was all that mattered. Providence was an ideal situation for raising our family. As soon as our fourth and last child was nearing college age, we left.

Brown from 1968 through 1989 never offered much intellectual stimulation. In place of Penner and Smith I found no one of philosophical depth or methodological sophistication. In place of Dartmouth's New Testament professor, Robin Scroggs, with whom I studied Greek and from whom I learned much else, they had an unproductive and anti-Christian Josephus scholar of German origin and education, who despised the Jews and Judaism only less than he hated Christians and Christianity. In place of Fred Berthold, one of the academy's exemplary citizens, I came among politicians and conspirators, people who had no important scholarly program for themselves and who were quick to take coffee breaks and long lunches and hours in the library reading newspapers and who happily accepted every committee assignment they could finagle; they would boast they'd never missed a Brown faculty meeting in decades. I never went. It was not a good fit.

At Brown I accomplished my goals despite a strange and arid environment. I can say nothing good of my 'colleagues' there; I did my best to work despite them. This I did through my graduate teaching and an on-going program of organizing conferences from year to year, to which I invited everyone I could imagine; foreign lecture and travel, from 1971 onward; attending conferences elsewhere; organizing multi-year study sessions at the American Academy of Religion; and, above all, endless telephone calls with interesting, patient people. As the years unfolded and our children grew more self-reliant, I took every chance I could to get out of Providence, and, when at home, I spent at Brown only those hours I had to for teaching and office hours; I taught my graduate seminar at home. Brown was the color of my paycheck, but not of my mood, ever.

THE DOCUMENTARY READING OF RABBINIC JUDAISM IN ITS FORMATIVE AGE

At this point – in the earlier 1970s – my scholarly program veered sharply away from historical study, to which I never returned. I determined that the arena for study could not find its limits beyond the texts but only within them. That is to say, I could not bring to the documents a program of study of my own invention but had to learn from them what they wished to teach. I further reached the conclusion that the analysis of the formal (rhetorical) traits of the document would provide a commentary, in the theory that the way people say things, as much as what they say, conveys their statement. I further determined that the description of the documents, one by one, was now required. In New Testament studies such a statement will not raise eyebrows; after all, for generations people have recognized that the Gospel of Matthew formulates its theology, which is not the same as that of the Gospel of John, and that the first step in all learning must be the description of the document, its traits and viewpoint. But in the study of the classics of Judaism, to that time, few had ever asked any questions of documentary description, analysis, and interpretation.

I determined to start with the Mishnah, because that is the first document of Rabbinic Judaism after Scripture, and to end with the Talmud of Babylonia, the final one. When I began, with the 63 tractates of the Mishnah in front of me, and with the rapid recognition that the Tosefta had to be read in relationship with the Mishnah, I thought I had started the project which would keep me busy and off the streets for the rest of my life. I never hoped for more than to finish that one project. But from my *History of the Mishnaic Law* – the last work of mine to be called a 'history' of anything – I would go on to all of the Midrash-compilations of late antiquity, the Talmud of the Land of Israel, the Talmud of Babylonia, and so on and so forth: the whole of the canon of Judaism in its formative age.

It suffices to say that, after Brown and a year at the Institute for Advanced Study, I found a genuinely happy ending for my career at the University of South Florida, with scholarly colleagues who work together constructively and with goodwill. These years, also, I have served part time as a Visiting Professor at Bard College, where I have joined an equally benign community. I believe I hold the best job(s) of anyone in the entire academy.

The rest of this story I have outlined briefly in the opening paragraphs. To tell the whole in equivalent detail would prove tedious.

DECIPHERING THE WRITTEN FORMATION OF A JUDAISM

I have worked out ways of reading documents and developing a conception of the religious system upon which those documents draw or to which they refer. This is a method that focuses upon the smallest details of writing and moves inductively outward from syntax and grammar, repetition and recurrent pattern. It is a method that allows us to characterize whole writings, not merely cite them, and to see all together and all at once what a given authorship – the person or persons responsible for the final form and closure of a piece or writing – wishes to say as its fundamental message. That message is the religion that I claim to derive from a piece of writing. In the method I have worked out, I want to accomplish for religious writing what others have done for religious emotions and feelings. That is why I claim to show how to study a religion that is attested only by written evidence, books written down in the formative time of that religion and preserved thereafter by the choice of the continuators and heirs of that same religion and in institutions that saw themselves as continuous with the original institutions of that religion. And that accounts for the problem at hand, and it further explains why I believe my methods serve in the study of other religions attested principally or only by written documents in a sizable corpus.

Before proceeding, let me offer definitions for terms that have already made their appearance and that appear throughout. In all that follows, two usages predominate, first 'system', then 'religious' or 'Judaic' system. Let me define these matters at the outset. With this matter of 'system', I refer, in particular, to ethos, ethics, and ethnos. For I understand by a religious system three things that are one:

(1) ethos: a worldview, which by reference to the intersection of the supernatural and the natural worlds accounts for how things are and puts them together into a cogent and harmonious picture;
(2) ethics: a way of life, which expresses in concrete actions the worldview and which is explained by that worldview;
(3) and ethnos: a social group, for which the worldview accounts, which is defined in concrete terms by the way of life, and therefore which gives expression in the everyday world to the worldview and is defined as an entity by that way of life.

In these categories I adapt for my purposes in working with literary evidence the ones put forth by Geertz. A religious system is one that appeals to God as the principal power. A Judaic system is a religious system – ethos, ethics, ethnos – that identifies the Hebrew Scriptures or 'Old Testament' as a principal component of its canon. A Judaism, then, comprises not merely a theory – a book – distinct from social reality but an explanation for the group (again: 'Israel') that gives social form to the system and an account of the distinctive way of life of that group. A Judaism is not a book, and no social group took shape because people read a book and agreed that God had revealed what the book said they should do. A Judaism, that is, a Judaic system, derives from and focuses upon a social entity, a group of Jews who (in their minds at least) constitute not *an* Israel but *Israel*.

Writings such as those in the Judaic canon of the dual Torah have been selected by the framers of a religious system and the community that embodies the system, and, read all together, are deemed to make a cogent and important statement of a system, a Judaism. I call that encompassing canonical written picture a 'religious system', when it is composed of three necessary components: an account of a worldview, a prescription of a corresponding way of life, and a definition of the social entity that finds definition in the one and description in the other. When those three fundamental components fit together, they sustain one another in explaining the whole of a social order, hence constituting the theoretical account of a system. Systems defined in this way work out a cogent picture, for those who make them up, of *how* things are correctly to be sorted out and fitted together, of *why* things are done in one way, rather than in some other, and of *who* they are that do and understand matters in this particular way. When, as is commonly the case, people invoke God as the foundation for their worldview, maintaining that their way of life corresponds to what God wants of them, projecting their social entity in a particular relationship to God, then we have a religious system. When, finally, a religious system appeals as an important part of its authoritative literature or canon to the Hebrew Scriptures of ancient Israel or 'Old Testament', we have a Judaism.

CURRENT WORK

Let me now return to my own work of the late 1980s and 1990s by way of example of how in the study of religion to move from literary evidence to a theory about the nature of the religious world that produced the evidence in hand, and thence to set forth hypotheses of general intelligibility about religion. I summarize this process as a move from (1) text, to (2) context, to (3) matrix. It is that first step, text to context, the theory of which I present in this essay. For reading a text in its context and as a statement of a larger matrix of meaning, I propose to ask larger questions of systemic description of a religious system represented by the particular text and its encompassing canon. What is to be done to achieve this goal?

First, I place a document on display in its own terms, examining the text in particular and in its full particularity and immediacy. Here I want to describe the text from three perspectives: rhetoric, logic, and topic (the standard program of literary criticism in the age at hand). Reading documents one by one represents a new approach in the study of a Judaism. Ordinarily, people have composed studies by citing sayings attributed to diverse authorities without regard to the place in which these sayings occur. They have assumed that the sayings really were said by those to whom they are attributed, and, in consequence, the generative category is not the document but the named authority. But if we do not assume that the documentary lines are irrelevant and that the attributions are everywhere to be taken at face value, then the point of origin – the document – defines the categorical imperative, the starting point of all study.

Second, I seek to move from the text to that larger context suggested by the traits of rhetoric, logic, and topic. Here I want to compare one text to others of its class and ask how these recurrent points of emphasis, those critical issues and generative tensions, draw attention from the limits of the text to the social world that the text's authorship proposed to address. Here too the notion that a document exhibits traits particular to itself is new with my work, although, overall, some have episodically noted traits of rhetoric distinctive to a given document, and, on the surface, differences as to topic – observed but not explained – have been noted. Hence the movement from text to context and how it is effected represents a fresh initiative on my part.

Finally, so far as I can, I want to find my way outward toward the matrix in which a variety of texts find their place. In this third stage I want to move from the world of intellectuals to the world they proposed to shape and create. That inquiry defines as its generative question how the social world formed by the texts as a whole proposes to define and respond to a powerful and urgent question, that is, I want to read the canonical writings as a response to critical and urgent questions. Relating documents to their larger political settings is not a commonplace, and, moreover, doing so in detail – with attention to the traits of logic, rhetoric, and topic – is still less familiar.

CONTINUING CHALLENGES

This brief statement has carried us far from the autobiographical point at which I began. I should be disingenuous were I to omit reference to the response to my *oeuvre*, now passing 675 books and no one can know how many articles. That response has proved mixed, much evidence of broad and appreciative reception, much evidence of systematic *Todschweigen* – murder by silence, sedulous 'ignoring', and the like. None of this has held my interest for long; where people have offered interesting criticism, I have listened and responded, if not on the spot, then over time. Where people have afforded a cool or even rude reception, I did not tarry. None of these epiphenomena of scholarship matter. They never got in my way.

What always concerned me, certainly from the mid-1970s and intensely in the mid-1980s, was two fates. The first was that my brain would turn to mush. The second was that I might run out of ideas to contemplate, problems to solve. To solve the former, I began studying languages – three years of Portuguese, two years of Swedish, three years of Spanish, more French, German, Italian, and so on. I always found native-speakers in the university to teach me. With my young tutors over the years, I could make sure that my memory still worked.

But making sure that I would not intellectually retire and begin to praise my old work rather than criticizing it in favor of new proved a sterner challenge. Being my own harshest critic could carry me just so far. I worried that, at some point, I should simply set foot in my personal Ganges and, imitating Alexander, weep at the prospect of no new worlds (of my own invention) to conquer. Indeed, the self-doubt was so real that, in the mid-1980s, when I got a call from the White House, asking whether I might wish to be considered by President Reagan for the position of Librarian of Congress, I actually went to the White House for interviews. Now it is difficult for me to imagine a position for which I might be less qualified (except as a pulpit rabbi or a head of a Jewish seminary, I suppose), let alone one that would offer me fewer satisfactions. I had been, after all, a book writer and library-maker, not a book collector and library-custodian.

But I agreed to come to the White House and talk with the Office of Presidential Personnel. When the interviewer – a wonderful woman, who came from the town, Beverly, Massachusetts, where my father had grown up, and whose family belonged to the synagogue that my grandfather had helped to found there – asked me why I might want the job, I told her, 'Because I think I might run out of ideas, so I ought to consider another career'. Through her indulgence I survived the first cut and came for a second interview. The head of Presidential Personnel asked me the same question, though, out of a different cultural milieu, he did not find the answer comprehensible. Nor did the President.

At any rate, God had other plans for me and for the Library of Congress, I reckon, since I did not get the job and a highly qualified person did. And to date, I also have not run out of ideas.

7

Theological Autobiography
JAMES M. ROBINSON

My childhood was the very sheltered existence of faculty housing on the campus of a Presbyterian seminary in a suburb of Atlanta, where my father was Professor of Church History and Polity for over 40 years.

My father was an orthodox Calvinist. I recall him reporting at the dinner table that the Chairman of the Board of Trustees and the President of the Seminary had called him in to tell him to desist from writing, in church magazines, articles opposing the published positions of our next-door neighbor, who chaired a committee of our denomination to update the standards of the church, such as the Westminster Confession of Faith. My father replied that he had taken an ordination vow to defend these standards and would not desist from honoring his commitment – they would have to fire him (which of course they did not do). I was thoroughly impressed by his courage and integrity, without really being aware of or interested in the issues themselves.

When later I was a student at this same seminary, I was conscientious in making a good grade in the required course in Calvinist doctrine (Bavinck), but did not really get involved in specific doctrines. Walter Lowrie was just then translating Kierkegaard, and I avidly read what had been published by then. Kierkegaard seemed to have a more relevant way to come to grips with the human dilemma. Though I did not realize it at the time, a pattern was already being pre-formed.

Before going on to graduate studies, I taught for a year at my college (Davidson)...a quite literal Old Testament. My students were mostly returning veterans, who must have experienced me as hopelessly naive. Whether or not they actually believed anything I said, by the end of the year I no longer did. I had tried to make sense of my childhood theology to myself, and had failed. But that year was decisive, in that I had become at least open to the strange new world of reality.

My brother (himself a returning veteran) and I went together for a year to study at the University of Basel, where our father had spent a brief sabbatical just before the war. For Basel had assembled perhaps the most distinguished theological faculty of the day, having become during the 1930s and 1940s a haven of refuge for distinguished German and Swiss theologians who had lost their professorships in Germany because of their resistance to Nazism.

During two periods of study at Basel, Barth happened to be lecturing once on supralapsarianism/infralapsarianism, once on angels. My only lasting impression was that Barth talked about certain valid values protected by one side of the debate, and other valid values protected by the other side of the debate. It later occurred to me that he did not really believe in the doctrine itself (whichever side he came down on), but only in those values expressed in that arcane language. I became convinced (only in retrospect) that he had demythologized dogmatics (and what about the angels?), without actually realizing it – no doubt he would not have accepted this interpretation.

This soon after the war, German students were not yet allowed to live in Basel, but were permitted to live just across the border (Lörrach) and come over each day for classes (with a free midday meal in kind Christian homes). Whatever else they may or may not have smuggled across the border, they did import demythologizing. Our father had told us of the Barth–Brunner debate (he of course was on Barth's side), but had not known what he would be exposing us to in the post-war debate. When another American studying at Basel (Paul Meyer) explained to me what it all meant, my first reaction was that, formulate it as one might in sophisticated Heideggerian German, what they were saying was not the resurrection. (It had not yet occurred to me that Barth's doctrines of the fall and of angels were not really seriously affirming these as facts either.)

Barth's debate with his Swiss co-founder of dialectic theology, Emil Brunner (whom I commuted to Zürich to hear), had stayed, so to speak, within doctrinal confines: the old problem of synergism vs. salvation as wholly an unearned and undeserved gift of God. Since Brunner's view that people have a certain capacity for receiving God's revelation seemed to Barth to open the door for a synergistic aberration, Barth had stoutly replied: Nein! But this pre-war sparring had been completely forgotten by the post-war generation, for whom theology, if it had anything at all to say, must mean something about people's actual existence.

After the year in Basel, I returned to Princeton, where I had all along planned to get my doctorate in New Testament. But I found that a boring field of study, and after a year returned to Basel, with Barth as my *Doktorvater*. I told him I would like to have a topic tracing the transition from Protestant Liberalism to the two alternative outgrowths of Dialectic Theology, his own Theology of the Word and Rudolf Bultmann's Existentialistic Interpretation. He said I should read Ernst Troeltsch, Rudolf Otto, and Wilhelm Herrmann, and then we would talk about settling on one as the focus of the dissertation. By the end of the nineteenth century the metaphysical theology that had been ended once for all (one would have thought) by Kant, and the deification of the historical process by Hegel, had given way to the neo-Kantian ethical definition of God as the good. I proposed for my dissertation area Herrmann, whose focus on the path to faith seemed to have brought Schleiermacher's interest in the religious person's experience into this ethical religiosity, for it was in one's ethical experience in interpersonal relations that God, or at least religion, is inescapable and indispensable.

Actually the end of the First World War had brought (German) Christendom to an end, with the abdication of the Kaiser ending the 'Holy Roman Empire of the German Nation'. Rather than Christian culture being the progressive revelation of God through (Western) history, German culture had in fact collapsed – just think of the million-Mark German postage stamps! But, paradoxically, this had cleared the ideological air of the cultural pride that practically deified the state (which 'established' the church). Hence it would seem that God, rather than man, could for a change be heard, a unique chance to hear God 'between the times', before a new culture emerged of which Germans could be 'justifiably proud'. Friedrich Gogarten interpreted the German collapse as just such a brief moment uncluttered by human self-assertion. Thus it was in the negation of Christian culture that the positive revelation of God was – dialectically – to be heard. (Heidegger: One becomes aware of the basic but forgotten insight that there is anything at all – 'being' – precisely when one realizes that there could equally well not be anything at all – 'nothingness'.)

It was of course the very antithesis of this emerging 'dialectic theology' of the 1920s when, in the 1930s, the German *ressentiment* over the French revenge-taking in the Versailles Treaty provided a bed of ideological discontent that triggered the nationalism-with-a-vengeance that Hitler exploited – precisely what Woodrow Wilson had feared. The mainline 'German Church' became a tool of this self-assertive nationalism, while the seceding 'Confessing Church' followed Barth in the direction of resistance.

Barth had told me he could speak out publicly in Germany during the Third Reich on behalf of Jews only by deriving what he wanted to say from a biblical text, since the Confessing Church had paid the price for maintaining its freedom to proclaim the word of God. This inevitably modulated Dialectic Theology, as culture criticism, into the Theology of the Word of God.

This of course needed decoding, for something very basic was being said: The inalienable core of the humanity of humankind is the right and freedom to blurt out the truth, even when unwelcome and painful, as sometimes the last form of resistance to evil. I heard Karl Jaspers lecture on the difference, during the Inquisition, between the appropriateness of recanting a 'heresy' that was irrelevant to one's very being, and on the other hand dying for a cause upon which one's own understanding of existence, constitutive of one's being, stood or fell. My father's refusal to be silenced, Herrmann's encounter with the good as God in interpersonal responsibility, the Confessing Church's 'word of God', Bultmann's 'authentic existence', the new hermeneutic's 'word event', though all buried somewhere back in my past, have nonetheless left their mark on what still today seems to me decent.

Given the retreat into traditional dogmatic language when called upon to speak out, it is no coincidence that Rudolf Bultmann, who had been convinced by Barth's *Römerbrief* that dialectic theology was in fact the best modern translation of Pauline, and hence Lutheran, theology, presented his demythologizing essay in 1941, just when the Confessing Church (of which he was part) was rigidifying into Neo-Orthodoxy. Whereas Barth had been a product of Ritschlian Liberalism (what we call the 'social gospel'), Bultmann had been trained in the even more radical history-of-religions school. Here the competing mythologies of the mystery religions had all become open to relevant interpretation as mythological objectifications of solutions to the human dilemma, languaged in terms of dying and rising gods – including the dying and rising Christ the Lord (what later was restated as the 'kerygma'). Whereas the New Testament's message was so enshrouded in such mythological jargon as to be offensive to modern people's better judgment (and thus to justify the widespread ignoring of whatever the church had to say), Bultmann argued that the kerygma as understood by Paul and John did have a strikingly compelling and intelligible meaning when put into the 'scientific' language of existentialism. For Bultmann's philosophical colleague at the University of Marburg, Martin Heidegger, had in fact produced a table of categories for interpreting human existence scientifically, worthy of being put alongside Aristotle's table of categories for understanding natural phenomena, upon which natural science had been so successfully built. When thus reformulated in modern scholarly terms, the Christian message turned out to be the most convincing presentation of authentic existence. Or so it seemed at the time.

Since Herrmann had taught at Marburg, and hence the library there would have what I needed to flesh out the context of his career, I proposed to Barth that I go for a time to study there – of course, to hear Bultmann. When I talked to Bultmann later about my dissertation topic ('Das Problem des Heiligen Geistes bei Wilhelm Herrmann'), he commented with some surprise that, after all, Herrmann had had very little to say about the Holy Spirit. When I explained that this was of course the doctrinal category where religious experience comes up for discussion, he no doubt forgave my *Church Dogmatics* lingo (see Robinson 1952).

I asked Marburg classmates where things were moving in the Bultmannian stream, and they said the most exciting Bultmannian, Ernst Käsemann, had just begun his teaching career at Mainz. I wrote him requesting an interview in passing through Mainz on my way out of Germany. We met for an hour in the train station. This was in 1951, two years before he proposed what I later called a new quest of the historical Jesus (see Robinson 1959). I thus became a 'post-Bultmannian' (to use a term I coined to express the defections among Bultmann's pupils) before I actually became a Bultmannian. In effect, my theological trajectory over half a century has moved step by step from right to left. Käsemann provided a crucial early transition, once it had become clear to me that Oscar Cullmann, my house-father at the Alumneum in Basel, was hopelessly out of it. For my future lay not in dogmatics but in New Testament studies, which I taught first at Emory University (during which time I belatedly completed a second doctorate in this field at Princeton after all; see Robinson 1957b).

I had, by this time, become Professor of New Testament and Theology at the School of Theology at Claremont, and then, as an inducement not to accept a professorship at Harvard, Professor of Religion at Claremont Graduate School. Here I founded the Institute for Antiquity and Christianity of which I am still Director.

It was clear to me at the time that the main centers of theological scholarship, where the basic tools of the discipline were created in massive tomes, were in Europe and the Ivy League (plus Chicago), whereas the West Coast was at best involved in popularizing at the retail level. My intention was to create a center of basic research in the roots of Western civilization, out of which the medieval synthesis of Christendom and then the modern world have emerged. The approach, more culturally than theologically based, had been launched in Germany by Franz Dölger at the University of Bonn, out of which emerged the massive many-volumed *Reallexikon für Antike und Christentum*. For his approach had been to trace antiquity through to its medieval and modern transformations as '*Christentum*'. After his death an institute was founded to carry on his legacy, and hence named the Franz-Dölger-Institut. This left the technical term he had made famous, *Antike und Christentum*, available as the most suitable name for the institute I had in view at the secular institution Claremont Graduate School: The Institute for Antiquity and Christianity.

Since I had taught a semester as a visiting professor at Göttingen in the chair of the retired New Testament lexicographer Walter Bauer, I negotiated after his death the purchase of his library for Claremont. Among the pamphlets that were part of his holdings were three editions of the statutes of the Göttingen Academy of Sciences – before Hitler, during Hitler, and after Hitler. I studied these to get a grasp of how such a research center could function. Our crucial point of departure in Claremont was a small cluster of young Turks ('Project Directors') in the biblical and patristic fields who shared my vision.

What we lacked (and still do) was funding. Normally such enterprises are not authorized by a university unless there is some assurance that funding will be available. I wrote an application to the newly created National Endowment for the Humanities to launch the six initial Projects (each directed by a different professor) with which the Institute began. Only my Nag Hammadi project was successsful in obtaining modest funding (for three years, for a total of about $50,000), but that was enough for the well-wishing (and soft-hearted) president of the Graduate School to let us come into existence.

Actually, he never sought approval from the Board of Fellows of Claremont University Center to launch such a venture, since he knew they would not approve. Instead, he invited them, in a printed invitation stating the invitation was from the Board itself, to a gala opening ceremony at the newly created Music Center in Los Angeles.

My mentor, Ernest Cadman Colwell, who had been President of the University of Chicago before moving to Emory, and then assumed the presidency of the School of Theology at Claremont (taking me along with him), had reported the following anecdote about Chicago's pioneering Orientalist James Henry Breasted: He had interested the McCormick family in building and endowing the Oriental Institute, by bringing a huge stone winged bull from Babylon and storing it in a dark, dank, cramped basement room. Mr McCormick agreed it was so magnificent it should be in better accommodations! – I did in fact succeed in flying over from France, to put on display at that opening banquet, a (much smaller) bronze bull from Dan (infamous in the Old Testament for erecting just such an idol). But the $35,000 for which we could have acquired it was not forthcoming.

Yet, in spite of the Achilles' heel of hardly any research funds, the Institute has published in its first 30 years of existence some 50 massive tomes. At first, projects were published at distinguished European publishing houses where the public was already accustomed to finding serious publications in that specialty, such as E. J. Brill, the Pontifical Biblical Institute, Oxford University Press, and Patristische Texte und Studien. But such scattering made the publication achievements of the Institute, as such, less visible, and newer projects have tended not to continue European publishing traditions. Hence our own monograph series, Studies in Antiquity and Christianity, has been publishing about a volume a year from various of our Projects for the past decade (see Asgeirsson 1994).

I taught modern theology only to a limited extent: A course on 'The Beginnings of Dialectic Theology' traced through the 1920s my own trajectory a generation later from Barth to Bultmann (with the help of Jürgen Moltmann's two-volumes of collected essays under that title, whose English translation I edited). A course on 'The New Hermeneutic' traced the development within the Bultmannian school from the 'existentialism' of *Being and Time*, to the language philosophy of the later Heidegger (see Robinson and Cobb 1963:3–76) as theologized by Gerhard Ebeling and Ernst Fuchs (see Robinson and Cobb 1964:1–77).

The sayings of Jesus played the central role of the 'language event' (= the word of God) in the new hermeneutic. Thus the Bultmannian school's focus on kerygmatic texts, such as the confessions and hymns imbedded in the New Testament (Robinson 1957a), gave way to a revival of interest in the Sayings Gospel Q (Robinson 1962). For, by this time, the new hermeneutic had in effect gone behind the kerygma's coded mythological language, which had made Jesus's decisive significance intelligible back then, but unintelligible today (Ebeling). It found a new basis in the word of Jesus as the language event constitutive of Christianity. It was Ernst Fuchs who, in his garbled pious jargon that few went to the trouble to try to understand, spoke of Jesus's sayings as gifts God lays on the table before us. Bultmann's famous or notorious one-liner to the effect that Jesus rose into the kerygma needed to be updated to read that Jesus 'rose' into the continuing validity of his own word.

Bultmann's own existential interpretation of Jesus, his *Jesus and the Word*, published in 1924 for a popular audience, had painted a humanly very authentic picture of... a Jew. As Bultmann moved via Barth into his kerygmatic theology, this Jesus came to have a rather awkward position in his system as a whole – not part of New Testament theology, but only a presupposition of it, whatever that means. For he had sought to maintain that only through the Christian kerygma does one reach authentic existence... like the pre-kerygmatic Jesus the Jew?

Käsemann's proposal to revive the theological relevance of the historical Jesus did not, in fact, face up to this problem. Rather Käsemann argued, via the threat of modern docetism, that neglecting as irrelevant what can be known through historiography about Jesus, that is to say, neglecting what in our modern world has the ring of reality about it, is tantamount to the early church's heretical denial of real humanity to Jesus. But the avoidance of docetism turned out not to be a major concern in the modern world, since that orientation was still grappling with validating the history of dogma rather than the historical Jesus.

It is only the relatively new ecumenical dialogue between Jews and Christians that makes Jesus the Jew not a theological liability, but rather the central meeting-ground for that dialogue. If Jesus was one of the greatest persons Judaism has produced, and yet was quite critical of the Judaism of which he was a part, the Jesus whom Christianity has exalted to high heaven would be at least as critical of what today is passed off in his name as Christian. Thus Jews and Christians share a valid claim to Jesus, but also share an awkward claim of Jesus upon both.

I had entered into the rehabilitation of Q by arguing it belonged to a literary genre in its own right, rather than just being a catechetical appendix to the kerygma (Robinson 1964). My insight had been triggered by the discovery of another gospel of the same sayings genre among the Nag Hammadi codices, *The Gospel of Thomas*, which at first had often been dismissed as no more than excerpts from narrative gospels long since available in the canon.

Yet this new access to Jesus was promptly sidetracked by my following up on another strand in the Bultmannian synthesis, his view that the Gnostic Redeemer myth was presupposed in and influential upon the New Testament. In order to ensure that the New Testament was free from such contamination, more conservative scholarship had all along argued that Gnosticism itself was a secondary product of post-apostolic Christianity, where system-building Gnosticism after all was first documented. No texts, no history! But then, the claim was made (Alexander Böhlig) that a Nag Hammadi text he published, the *Apocalypse of Adam*, documented pre-Christian Gnosticism! Though this claim itself later became controversial (as was inevitable), it was enough to send me to Cairo (while on a sabbatic, as Annual Professor at the American Schools of Oriental Research in Jerusalem), to see when the bulk of the new gnostic texts, still inaccessible to scholarship, might become available.

The answer was quite dismal: First a French, then a German monopoly had blocked access to the material for a generation. As long as a French Abbot headed the Department of Antiquities of Egypt and a Paris-trained Copt directed the Coptic Museum in Cairo, only French scholarship had access. Indeed the head of the Paris establishment literally gloated over his 'revenge' on the Germans, who had not been able, during the period of the two World Wars, to publish a Gnostic papyrus codex in Berlin to which we wanted access. Then when the Suez Crisis expelled the French, and a Berlin-trained Director took over the Coptic Museum, the Germans moved in, and assignments went only to Germans (even to the exclusion of East Germans). And all these impediments to the advancement of scholarship in favor of one or another first-world nation's hegemony over a third-world nation's culture, and one scholar's professional advancement at the expense of the rest of the scholarly community, was clothed in the loftiest terms. I entered the real world of scholarship quite abruptly.

The French had counterattacked by motivating UNESCO (which of course was based in Paris and hence used French scholars as consultants) to intervene. But when they learned that the Coptic Museum had assigned the plums to the Germans, indeed were told that many were already published (a claim which turned out to be false), the French, and hence UNESCO, lost interest. UNESCO's involvement was pruned down to the plan to photograph the material and publish it in a facsimile edition, thus making it available to all (which the French, now on the outside, had come to favor). But at UNESCO the whole undertaking got enmeshed in the bureaucracy, and was not moving forward. It only meant that no one had access, neither the French, nor the Germans, nor myself.

To speak of 'methodology' in connection with my frantic expedients to put the material in the public domain, enmeshed in the utter chaos of the Nag Hammadi situation, would seem to be quite an overstatement. Only if one recalls that, etymologically, method has to do with a path directed toward a goal, would it seem faintly appropriate to describe what I did as methodical. In any case, the first thing that would have to be said is that in such circumstances a method must be worked out ad hoc, from inside the situation, and would be largely inapplicable to other circumstances. It was only the basic commitment, the dogged determination, the willingness to do what it took, even to take risks, play a subservient role, have endless patience, be exploited by doing the chores no one else would do, seize every opportunity, go to any length, that made success in such a hopeless situation even remotely possible.

When I asked at the Coptic Museum to see the texts, I was told that they would of course have been glad to let me see them, had they not turned control over to UNESCO. I should address myself to the Center of Documentation in Cairo that administered the UNESCO photographic project. There I was told that UNESCO only controlled the photography, not the papyri themselves, which of course were under the control of the Coptic Museum. If I wanted to see the photographs, I should go to UNESCO in Paris.

Since I was at the moment not in Paris but in Cairo, I followed a lead from the pastor of the German church there, to ask about previously-made photographs at the German Institute in Cairo. I was indeed given access to a rather large number of photographs by the Acting Director, who told me I could study them while he was gone for three days to visit an archaeological excavation. I took the photographs to my inexpensive lodging in the Presbyterian Mission, and there transcribed the photographs 24 hours a day for three days and nights, finishing them all in time to return them before the Acting Director arrived back in town.

I attended on that same trip a congress of the International Association for the History of Religions in Messina, Sicily, on the origins of Gnosticism. Here I was suddenly hailed as an authority on the photographic project in Cairo, from which I had just come. Hence I was assigned to a committee to draw up a telegram that the congress officially endorsed and sent to UNESCO, urging the completion of the photography and the publication of a facsimile edition. I went to Paris to inquire at UNESCO how the telegram I had composed had been received. I was assured the photography had indeed been completed and the publiction of a facsimile edition was imminent. In retrospect, when it became clear that nothing was happening, I realized that this good news was merely a convenient maneuver to get me out of the functionary's office.

I then visited the German university where the leading German Nag Hammadi specialist I had met in Sicily taught Coptology. For, on learning that I had plans to visit his university, he had acceded to my request to let me copy when in Germany his transcription of a short Nag Hammadi tractate (after I had sat up all night in Messina producing a translation of a sample page, to accredit myself as qualified – which I actually was not).

On arrival in Germany I was told by my host (the textual critic Kurt Aland of the Theological Faculty) that, unknown to myself, I was to be the guest speaker the next day at a joint meeting of the university's Theological Faculty with a nearby Theological Seminary. In order to give me a chance to prepare something to say, once it became clear I had never received the written invitation to speak, he made the kind offer to xerox the transcription I had planned to re-transcribe all that evening. But, since the notebook containing that transcription contained other transcriptions as well, I sat up all night transcribing those texts that had not been xeroxed. The next day I gave as my German lecture an introduction I had written for the German paperback edition of Albert Schweitzer's *Quest of the Historical Jesus* (see Schweitzer 1966:7–24), which, after all, was (I thought) in the area of my ongoing scholarship.

My innocent inquiries in Cairo had thus enticed me bit by bit into the whole morass, ending in my investing almost 20 years (in my case the prime of life) in breaking the monopoly.

After returning home, I was alerted to the problem that the UNESCO photographs were probably not usable for a facsimile edition, since presumably the many fragments had not been reassembled into legible pages. I wrote UNESCO to inquire if that was the case. On getting no reply, I had to return to Paris to ask in person. When I made a mild complaint to the functionary's superior that he did not answer letters, I was informed that I was not a citizen of the country (in UNESCO jargon: 'member state') whose cultural heritage was in question, and, besides, the functionary in charge of the photographic project was from an oral culture (Afghanistan). But when I went to his office, he graciously received me, listened to my problem, and suggested I spend a weekend working in an adjacent office finding for myself the answer to my question. He was kind enough to put at my disposal the negatives of about half the texts, and enlarged glossy prints of the other half (presumably so that I would not have a complete file of either, and hence would not be tempted to abscond with them).

I returned Saturday morning to my new office, got the negatives, and took them to a suburb of Paris, where I knew a photography shop, and paid dearly to have them make two enlargements of more than 500 negatives by Sunday evening. I then hurried back to Paris and, with a simple tripod and tourist's 35 mm camera, photographed the glossy prints one by one as I laid them on the floor beneath the tripod. UNESCO was of course completely empty on the weekend. I had finished just in time to return to the Paris suburb, pick up the enlarged prints, and return the negatives to the UNESCO office before the leisurely tempo of a bureaucracy's Monday morning began. Thus I was finally in possession of good photographs of all the Nag Hammadi codices, and to this extent was in a position to break the monopoly. But I still had no publication rights! On my return home I studied the photographs enough to write up and send to UNESCO a report answering my question: The leaves would indeed have to be reassembled from fragments before a facsimile edition (that would finally break the monopoly) could be published.

The facsimile edition planned by UNESCO envisaged an international committee of Nag Hammadi experts that would organize the publication. But the committee had never been convened. I wrote repeatedly to inquire when that would take place, and, after my patience had worn out, arranged to live during a sabbatic year at the American Church in Paris, as scholar in residence, within walking distance of UNESCO. Although I had gone to the trouble to attend a follow-up meeting of the International Association for the History of Religions in Sweden, and persuaded them to authorize its Secretary to write UNESCO on my behalf, I discovered on presenting myself again at UNESCO that the letter had never been sent. I was nonetheless provided with an office, where I spent all autumn labeling the photographs at UNESCO with the identification of fragments and page sequences that the team of young American scholars I had organized had established. We had in fact prepared draft transcriptions and translations of all the material. Hence when, in November, I had persuaded my superior at UNESCO to name a committee (including myself as the American delegate) and schedule a meeting in Cairo for December, I was able to send to each member of the committee, in advance of the meeting, this rough draft of everything. The net effect of that gesture was that I was later elected Permanent Secretary of the International Committee for the Nag Hammadi Codices, which meant I was authorized to do all the work for the committee.

The publishing house E. J. Brill in The Netherlands had had the good fortune some years earlier to publish *The Gospel of Thomas* in an inexpensive 'preliminary edition' that sold over 40 000 copies in the Christmas rush. Hence the head of the firm, F. C. Wieder, Jr, was eager to publish the whole, and had become my decisive, trustworthy, and effective partner. We had an unspoken agreement that, come hell or high water, we would publish the texts. And we had made the following concrete plan: Brill would hire a photographer and make for him a plane reservation to Cairo for the day after the UNESCO meeting convened, so as to photograph everything while the papyri was available to the UNESCO committee. For, since Egypt was technically at war with Israel, all the papyri, conserved each between panes of plexiglass, was in safe keeping. Bringing it to the Coptic Museum for the meeting was the one condition I had been able to have honored – I pointed out that otherwise we might meet less expensively and more conveniently in Paris rather than in Cairo, which of course Egyptian officialdom did not want to do for reasons of national prestige.

What I had not counted on was that the first day of the Cairo meeting of the UNESCO committee was filled with pomp and ceremony, such as newspaper reporters photographing the Minister of Culture with officials of the Coptic Museum (not with world-famous European scholars). He was then given a guided tour of the Museum to impress upon him that next year's budget should include funds for renovating the Museum (a very worthy cause, unfortunately not honored). But I had to get the committee down to business at least long enough to choose Brill (rather than some Egyptian publisher) to do the facsimile edition! For a delay of even a day would frustrate our best-laid plans, since by now the tourism just before Christmas had booked up all plane seats to Cairo. I appealed (while we were cooling our heels during the pomp and ceremony) to the very distinguished Swedish delegate, one of the committee's several honorary Presidents, to shift that item to the top of the agenda, and to call upon the committee to come to order long enough to handle at least one item on the agenda.

Once this was thus achieved, all I had to do was telegraph Brill to put the photographer on the plane the next morning. Only then did I learn that one could not normally send telegrams to addresses outside of Egypt. The Nile Hilton Hotel had its own telegraphic service, for persons staying there (but we were of course in a different hotel, one owned by the Egyptian government), except in dire cases of emergency. I conjured up a big enough emergency that my telegram was accepted. The photographer arrived the next day and photographed steadily while the committee met. I proposed a 'Technical Sub-Committee' stay to work on assembling fragments (on the basis of the lists of placements the American team had provided), along with the photographer, once the official meeting adjourned, which did take place. Then we broke for Christmas, but returned again in early January for another ten days of work. By the time the Technical Sub-Committee adjourned, a complete updated file of photographs was at Brill – and at Claremont. But we were far from completing placing all the fragments.

The Technical Sub-Committee returned each year for a couple of weeks to work further on the fragments. Since UNESCO paid for the trips by issuing the plane tickets, we had to have its approval, which in turn meant the functionary there had to have the approval of the

President of the Egyptian Antiquities Organization. When I received no replies to my letters to Paris and Cairo, I went to Cairo and made arrangements with the official there, even getting him to initial a draft contract with Brill that Mr Wieder and I had worked out.

In a subsequent year I had to fly to Paris, to handle a last-minute snag: The Egyptian official was to be out of the country (receiving an honorary doctorate in France, part of the French counter-attack), and hence the planned time for Cairo did not suit. The UNESCO official explained he had talked by phone with the Cairo official, who had requested that the time should be changed if that was not an undue inconvenience to the Technical Sub-Committee. I explained that indeed it was quite inconvenient for us, since we had each made arrangements for absenting ourselves from our classes, and I was already in Paris, with the others on alert awaiting momentarily their plane tickets. I insisted he phone Cairo again for clearance, and sat in his office several hours until he did in fact get through by phone to Cairo and got its approval for the trip to proceed.

In Cairo things were equally chaotic. Once the wrong crate had been brought from 'security' (the unlighted basement of the Egyptian Museum, a state secret we were not supposed to know until it became necessary for us to produce a truck to return the wrong crate and bring the right one). We also found the lights had gone out at the Coptic Museum, and so had to wait until the official, now *Dr* Gamal Mokhtar, returned from France, to authorize bringing in a generator and stringing electric wires all over the floor and tables in our work area.

We imported from London rat poison to cope with the uninvited guest that prevented the Museum staff from walking into one half of our work area. The resultant odor which over the years only gradually went away was hardly an improvement.

Each year I brought with me members of the American team to assist the Technical Sub-Committee in the placing of fragments and the establishment of page sequences. When the UNESCO money ran out and of course the Technical Sub-Committee stopped working on its unfinished assignment, I brought some of the American team for seven months non-stop to get the job completed. Our pressure on the Museum staff to arrive when the Museum officially opened and stay until the official closing time led them finally to move us into a room by ourselves and give me the key.

When it comes to reconstructing a papyrus codex, one can with more justification speak of scholarly method. On the basis of photographs, we had initially been dependent on the lettering, placing fragments where the resultant text made sense. Sometimes, as in a jigsaw puzzle, the broken edges fit exactly, but often the fragment did not actually touch the leaf to which it belonged, but stood off by itself, in what we called an 'island placement'. When in Cairo we finally had access to the papyrus itself, each such placement had to be verified by the fiber patterns (as distinctive for a trained eye as fingerprints), horizontal on one side and vertical on the other. Most of the 'easy' placements based on the text had already been done on the basis of the photographs by the time we began, but with painstaking and prolonged effort (one team member stayed over a couple of years more), all fragments larger than a fingernail were ultimately placed.

The sequence of leaves in several codices was completely unknown, due to the disorder in which the material had been conserved. We discovered that the horizontal fibers not only aided in placing a fragment on a leaf, but also made it possible to identify which leaf in the other half of the quire had joined it, at the (now broken) fold at the spine. This double-leaf had then horizontal fiber continuity with the next double-leaves above and below it in the quire, since in effect these double leaves had been cut in sequence one after the other from a papyrus scroll and laid one on top of the other in a stack that, when folded down the center, had produced the quire.

The roll itself had been manufactured by pasting end to end long strips of papyrus – when the horizontal fiber continuity on our leaves ended, we found a half-inch wide overlap where one papyrus strip had been pasted to another. When there was no such pasted overlap, we knew we had reached the end of a roll. Thus we had to reconstruct the rolls from which the codex had been manufactured to be sure we had established the correct sequence of leaves, especially in fragmentary codices where the text itself no longer made the sequence clear.

Ultraviolet lamps, which we had brought from California, aided in transcribing the text (once we produced a dark setting under a blanket in the sweltering heat), since the ink had included iron and hence showed up as purple stain even when the ink itself had flaked off.

The monopoly was completely broken by the end of 1977, when the last of the 13 codices was published by E. J. Brill for UNESCO in the facsimile edition of the Nag Hammadi Codices, just seven years after I had first seen the originals in Cairo. At the same time we published a one-volume English translation, which has subsequently sold over 100 000 copies (Robinson 1977); the 14-volume critical edition was completed and published by E. J. Brill in 1995.

Part of the broader responsibility put on me by the UNESCO committee had been to verify the site of the discovery. I had once already (on my way to Sicily) made a hurried trip to Nag Hammadi, where my procedure was to turn myself promptly in to the police, and ask them to engage for me a taxi and translator, to help me visit the presumed site of the discovery. It was my good fortune that the translator was a godly Copt (he refused a generous tip, but did take me to church), who taught math at the local Boys Preparatory School. He mentioned that his father had been offered one of the books, but had not bought it, since he owned a Bible and that was all he needed.

Once the law was lifted that had subsequently made Upper Egypt (except for tourist traps like Luxor) inaccessible to foreigners (while the Soviets built the High Dam), I immediately returned to Nag Hammadi on behalf of my assignment from the UNESCO committee to investigate the site of the find. I found agreeable lodging at the Guest House of the nineteenth-century Belgian Sugar Factory. I first inquired at the Boys Preparatory School for my interpreter, since he was also connected, via his father, with the marketing of the codices. The Principal told me he had moved to Cairo, and wrote down the Cairo address for me.

I then tracked down that address, but no one there had ever heard of the person I sought. In desperation I came up with a wild hunch: Since in Arabic one writes in the opposite direction from English, except for numerals, perhaps the Principal had reversed the numbers of the street address, unfamiliar as he was with writing for an English reader. So I asked my driver to turn around and drive to the other end of the street, where the reversed number would be located. There we found not only my former translator, but his friend the Principal, on a visit from Nag Hammadi. Sometimes a wild hunch does pay off! But you also have to earn your luck.

The Principal said his teacher of English at the Boys Preparatory School lived in the same village as did the discoverer of the Nag Hammadi Codices, and knew not only who the discoverer was, but would be willing to put me in contact with him when I went to Nag

Hammadi the following week. I also mentioned the previously unnoticed name I had found in the Registry of Acquisitions of the Coptic Museum, as having sold the first codex to the Museum. The Principal said of course he, and any other Copt of the region, knew that name, since the person had taught English and History, on a circuit of Coptic parochial schools, before Nasser closed Coptic schools to replace them with public schools. Thus I was put on the track of both the discoverer and first middleman, leads which I did in fact follow up year after year, drinking tea endlessly in villages of the Nag Hammadi region, until I had interviewed repeatedly each person still alive who had been involved in the discovery and trafficking. This is, I think, the first time that the details of an important illicit manuscript discovery have been tracked down with such patience and care that the story could be accurately recorded, from the illiterate Muslim camel driver who made the discovery, through villagers who acquired for cigarettes or oranges one or more codex, to the final conservation of the material in the Coptic Museum (for further details, see Robinson 1979 and 1981). There was of course a less scientific, more dramatic side of the story, having to do with the discoverer, Muhammad Ali, having been involved in a blood feud at the time of the discovery.

One night his father, a night watchman for valuable irrigation machinery that had been imported from Germany, killed a marauder from the nearby village Hamra Dum, a village that had an ongoing blood feud with Muhammad Ali's own village al-Qasr. The next day that murder was avenged, in that Muhammad Ali's father was found shot through the head, lying beside the remains of the man from Hamra Dum he had killed. Muhammad Ali's mother, beside herself, told her seven sons to keep their mattocks sharp so as to be ready when an occasion for revenge presented itself.

Some six months later someone ran to the house of Muhammad Ali to tell the family that the murderer, Ahmad Ismail, was asleep in the heat of the day on a dirt road nearby, with a jug of sugar cane molasses, the local product, by his side. The sons grabbed their mattocks, fell on the hapless person before he could flee, hacked him up, cut open his heart, and, dividing it among them, ate it raw, the ultimate act of blood vengeance.

The story of the blood feud came out in connection with Muhammad Ali explaining why he would not accompany me to the cliff to show me the site of the discovery: The hamlet of the opposing clan lay just at the foot of the cliff, and controlled it as its turf. He had avenged his father's murder just about a month after the discovery, and hence had been afraid ever since to return to the site. So I had to go to Hamra Dum myself, find the son of Ahmad Ismail, the man Muhammad Ali had butchered, and get his assurance that, since he had long since shot up a funeral *cortège* of Muhammad Ali's family, wounding Muhammad Ali and killing a number of his clan, he considered the score settled. Hence he would not feel honor-bound to attack Muhammad Ali if he returned to the foot of the cliff. I took this good news back to Muhammad Ali, who opened his shirt, showed me his scar, bragged that he had been shot but not killed, yet emphasized that if he ever laid eyes on Ahmad Ismail again, he would kill him on the spot. As a result of this display of a braggadocio's fearlessness, I called his hand and thus persuaded him to go to the cliff, camouflaged in my clothes, in a government jeep, with me sitting on the bullets side facing the village and him on the safer cliff side, at dusk in Ramadan, when all Muslims are at home gorging themselves after fasting throughout the daylight hours.

One false lead from a local priest was that the papyri had for a time been in the nearby city of Dishna, in the possession of a deceased priest he had known. In tracking down that lead, a representative of the Department of Agriculture (who was interested in what came out of the ground, and not just the local crop of sugar cane) told me the name of the antiquities dealer in Alexandria to whom some of the papyri had been sold (presumably by this person himself).

I went to Alexandria and found the shop, but the original owner had died. I visited his son in his sumptuous home (dealing in antiquities paid off). He showed me a stack of photographs of objects his father had sold. In thumbing through them, I found two photographs of manuscript pages, and asked if I might borrow them. I had them photographed in America and then mailed them back to him.

One that contained the Psalms in Greek was identified as a Bodmer Papyrus by a specialist in the Septuagint whom I knew (John Wevers of Toronto). The other, a page from the Song of Songs in Coptic, is a text that had been reported to be also in the Bibliothèque Bodmer, but not yet published. I asked a German Coptologist at the Pontifical Biblical Institute in Rome (Hans Quecke), on his way back to Germany for summer vacation, to pass by

Geneva and verify whether this picture belonged to that codex, which it did.

Thus I had by mistake floundered upon the story of the discovery and marketing of the Bodmer Papyri, among which the best papyrus manuscripts of Luke and John are found, which I pursued with similar energy, until the site of the discovery and the middlemen had all come to light (for further details see Robinson 1986). As a result, I was able to show that the Bodmer Papyri are the remains of the library of the Pachomian Monastic Order.

In the case of the discoverer, my trusted Principal of the Boys Preparatory School of Nag Hammadi later wrote me that he had been sent to examine students applying for graduation from the High School of a small hamlet near the cliff behind Dishna, and had tracked down the discoverer, whom we had heard lived in that hamlet. I made an extra trip to Egypt to follow up that lead.

The hamlet had its first electric light bulb, functional and obviously on display, in a large public room – the High Dam had just generated enough electricity to permit rural electrification! The room was crowded full of curious (male) villagers. The discoverer had just finished telling us his story, when someone from the back of the room spoke up to the effect that he too had been involved in the story, since he had once had one of the books. I asked (through the Principal, functioning as my translator) for his name. He gave me, in standard Arab style, his name and that of his father. I immediately recognized the name as one that had been repeatedly mentioned to me as that of a middleman. Often Arabic names include in third place the name of the grandfather. This had been the case when, in previous interviews, persons had narrated this person's role in the story. So when he gave me two names, I, without waiting for the translator, immediately threw in the name of his grandfather. There was dead silence in the over-crowded room. How could an American, who could not even speak Arabic, and who, for the first time, was in their hamlet, know the name of this unknown peasant's grandfather? Obviously I must have all the facts, in an almost magic way! (The discoverer had just reported that he thought the books had been written by monsters – no doubt his sense of alienation, at seeing a script that did not look like Arabic, was objectified in mythological terms.) I was, to put it mildly, in a pre-Enlightenment setting.

Since my involvement had escalated far beyond my initial intentions, and had necessitated acquiring such competencies as

Coptology, Papyrology and Codicology (not to speak of Archaeology as a cover for espionage), for which I had no previous preparation, it became an all-consuming investment of time that meant an almost total hiatus in my previous scholarly career. But this kind of scholarship was not really where my heart lay.

I did in fact subsequently get involved in publishing a two-volume facsimile edition of the unpublished fragments from Cave 4 of the Dead Sea Scrolls discovery, in order to break that monopoly, but that involved only a minor investment of energy, a project on the side, once I happened to get access to the photographs and felt morally bound to publish them (see Robinson 1994).

When at the age of 60 I had completed the bulk of my Nag Hammadi responsibilities, the question arose as to what next, since neither I nor my field were the same. The quite distinguished New Testament scholar Ernest Cadman Colwell, in many ways my academic mentor, had, after investing a generation in academic administration, sought to re-enter New Testament scholarship, but was forced to the painful conclusion that it was no longer possible in his case, and so retired to his favorite fishing pier in Florida. Was there anything that I could actually do in my field that was also worth doing?

The change in myself consisted not just in new scholarly methods and skills I had to acquire, but in the basic shift out of the ivory tower and into the feuding villages of Upper Egypt, where my excavations of the site of the Nag Hammadi discovery put me year after year all too literally into the line of fire, but also into the intrigues, selfishness and phoniness of distinguished European colleagues. To give but one example: The last holdout in the monopoly had been the Jung Codex (Nag Hammadi Codex I), since it was in a bank vault in Zürich, accessible only to its lethargic editors, but not available to the UNESCO Committee in Cairo. I was told by the Swiss representative on the Committee that the long-standing agreement to return the Codex to Egypt when the editors had completed their transcription had not been honored, because the heirs of Jung knew of its high financial value. I contacted the spokesperson for the heirs, who said they were ready to return it to Egypt as soon as the editors would give their approval. He even agreed to write them requesting their permission to return it. But then he had to write me back that one editor had blocked their good intentions: The Swiss representative on the UNESCO Committee!

Such scholars looked down condescendingly on the Egyptians as natives one could never trust; yet they themselves, once their own behind-the-scenes machinations had become clear to me, turned out to have absolutely no high ground from which to pontificate such (in any case outdated) colonialist views. The awe with which I had automatically held European scholars turned into disdain for some for whom I could no longer have respect. All this coincided with the Watergate scandal that toppled an American president for just such behind-the-scenes machinations. I found myself mired in what I gradually had to concede was the prevalent reality. Reporting on what great European scholars were doing could no longer be my thing. I had to strike out on my own.

The Gospel of John has always been associated most closely, among New Testament texts, with Gnosticism, and hence the question had been in my mind for some time as to whether I should not seek to write the Hermeneia Commentary on John. But I could not convince myself that the progress in Johannine scholarship, which my working the Nag Hammadi texts into the scholarly literature would effect, was ultimately worth the effort on my part (quite apart from the fact that my competence was really not in the History of Religions and Gnosticism). Instead, I decided to return to my new beginning that had been aborted with the Nag Hammadi intrusion, the Sayings Gospel Q.

The nineteenth century's quest of the historical Jesus had been a driving force behind Liberalism in German theology. The outcome had been, by the opening of our century, the Two Document Hypothesis: Matthew and Luke were so similar, so 'synoptic', because where they agreed they were copying out Mark, or, when the material on which they agreed was not in Mark to be copied, they must have been following a hypothetical second source nicknamed Q, the acronym of the German word *Quelle* meaning 'source'. It was thought (Adolf von Harnack) to be early enough not yet to have been corrupted by (Pauline) theology, and hence a reliable source for Jesus's teachings, just as Mark was for Jesus's biography.

Albert Schweitzer attacked all this, not because he did not share Liberalism's trust in the reliability of the sources, but rather because he thought that the sources presented Jesus not as a modern social reformer, but as a hopelessly obsessed apocalypticist. Schweitzer was the last to take the Gospels as chronologically accurate literal historical narration. In this regard, and hence in his picture of Jesus, he was as wrong as those he so eloquently criticized (see Schweitzer 1968: xi–xxxiii).

Then all this had changed after the opening of the century. It became clear (William Wrede) that Mark was obsessed by the dogma of the 'Messianic secret', and hence was narrating anything other than objective history or biography. The form critics (Martin Dibelius and Rudolf Bultmann) next argued that Jesus's sayings were first of all products of the transmitting church, whose use of such traditions had led to their reformulation and even in many cases their creation, so that what Jesus actually said is hardly more than a faint echo or whisper behind what the church said he said. It is impossible to write a biography of Jesus, since all the traditions about him were 'kerygmatized', and one cannot really get behind that prism to the objective facts themselves.

Q's relevance had earlier been played down, as merely the ethical, catechetical instruction for newly baptized converts to the kerygma, no more than its 'application'. But then it became clear that Q did not build on the kerygma of Jesus's death and resurrection at all, but had its own 'kerygma' ('greater than that of Jonah'). It was the document of a distinct branch of primitive Christianity, for which 'the' kerygma was not the all-inclusive 'unity' with which Christianity was supposed to have begun (Heinz Eduard Tödt). Form criticism's 'history of the synoptic tradition' (the title of Bultmann's book), with its focus on oral tradition, had in fact not written the history of the Q tradition. But Q's layering can after all be traced back to a core of authentic sayings of Jesus (roughly comparable to the Sermon on the Mount). The oldest layer in Q is the nearest to Jesus that one can get, and hence may well prove to have pay dirt!

Of course it can always be said that the oldest layer of tradition is after all a layer of the church's (or: the Q community's) transmission, which may or may not consist of actual quotations of Jesus. But as one works back from Matthew and Luke's editing to the final redactional level of Q itself, and from that back to pre-redactional smaller clusters and collections, and then to the individual saying, one can see a directionality in which the tradition was moving:

When looking forward in time, the tradition is moving toward a more moralizing, spiritualizing, christologizing, domesticating way of imagining Jesus, an amazingly successful enterprise that produced the image of Jesus most Christians still have today. But then those interpretive stages can be traced in the reverse direction, pointing back toward Jesus, the point of departure of this 'whole procedure. These arrows back through the layers of tradition do point to a convergence point, even if that point itself remains, so to speak, enclosed in a black box of uncertain authenticity. Such arrows do make it possible to know, not quite Jesus's *ipsissima verba* (Joachim Jeremias), but at least what he was up to, what he proposed, and what made such a dramatic impact on those who heard him.

There is then really no cogent reason not to ascribe to him such striking sayings that crop up rather densely in this oldest material. Its basic authenticity is all the more probable in view of the fact that the editing by Matthew and Luke was moving away from resolving the desperate plight of the needy, into an endorsement of the disciples, and a clearly discernible spiritualizing rather than con-cretizing (Robinson 1995). Hence, in view of the directionality of the flow, the point of departure in Jesus shows a remarkable con-sistency with the material in the oldest layer of Q itself.

Jesus really is not a shadowy founding figure beyond our reach, comparable to Qumran's 'teacher of righteousness', but rather is someone who can be encountered as an historical figure. The problem the historical Jesus poses is really not that we do not know what he had to say, but rather that, when we get wind of it, we do not know how to handle it. Rather bear those ills we have than fly to others we know not of! And so the church prefers to whistle in the dark.

In my case, this working hypothesis of pursuing Q back to Jesus seemed quite worth pursuing. After all, some sayings seem to pick up just where I had left off: 'Why do you address me Lord, Lord, and do not do what I say?' 'Do not fear those who kill the body but are not able to kill the soul.'

My return to New Testament scholarship thus took the form of organizing a decade ago the International Q Project (consisting of a new team of some 40 younger scholars) to establish a critical text of the Sayings Gospel Q. For this written Greek collection of a couple of hundred sayings ascribed to Jesus had been used by the authors of the Gospels of Matthew and Luke, who in the process had 'improved' the wording of Q to make it more clearly reflect their own understanding of Jesus's sayings. It was this damage that needed to be repaired.

Our method for reconstituting the wording of Q has been to get deeply enough into the vocabulary, grammar, style, and slant of those two Evangelists to be able to detect, in the many small divergences of the Matthean and Lukan text from each other, which Evangelist is responsible for the 'improvement', and then to undo that good work by restoring the way the text of Q originally read.

Previous scholarship's studies of Matthew and Luke's editing of Mark had already provided detailed information about their vocabulary, syntax, theological tendencies, and the like, so that there was already available a vast amount of information to apply to our task. When Matthew and Luke disagreed in the wording or word order of Q sayings, the 'fingerprints' of one Evangelist or the other made clear that this Evangelist had changed the text. This did not automatically mean that the reading of the other Evangelist was that of Q, since both Evangelists could have, and in fact often did, 'improve' what both sensed to be 'deficient'.

Since I was coming at the task directly from manuscript study, I applied to the reconstruction of this text, though no manuscripts survived, methods familiar to the textual criticism of the New Testament text itself: When a scribe makes a scribal error (in our case read: 'improvement'), the error often consists not just in a single word, but includes whatever consequences in rewriting the one change may have made. A different preposition requires often a different case ending. Sometimes the consequences are more subtle and far-reaching. Indeed we have found the task of delimiting precisely the 'variation units' within each saying to be a very time-consuming enterprise, requiring that one get to the bottom of each of the Matthean and Lukan reformulations.

Each saying in Matthew and Luke had to be coded with numbered sigla, making each variation unit discrete, so that the documentation for precisely that variation unit, on which our decision as to how it read Q at that precise place was based, could be amassed in a voluminous database. The database itself went *seriatim* through the numeration of the discrete variation units, each of which was divided into four subdivisions: Luke = Q, Pro; Luke = Q, Con; Matthew = Q, Pro; Matthew = Q, Con. Then German, French and English scholarly literature over the past century and a half was gleaned for opinions as to how Q read for each variation unit. The verbatim quotations in all three languages were printed in chronological order in these four sequences. Then the person who had collected all this data presented a written Evaluation of the data, stating how that person thought the Q text actually read for each variation unit of one's assignment. Then two other members of our team read this database and Evaluation and wrote their own agreeing or disagreeing Evaluations. All this was then distributed by mail, sometimes in rather massive mailings, to all the members. Each variation unit on which the three Evaluators did not agree was then discussed at our next semi-annual meeting, and a vote was taken. The resultant text of Q, for the sayings treated the previous year, was published each October in the *Journal of Biblical Literature*. It has taken eight years to work through the whole Q text in this way.

We have now revised our procedure, in view of a one-volume second edition of the critical text of Q. In addition to Claremont, two subsidiary centers have been created in Toronto, Canada, and Bamberg, Germany. The leaders of those two centers and myself have become General Editors, who go through the previous results and re-vote to establish an improved critical text. Meanwhile four younger Managing Editors are revising the databases into publishable form.

The outcome of this new phase of the project is to be a one-volume synopsis of the critical text of Q flanked by the Matthean and Lukan texts, formatted so that users can see for themselves each divergence between Matthew and Luke and the degree of certainty, in our judgment (graded A to D) with which the Q text has at each such juncture been reconstructed. It should become a standard tool in the discipline, much as the Nestle-Aland *Novum Testamentum Graece*, or Aland's *Synopsis Quattuor Evangeliorum*, or Bauer's *Greek-English Lexicon*, are assumed to be on the desk of anyone involved in serious work in our discipline. As a back-up to the critical edition, the database of citations from scholarly literature of the past hundred or more years, on the basis of which the final decisions for each variation unit have been determined, is being published in a series estimated to comprise 31 volumes between now and 2002 CE (see Robinson, *et al.* 1996).

It now appears to be the case that the final editing of Q took place at about the time of the fall of Jerusalem, but that it contained not only isolated sayings ascribed to Jesus, but even small clusters of his sayings that had previously been brought together. For there is rather general agreement that this final redaction was preceded by some layering procedure in which smaller collections were already involved, although no specific proposal has received general acceptance. Yet enough such pre-redactional layering has become apparent to make it possible to trace the broad lines of the Jesus movement, as it has come to be called, from Jesus, through Q, to the Gospel of Matthew, and thus into the main stream of the Christianity of which we are heirs.

It has usually been overlooked, what gaping holes there have traditionally been in our knowledge of primitive church history. For in our mind's eye, we have normally moved from Jesus via Easter to the church history of Acts (to whatever extent reliable historical sources can be presupposed there): the Jerusalem church and its expansion to Antioch, then the Pauline mission as also reflected in Acts, with the Pauline and Deutero-Pauline Epistles providing a parallel and, as needed, a corrective source of such information, until the Paulinist Ignatius of Antioch brings us to the second century, where the church historian can take over.

What is overlooked in this overly reassuring projection is the fate of Jesus's disciples who stayed in or returned to Galilee – there is only a single passing reference in all of Acts to a church in Galilee! Unwritten is the history of a Jesus movement whose variety of religious experience was primarily the reproclamation of the sayings of Jesus (which is not a variety attested in Acts), until ultimately the Galilean Q movement became the Matthean community of Antioch. Indeed, what happened in Antioch between Paul's crisis there in mid-century and the composition of the Gospel of Matthew a generation or so later?

Actually, there would appear to be imbedded in Matthew, discernible from a rather clear seam between chapters 11 and 12, an echo of a transition from a primarily Jewish Christian community based on Q to a Gentile Christian community based on Mark. Thus we can begin to mock up, in the layering of Q and Matthew, the course of Jewish Christianity from its first beginnings, recorded in early chapters of Acts and in Paul, to its absorption into mainline Christianity, no doubt at the expense of losing some of its membership to emergent normative Judaism and what we have come to consider heresies, such as the Ebionites and Nazarenes. But yet it is also here that the historical connection between Jesus himself and all subsequent Christianity has for the first time become discernible in the Q trajectory.

The predominance of Matthew in the early church is well attested statistically by the number of surviving manuscripts of Matthew, the quantity of quotations from Matthew in early Christian literature, and the assimilations by scribes copying Mark,

Luke and John to the more familiar readings of Matthew. Paul and John provided the main line of development for the intelligentsia, be they orthodox or Gnostic. But Matthew provided the substance for the Christian living of most Christians, and therein survived the Judaism of Jesus and his earliest followers.

The problem of relating Jesus to the church used to be posed in terms of how Jesus's only implicit Christology became explicit in the church, or how his indirect Christology became direct, or how the proclaimer became the Proclaimed (Bultmann). All such ways of posing the problem (for which no really satisfactory answer emerged) had in view, when speaking of the church, the kerygmatically-oriented church attested in Paul and Acts, which built not on Jesus but on Easter. But when one realizes that the Matthean church is really the precurser of the bulk of Christian believers, the problem is posed differently, and is subject to a different resolution: The miracle ('Easter') is that, with Jesus's awful death, his talk of a loving, caring God who supplies our every need was not simply dumped as tragically misinformed, but instead continued to be proclaimed, believed, and put into practice.

The best-known early collection imbedded in Q, and no doubt its most important, is the Sermon, which seems to have held pride of place from the very beginning as representing the epitome of Jesus's teaching (though not an actual sermon he ever held on a given occasion on a Mount or Plain). It is here that one finds the blessing of the poor and hungry, the love of enemies, turning the other cheek, giving the shirt off one's back, hearing and doing rather than just talking high Christology. When one associates other equally early collections, which have much the same gist, such as the Lord's Prayer, the Caring Human Father who gives bread and fish, not stones and snakes, and the Ravens and Lilies whom God takes care of so splendidly (whose affinity Matthew still sensed strongly enough to move them all into his Sermon on the Mount), one catches sight of what Jesus meant.

The basic problem for focusing in on the center of what Jesus had to say, even for critical historical scholarship, has been that Christian research has been too much determined by an apologetic interest, somehow to root one's own Christology in Jesus himself. Now that there is general agreement that most christological titles do not go back to Jesus, a last-ditch stand has been taking place about his use of the Aramaic idiom for 'human', literally 'the son of man'. On Jesus's tongue, was this a non-titular generic reference to a human, who, for instance, in distinction from birds and foxes has no place to lay his head, or was it already for Jesus a titular understanding of the (originally non-titular) use in Daniel, hence referring to Jesus as a heavenly figure, the final Judge, such as is the case in Mark and even more explicitly in Matthew?

In the oldest layer of Q, Jesus claimed no title, and seemed not to have been involved in our christological reflections at all. (The Gospel of John has misled us into thinking he was obsessed with his own status, which is almost all Jesus talks about there.) He exorcised not through some distinctive role he played, but by *God's* finger, as evidence of *God's* kingdom, much as he thought other exorcists functioned (a completely overlooked/avoided saying in Q). Faith for him was not belief in certain beliefs, but trust in God to be there when needed. One would be acquitted in the judgment not on the basis of certain beliefs, but for actually doing what Jesus said one should do. However, even the rationale for this does not come to expression through a christological title, but apparently, at first, through imagining Jesus functioning at the judgment as a character witness. Even this function ascribed to Jesus may not go back to Jesus himself, but might be a subsequent mythological objectification based on Jesus's conviction that doing what he said would acquit in the judgment. For him, this was really enough.

The problem with this position advocated by Jesus is not just that it does not satisfy one's interest to find roots for one's Christology, but, perhaps still more basically, that people do not have the slightest intention of doing what Jesus said one must do to be acquitted. Rather we prefer to exalt Christ as our savior. Thus Paul provided the core of our Christian faith, not Jesus. Even such a Pauline concession as his comment that we will all stand before the judgment seat of God to give account of ourselves is easily passed over. The church at any given time tends to hear only what it wants to hear.

I am often asked by Christians who are not academics the leading question as to how a lifetime of critical biblical scholarship has affected my faith as a Christian. The implied answer is that such 'higher criticism' obviously destroyed it. Hence my standard reply has been that, if I had entered upon a quite unrelated profession, I would no doubt have abandoned Christianity completely as hopelessly outdated and irrelevant. After all, the godly Christianity in which I grew up did not catch sight of racial segregation, militarism, or the plight of share-croppers, as problems to be addressed.

It is of course true, as has already become abundantly evident in what I have said thus far, that my objective scholarship has not been disinterested, and that my personal convictions have evolved not independently of the intellectual trajectory sketched above. I surely have reached my seventies with a different faith than what I had when I began. Let me therefore conclude this theological autobiography with a summary of where my scholarship and my faith now tend to converge:

What Jesus had to say centered around the ideal of God's rule ('the kingdom of God'), the main 'theological' category Jesus engendered. Calling the ideal *God's* rule puts it in an antithetical relation both to other political and social systems, and to individual self-interest, 'looking out for number one'. The wild birds and flowers prosper without working to secure their needs. God cares about every sparrow sold a dime a dozen. For God will not give a stone when asked for bread, or a snake when asked for fish, but can be counted on to give what one really needs. Indeed, people should trust God to know what they need even before they ask. This 'utopian' vision was the core of what Jesus had to say. It was both good news, reassurance that the good would happen to undo one's plight in actual experience, and the call upon people to do that good in actual practice.

For the Jesus people this was their gospel – what they called evangelizing the poor, a kerygma greater than that of Jonah. But since Paul anathematized any other gospel than his own, even if proclaimed by angels, and said that persons who had known the human Jesus (as Paul had not) need know him that way no longer, the acknowledgment that Jesus's gospel should be accorded at least equal status with *the* gospel has only slowly gained ground among Christians (Francis of Assisi, Tolstoy, M. L. King, Jr, ...).

Jesus was, after all, a real idealist, a committed radical, in any case a profound person who had come up with a solution to the human dilemma that is at least worth listening to.

The human dilemma is in large part that we are each other's fate, the tool of evil that ruins the other person, as we look out for number one, having wised up with regard to any youthful idealism we might once have cherished. But if I would basically cease and desist from pushing you down to keep myself up, and you for your part would do the same, then the vicious circle would be broken. Society would become mutually supportive, rather than self-destructive. Count on God to look out for you, to provide people that will care for you, and listen to him when he calls on you to provide for them. This radical trust in and responsiveness to God is what makes society function (as God's society). This is what, for Jesus, faith and discipleship were all about. Nothing else has a right to claim any functional relationship to him.

Put in language derived from his sayings: I am hungry because you hoard food. You are cold because I hoard clothing. So we are all to get rid of our backpacks and wallets! Such 'security' is to be replaced by 'God's rule', which means both what we trust God to do (to motivate the other person to share food with me), and what we hear God telling us to do (to share clothing with the other person). One does not carry money while bypassing the poor (literally: 'the beggars'), or a backpack full of extra clothes and food, while the cold and hungry lie in the gutter ignored. This is why the beggars, the hungry, the depressed, are actually fortunate ('blessed'). God, that is to say, those who hearken to God, those in whom God rules, will care for them. They are called upon to trust in God's rule as being there for them ('theirs is the kingdom of God'). One does not even carry a club for self-protection, but rather returns good for evil even with regard to one's enemies. One turns the other cheek. God is the kind of person who provides sunshine and rain even to those who oppose him. So it is those who care for ('love') even their enemies who are God's children.

In the original form of the Lord's Prayer, what followed directly upon 'Thy kingdom come', as its concrete meaning, was: 'Give us this day our daily bread'(Q 11:2b-4, see Robinson, *et al.* 1996). People should ask for no more than a day's ration of food, trusting God to provide for today, and then tomorrow trusting for tomorrow.

God's rule was interpreted by Matthew's community to mean: 'Thy will be done on earth as it is in heaven'. This petition added to the Lord's Prayer is, technically speaking, not a call for action, but, like 'Thy kingdom come' which it interprets, an appeal to God. When one prays, one trusts in God to answer. But God answers through motivating people to turn the other cheek; to give the shirt off one's back; to lend, expecting nothing in return. The person who prays to God for help is the same person whom God motivates to help: 'Forgive us our debts *as we forgive our debtors!*'

Part of God ruling in one's life was helping the disabled with whatever the primitive psychosomatic medicine of the day could provide. One went from door to door, and, if admitted for bed and breakfast (the answer to the prayer for a day's bread), one placed God's *Shalom* on the house, which meant one healed as best one could, as God ruling, the infirm there ('Heal the sick and say: The kingdom of God has drawn near').

Just as the sharing of food and clothing, the canceling of debts, the non-retaliation against enemies, were not seen as human virtues, but rather as God acting through those who trust him, just so healings were not attributed to some witch-doctor's or magician's individual technique or skill, but to God's finger that made use not only of Jesus's fingers, but of the hands of others as well. Clearly, all this that one could not oneself do, from renunciation of self-interest to healing disease, took place because God was doing it. God was ruling in this unusual human society – this was in fact the 'coming' of 'the kingdom of God'! For Jesus was a 'faith healer' in the sense that he trusted God to interject his 'finger' into the human dilemma, to overcome the plight of the disadvantaged.

But not everything had been done: Not all people lived such trust in God, not all the helpless had been helped, not all the disabled were healed. Of course, one trusted God to follow through to completion ('eschatology'). But Jesus's 'eschatological' message was not to distract from grim reality by means of the utopian ideal of 'pie in the sky by-and-by', but rather to focus attention on trusting God for today's ration of life, and on hearing God's call to give life now to one's neighbor.

All this is as far from mainline Christianity as it was from the Judaism practiced in Jesus's day. The 'hardest' saying of Jesus is: 'Why do you address me Lord, Lord, but do not do what I say?' One laments the absence of a 'high Christology' in the sayings of Jesus. But what could be 'higher' than maintaining that doing Jesus's word is what acquits in the day of judgment? A Neo-Platonic metaphysical speculation secondarily Christianized? Christological creeds may be no more than pious dodges to avoid this unavoidable condition of discipleship: Actually do what he said to do!

People do not do what he said, not simply because of the shift in cultural conditions, for which an adequate hermeneutic might provide a solution, but, ultimately, because people do not trust God as Jesus did (though of course one claims to have Christian 'faith', that is to say, a traditional ideology). This is what should be unsettling about finding out what Jesus had to say.

All this of course sounds incredibly naive. Once Jesus launched himself into this lifestyle, practicing what he preached, he did not last long. A reality check is called for! Yet the bottom line is not necessarily so cynical. In concentration camps, cells of a few who can really trust each other, due to a shared ethnic, religious, or political commitment, and who are hence willing to give an extra portion of their meager food and other necessities of life to the feeblest, have turned out to have a higher chance of survival than do individuals looking out only for number one. Selfishness may ultimately turn out to be a luxury we can ill afford. There is a paradoxical saying to the effect that when one saves one's life one loses it, but when one loses it one saves it. To be sure, this has in view less longevity than integrity. It is all the more worthy of serious consideration.

References

Asgeirsson, Jon Ma. 1994. *The Institute for Antiquity and Christianity: Publications of the First Quarter-Century* (Occasional Papers 29). Claremont: Institute for Antiquity and Christianity.
Robinson, James M. 1952. *Das Problem des Heiligen Geistes bei Wilhelm Herrmann*. Marburg an der Lahn: Karl Gleiser Inhaber der R. Friedrichs Universitäts-Buchdruckerei.
——1957a. 'A Formal Analysis of Col. 1,15–20', *Journal of Biblical Literature* 76:270–87.
——1957b. *The Problem of History in Mark* (Studies in Biblical Theology 21). London: SCM; Naperville, IL: Alec R. Allenson.
——1959. *A New Quest of the Historical Jesus* (Studies in Biblical Theology 25). London: SCM; Naperville, IL: Alec R. Allenson.
——1962. 'Basic Shifts in German Theology', *Interpretation* 16:76–97.
——1964. 'LOGOI SOPHŌN: Zur Gattung der Spruchquelle Q'. pp. 77–96 in *Zeit und Geschichte: Dankesgabe an Rudolf Bultmann zum 80. Geburtstag*, edited by Erich Dinkler. Tübingen: J. C. B. Mohr [Paul Siebeck].
——1979. 'The Discovery of the Nag Hammadi Codices'. *Biblical Archeologist* 42 (Fall):206–24.
——1981. 'From the Cliff to Cairo: The Story of the Discoverers and the Middlemen of the Nag Hammadi Codices'. *Colloque international sur les textes de Nag Hammadi (Québec, 22–25 août 1978)* (Bibliothèque copte de Nag Hammadi, Section 'Etudes' 1). Québec: Les presses de l'Université Laval; Louvain: Peeters, 1981 [1982]:21–58.
——1986. 'The Discovering and Marketing of Coptic Manuscripts: The Nag Hammadi Codices and the Bodmer Papyri'. pp. 1–25 in *The Roots of Egyptian Christianity*, edited by Birger A. Pearson and James E. Goehring. Philadelphia: Fortress.

—— 1994. 'Ethics in Publishing Manuscript Discoveries: Panel Discussion'. pp. 468–71 in *Methods of Investigation of the Dead Sea Scrolls and the Khirbet Qumran Site: Present Realities and Future Prospects* (Annals of the New York Academy of Sciences 722), edited by M. O. Wise, *et al.* New York: New York Academy of Sciences.

—— 1995. 'The Jesus of Q as Liberation Theologian', pp. 259–74 in *The Gospel Behind the Gospels: Current Studies on Q* (Supplements to *Novum Testamentum* 75), edited by Ronald A. Piper. Leiden: E. J. Brill.

Robinson, James M. (ed.). 1977. *Nag Hammadi Library in English.* Leiden: E. J. Brill; San Francisco: Harper & Row.

Robinson, James M. and John B. Cobb. 1963. *The Later Heidegger and Theology* (New Frontiers in Theology: Discussions among German and American Theologians, vol. 1). New York: Harper & Row.

—— 1964. *The New Hermeneutic* (New Frontiers in Theology: Discussions among Continental and American Theologians, vol. 2). New York: Harper & Row.

Robinson, James M. , Paul Hoffmann, and John S. Kloppenborg (eds). 1996. *Documenta Q: Reconstructions of Q Through Two Centuries of Gospel Research Excerted, Sorted, and Evaluated.* Leuven: Peeters.

Schweitzer, Albert. 1966. *Die Geschichte der Leben-Jesu-Forschung* (Taschenbuch-Ausgabe). Munich and Hamburg: Siebenstern Taschenbuch.

—— 1968. *The Quest of the Historical Jesus.* New York: Macmillan.

8

Half a Life in Religious Studies: Confessions of an 'Historical Historian'

MARTIN E. MARTY

When people ask whether I am in 'religious studies', 'history', or 'divinity', I answer 'Yes'. It all depends upon what question is being asked at any moment, in what context, and toward what end. We all express ourselves through various modes of being or universes of discourse. When asked at this moment to reflect on what someone in my generation of historians, particularly me, might wish to pass on to scholars in the two generations that are at work succeeding ours, I pause. Given my peculiar history *vis-à-vis* religious studies – a curricular zone for which I never consciously prepared myself – will not everything seem idiosyncratic if not idiopathic?

Attempting to answer that question, I looked around me at colleagues in my generation and in those that were our students, in theirs, and then it dawned on me: the professions of most of us are idiosyncratic; that is, they bear 'structural or behavioral characteristics peculiar to an individual'. At least some of us display 'idiopathic' career patterns, which means that the cause of the disease that led us into our fields is not fully known. Rather than be disturbed by that feature, I make a virtue of the necessity of showing how different from each other we all are.

In a lifelong battle against conformity to a single model of what religious studies is and how scholars in it are to think and behave, I will unembarrassedly drop any masks that academics are trained to hide behind, and accept the invitation to be autobiographical. This means that, no more than any other colleague would I be able to offer my career, outlook or achievement as a template, a gauge or pattern others could follow even if they would. Instead, it is designed to be an emboldener: if I could get to this curricular area

151

through routes this circuitous and have this much enjoyment in it, why not 'be yourself' and make the most of the routes you have taken, have to take?

Right off, I am all but violating a norm of the humanistic culture we are supposed to share, since the study of religion belongs to humanistic culture. Humanistic cultures, philosopher Ernest Gellner reminds us, are cultures based on literacy. Pre- or non-literate cultures rely on a kind of tribal wisdom, passed on from seniors and sages to successive generations. I am being asked for this moment to act the role of the senior sage and to address some who are in the figurative tribe of religious studies professionals. But since those who come to what is being 'passed on' here do so not in front of my rocking chair but through a text, this text in this book, I suppose we check out all right in respect to what the humanities intend to be.

Still, one is uneasy for reasons that have already begun to show. In the academy we are trained to suppress reference to the 'I' of the scholar, yet this invitation calls for an orgy of 'I'-ism. We are so accustomed to humanistic culture's dependence on texts and their analogues – town maps, monuments, dance charts, cathedral floor plans, and the like – that it is hard to make an intellectual case without constance reliance on footnoted authorities; yet here we must. Also, regarding one's self as a senior or a sage is a difficult act for a person who thinks of himself as a perpetual 35-year-old who is not sure what he wants to be when he grows up. Picturing juniors gathering around the metaphorical campfire of our teaching and writing tribe, in eagerness to hear valuable anecdotes that might instead reveal signs of anecdotage, demands a strongly developed sense of fantasy. Yet here we are, you and I, transacting. Pope Leo X once said, 'God has given us the papacy; let us enjoy it.' I have been given this forum and intend to enjoy it.

To begin at the beginning, it strikes me that most people in religious studies are still self-conscious about the study of religion and its closeness to the expression of faith. Folklore at the American Academy of Religion, in tried and trite and true tellings, finds AAR scholars wearing AAR badges on elevators in hotels they share with Rotarians or Kiwanians. 'What religion are you?' they are asked. Or they hear joshing: 'Oh, oh, we better behave and not be profane. We are sharing the elevator with you religious folk!' To which the responses are: 'We're not religious! We *study* religion. We don't behave. We're profane. Don't get us wrong!'

The roots of this more-secular-than-thou attitude, which often extends from elevators to curricular discussions, are usually in the childhoods of the scholars. Interview almost anyone who is emphatically distanced from religion and you will find that, more often than not, they are dealing with what John Dewey called his childhood religion: a 'laceration', old wounds. Or they are embarrassed by the provincialism of their adolescent spheres, where commitments were forced on them, or had been made naively – and necessarily were later broken. Temple Emanu-El or Old First Church was the symbol of boredom, niceness, repression, and narrowness, precisely the elements of life we, the liberated, spend our lives rejecting. For those of us in religious studies who remain in continuity with their childhood faith tradition or have been 'born again' and habituated into another, most find it discreet and civil not to bring the subject up, lest we look pious or sound apologetic.

Here comes my own religious studies-based caveat: don't get me wrong, I find myself saying. I am not suggesting that one must be pious or apologetic, a believer or a practitioner, to be a good religious studies scholar. I am only promoting a notion forged by experience of decades in encounters, at AAR conventions and on the site visits that this wanderer has made, that we do best if we are ourselves, and use attitudes toward or against faith that are part of the accidents and contingencies of life to understand what we are teaching. This would be opposed to artificial and militant distancing in the name of an objectivity that only other cultural laggards in the academy are still looking for.

I think of how many North American scholars of religion, now liberally at home in pluralist societies, were brought up in fundamentalist Protestantism or in sheltered and often repressive ultraconservative Catholicism. To spend their life fighting their past is an activity interesting only to them. To spend it transforming the substance and structure of childhood training into adult and professional skills that encourage empathy, listening, and criticism, strikes me as the most mature and helpful use of such pasts.

THE ROOTS OF COMMITMENT TO RELIGIOUS STUDIES

My own first path to religious studies had four elements: familial, catechetical, ecclesial, and confessional training combined to form a matrix that I did not experience as repressive, though many peers found it so. Translate my four adjectives ending in '-al' to real life, beginning with *familial*. I was brought up in a family that fused the heritages of Swiss Reformed and German Lutheran nurture. This occurred in Dust Bowl and Depression Era Nebraska, in a county that even today, according to the denominational censuses, is listed in the atlas as being 100.2 percent 'churched', mainly Catholic and Lutheran.

A clue to what one does with beginnings like this in religious studies: We scholars have to remember or learn that the faith, in cases where there was faith, that elders like mine professed and taught us did not look to them like anything we now call 'religion', let alone a subject for 'religious studies'. The universe of meanings and practices were fired point blank at us children. In a gentler picture, it was presented as a world of threat and promise, divine law and divine grace. The tone of teaching was somewhat polemical, but not grievously so. Others of faith or of no faith were simply 'others'. They and what they believed and practiced were simply 'out there', serving neither as subjects for copying nor even as objects for studying. 'We' had to make sense of our own ordinary and sometimes desperate lives, and the adult world set out to show us how they were doing so.

As children of the Enlightenment, even when as respectable postmoderns we repudiate 'the Enlightenment Project', we often forget that our parents and teachers and rabbis and chaperones were also children of the Enlightenment, but they often found ways also to be people of faith – as the vast majority around us profess to be (ask Dr Gallup!).

The advantage for religious studies of the kind of background I have described was available to many in my generation and may be repeated in the experience of a minority of scholars who are younger. I recognize that thousands of others in religious studies now have the opposite kind of past: religionless, marked by parental apathy, nurtured in college along a bewildering cafeteria line of options, none of which one could take seriously, and none of which provided grounding. To such, many in my generation's kind of experience may seem antique, but I hope not worthless.

This personal background has helped me and my kind, lifelong, to remember that the people who believe and practice what we scholars classify and analyze as 'religion' for 'religious studies' is to them simply immediate experience, a given world. My childhood reference does not mean by any means that our family and the families around us thought we had all the answers. We and they could be benumbed, stupefied, silenced, or angered by the presentations of the mysteries of faith in that stark climate, just as we could be quickened, enlightened, moved to speak, or filled with delight by unwarranted benignities and mercies. So it is, I have always thought, with most of the folk that scholars of religion study. I wish more of the scholars would take the risk of manifesting that enlivening ambiguity in their teaching and public expression.

Secondly, I mentioned *catechetical* formation, an element that I expect and almost hope many will find idiosyncratic and esoteric – which means, ripe for retrieval. The study of *a* religion, *our* religion, came to us in a form that was both static, in the form of monologues expounding scriptures or traditions *and*, at times, dialogical, prompting conversation. We memorized *a* catechism and, already as children, were taught to use its question and answer form as a stimulus to our own inquiries, expressions of doubt, and affirmations. Recall that etymologically 'catechetical' has to do with 'resounding in the ear of'.

The catechismal was also, in its way, systematic. Paul Tillich often said that he liked to teach in classrooms where students had long and deep steeping in Catholic, Lutheran, Reformed, or other scholasticism. They at least had something arranged that he could help them rearrange. Those who lacked all acquaintance with system were interesting – Tillich liked to work with chaos – but were at a disadvantage when it came to experimenting with the new.

The advantage of this catechismal background for religious studies has also always struck me as clear, and I hear similar affirmations from others, whether they critically affirm 'their' catechism or its analog, or reject it. The religions we study, be they 'primitive' or 'high', folk or sophisticated, tend to have a substance. In faiths such as that professed in my parental world, there is some accent on 'belief *that*' as well as 'belief *in*'. I would argue in other contexts, including with historians of religion or anthropologists who stress ritual and behavioral elements, that *all* the expressions we call religion exhibit some sort of cognitive or substantive dimensions that undergird their practices. It strikes me as romantic on one hand or condescending on the other to suggest that 'primitives' have no intellectual structure to their ritualized lives.

Whatever it was intended to do centuries ago, the catechetical approach now at least potentially empowered us and inspired us less to argue than to converse. In recent years we note much attention among philosophers like Michael Oakeshott and theologians like David Tracy who use the model of conversation in religious thought. We had a head start on this. I hope that the next two or three generations of religious studies experts refine the approach that combines both substance and conversational encounter.

Third, the childhood approach to religious studies was *ecclesial*, and, in ways, often misunderstood by some; decades later it remains so. At the gatherings or convenings of the American Academy of Religion and other scholarly societies one senses a company of scholars disdaining the idea of being found present at mosque, synagogue, or church. Away from the gatherings and conventions, I visit hundreds of campuses and find many of the same scholars positively related to local worshipping congregations. One thing tends to happen to many when we scholars gather and something different happens when we disperse. Maybe something about professionalism is here revealed.

On ecclesia and community: I underwent training for pastoral ministry in the context of churchly prep school, college, and theological seminary. This meant that the study of religion was provincial and professional. Provincial means that we explored scriptural, historical, and theological texts within a defined (and prejudicial) province, in this case conservative Lutheranism. Professional means that the learning was designed to make graduates effective practitioners and leaders of religious communities. All this occurred without much reference, or certainly without much positive reference, to the non-Lutheran or non-Christian surroundings that made up our culture, or world culture. Of course, that approach therefore represented some disadvantages later on, when it became urgent to make sense of the larger environment, the different, the other.

I am not sure that the positive values of the ecclesial or communal experience have been understood or appreciated among generations where late-Enlightenment hyperindividualism in religion and other spheres came to be taken for granted. I like to make the case that the scholar, if moved by faith, may benefit from putting to work his or her complex and ambiguous mix of faith and nonfaith, communal experience and private search, when trying to understand others. Many suppress the experience of religious communities while trying to impart to students a sense that religion past and religion elsewhere cannot be grasped apart from comprehension of this communal dimension.

That paragraph might sound like an injunction, 'Go to church!' I am not forthright or self-assured enough to preach that, though I have had African-American religious studies colleagues who were emboldened to shout it as part of their contribution to religious studies. At least a willing suspension of disbelief or dispractice, a bracketing of the hermeneutics of suspicion long enough that one might experience and understand the minuses and pluses of religious congregating, can be a plus. When speaking of possible values in congregating, I hasten to add that those of us who are members of religious communities, and as many juniors as seniors in the profession may be such, are not likely to initiate bed-checks and scoldings in a search for Sabbath or Sunday slugabeds in order to increase empathy and nuance in religious studies!

The advantage of the kind of background of ecclesial practice for religious studies I have described here was not as clearly advantageous in this case as were the other two, familial and catechetical backgrounds. But something vital could be rescued from it, and thousands of scholars in religious studies who share rootage in ecclesial and professional training have done such rescuing.

Lifelong after such training, whether later it is reaffirmed or rebelled against, our kind has reflexively been poised to be sensitive to the forms of community in which religious meanings have characteristically developed. In an era when academics perceive and perhaps experience individualistic 'spirituality' at most, the ecclesial framework makes possible analogical thinking about communal expression, so easily forgotten in the postindustrial and postmodern West, where most of what we call 'religious studies' goes on.

Now it is time to note the most problematic of the four inherited marks of so many in religious studies: the *confessional*, not in the sense of 'true confessions' but of creeds. This was my fourth mark: from age four to 24 I experienced teaching in the confessional context. This had to be and was radically transformed when I entered religious studies in a pluralist and partly secularized cultural context. Our self-enclosed confessionalism had often been perverted into an orthodoxy of 'this you have to believe in order to belong and be right'. Confessions had instead been intended chiefly to say 'this we believe, and if you want to understand us, you have to hear and understand this'. I was pleased to find such a note in one of my theological heroes, H. Richard Niebuhr, who helped me make a transition from the cocoon version to the expressive and expansive interpretation of confession.

Some in religious studies will say that any vestigial trace of a confessional bias, and of course it is a bias, is detrimental in at least two ways. It first assumes that 'belief *that*', the content of confessions connected with dogma, colors all the things we call religion. This it does not or, at least for most of us, need not do in any exclusive way, at least not in our Western ways of apprehending belief. Second, because the confessional mode is prejudicial, biased, and subjective, it may blind the confessor, the creedalist, so that she or he cannot express empathy for the different, the other.

Such threats to integrity from confessionalism or such biases are obvious dangers to learning, of course, and they have often properly evoked a response of suspicion or rejection in my generation, just as they have among those who are younger but who also experienced similar modes of teaching. But I would argue that varying prejudgments or biases color the thinking of *everyone* in religious studies, no matter their background. Robert N. Bellah and any number of other analyzers have rather provocatively but, in my understanding, successfully suggested that the ethos of Enlightenment era and postmodern academic study of religion alike generate and depend upon a kind of religious ethos, almost a quasi-religion itself. Such a creed might be rooted in Enlightenment rationalism, Nietzschean or Marxian or Darwinian or Freudian precommitments, gender, class, ideology, or postmodern relativisms. To those who stand outside any of these, each looks like an informal and thus especially formidable confession that also colors religious studies.

Though I have some psychological and biographical clues, I have not been swayed by any intellectual case that suggests why prejudgments or perspectives shared in their awesomely broad spectra of options ('Judeo-Christian') by over 80 percent of the North American people can be almost uniquely the subjects of suspicion and scorn by many in the academy. Tell someone that you have adopted Zen Buddhist ways, are on an individualized spiritual search or, like me, are an Aquarian, and you will be honored, or at worst smiled at with measured condescension. I'd like to think that Mennonites, Catholics, or Conservative Jews could get off so lightly.

That paragraph may sound defensive, as I do not wish to be. More positively: an advantage of the confessional background is therefore ambiguous, but there are compensations in it. One can acquire from it both the impulse and the skill to engage in what some colleagues at the University of Chicago have called 'meta-physical crap-detection'. On the basis of the saying about the thief, 'it takes one to know one', one might observe those brought up in confessional settings 'knowing one' who may not know that she or he is some sort of confessionalist. H. Richard Niebuhr among theologians later taught us to look at history or at anything else from within and from without, as insider and as outsider. The phenomenologists among religious studies experts later taught us to bracket our precommitments and prejudgments in order to begin to understand a phenomenon. We at least knew what some of those presuppositions were that we had to suspend, to bracket, to make the subject of the Husserlian *epoché*.

THE ROLE OF CONTINGENCY AND ACCIDENT IN PROFESSION

We are not simple objects of fate, bound by childhood, adolescent, and collegiate experiences. But we are not simply masters of it either, thanks to the role of accident, contingency, luck (good and bad), and serendipity, as my case illustrates. Nothing in the four elements already mentioned directly or intentionally led me to what we mean by 'the study of religion' in the academy. Here begins an account of the second path, one that I find many in my generation and successive ones have walked, but one that is not always identified or celebrated. My version of contingency is perhaps more bizarre than many, so I shall bring it up and hurry past it, hoping readers will thereupon explore the value and meaning of their own accidental tours on the blurry map that leads to religious studies. Again, I think 'luck' has its place in philo-sophical and theological speculation, but I bring it up here as an historian who is unmoved by what are called 'covering laws' of the sort certain schools of sociology would impose on human behavior, especially in religion. Here is my improbable course:

I coinvented and helped promote the pretend-theologian Franz Bibfeldt (see Marty and Brauer 1994) while I was a theological student, and therefore was seen by seminary administrators and ordination boards as being too immature and irresponsible to represent their church in the United Kingdom, where I had been informally scheduled to go (to minister to post-World War II displaced people from the Baltics). I was instead sent to assist a mature and responsible senior minister near Chicago. He and the congregation we together served compelled the assistant ministers to do graduate work toward the doctorate. Speaking therefore of accident: I ponder and look around: how many others entered religious studies as a punishment, a disciplining before there was a discipline? The Polonius in me is tempted to say, and says: 'If I could make something of such a bizarre route to religious studies, so can you transform your accidents into purpose.'

Back to my plot: so it was that for two years after ordination and before seven more years of pastoral ministry after the doctorate, I was coerced and attracted to study at the University of Chicago where Sidney E. Mead and Jerald C. Brauer in religious history and Daniel J. Boorstin in history history, among others, became my mentors. At age 26, in 1954, I finally and for the first time and utterly without forethought encountered the bewildering world of religious studies. Joachim Wach, a pioneer in the History of Religions, and one who focused on *Verstehen*, understanding, was the prime influence at Chicago in those years. While I took no courses under him, his approach provided a climate in which I could appraise the 'process theology' then regnant among the theologians, who provided the other pole in divinity at that time and place. Between those two poles I pursued the questions of what it was to be an historian in religious contexts and a religionist in historical contexts, but without having developed much of a teachable or scholarly framework for understanding how to go about pursuing these questions systematically or vocationally.

I am supposed here to address particularly the historians in religious studies, but I hope to write in such a way that I do not lose readers from other disciplines in the paragraphs ahead. I like to compare the necessary and inevitable muddiness of disciplinary outlines historians have to use with those who can enjoy neatness. Historians have to work with and might as well enjoy messiness and blurring of lines. So we ask: Do we represent a definable subdiscipline within religious studies? Do we historians simply offer an enriching 'provision of historical perspective' for all the other subdisciplines? Is our contribution, if any, the result of what we can bring from foreign disciplines as we make our intrusions from 'secular' social sciences and humanities?

Whatever the intention, I have tried to make a virtue of this disciplinarily messy necessity and like to counsel others, 'you' in whatever your discipline, to do the same. That is, lifelong one tries to perfect the inherited subdisciplines of one's discipline and, lifelong, one learns to turn to advantage the fact that it is hard to define the borders of those disciplines or to isolate and define them. The advantage of this? One gains some contentment with that ill-defined discipline of history and this equips one for religious studies, none of whose subjects or objects ('the religious' people) experiences or expresses religion on lines that match the academic curricula's disciplinary outlines.

Again, back to autobiographical plotting: in 1963, seven years after receiving the doctorate, at age 35, the proverbial, or at least biblical and Dantesque, middle of life, I was invited to return from a parish pastorate to the University of Chicago to teach. The path was again indirect, not intentionally chosen. This fork in the path did not demand repudiation of the familial, catechetical, ecclesial, or confessional life that was now part of my autobiography. At the same time, in the pluralist and in many ways secular setting of a Divinity School that is physically positioned at the *axis mundi* of the campus flagpole and at home in the secular university, little of my background made much difference to colleagues or students. It *had* done so to those who had appreciated or rejected my pastoral ministry in the pluralist and in many ways secular setting where I had been ministering.

It has always been good for my historical work that no colleagues or students, no citizens of the city or the university community, bowed or saluted or honored any part of my four background contexts for religious studies. Some in the academy, as noted, might *dis*honor such backgrounds, perhaps to cover up for aspects of their own autobiographies that paralleled mine.

Schopenhauer once said that you spend the first half of your life writing its script and the second half interpreting it. From exactly age 35 until exactly age 70, when I plan to retire from teaching, I have been doing that interpreting and intend to interpret on a set of three curricular routes that together make up the third path of my scholarly life. This works itself out in the context of a *professional* school of divinity, a *social scientific* history department, and a *humanistic* committee on the history of culture. These are three PhD granting routes in three disciplinary contexts at the University of Chicago. I found and find them ideal vantages to pursue the substance and the methods of religious studies, though I am aware that most scholars and teachers will work in only one of the three. We mixed-up ones do have to be reflective concerning our vocation and disciplines in special ways.

Back to the life course: For those who need proper names to go with themes such as 'substance and methods of religious studies' I should report that by 1963 Joachim Wach was gone from the university, but his influence lived on in Joseph Kitagawa. By then Mircea Eliade, who brought his distinctive approach, was the strong influence, though the then and always since provocative African-American scholar Charles Long did more to stimulate my historical approach to religious studies. In passing, let me express at least mild discontent over the fact that Eliadeans and their counterparts appropriated the word 'history', as in 'History of Religions', for their *Religionswissenschaftliche* studies, colored though these were by various structural, synchronic, and symbolic bypassings of what ordinary historians call history. Compensatorily, these historians of religions taught this historian of religions to deal with the different, the other, the sacred, in terms that differed widely and wildly from the modes of dealing I had brought to Chicago at midlife.

Disciplinarily, my own intellectual history has led me through a vocation of teaching and scholarly writing on modern, Western, originally North Atlantic oecumenical (northwest Europe, British Isles, North America), and finally United States religious history. All this occurred within a genus whose species used to be called 'church history'. At Chicago it was called History of Christianity. But more properly, if our colleagues had not camped on the words History of Religions, we would better describe our work in that category. The numbers of Jewish students or students of Judaism whose dissertations I have mentored have the oxymoronic, idiosyncratic, and, were they ungenerous, they would have to say, sometimes ignominious experience of living with this anomaly: their histories of Judaism occurred in the History of Christianity area!

I have also spent almost as much energy studying what Benjamin Franklin called 'publick religion' and what others from Rousseau through Durkheim and beyond Robert Bellah have called 'civil religion', as I have probing the history of Christianity. Still, 'church' as concrete object or Thing provided a skeleton, 'Christianity' as a cultural complex has been a fleshing out, and 'religion' has been the breath of ethos in the body of much of the West that I studied multiculturally in premulticultural days, and still do.

Not assuming that readers know my works, I should mention that the history endeavor has issued in the publication of my books on the EuroAmerican church complex (such as *The Modern Schism*); on United States Christianity, in one case on the assigned topic of the Protestant mainstream alone (which means *Righteous Empire*); on American religion in the broadest sense (in *Pilgrims in Their Own Land: 500 Years of American Religion* and the by now three-volume *Modern American Religion* on the 20th century pluralist experience). On occasion I have been asked to do some generalizing, some mapping work that verges on the discussion of method (as in *A Nation of Behavers*).

Sometimes I have also been asked to write historically-informed essays that throw oblique light on issues in religious studies, as in the textbookish *Protestantism*, the edge-of-religion *Varieties of Unbelief*, and the publick religionist *Religion and Republic*. Note that twice I have used and shall again use the verb 'asked': except for filling assignments in periodicals where I am an editor, such as, currently, *Church History*, *The Christian Century*, *Context*, and *Second Opinion*, I have never written an article or book unless it was 'asked for', solicited, commissioned. Editors, publishers, or commissions have made requests that I take up this or that subject matter in this or that medium. Doing research for such assignments has contributed greatly to my continuing education, serendipitously.

WORKING IN SEVERAL MODES, INCLUDING THE COMPARATIVE

Here is where contingency led me to the somewhat idiosyncratic point of having to write, and then choosing to write, in a variety of modes. Sometimes, editors of journals, tenure committees, cautious colleagues in numerous disciplines, and those who strike me as affectatious in their ambition to be known as 'scholars' scholars', 'theologians' theologians', and the like, or to 'protect the integrity of academic disciplines', often school and advise younger scholars to be conformist, to restrict themselves to the impenetrable style and formal academese favored by some in the disciplines.

Polemical point: they thereby lose credentials when they complain either that a) amateurs alone are ministering to public hungers for humanistic discourse or b) that the public has no hunger for humanistic discourse. So, in my case:

In the instances of *Righteous Empire* and *Pilgrims in Their Own Land*, for instance, the series formats included a 'no footnotes' stipulation. As senior or sage now – I smile my ironic smile – I picture being asked whether a young scholar should take the risk of writing in such modes. I answer: it depends, but, yes. Let's see a bit of *chutzpah*. Ask anyone who has complied with such demands and they will tell you what I have to say: that the above mentioned propless, unfootnoted works, were more exacting and demanding than have been those with scholarly mien and apparatus, those whose footnotes have footnotes. At the same time, I recognize the frustration one causes and the scholarly limits that go with non-documentation. In order are different strokes of the computer keyboard for different folks, or for the same folks on different days.

So here comes another plug based on my own experience as someone who believes in a public mission for the humanities. Scholars would do well to try to help create a climate in which more and more humanists and social scientists would take some risks on writing clearly, which is the hardest kind of writing, and for the public, which is the most demanding audience. I hope to learn how to do better myself.

While on the 'asked to' theme, I introduce one other dimension of scholarly work with which I became accidentally but, I hope, productively associated: the formally comparative mode. Two vast projects which drew on my being-commissioned way of life and comparative instincts were asked of me as an editor. The two differ drastically from each other but, taken together, define poles of religious studies. Someone observed that I get interested in religion only when it 'heals or kills', but not often in between. Documentation:

There has been on one hand my comparative work on history and healing. The Park Ridge Center for the Study of Health, Faith, and Ethics, where I am senior scholar in residence by dusklight, asked me to edit some series of books and collections of essays whose authors compare approaches to illness and health, well-being and suffering and death, in the religions.

At the other extreme, the American Academy of Arts and Sciences asked me by moonlight to direct its The Fundamentalism

Project. It took over six years and its findings appear in six volumes coedited with R. Scott Appleby. This project led Appleby and me to pursue a strand or expression that courses through and colors religion in everything from Sikhism and Shi'ism through Latin American evangelicalism and the Gush Emunim in Israel and Judaism.

This experience has poised me to ask first a substantive question about the religion in religious studies and then a formal question about how to pursue it. I have been impelled to ask, What is it about what we call religion that makes the same phenomenon capable of being, through most of history in most cultures, the prime instrument of both healing and murderous activity?

Here the *Religionswissenschaftlicher* sorts like Wach and Eliade, Kitagawa and Long, and the masters like Durkheim and Weber and Otto, have informed this ordinary historian. They have forced or enabled me to contemplate 'the sacred', the numinous, the Other, and to hypothesize that somehow it is the subject matter of religious studies. Or if the sacred is something else, it colors the subject matter of religious studies, whether or not religious studies has or should have a corner on the disciplinary market when it comes to the sacred. In this understanding, people, in awe, experience the sacred. It fascinates, frightens, and empowers them. In its name and realm they find company, employ symbols, create artifacts, and engage in activities which historians, among others, then study. I would like to see the generations ahead put more energy into isolating what 'the sacred' can mean in emergent, postmodern cultures.

The other element to be teased out of the sentences several paragraphs ago was signaled by the word 'comparative'. A disciple at a distance of the great French social historian Marc Bloch, I have learned to think self-consciously in comparative terms when writing narrative. My students know they cannot get through doctoral qualifying exams with me without being able to respond to a first question: Compare such and such a phenomenon in a period of your choice in at least three nations that you choose, nations with three differing religious expressions. Thus, compare spirituality or piety or intellectual challenges or religion and regime or religion and art or institutional development in, say, the United States, Brazil, and Belgium.

Bloch reminds us that we all naturally and inevitably think comparatively in our reach for the sizing adjectives and the qualifying adverbs, but we normally do this without reflection or sophistication. In my understanding of religious studies, we have to help students think, and we have to think, in terms of more than one tribe, even if we write on but one. This understanding recalls the motif: 'Wer ein Religion kennt, der kein Religion kennt', whoever knows but one religion knows no religion. After having worked on the Fundamentalism Project, I can never write the story of American Protestant Fundamentalism, which had earlier been familiar to me, without mentally and sometimes verbally comparing it to Sikhism in the Punjab for one feature, or the Muslim Brotherhood in Egypt for another. Not knowing the languages needed, I would never write a chapter explicitly on Sikhism or Islam, of course. But comparing the phenomenon one is centrally equipped to study with something more remote strikes me as being a valid exercise.

My curiosities, at least those relevant to religious studies, have focused on the spheres that have been named and thus partially misnamed 'secular' and 'religious'. As with most pursuits of whatever it is that inspires curiosity, these curiosities have led to some surprises. It may be the familial-catechetical-ecclesial-confessional orbit of my younger years that first painted the world of the different and the other as secular, and almost simply so. Most academic colleagues in other disciplines keep referring to most of the society or culture as being secular. Through all these years I have kept pondering, studying, and writing about what the secular is, especially in the academy, media, government, commerce, and ordinary ways of the West. What has led so many in the academy to describe individuals, collectives, and complexes of ideas as 'secular?' Certainly these reveal a dimension that wears a secular guise, if by secular we mean what theologian Karl Rahner pointed to. He spoke of the understanding by which the world figuratively 'rounds itself off' without occasioning reference to the transcendent. But is that the whole story, as historians find and tell it?

To my surprise, it was difficult then to isolate simply secular social and cultural phenomena. Eliade's influence was there, too: the modern person was modern, in some respects at least, precisely because she chose to live in a dis-enchanted, *Entzaubert*, universe of meanings. We postmoderns may be secular in our operations but most are also religious in our passions. Not shy about fashioning neologisms with some always thwarted hope that one or another might make it into the dictionary, I am embarrassed not to have come up with anything more elegant than the unsalable coinage 'religiosecular' to describe this. That is, in some modes or dimensions almost everything of cultural importance represents an inextricable bonding and interwebbing of some elements conventionally called secular and others conventionally called religious.

All of which makes religious studies an area, field, or emphasis that cannot have clear 'No Trespassing' boundaries around it, ruling out other disciplines, just as religious studies will constantly be a trespasser in other disciplines, such as my own, history. Think of me, then, if you think of me at all in religious studies, as someone who, by studying the religiosecular or the secular-religious fusion, will insist on messiness at the boundaries of the discipline.

ON METHODOLOGY AND HISTORICAL INQUIRY

Thinking of the visual metaphors for postmodernity – assemblages, montages, collages, bricolages (Chuck Long would add, in French pronunciation also, garbages) – it may be that we in religious studies were the pioneer postmodernists, necessarily eclectic, acquainted with many conventional disciplines without having clearly invented – which means both 'made up' and 'found' – our own, and also without having become fully reposed in any. I'd like to see that theme developed.

In the Divinity School at Chicago we ask, which means we force, students of history to include some reference to method and awareness of trends in their dissertation proposals. They and their advisers often wrestle at length with this requirement. Thus on one level or in one mode or dimension, I try to embody the naive simplicity involved in an epithetical dismissal of Leopold von Ranke, the father of us all as historians, by Hegel, the father of them all as philosophers. Hegel said that Ranke was *'nur ein gewöhnliche Historiker'*, just an ordinary historian.

An ordinary historian: I've taken inordinate pride in the designation on the plastic badge provided for my identification at a conference of theologians in Tübingen to which a dozen Chicago divines were airlifted some years ago. Other colleagues were, in the English on their badges, described as 'Theologian' or 'Historian of Theology' or 'Historical Theologian'. Marty was 'Historical Historian'.

No one gets past our Divinity School's interarea, interfield, interdisciplinary doctoral proposal committees with apparently jejune self-descriptions like that one. We must wrestle with and become self-conscious about so many methods and trends, that one religious studies enthusiast advocated 'polymethodology'.

In the spirit of colleague Wendy Doniger, who dismissed 'polymethodoodling all the day', I have tried to teach students to take 'methods and trends' very, very seriously – but not too seriously. If historians are reporting on events, they have to be good at being aware of trends in times past; can they be trusted if they are not alert to those present? So one demands and hopes to acquire relative acquaintance with what is passing – we historians *know* each is passing by way of method. Just you wait, and we'll tell the story of their demise and fall into disfavor: deconstructions, poststructuralisms, Lacanisms, Foucaultisms, and the like will pass. Should we be attached to one or another of them along the way?

Let me borrow the spirit and framework of reference once mentioned by philosopher John Searle first in a formal article and, as reported here, in informal conversation: 'Here I am in my sixties, and I have already outlived eight permanent, all-purpose, final explanations of... [fill in the blanks].' From each of these one learns that most of us cannot refute or dismiss or even intelligently criticize most of them. But when it comes down to the work of 'ordinary history' or being an 'historical historian' of religion, a partner in religious studies, one does a critical reading of sources and composes some sort of narrative, with methods and trends absorbed but put from the front of the mind. To speak thus is to leave real problems with a new generation, since in the budget of downsized humanities departments, religious studies departments will have to justify the presence of a particular subdiscipline or scholar in their department. What is an 'historical historian' doing there?

As I write that, I am aware of how complex the theory of narrative has become, and have no interest in chasing away members of new generations from acquaintance with such theory. We have to reflect on how historians can work with synchrony or how relative the very concept of story has become. Yet my own methods and trends analysis suggests that postmodern history will also keep including story, narrative.

ISSUES THAT PUZZLE OR PLAGUE

My reference to awareness two sentences ago, however, does suggest an element of something I have been asked to speak about: some 'issues that have plagued' me. In the company of theologians I have to reflect on this one: I know no way to break what I call 'the circle of immanence' when writing history as history. This means that the empirical methods and assumptions one brings to an enterprise if he or she wants to call it history and have it somehow recognized as such, provide no certifiable means of dealing with the Absolute, no special access to the Mind of God, no result of research that offers the Metaphysically Certain.

All of which means that religious studies, also and maybe especially in its historical aspects, cannot verify or validate its own enterprise. There is no way of knowing, within the issues of the discipline, whether our stories are full of fury and sound, signifying nothing; whether the only meanings available are meanings we fabricate or bring to the perceptions of reality around us; whether the study of religion is entirely self-enclosed and self-referential, which means whether religion points to anything but itself, or whether it can be and has to be reduced to something else, to be pursued in the late-modern, still self-defined as secular, university.

What theoretical assumptions guide me at this crucial positioning in religious studies? That is, what is assumed by someone who does not believe religion has to be reduced, rendered something else, until it is 'nothing but...' this or that? Which means, for example, not reducing religion for scientific study reasons to nothing but Marx's materialist understanding that it is nothing but bad faith; nothing but Freud's psychoanalytic or Darwin's evolutionary or Nietzsche's promethean 'nothing buttery'. My assumption is that such an issue can ultimately be addressed only metaphysically, and penultimately only pragmatically and existentially. That is, whether or not there is 'something there', as William James would say, cannot be settled by history or *any* of the approaches to religious studies.

Therefore, pragmatically, we go about the business of studying, using any number of criteria to test our results, without having settled things metaphysically. And existentially, we may be better or worse students of religion depending upon whether we 'believe' *or* disbelieve. Neither belief nor disbelief, 'appreciation' of the objects of religion or a priori and total dismissal of these, by itself makes one a better or worse scholar. The appreciator of religion has to compensate by developing critical sensibilities, and the dismisser, I believe, does well to cultivate arts and acts of empathy.

THE COMPANY WE KEEP

From what I have said above about familial influence, conversation inspired by a catechetical approach, and ecclesial or communal thinking, it should be obvious that this critical non-rebel has kept talking to family, to spiritual mentors, to the community of faith, and to ordinary friends who never heard of religious studies and would be unmoved by what it represents. I cherish roots and trying to have my feet on the ground, love 'the minute particulars' of concrete life, and like to think that they bring with them the possibility to a scholar of keeping a special note of realism in religious studies. I do not judge those who distance themselves; who think they *can* distance themselves, or spend their lives trying to distance themselves from such influences. The ideal religious studies house is catholic, cosmopolitan, and many mansioned. It welcomes what William James called 'a republican banquet'. I'm glad to have been given one seat there.

Next, from what I have said about teaching in three university faculties, professional divinity, social scientific history, and humanistic history of culture, it should be obvious that I converse with colleagues and students who spend their lives refining the historical element in the professions, society, and culture. Closest to home in Chicago, this has meant people like Jerald C. Brauer, the late Arthur Mann, and Neil Harris – to take one from each of the three spheres – and, beyond them Bernard McGinn and Brian Gerrish or, looking toward tomorrow and two new generations, W. Clark Gilpin and Catherine Brekus in Divinity; or, back again, to John Hope Franklin, Katherine Conzen and Karl J. Weintraub in the other faculties.

In the American Society of Church History, the American Catholic Historical Society, and the American Academy of Religion, three professional societies over which I have taken a turn presiding, we historians cherish the notion that, by and large, we are a very critical group of scholars but are also almost familial in our regard for each other as persons. This has meant that my critical conversations, often very intense, have been with friends like the two Sids/Syds, Sidney E. Mead and Sydney Ahlstrom and their colleagues and successors. Which ones, since I cannot name them all here? All of them, any of them, any who will talk, criticize, be a friend.

Election to fellowship in the American Academy of Arts and Sciences, and to membership in the American Antiquarian Society, the Society of American Historians, and the American Philosophical Society – this is getting to sound like a paragraph in my curriculum vita but, then, I *was* asked to be autobiographical, and I do mount the certificates on the wall! – has brought me into surprising humanistic conversations with scholars in many disciplines. If an entity has the word 'Humanities' in it, I am often among the religionists who have been graced – no merits for this Lutheran! – to be among the invited.

Colleagues from religious studies in all these companies report on the experience we together often have: one first experiences an assumed distance by the majority of the invited company from or a dismissal of religion and what it signifies in these academies, which are putatively and self-descriptively secular. But these colleagues and I take delight in the challenge we thereupon offer: we can mess up any seminar, cocktail party, dinner, or program by bringing up religion, what we study, and the ways we study it. Then there emerges from the company of academics all kinds of long-forgotten or repressed, subliminal or subterranean, supra-intellectual and passional elements of curiosity about religion, which soon tend to take over the topic. I do not mean that as triumphalistically as it sounds. No, one whispers, hints, and peeps more than one stands on a soap box and shouts in such settings: we have much to learn and there are rules of etiquette. And we can often be as wrong or, worse, as foolish as many of those uninterested in religion in such company.

Who have been my intellectual opponents, I am asked for definitional reasons. I am bored by and abhor literary and scholarly feuds, which obscure true critical faculties and endeavors, so I have no Enemies List or register of opponents in historical zones of religious studies. One cannot have critically reviewed as many articles or books in manuscript or print as I have through the years without having done some bruising and, no doubt, quickened some bruisers. But, frankly, I would not know in whose presence to keep a guard up to protect against getting bruised.

However, if I had to point to members of a genus of opponency in the intellectual and postural aspects of religious studies I would list these as the probably irritated: first, the 'more secular than thou' sorts who believe one can establish religious studies more respectably by culturally laggish regress into distanciated and objectivist modes. Ironically, it is such as these that are being themselves called into question by much of the rest of the academy long after the prime of the Enlightenment Project.

Second, if I were a reductionist in religious inquiry, one who was ungenerous to those who bracket the issues of reduction, I would find fault with Marty.

Third, those who see no place for ordinary historical historians in religious studies on one hand and, on the other, those historians who allow no place for religious inquiry should find fault. But I would have to disappoint the reader who might be searching for names to draw some plot of the drama of conflict out of this essay. There is no gallery of personifiable villains in my mind.

THE PERSONAL ASPECTS OF TEACHING AND SCHOLARSHIP

Of course, my views keep changing constantly; historians are in the business of chronicling and discerning change. They, we, may be as set in our ways as are scholars in any other discipline. But some of us at least theoretically are given to what Gabriel Marcel described as *disponibilité*. This means making one's self available to the different, the other, to the one or to the event that might induce a person to change.

And at the same time, in order to be secure enough to be free for intellectual change, I have also cherished ties to roots: to continuity with the mental and physical landscapes of a Nebraska youth and an adult life in Chicago. Intensely, and gratefully almost beyond words: to family and friends. To *The Christian Century* for almost 40 years and the University of Chicago for, one hopes, 35 preemeritus years and more from a distance thereafter. These are the externals: to take another Marcel term, I aspire to show 'creative fidelity' to certain beliefs, communities, and ideas. Most of them are not relevant in this essay on religious studies except in the personal self-description of one scholar in that sphere. 'Fidelity' means continuity; 'creative' implies criticism and innovation.

The key change apropos religious studies themes, but relating to the ecclesial or theological understanding of religion and my later developed religious understanding is this: my generation of my sort was brought up during the neoorthodox Protestant, neo-Lutheran, Barthian, Bonhoefferian prime. In those four companies, religion was, shall we call it, a dirty word. It was seen as a human artifact, a construct or complex that prematurely satisfied its creators. But that meant it necessarily kept them insulated from and deaf to divine revelation, prophetic judgment, salvific proclamation. That notion of religion was a stringent concept, an astringent medication for anyone who wanted to understand religions as an historian in religious studies might and must. Wach is relevant here again: *Verstehen*, understanding is the goal. Or Spinoza, who in paraphrase provided the motto for the Fundamentalist Project: when setting out to understand human action, I have made a sedulous effort not to laugh, not to cry, not to denounce, but to *understand*.

I am not sure if a single incident or episode led to the turning toward appreciation of religion, of apprehensions of the sacred, of the spiritual search beyond the scope of specific revelation as one conceived it, or one's own ecclesial or confessional understandings. People, embodiments, were exemplars: people like Wach and Kitagawa among historians of religion were influential, as were most of the historians I knew in religious studies, few of whom operated in a confessional orbit.

A mix of scholars and writers including Alfred Schutz, William James, Paul Valery, and Michael Oakeshott have been mentors on the printed page. They have taught me to operate with a variety of 'modes of experience', 'nonparamount realities', 'multiple realities', 'universes of discourse', 'provinces of meaning', 'worlds', and spheres of 'attentiveness', each of which is not or need not be in conflict with or in contradiction with the other. This variety exacts consistent intellectual endeavors until such endeavors begin to become second nature. It exacts consistent behavioral discipline until it comes to be reflexive.

Thus in one 'universe of discourse' one can be, or can aspire to be, a scholar's scholar and in another the same person can talk in the discourse of the public intellectual, without creating internal conflict (though perhaps presenting an image that will confuse the stereotypers). Thus also one can operate within ecclesial and confessional contexts which allow one to say 'I believe' and then to move to scholarship without confusion or any more prejudice than any other good bracketer brings.

One is ready then for the questioner to ask, as one must in religious studies: 'what do you mean by "believe"' and 'how are you sure' and 'how do you find warrants for faith' and 'don't you notice that the different, the other, also believes and practices – with integrity?' To be alert to these multiple realities, universes of discourses, and modes of experience, it seems to me, is to help form the *habitus* and habits of scholars in religious studies. Such scholars then would move eagerly and full of expectation, as this historical historian among them always has and would, to the religious subject matter to which they are committed and to which they are commended by their discipline and their vocation.

Reference

Marty, Martin E. and Jerald Brauer (eds). 1994. *The Unrelieved Paradox: Studies in the Theology of Franz Bibfeldt*. Grand Rapids, MI: Eerdmans.

9

On Theory-Driven Methods
RODNEY STARK

Social scientists typically are trained to prefer a single methodology, hence they commonly identify themselves as experimentalists, survey researchers, participant observers, or demographers and they predicate their research on the basis of their methodological commitments. It is common to hear them wonder what they should do a survey on next, what experiment they could do, or what social scene they might observe.

This is backwards. And it is the major reason why so much pointless research is conducted. The fact is that research questions must determine what method or methods are suitable – *how* to find out depends on *what* you want to know. When one's primary commitment is to a particular methodology, one's ability to pursue important questions is severely limited.

When I was asked to contribute to this volume I was told to focus on methodological issues. Although I regard my theoretical work as my primary contribution to the social scientific study of religion, the idea of recounting my methodological odyssey was very appealing. Over the course of my career I have used every legitimate social scientific method of research, not because I get bored easily, but because I have always been theory-driven. I have selected research questions because of their theoretical importance and have selected methods because they were appropriate. Not only has this experience yielded a fund of cautionary tales which may usefully be shared, but it may help others see how to overcome what may appear to be insurmountable barriers to research.

CONVERSION: OBSERVING THE MOONIES

The year before I began graduate school at Berkeley I worked as a reporter for *The Oakland Tribune*. After writing a very well-received feature story about a speaker at the Oakland Space Craft Club who recounted his trips to Mars and Venus as a guest on a flying saucer, I was routinely given stories concerning various occult gatherings and new religious movements. Thus did I become interested in why and how people converted to deviant religious groups. My initial efforts to find answers in the social scientific literature were unsatisfactory. For example, I found a book in the University of California library about an exotic religious movement that flourished in northern California during the late 1930s and early 1940s. The author claimed that, because the movement proposed an elaborate, state-supported pension scheme for the elderly, this movement's primary recruitment base was older people – especially elderly widows. It turned out that *The Oakland Tribune*'s morgue (a library of newspaper clippings and photos) had a voluminous file on this group. In it was a wide-angle photo of a public meeting of the group held in the ballroom of the Leamington Hotel during the late 1930s when the movement was at its height. There were 512 members in the picture and not only were there no grey heads among them, there were virtually no bald heads to be seen – the crowd was overwhelmingly made up of young adults, about equally male and female. Careful reading of this book and of other studies of similar groups made it evident that the authors had made their 'observations' in the library. They proceeded by seeing to whom a group's doctrines might most appeal and then they assumed that was who actually joined. It took no social scientific methods training for me to recognize that this was absurd. The only way to find out who joined such movements and to discover how and why they did so, was to go out and observe an appropriate group.

The next year I began graduate school and one of my classmates was John Lofland. We discovered a mutual interest in studying conversion. So we began to look for an appropriate group to study. We wanted a real social movement, not just a discussion group or lecture audience. We also wanted a group that was small enough so that the two of us could provide adequate surveillance and new enough so that it was in an early and optimistic phase of growth. After more than a year of sifting through many deviant religious groups in the San Francisco Bay area we came upon precisely what we were looking for – a group of about a dozen young adults who had just moved to San Francisco from Eugene, Oregon. The group was led by Young Oon Kim, a Korean woman who had once been a professor of religion at Ewha University in Seoul. The movement she served was based in Korea and in January 1959 she arrived in Oregon to launch a mission to America. Miss Kim (she was invariably referred to as Miss within the group) and her young followers were the very first American members of the Unification Church, widely known today as the Moonies.

As Lofland and I settled back to watch people convert to this group, the first thing we discovered was that all of the current members were united by close ties of friendship predating their contact with Miss Kim. Indeed, the first three converts had been young housewives who were next door neighbors who became friends of Miss Kim after she became a lodger with one of them. Subsequently, several of the husbands joined, followed by several of their friends from work. By the time Lofland and I arrived to study them, the group had never succeeded in attracting a stranger. All had been tied to group members through friendships.

Lofland and I also found it interesting that although all the converts were quick to describe how their spiritual lives had been empty and desolate prior to their conversion, many claimed they had not been particularly interested in religion before. One man told me 'If anybody had said I was going to join up and become a missionary I would have laughed my head off. I had no use for church at all.'

We also found it instructive that during most of her first year in America Miss Kim had tried to spread her message directly by talks to various groups and by sending out many press releases. Later, in San Francisco, the group also tried to attract followers through radio spots and by renting a hall in which to hold public meetings. But these methods yielded nothing. As time passed Lofland and I were able to observe people actually become Moonies. The first several converts were old friends or relatives of members who came from Oregon for a visit. Subsequent converts were people who formed close friendships with one or more members of the group.

We soon realized that of all the people the Moonies encountered in their efforts to spread their faith, the only ones who joined were those *whose interpersonal attachments to members overbalanced their attachments to non-members*. In effect, conversion is not about seeking or embracing an ideology, it is about bringing one's religious behavior into alignment with that of one's friends and family members. Lofland and I saw many people who spent some time with the Moonies and expressed considerable interest in their doctrines, but who never joined. In every instance these people had many strong attachments to non-members who did not approve of the group. Of persons who did join, many were newcomers to San Francisco whose attachments were all to people far away. As they formed strong friendships with group members these were not counterbalanced because distant friends and families had no knowledge of the conversion-in-process. In several instances a parent or sibling came to San Francisco intending to intervene after having learned of the conversion. Those who lingered, eventually joined up too (keep in mind that becoming a Moonie may have been regarded as deviant by outsiders, but it was an act of conformity for those whose most significant attachments were to Moonies).

Since Lofland and I (1965) first published our conclusion that attachments lie at the heart of conversion and that conversion therefore tends to proceed along social networks formed by interpersonal attachments, many others have found the same to be true in an immense variety of religious groups all around the world. A recent study based on Dutch data (Kox, Meeus, and 't Hart 1991) cited 25 additional empirical studies, all of which supported our initial finding. And that list was far from complete.

Although several other factors also are involved in the conversion process, the central sociological proposition about conversion is: *Conversion to new, deviant religious groups occurs when, other things being equal, people have or develop stronger attachments to members of the group than they have to non-members.*

A second aspect of conversion is that people who are deeply committed to any particular faith do not go out and join some other faith. Thus, Mormon missionaries who called upon the Moonies were immune, despite forming warm relationships with several members. Indeed, the Moonie who previously had 'no use for church at all' was more typical. Converts were not former atheists, but they were essentially unchurched and many had not paid any particular attention to religious questions. Thus the Moonies quickly learned that they were wasting their time at church socials or frequenting denominational student centers. They did far better in places where they came in contact with the uncommitted. This finding has received substantial support from subsequent research. Converts to new religious movements are overwhelmingly from relatively irreligious backgrounds. The majority of converts to modern American cult movements report that their parents had no religious affiliation

(Stark and Bainbridge 1985). Let me state this as a theoretical proposition: *New religious movements mainly draw their converts from the ranks of the religiously inactive, discontented and those affiliated with the most accommodated (worldly) religious communities.*

Had we not gone out and watched people as they converted, we might have missed this point entirely, because when people retrospectively describe their conversions they tend to put the stress on theology. When asked why they converted, Moonies invariably noted the irresistible appeal of the *Divine Principles* (the group's scripture), suggesting that only the blind could reject such obvious and powerful truths. In making these claims converts implied (and often stated) that their path to conversion was the end product of a search for faith. But Lofland and I knew better because we had met them well before they had learned to appreciate the doctrines, before they had learned how to testify to their faith, back when they were not seeking faith at all. Indeed, we could remember when most of them regarded the religious beliefs of their new set of friends as quite odd.

When Lofland and I came to write up our results I recognized another important lesson. While it was clear that our research questions had dictated that we do a field observation study of a religious movement, it became equally clear that the 'field' is a place, not a method. Lofland was convinced that the only good work is qualitative work, but I knew better and should have forced the matter. True, we could not have discovered many things had we not gone into the field, but once there we should have availed ourselves of the opportunity to collect data in a way suitable for quantification and this was especially true for those who nibbled at joining, but did not. Since, soon after we began our observations we were given official permission from Miss Kim to conduct a study, there was no reason whatever to have limited ourselves to observational notes. At the very least, we should have administered a brief questionnaire. For, if observation is the only good way to answer some questions, it is useless (or at least untrustworthy) for answering many others.

SURVEYING RELIGIOUS COMMITMENT

While Lofland and I were doing our field study of conversion, I was a project director at the Survey Research Center of the

University of California preparing the first major surveys of American religion (the appointment came at the end of my first semester of graduate school). The funding was from the Anti-Defamation League which had commissioned a package of studies of anti-Semitism. The study in which I was involved, with Charles Y. Glock, was meant to determine whether Christian beliefs and participation sustained religious images of Jews that led Christians therefore to accept secular anti-Semitic beliefs as well.

Such questions cannot be answered by field research or by experiments, they require that properly selected samples of the population(s) of interest be asked valid questions about their beliefs, attitudes and activities. So I spent two years preparing and pretesting a questionnaire and, in the spring of 1963, copies were distributed to about 6000 Christian church members randomly selected from all churches in four northern California counties (centered on San Francisco). Then, in the fall of 1964, a selection of the best questions were used in interviews conducted with a national sample of more than 1700 adults.

Once the data were collected, we gave our initial attention to the study of Christian beliefs and anti-Semitism, producing a book that is acknowledged to have played a role in the deliberations of Vatican II concerning a new statement exonerating Jews from guilt for the Crucifixion (Glock and Stark 1966). However, from the start I had planned to address a number of basic questions about religious commitment having nothing to do with anti-Semitism. Perhaps the most interesting of these was the current state of denominationalism.

The late 1950s and early 1960s were the era of ecumenical consultations among major Protestant bodies. There was such widespread confidence that the major Protestant denominations soon would merge that books were written in advance to explain why it had happened (e.g., Lee 1960). The most cited reason was that 'old doctrinal cleavages' had become 'irrelevant in American thought today' (Lambert 1960:155). Or, as Peter Berger put it, denominational differences had become nothing more than 'functionally irrelevant embellishments and packaging' since American Protestantism had undergone a 'process of intense product standardization' (1963:89).

I wasn't convinced. In fact, as I had visited churches in order to create the frame for our northern California sample of Christians, I encountered important denominational differences. But, of course, that was only impressionistic evidence – if scholars really want to know how a population stands on an issue, they must sample them properly and ask them valid questions.

The very first thing we did when the data were in the computer was to cross-tabulate denomination against everything else. The results were overwhelming: the ecumenical conviction that denominationalism was dead in terms of belief and practice was nonsense! Differences across denominations on member belief in such central theological matters as the divinity of Christ, the virgin birth, the second coming, heaven and hell could hardly have been greater. Indeed, the 'new denominationalism' as we labelled it in our initial article, fragmented 'the core of the Christian perspective. ... In light of these findings it is difficult to account for the hopes and activities directed towards a general ecumenicalism' (Stark and Glock 1965:14). And, of course, the mergers did not take place.

During the next several years I explored many other aspects of the data (see Stark 1968 and Stark 1971, and Stark and Glock 1968), pursuing in depth many interesting correlates of religious belief and participation, including sex, race, education, income, and age. But, in all instances these social-psychological findings were dwarfed by denomination. That is, educated and uneducated Southern Baptists were far more alike than were educated Southern Baptists and educated Presbyterians. It could only be concluded that religion is primarily a group, not an individual phenomenon. As a sociologist, this finding was much to my liking and, of course, it jibed with what I had discovered about conversion.

Thus my interest shifted to religious groups. How do they form? What factors influence their fate? More specifically, how and why do sects form, and why, and how often, are they transformed into churches? Do novel religious movements, such as cult movements, arise in the same places and under the same circumstances as give rise to sects? The available literature on religious groups was relentlessly descriptive – case studies of one or several groups based either on field work or library research. This literature could not adequately answer my questions. But, for a while, it seemed to me that I would be unable to get the necessary financial means to study religious groups in the comparative and quantitative fashion required by my questions. I was blinded by my methodological experience with survey data which caused me to think that in order to study a group I first needed to survey an adequately large sample of its members. That approach would have cost huge sums of money since I would need to conduct comparable surveys of scores of religious groups, perhaps of hundreds of them.

Then one day it occurred to me to use trustworthy published data, including field work studies, to *create* the needed data bases.

CODING SECTS AND CULTS

Sitting in the breakfast room one day in 1978, going over my mail, I noticed a flier for *The Encyclopedia of American Religions* by J. Gordon Melton. This work purported to include comparable information on more than 1200 separate American religious bodies, from the largest to the most obscure groups. As I recall, this two-volume work could be had for $90 as a pre-publication offer – the post-publication price being $130. I remarked to my wife, that 'If this is half the book they claim it is, it would be very valuable. But these things are always hyped.' She responded that it was hardly an expensive purchase. So I ordered my copy. Soon my two volumes arrived and they were all I could have hoped for. They were so complete that soon I used them to create two primary data sets.

The first of these consisted of 501 cult movements, defined as groups outside the conventional religious tradition of the society in which they are observed – in this case, groups beyond the limits of the standard Judeo-Christian tradition. For example, Christianity would be classified as a cult movement in a Hindu society and Hindu groups would be so classified in a Christian society. I spent the first week of July 1978 coding many facts about each of these movements from Melton's encyclopedia: including location (most consisted of but one group in one place, otherwise I coded the location of the headquarters) when founded (and where), 'theological' family (New Thought, Flying Saucers, Magick, Pagans, etc.), size and growth curve over time and other facts. One of the most interesting things I coded was how conventional-sounding was the group's name? Groups named Society of Christ or Universal Christ Church (both spiritualist bodies) were coded as conventional-sounding. Should someone give that as their religious affiliation, no eyebrows would be raised. That is not the case with groups named Ruby Focus of Magnificent Consummation or the Enchanted Moon Coven. An interesting finding was that groups founded more recently tended to have a higher proportion with unconventional sounding names – suggestive of an increasingly permissive religious environment (Stark, Bainbridge, and Doyle 1979).

The second data set consisted of 417 American-born sect movements – movements that originated by splitting from another religious body within the conventional religious sphere and which remained within that sphere. Initial analysis of these data revealed that sects are, on average, older and larger than cult movements. But the more impressive finding was that most sects not only began as very small groups, but most remained small – 56 percent had never exceeded 2000 members during their history. Moreover, most sects were as large the day they began as they ever were. That is, 51 percent had experienced a steady decline in membership since they were founded and another 18 percent had remained the same size. Only six of the 417 sects had sustained a rapid rate of growth since the beginning. This revealed that the famous sect-to-church process seldom actually takes place since very few sects grow and prosper and therefore very few ever experience the pressures that would transform them from higher to lower tension with their environments (Stark and Bainbridge 1981a).

I discovered that one reason for their lack of growth is that most sects originate in a state of such high tension with their environment as to cause their early social encapsulization. Once encapsulized, a sect may persist for centuries (as the Amish have done), but they will not grow (except sometimes via fertility) because they are unable to form or sustain the close interpersonal bonds with outsiders through which converts come.

ASSESSING RELIGIOUS ECOLOGIES

As I reflected further, it seemed likely that the success or failure of sects and cults is greatly influenced by factors beyond their control, that aspects of the social and cultural environment of such groups often seal their fate. I concluded that the most important environmental factor had to do with the vigor of their religious competitors (just as Lofland and I discovered that people already committed to one religious group do not join another one, so too in communities where the conventional faiths are strong, novel religious movements will make little headway).

But, where to get data to test this thesis? Again, theoretical issues pushed me toward new data sources and techniques. The easy part was church membership rates which could be calculated on the basis of data collected by the Glenmary Research Center from the nation's denominations every 10 years since 1970 and published broken down by states, counties, and standard metropolitan areas. Having decided to work with states, novel religious activity could be assessed in many ways. First, from the number of cults per 100 000 population based on the data set on cults discussed previously. Secondly, on the basis of various lists and guidebooks of 'New Age' and psychic groups. Third, from subscription rates for *Fate* magazine, a leading occult periodical, and from coding the home state of thousands of people whose letters to the editor have appeared in *Fate*. Finally, from data on 735 280 persons who were initiated into Transcendental Meditation during the period 1967–77. In all cases there was a very strong, negative correlation between church membership rates and measures of the strength of alternative faiths (Stark and Bainbridge 1980 and 1985). Next we used data from the Canadian Census, which asks religious preference as the US Census does not, to repeat the test and got the same results (Bainbridge and Stark 1982). Novel religions did best where the proportion giving their religious preferences as 'none' was highest.

It was at this juncture that I discovered the US Census reports on Religious Bodies which, since 1890 and continuing through 1906, 1916, 1926, and 1936, report membership statistics, broken down very finely by denomination, for states and for major towns and cities. These statistics had long been ignored by demographers on the assumption that since the data were supplied by the local churches to the local census takers, they would be hopelessly fraudulent. It was easy to show that the data were quite valid. And, because the census had taken pains to include the tiniest and most unusual religious groups, these census volumes contained everything needed to extend our research back in time. Data for 1926 showed once again that where church membership was higher, membership in groups such as Theosophy, Christian Science, Divine Science, and Baha'i was lower (Stark and Bainbridge 1981b).

Subsequent use of data for Europe, assembled from many unlikely sources including the back cover of an ISKON magazine, from a Mormon almanac, and from a New Age guidebook, yielded these same results. Religious novelty thrived where the conventional churches were empty (Stark 1985a).

Social scientists have long admired religious monopolies, believing that religious competition called all faiths into question for if truth is disputed it is open to question. For a variety of theoretical reasons, I have long rejected that argument in favor of the standard economic proposition that competition results in vigorous, efficient, specialized firms that will, together, be able to appeal to a far greater proportion of consumers than can be the case when only one faith is available without risk of sanctions (Stark 1985b). Moreover, because so much of the religious product necessarily is intangible and concerns the far distant future, vigorous marketing activity is needed to achieve high levels of consumption. But that is not how state-supported monopoly firms function. It is a major proposition of economics that such firms tend to be inefficient.

Here, too, the need was for data on aggregate social units such as cities, counties, states and nations. From the *Catholic Almanac* came data on the number of Catholics and the number of priests for each of 45 nations in which the Roman Catholic Church is active. My theory predicted that the ratio of priests to nominal Catholics (a measure of local Catholic commitment since it reflects both the ordination rate and the demand for priests) would vary across nations *inversely* to the proportion of Catholics in the population. That is, the Catholic Church will be more effective in mobilizing its members where it is confronted either by pluralistic religious economies or by Protestant semi-monopolies and will be least effective where it most closely approximates a monopoly. The correlation between the ratio of priests and the percent nominally Catholic was −0.73. Suitable controls did not reduce the correlation (Stark 1992).

This prediction was replicated when it was found that rates of Catholic ordination, seminary enrollments, and conversion varied inversely to the proportion of Catholics in the community, based on the Roman Catholic dioceses in the United States (Stark and McCann 1993, and Stark [in press]). Then states were used as the units of analysis and it was additionally found that the circulation rate of the *Catholic Digest* was higher in states with proportionately smaller Catholic populations. The same holds for a rate based on the number of centers devoted to apparitions of the Virgin Mary per 100 000 Catholics in a state's population and the number of Catholic converts per 100 000 Catholics (Stark [in press]).

To test the more general thesis that pluralism *per se* generates increased religious participation, Roger Finke and I (1988) turned once again to census data to show that for American cities in 1906, there was a very strong relationship between religious pluralism (the greater the number of religious bodies having a significant share of the market, the greater the pluralism) and rates of church membership. Subsequently we discovered the rich religious details included in the 1855 and 1865 censuses of New York State. Basing our analysis on 942 towns and villages, we found that both church membership and church attendance rates rose remarkably in proportion to the diversity of the local religious market (Finke, Guest, and Stark 1996). I also discovered that a complete religious census had been conducted in England and Wales in 1851. Here too we found that the greater the local pluralism, the higher the overall community rate of church attendance. As of August 1996 there were at least 20 independent studies, based on a variety of times and places, all reporting that religion is strengthened by competition (the one contrary finding cannot be duplicated on the same data on which it was based).

This use of older data reflected my growing involvement in historical applications of some of my more central theoretical propositions.

HISTORICAL METHODS

Aside from using a variety of older data to test my theories, I have been involved in two major historical projects, both of which applied portions of my theoretical work on religion to explain religious change and in both instances methodological innovations were required.

1 The Churching of America

The first of these projects arose because Roger Finke and I (Finke and Stark 1986 and 1988, and Stark and Finke 1988) were able to reconstruct reliable statistics on church membership spanning the period 1776 to 1990. As these were entirely incompatible with the received historical wisdom they pushed us forward.

Standard historical accounts report cycles in American religion during which religiousness increases or declines. The standard works uniformly have described a great decline in religious participation subsequent to the American Revolution, a 'Great Awakening' at the start of the nineteenth century during which religious involvement sky-rocketed, another revival after World War II, followed by a sudden decline in membership of the so-called mainline denominations beginning in the 1960s. Our data showed no cycles. Instead, the proportion of Americans affiliated with a specific religious body has increased steadily from the start. In 1776 only about 17 percent of Americans were 'churched'. Today about 62 percent of Americans belong to a church.

The churching of America cried out for explanation. How was it done? And which groups benefited? In the end, Roger and I spent a great deal of time reading obscure books and diaries to become sufficiently familiar with the primary sources. But our aim was not to master the detail on which the traditional narratives of American religious history depended. Rather, we meant from the start to test fundamental theoretical notions about religious ecologies. Specifically, we expected to be able to show that the percentage of Americans activated by the churches increased as the extent of American pluralism increased. The churching of America was the result of religious competition and those religious bodies prepared to compete vigorously for souls grew, and those unable or unwilling to exert such effort lost out. Moreover, theology (or faith) is central to our model. As we wrote on the first page of our book: 'to the degree that denominations rejected traditional doctrines and ceased to make serious demands on their followers, they ceased to prosper. The churching of America was accomplished by aggressive churches committed to vivid otherworldliness' (Finke and Stark 1992:1). Discussions of the vital role played by faith and, indeed, by conceptions of God, fill many pages. Thus, rather than reduce the churching of America to a marketing phenomenon, we note how fundamental *religious* factors determine which religious organizations are energetic and effective.

Our efforts to explain major trends in American religious history utilized a lot of statistics. Many of these statistics weren't just 'there', waiting for someone to use them (although many were). It took imagination, some luck, and reasonably sophisticated statistical methods to reconstruct our primary data.

The US Census actually began to collect statistics from the churches during the census of 1850 and repeated the process in 1860, 1870, and 1880 (although the 1880 data were lost). Thus, for every church in the nation, we know the estimated value of church property, the number of organizations sponsored by each, and the seating capacity of the church. But, until 1890, the census never asked how many members there were to sit in the seats. Thus it appeared that time series data on church membership rates could only go back to 1890 – unless we could find a way to turn pews into people. And that's exactly what we were able to do.

Because the questions asked of the churches in 1850 through 1880 were all included in the 1890 census of religious bodies, we tried building regression equations that would accurately predict actual membership from data on value, organizations, and seating capacity. This effort was far more successful than either of us could have hoped, producing R^2 values from 0.93 to 0.99 for various denominations. We then used these same equations to 'predict' the membership of churches in 1850, 1860, and 1870 – thus turning pews into people.

To further validate these estimates we secured actual membership statistics from some denominations in various times and places and compared these with our projections of membership. Here too the accuracy of our projections was remarkable. Later, we used equally imaginative techniques to recreate a trustworthy church affiliation rate for 1776 and, in addition, we were able to dig up many remarkable statistics: on seminary enrollments in the mid-nineteenth century; on the proportion of Roman Catholic services in languages other than English in 1906; on the average salary of ministers by denomination; and on and on. If the superstructure of the book is theory and the focus is historical, the hard underlying structure is quantitative.

Admittedly, *The Churching of America, 1776–1990: Winners and Losers in Our Religious Economy* (Finke and Stark 1992) was a very revisionist work. We found no cycles. We discovered that the 'mainline' Protestant bodies did not begin their decline in the 1960s, but in the 1700s. That is, while the nation's population grew and as a larger percentage of Americans joined churches, the market shares of the Congregationalists, Presbyterians, and Episcopalians declined. Meanwhile, the Methodists and Baptists – the truly American upstart sects – grew at an incredible pace. Then, as the Methodists became respectable and watered down their preaching and practice, they began a long downward slide that continues to this day. In contrast, the Southern Baptist Convention continues to grow, recently joined by a whole new group of vigorous upstart sects such as the Assemblies of God. We tried to say why. We also tried to explain why ecumenism only attracts declining denominations. And we criticized many of the standard histories, not only for ignoring easily available statistics that invalidate some of their most significant claims, but even for failing to consult the original sources of their stories.

Not surprisingly, several well-known church historians were quite put off by our book. Indeed, they responded in much the same way that those identified with the received narratives of secular American history responded when quantifiers entered their field a generation ago – with surprisingly personal, if rather irrelevant, attacks. The earlier historical quantifiers won because when quantitative questions arise, numbers always beat stories. And, judging by the overwhelmingly positive reviews (and awards) we have received, the same outcome is to be expected in this case.

2 The Rise of Christianity

About ten years ago I became aware that many historians of the early church were attempting to use social science to help illuminate their subject and to infer 'what must have happened' in order to fill blanks in the historical and archaeological record. As Robin Scroggs (1980:166) pointed out in an influential essay:

> ...there may be times when a sociological model may actually assist our ignorance. If our data evidence some *parts* of the gestalt of a known model, while being silent about others, we *may* cautiously be able to conclude that the absence of the missing parts is accidental and that the entire model was actually a reality in the early church.

Since those lines were published, the practice Scroggs suggested has become common. As I examined this literature I had quite mixed reactions. Some studies I have read with pleasure and admiration. Other examples have made me very uncomfortable because the social science 'models' utilized were so inadequate.

It seemed to me that what historians of the early Church most needed was someone to provide them with more modern and sharper social scientific tools. Since I had become fascinated with the subject of early Christianity I nominated myself for the job of demonstrating real social science (as compared with the dated and empty typologies that too often are mistaken for theories – even by social scientists, sad to say). But beyond better theories, I rapidly discovered that the field desperately needed quantification – to the extent that even hypothetical data are better than nothing.

The focus of my work on the early Church was to reconstruct the rise of Christianity in order to explain how it all came to pass – how did an obscure messianic movement from the eastern edge of the Roman Empire dislodge classical paganism and become the dominant faith of Western Civilization? But, before any useful social scientific work could proceed on the question of how it all came about, it was first necessary to eliminate the oldest and still-dominant explanation – that the Greco-Roman world was saved by mass conversions in response to public preaching and miracle working. From earliest days, mass conversions were central to the Christian story: crowds gathered, listened, marveled, and were saved. Thus, Acts 2:41 reports that after Peter preached to a multitude 'there were added that day about three thousand souls'. Writing in about 325 CE, Eusebius tells us that 'at first hearing whole multitudes in a body eagerly embraced in their souls piety towards the Creator of the universe' (III 37.3).

That mass conversions built Christianity has seemed obvious. Adolf Harnack put it plainly: how else can we understand the 'inconceivable rapidity' of Christian growth and 'astonishing expansion' of the movement? (1908,2:335–6). Indeed, Harnack reminded his readers of St Augustine's insight that the greatest miracle of all would have been for Christianity to grow as rapidly as it did without the aid of miracles. In his distinguished recent study, *Christianizing the Roman Empire*, Ramsay MacMullen also stressed the arithmetical necessity for mass conversions. Because 'very large numbers are obviously involved', Christian growth could not have been limited to an individual mode of conversion, but requires 'successes en masse' (1984:29).

This was all very troublesome because modern social science lacks any theoretical propositions to deal with spontaneous mass conversions. Instead, as noted early in this essay, conversion is explained by social science as the result of interaction processes within networks of interpersonal attachments whereby people come to accept new faiths in response to their social ties to those who already believe. Thus, from the perspective of modern social science, the kind of mass conversions described by Eusebius and accepted by historians ever since, would indeed be miraculous.

And if the rise of Christianity can be explained only by resort to miracles, then social science would seem to have little to contribute.

Fortunately, the 'facts' justifying the miraculous assumption were wrong. The only reason people believed that there was an arithmetic need for mass conversion, was because no one ever bothered to do the actual arithmetic. I have done so in considerable detail, taking care to verify my results with the pertinent literature (Stark 1996). A brief summary suffices here.

There is general agreement among scholars that Christians in the Greco-Roman world numbered somewhere between 5 and 7 million in the year 300 CE. How this total was reached from a tiny starting point of, say, 1000 Christians in the year 40 CE is the arithmetic challenge. At first glance, growth of this magnitude might seem a miraculous achievement. But, suppose we assume that the Christian rate of growth during this period was similar to that of the Mormon rate of growth over the past century, which has been approximately 40 percent per decade (Stark 1984 and 1994). If the early Christians were able to match the Mormon growth rate, then their 'miracle' is fully accomplished in the time history allows. That is, from a starting point of 1000 Christians in the year 40 CE, a growth rate of 40 percent per decade (or 3.4 percent per year) results in a total of 6 299 832 Christians in the year 300 CE. Moreover, because compounded rates result in exponential growth, there is a huge numerical increase from slightly more than 1 million Christians in the year 250 CE to more than 6 million in 300 CE. This gives further confidence in the projections since historians have long believed that a rapid increase in numerical growth occurred at this time (cf., Gager 1975).

The rise of Mormonism has been very carefully documented and their growth has been based on the conventional network processes understood by social science, while mass conversions to the Mormon faith of the kind described by Eusebius are unknown. Clearly, then, the rise of Christianity could easily have been accomplished in accord with our current understanding of why and how conversion takes place and social science is sufficient unto the task at hand.

In many other essays on the early Church I have utilized the arithmetic of the probable to demonstrate the importance of various factors in the rise of Christianity. But I have not always been forced to settle for hypothetical quantification. Indeed, I managed to create a data set based on the 22 largest Greco-Roman cities in about the year 100 CE (Stark 1991). Thus far, the data set includes seven variables (several other scholars promise they soon will contribute additional variables).

The whole thing began when I was looking through an atlas of the history of Christianity. One of the maps showed the location of Christian churches as they appeared during the first several centuries. Consulting the notes I discovered that locating and dating Christian churches had begun with Adolf Harnack (1908) and that many scholars had contributed to the project over the years. Unfortunately, it seemed that only atlas authors cared about this information, as I could not find it elsewhere. This caused me to examine many similar atlases. Eventually, I used five of them to construct a consensus view of when Christianity managed to establish a church in each of the 22 largest cities of the Greco-Roman world during the first several centuries of the Christian era. I then coded this information to create a variable I call Christianization. This is a measure of the expansion of Christianity based on three thresholds: cities that had a church by the year 100 CE were scored two; those with a church by the year 200 CE were scored one; the remainder were scored zero. Another variable was city-size, which came from the authoritative work of Tertius Chandler and Gerald Fox (1974). Then it was back to the maps as three distance measures were used to assess the eastern versus the Roman culture of a city. I used a map meter to measure distances from city to city, following the most efficient known routes which often meant travel by sea. The number of miles from Jerusalem measured the influence of eastern culture in each city. Miles from Rome measured the influence of Roman culture. Finally, a ratio of these two variables measured the relative extent of eastern and Roman influences: degree of Romanization. An additional variable gauged the size of the local Jewish population on the basis of whether or not there was a synagogue in the city. My initial data on synagogues also came from atlases, but was confirmed by the excellent summary of the most recent evidence by R. S. MacLennan and A. T. Kraable (1986). Finally, taking my data from Bentley Layton (1987), a measure of Gnostic presence was based on whether there is evidence of Gnostic activity prior to the year 200 CE, by the year 400 CE, or not at all.

Admittedly this all sounds rather crude and in fact it began as a bit of a lark. But the data displayed such robust and consistent statistical results that they deserved to be taken seriously. Thus, a three-variable regression using Jewish presence and Romanization (the ratio variable) as the independent variables and Christian-ization as the dependent variable resulted in an R^2 of 0.66. Of course, this is not news – everyone knows that Christianity grew more rapidly in the East than the West and that the diasporic Jewish communities provided the first flow of converts. But, because the results so strongly showed the obvious, they arouse more confidence in a far more controversial finding. Using Gnos-ticism as the dependent variable, regression results showed there was no significant direct effect of Jewish presence when Christia-nization is controlled. That is, the statistical results support the view that the Gnostics were a Christian heresy, not, as many current historians believe, a parallel movement rooted in Judaism.

In addition to suggestive results concerning the early Church, the data also offered strong confirmation of Claude S. Fischer's (1975) work on the subcultural theory of urbanism. A central proposition in the theory is 'the more urban the place, the higher the rate of unconventionality'. Fischer's thesis is that the larger the popu-lation, in absolute numbers, the easier it is to assemble the 'critical mass' needed to form a deviant subculture and he specifically included unconventional religious movements. The data showed very robust positive correlations between city size and both Chris-tianization and Gnostic activity. When he learned of the results, Fischer was not surprised that his theory prevailed, but he seemed rather startled about the data on which it was tested.

Looking back at the empirical research side of my career it might appear that I have a knack for finding appropriate data in strange places. But that's not it. I have gone on so many odd-seeming data hunts because my work has been relentlessly theory-driven. Because I knew what I needed to find out, it often was quite obvious where to look for data and fairly easy to spot what was appropriate. I conclude with one of my best examples.

Several years ago I supervised a master's thesis in sociology by Satomi Kurosu, a young woman from Japan. She had built a data set for the 47 Prefectures of Japan and was trying to explain why the suicide rate was higher in rural than in urban parts of Japan – a pattern opposite of findings in Europe and North America. She took her data from many sources including the *Japanese Statistical Yearbook* (which is published in both English and Japanese on facing pages). She believed that westernization had something to do with the lower rates in the cities, but she was having great difficulty finding an adequate measure of it. One day I came across a guidebook to McDonald's restaurants worldwide. In it was the address of every McDonalds in the world including a large number of them in Japan. To almost anyone else this would have been trivial. But, to me, here was a measure of westernization. Surely places with many McDonalds must be more westernized than places with few or none. Turned into a rate for each Prefecture, the number of McDonalds per 100 000 population turned out to be a potent measure of westernization. And, not only was it strongly, negatively related to the suicide rate, when entered into a regression, McDonalds reduced the effects of urbanism on suicide to insignificance.

And that's what it means to let theories direct the research process.

References

Bainbridge, William Sims and Rodney Stark. 1982. 'Church and Cult in Canada'. *Canadian Journal of Sociology* 7:351–66.
Berger, Peter. 1963. 'A Market Model for the Analysis of Ecumenicity'. *Social Research* 30:77–93.
Chandler, Tertius and Gerald Fox. 1974. *3000 Years of Urban Growth*. New York: Academic Press.
Finke, Roger, Avery M. Guest, and Rodney Stark. 1996. 'Mobilizing Local Religious Markets: Pluralism and religious Participation in The Empire State, 1855–1865'. *American Sociological Review* 61:203–18.
Finke, Roger and Rodney Stark. 1992. *The Churching of America – 1776–1990: Winners and Losers in Our Religious Economy*. New Brunswick: Rutgers University Press.
—— 1988. 'Religious Economies and Sacred Canopies: Religious Mobilization in American Cities, 1906'. *American Sociological Review* 53:41–9.
—— 1986. 'Turning Pews Into People: Estimating Nineteenth-Century Church Membership'. *Journal for the Scientific Study of Religion* 25:180–92.
Fischer, Claude S. 1975. 'Toward a Subcultural Theory of Urbanism', *American Journal of Sociology* 80:1319–41.
Gager, John G. 1975. *Kingdom and Community: The Social World of Early Christianity*. Englewood Cliffs, NJ: Prentice-Hall.
Glock, Charles Y. and Rodney Stark. 1966. *Christian Beliefs and Anti-Semitism*. New York: Harper and Row.
Harnack, Adolph. 1908. *The Mission and Expansion of Christianity in the First Three Centuries* (2 volumes) (trans. James Moffatt). New York: G. P. Putnam's Sons.
Kox, Willem, Wim Meeus, and Harm 't Hart. 1991. 'Religious Conversion of Adolescents: Testing the Lofland and Stark Model of Religious Conversion'. *Sociological Analysis* 52:227–40.

Lambert, Richard D. 1960. 'Current Trends in Religion: A Summary'. *The Annals: Religion in American Society* 332:146–55.

Layton, Bentley. 1987. *The Gnostic Scriptures*. Garden City: Doubleday.

Lee, Robert. 1960. *The Social Sources of Church Unity*. New York: Abingdon Press.

Lofland, John and Rodney Stark. 1965. 'Becoming a World-Saver: A Theory of Conversion to a Deviant Perspective'. *American Sociological Review* 30: 862–75.

MacLennan, Robert S. and A. Thomas Kraabel. 1986. 'The God-Fearers – A Literary and Theological Invention'. *Biblical Archaeology Review* 12 (Sept/Oct):47–53.

MacMullen, Ramsay. 1984. *Christianizing the Roman Empire*. New Haven: Yale.

Scroggs, Robin. 1980. 'The Sociological Interpretation of the New Testament: The Present State of Research'. *New Testament Studies* 26:164–79.

Stark, Rodney. [in press]. 'Catholic Contexts: Commitment and Innovation'. *Review of Religious Research*.

——1996. *The Rise of Christianity: A Sociologist Reconsiders History*. Princeton: Princeton University Press.

——1994. 'Modernization and Mormon Growth', in Marie Cornwall, Tim B. Heaton, and Lawrence Young, editors, *A Sociological Analysis of Mormonism*. Champaign, IL: University of Illinois Press.

——1992. 'Do Catholic Societies Really Exist?' *Rationality and Society*, 4: 261–71.

——1991. 'Christianizing the Urban Empire: An Analysis Based on 22 Greco-Roman Cities'. *Sociological Analysis* 52:77–88.

——1985a. 'Europe's Receptivity to Religious Movements'. pp. 301–43 in Rodney Stark (ed.), *New Religious Movements: Genesis, Exodus, and Numbers*. New York: Paragon.

——1985b. 'From Church-Sect to Religious Economies'. pp. 139–49 in *The Sacred in a Secular Age*, edited by Phillip E. Hammond. Berkeley: University of California Press.

——1984. 'The Rise of a New World Faith'. *Review of Religious Research* 26: 18–27.

——1971. 'The Economics of Piety: Religion and Social Class'. pp. 483–503 in *Issues in Social Inequality*, edited by Gerald W. Thielbar and Saul D. Feldman. Boston: Little, Brown and Co.

——1968. 'Age and Faith'. *Sociological Analysis* 29:1–10.

Stark, Rodney and William Sims Bainbridge. 1985. *The Future of Religion: Secularization, Revival, and Cult Formation*. Berkeley: University of California Press.

——1981a. 'American-Born Sects: Initial Findings'. *Journal for the Scientific Study of Religion* 20:130–49.

——1981b. 'Secularization and Cult Formation in the Jazz Age'. *Journal for the Scientific Study of Religion* 20:360–73.

——1980. 'Secularization, Revival, and Cult Formation'. *The Annual Review of the Social Sciences of Religion* 4:85–119.

Stark, Rodney and Roger Finke. 1988. 'American Religion in 1776: A Statistical Portrait'. *Sociological Analysis* 49:39–51.

Stark, Rodney and Charles Y. Glock. 1968. *American Piety*. Berkeley: University of California Press.

—— 1965. 'The New Denominationalism'. *Review of Religious Research* 7:8–17.

Stark, Rodney and James C. McCann. 1993. 'Market Forces and Catholic Commitment: Exploring the New Paradigm'. *Journal for the Scientific Study of Religion* 32:111–24.

10

On Studying Religion

ANDREW M. GREELEY

I suppose that I began my serious study of religion as something more than just a classroom exercise when I was in the seminary theologate during the early 1950s. I hasten to add that the reason for this beginning was not the course of studies in philosophy and theology that I endured there for seven years. My formal studies at the seminary consisted of an exposure to the most deadly kind of manualism one can possibly imagine, an adherence by instructors to the words of textbooks (in Latin, of course) without the slightest inclination to go beyond the words to the issues and the history which had been digested by the authors of the manuals. It was required that we memorize these words (in Latin) and give them back to our teachers in exams both written and oral. Anything more than that was considered dangerous for young men who were to be ordained for the service of a Church which was beyond change and whose role was to be dutiful and obedient assistant pastors for the rest of their lives. Such young men were not supposed to think too much.

One can imagine what happened to such young men when they discovered that they were to work with Catholic laity who were much better educated than they were and when the unchanging Church went through an exuberant and turbulent change a few years after they were ordained. Some of them left the priesthood, some of them hunkered down and refused to admit what was happening, others tried to 'update' themselves which often meant that they sought ways to persuade themselves and their laity that nothing had really changed.

I was lucky. A man the year ahead of me had left the seminary and enrolled in a graduate program at the University of Chicago. At that time – late 1940s shading into early 1950s – there was a flowering of Catholic intellectual life at the University as a group of self-consciously Catholic young men and women (many of them veterans of the War) strove to reconcile the Catholic faith they had learned in the neighborhoods growing up with the intellectual challenges of the University world.[1] My contact with that world was limited, though I did have sense enough to realize that they represented the emergence for the first time in the United States of a large and self-conscious intellectual elite. However, I did learn the names of their favorite theologians – Jean Danielou, Yves Congar, Henri de Lubac, and, though read only in manuscript, Pierre Teilhard de Chardin. I also realized that these theologians, whose thought would shape the Second Vatican Council only a decade later, had been condemned not by name in a papal encyclical in 1950.

However, some of their books were available if rarely read in the seminary library and could be bought by mail from English and French bookstores. Our Jesuit faculty viewed them all with suspicion but with one or two exceptions had not read them and raised no particular objections to my reading them – though their tolerance was for the most part the result of laziness and indifference and not principle.

Danielou, de Lubac, and Congar would all later become Cardinals. Danielou turned reactionary, de Lubac was deeply disturbed by the changes of the Council. Only Père Congar, the one whose writing most influenced me, never deviated from the course he laid out in *Jallons Pour Une Théologie du Laicat* and *Vraie et Fausse Reforme dans L'Eglise*. He was the last to be named a Cardinal and only when he was too sick to travel to Rome to receive the red hat. He never sold out to the Establishment, never regretted the energies he had set in motion, never turned against the Conciliar reforms.[2] I had the pleasure of serving with him for several years on the editorial board of the journal *Conciliu*.[3] I tried to explain to him how much his work had meant to me in my formative years and how much I admired him. But the barrier of language difference choked off the message.

Fascinated to discover a theology which was so completely different – and so much more interesting than what we were being taught in class – I began to explore for my MA and STL papers the writings of their immediate predecessors, the World War I generation of French Dominican and Jesuit theologians – Pierre Rousellot and Ambrose Marcheal especially. I discovered that faith was not a purely cognitive exercise by any means and that the propositional theology of the decadent scholasticism we were being taught was a poor excuse for religion. Rousellot's *Les Yeux de La Foi* was especially important in convincing me that experience prepared the way for the act of faith and was not a consequence of it. These men led me back to John Henry Newman, not the Newman of the *Apologia* but the Newman of *Essay on the Development of Doctrine*. His notion of assent being the result not of certain propositions but of converging probabilities appealed to me then and still does – and also provides an epistemological basis for the probability statistics that are the foundation of my sociology.

My work in the two papers impressed one of the Jesuits on the faculty, one that still thought that scholarship was important. He wanted me to be chosen as one of the two from our class who would do graduate work for the doctorate in theology. I would be assigned to read all the books in English and French written by converts to Catholicism in the 19th and 20th centuries and evaluate the discussion of the theologians on the nature of the act of faith in light of their writings. Even then I was tagged as an empiricist. His suggestion was voted down on the grounds that I was just a little bit too smart for my own good.

It would not be the last time in my life that I felt in retrospect that the Spirit intervened in my life with plans of Her own. I see now a direct trajectory between my discovery of the importance of experience in the mid-century French theologians and my eventual development of my model in the sociology of religion that religion is story before it is anything else and after it is everything else. Doctrinal propositions I realized even then were indeed important but there was more to religion than that.

I have described elsewhere[4] the joys of my work at Christ the King parish in the Beverly neighborhood of Chicago for the ten years I worked in that community. For the purposes of this essay, two dimensions of that crucial interlude in my life must be mentioned:

(1) I became convinced that the religious faith of my well educated parishioners did not fit the paradigm I had learned at the seminary. While they may have accepted a body of propositional truths, their Catholicism was deeper and richer and not constrained in practice by the demands of rigorous and systematic ordering. It was rather a faith deeply rooted in their experience of community and their experiences of the sacramentality of the Catholic liturgy (even before they knew that there was a word such as 'liturgy' and also before, heaven save us all, they encountered the ideological prigs who claim the name of liturgist). It was clear

to me even then that the Catholicism of the new professional class fit no one's theological model. For that matter, it still doesn't.

For example, Ellen Foley, in my novel *The Cardinal Sins* summarizes the appeal of Catholicism: 'I focused on all the ugly things and forgot about Father Conroy and Sister Caroline and First Communion and May crownings and High Club dances and midnight mass and all those wonderful things that I love so much.'

This appeal I would later remark was so strong that not even all the mistakes and the stupidities of Church leadership during the past 30 years could drive them from the Church. Catholics stay in the Church, I would argue in *The New York Times Magazine* in the summer of 1994, because they like being Catholic and they like being Catholics because of the stories.

(2) The same friend who had put me in touch with the Catholic group at the University in the late 1940s and early 1950s, also introduced me to several wandering French 'Sociologistes Religieuses' who were drifting around America in those days. I would later decide that they were not very well trained in their field, would derive vast *a priori* theories from a single finding (a tendency which has not been eliminated completely from French sociology of religion even today). They did not like what they saw in the American Church – too many people going to Mass, too many receiving Holy Communion. Hypocrisy, they said dismissively. Once the immigrant experience was over, Americans would drift from the Church just as the French had done. My experience at Christ the King suggested that they could not be more wrong.

When I went to the University in the autumn of 1960 (John Kennedy running for the Presidency, John XXIII reigning on the banks of the Tiber), I was determined to try to understand more about American Catholicism and especially the tenacious loyalty of American Catholics to their Church despite their social upward mobility and (later) despite the turbulence stirred up in the Church when Pope John opened his window and let the fresh breezes sweep in.

My initial work at the University (at the National Opinion Research Center under the benign and exciting direction of Peter H. Rossi) was empirical. I had the delightful experience of discovering that what everyone knew about American Catholics and about Catholic schools was not true – and that what I suspected about both subjects from my years at Christ the King was true.

These experiences alienated me, I very much fear, from the Catholic liberal ideologues (such as those who reigned at *The Commonweal*) who seemed to have a vested interest in believing in the inadequacy of all things Catholic and the anti-intellectualism of most Catholics other than themselves. They wrote me off as an 'optimist' and an ambitious young opportunist who wanted to be a bishop. (They still dismiss me after all these years, though with different epithets.) I wrote them off as ideologues, snobs, and anti-intellectuals who would not accept evidence that challenged their assumptions. (I still write them off and with virtually the same epithets. I'd add 'envious' now, however.)

For many years my principle research goal was to elaborate a description of the descendants of the Catholic immigrants in the later stages of the acculturation process, to discover empirically as much as I could about them generally in refutation of the conventional wisdom of both the right and the left. My experience was that the findings my colleagues and I produced about Catholics and their schools would be denounced on all sides when they initially appeared and then in a few years be accepted as truth by everyone, indeed as something everyone knew all along to be true – without any footnote references or any apologies.

The biggest surprise and the biggest controversy came because of the book my colleagues and I produced in 1976 which we called *Catholic Schools in a Declining Church*. The focus of the controversy was not on the finding that Catholic schools were even more important in a turbulent Church than in a quiet Church. Rather it was on our report that, despite the 1968 birth control encyclical, Catholics had changed from 50 percent opposition to birth control to 12 percent opposition. Anyone who had any meaningful contact with the Catholic laity could not have been surprised by the finding. Catholics had made up their minds that the Church had no right to prescribe to them acceptable and unacceptable means of fertility limitation. They would remain Catholics, but now on their own terms.

This was a change in the American Catholic population of enormous import, a change which has not yet been absorbed or understood by the elites, whether they be hierarchical or intellectual, right or left.

Instead of turning the tide, the papal intervention seemed to have accelerated the change. Moreover, although in the aftermath of the birth control encyclical, church attendance and financial contributions declined somewhat, there was no massive exodus from the Church. On the contrary there was no exodus at all. The defection rate of 15 percent had not changed since 1960 (and has not changed as of 1997).

While I had to fight off critics on both sides who dismissed our findings as my 'opinions',[5] I was more interested in the remarkable change in Catholic reaction to Church authority which I described as that of 'communal Catholics'. By that I did not mean merely men and women who did not receive the sacraments or attend Church services but still identified as Catholic but especially those who remained devout, but now on their own terms. It was only a couple of years after the 1976 book that I wrote the dialogue between Kevin Brennan and Ellen Foley that I cited above. I knew what was going on, but I had yet to elaborate it into a full-fledged theory (of the 'middle range').

I was not merely a 'naive empiricist' (as *The Commonweal* dubbed me). I was struggling to discover a theory of the sociology of religion – indeed a theory of religion – that could account for the findings that I was reporting. Several major influences would shape this pilgrimage.

(1) While I was still in graduate school (1961 I think), a young anthropologist on the University faculty substituted for our regular teacher (who was away, I presume at a meeting) and gave a lecture based on a paper he was writing. His name was Clifford Geertz and the paper would later be published as 'Religion as a Cultural System'. I was dazzled by Geertz's prose style (so different from that of the usual flat, crabbed style of social science discourse) and even more by his theory that religion was a system of symbols which purports to explain uniquely the meaning of human life. The word 'symbols' was critically important. Religion was image, symbol, sacrament before it was anything else. Theological and catechetical articulations of a religious faith were nothing more than derivations (necessary derivations I hasten to add) drawn from reflection on the symbols. If you want to measure someone's religion, you had better get a profile of his religious imagery.

(2) A year or two later I read Michael Polanyi's *Personal Knowledge* which persuaded me that the 'scientific method' as propounded in textbooks and as practiced in journal articles was either phony or a pose required by journal editors and reviewers which no one takes seriously. Intellectual 'instincts', hunches, half-formed ideas, findings vaguely remembered, notions that spring

up from the preconscious – this is what 'science' is really like, even if one has to pretend otherwise when one is reporting one's work. Science, like religion, is first of all story. I wouldn't have used that sentence then, but it conveys something of the illumination I received from Polyani.

(3) In the late 1960s I had begun to be interested in religious experiences (not my own) after reading a book by Margarita Laski about a non-representative sample of people with ecstatic experiences. I then tackled William James again and understood him for the first time. *The Varieties* is one of the great books of American religious scholarship and James perhaps the most distinguished original religious thinker in our history. In a project we were about to launch in 1972 for the Henry Luce foundation – designed as my first attempt to operationalize Geertz's theory by measuring imagery of God – we also asked questions about ecstatic and paranormal experiences. Contrary to research reported by the Group for the Advancement for Psychiatry, those who reported intense religious experiences (32 percent of Americans) were not psychological misfits (the GAP findings were based on non-representative samples of patients encountered in clinical situations while our findings were based on representative population samples) but paragons of mental health.[6] As I would summarize our findings, the paranormal was normal and ecstasy was good for you.

At that point, 25 years ago, I had clearly wandered beyond the boundaries of acceptable social science. Neither American Catholics nor mysticism were approved areas of social research, nor the sort of subjects that journal editors would think twice about rejecting out of hand.[7] One of the reasons it took so long for me to develop my theory is that I had always insisted that I would publish it only when I had enough data to prove that it was a useful approach to the study of religion. Since none of the major public or private funding agencies believe that religion is an important part of American life (their staff members apparently do not read the newspapers), it has proven very difficult to collect data.[8] A combination of the annual NORC General Social Survey, the International Social Survey Program, and royalties from my novels finally produced enough data for me to articulate and test the theory in the late 1980s and the early 1990s.

It was not easy. Thus, in the 1972 study, we established that more than half of the American population prays every day. A prayer question included in the GSS after 1983 enabled me to prove that frequency of prayer is the most powerful of the ordinary religious predictors and that in any choice between Church attendance and prayer, the later should be chosen. Nonetheless my colleagues at NORC venture forth with research projects that involve variables on which I have shown prayer has a strong effect (as social science effects go) and don't ask the question. There is no malice in this behavior, only forgetfulness.

In the early and middle 1970s I encountered work (and men) who have had powerful influence on my scholarly (and personal) thinking about religion: the work of David Tracy and John Shea. The latter is as much an outsider to the academic enterprise as I am. No, he is far more an outsider because he does not choose to get involved in the academy at all. While 'narrative theology' was a passing fashion and academic theologians may write about stories but never tell them, and, while few of them are willing to see that religion IS story, Shea has never considered narrative to be a fashion, tells stories (usually in powerful poetic form as in the final chapter of his wondrous book *Starlight*), and understands perfectly well that religion IS story. His as yet unpublished work on the 'literary-spiritual' interpretation of the Bible is as revolutionary an approach to the study of the Scriptures as has appeared in a long time. His insight is that the Bible stories as they are presented to us are stories and indeed skillfully told stories with powerful spiritual insight that demands hearing in addition to analysis. From his work I learned of the importance of story as a continuation of experience. Religion is founded in experience and shared with others in story. The images which encode the experience and imprint it on our memory are in fact narrative images.

Shea's work is also strongly tinged with mysticism, especially the poetic conclusions of *Stories of Faith* and *Starlight*. He has persuaded me not only of my own mystical nature, but also even more strongly than James of the experiential dimension of all religion. Shea is the kind of writer who professional theologians of the present ignore completely because he does not play their academic game and who professional theologians of the future will study because they will realize that he was one of the few of our time who got it right.

Tracy is in some respects just the opposite, an academic theologian (probably the best of them in the world today) who is also aware of the pastoral implications of his work and preaches fine sermons at the Catholic center of the University of Chicago every week.[9] From his first two books, *Blessed Rage for Order* and *The Analogical Imagination*, I learned more about the philosophical background of my speculations about religious imagery and story and also identified that which was unique about Catholicism – a quality which Tracy calls 'The Analogical Imagination', the propensity to see the Transcendent disclosing Herself in the objects, events, people and communities of everyday life (as over against the Protestant 'Dialectical Imagination' which strives to distance the transcendent from these realities lest religion degenerate into idolatry). Hence Catholics have saints and angels and souls in purgatory and statues and stained glass windows and elaborate rituals and a vast, if often monumentally incompetent, church structure while (many) Protestants view these devotions as idolatry if not the work of the devil. I shall leave the refinements and the developments of Tracy's work to his own expositions of his theories. However, I recognized in it the first fair and accurate description – though at a very abstract level – I had encountered in contemporary theologians of the Catholicism I had encountered while I was growing up and in parishes in which I worked (and continued to work). No longer were American Catholics being urged to look to France or the Netherlands or Germany or South America to find models to imitate. Rather Tracy was pointing, however implicitly, to an older and richer Catholic tradition which was still alive and well in the United States, however unappreciated it might be.

In the middle 1980s it occurred to me that the proliferation of international data files from the European Values Study and the International Social Survey Program (in which I would later become deeply involved) provided a possibility of testing Tracy's thesis with cross-national empirical data. Did Catholics still imagine reality differently than Protestants did? Was Tracy's description of the two 'Imaginations', drawn from his study of the 'classics' of the two traditions, also an accurate description of Protestant and Catholic imaginative propensities today? Was the difference between Catholics and Protestants outlined by Weber and Durkheim in fact a 'superstructure' based on different styles of imagination?

Tracy admitted later that he was uneasy about such testing of his theories. Would they stand up to the data? In fact, his theory, based on the 'classics', depended for its validity on its accuracy in describing and interpreting the 'classics' and did not need empirical validation from the social sciences. If, however, it turned out that the imaginations of ordinary Catholics in many countries today were influenced by the 'classics' or more properly by the same heritage which had shaped the classics, then Tracy's theory had implications which were very broad indeed.

In the lead article in the summer 1989 issue of the *American Sociological Review*, I reported my analysis under the title 'Is the Analogical Imagination Extinct?' (Part of the analysis was repeated in my summary, *Religion as Poetry*.) Analogical styles of imagining were not at all extinct. Tracy was right, even more right than he had expected.

By that time I had the three elements of my theory in place – religion is experience, story, and imagination before it becomes anything else and after it has become everything else (Paul Ricoeur's 'First' and 'Second' Naivetés'); Catholics still imagine differently in most countries; and religion is still important.[10]

A decade before that, however, I had tried to integrate the theory by combining the work of Tracy and Shea to establish a sociological paradigm for the study of the role of Mary the Mother of Jesus in the Catholic tradition. The book I wrote as a result of this analysis, *The Mary Myth*, was one of the most important works I have ever written for my own thinking. It became clear to me that Mary was enormously popular with Catholics because she represented the Mother love of God, the womanly dimension of God. Since I didn't have any survey data yet, I used as my data the art and the poetry of Catholicism. Only later in a study of young Catholics commissioned by the Knights of Columbus did we come upon empirical data which established that the Mary Myth still was enormously attractive to young Catholics (and also to those who were not Catholic but married to Catholics). Indeed the Mary image was 'warmer' than that of both God and Jesus. As St Bernard had remarked, 'If you fear the Father, go to the Son. If you fear the Son, go to the Mother.'

Mary was an enormous resource for the Catholic imagination and indeed defines how the Catholic imagination differs from other imaginative heritages. Perhaps that ought not to be surprising. She is the only 'mother goddess', the only 'spring goddess', in the Western market place of deities.[11]

Although the Mother of Jesus had been abandoned by much of the Catholic elite as offensive baggage in an ecumenical era, there was no evidence that she was any less popular among the Catholic laity. Small wonder: any narrative symbol that God loves us like the Madonna loves her new-born child in the Christmas story is bound to have permanent appeal. Ultimate reality may not be of that sort, but the possibility that it might be is simply too attractive to dismiss.

The book was for the most part ignored, as were the later empirical validations. A sympathetically disposed archbishop wondered why I would not say at the very beginning that Mary was the mother of God. His question confused the propositional with the poetic and the sociological with the theological. Moreover, it demanded of the reader an understanding of the complex rules of the Communication of Idioms from Christology, abstract Greek philosophy being deemed more important than the image of the Madonna and child.

A serious public attack appeared in *Theological Studies* by Elizabeth Johnson, a much admired 'feminist' theologian. Johnson's position seemed to me that no male and certainly no celibate male had any right to analyze the womanly love of God in general and the role of Mary in particular. In fact, Johnson rejected all other approaches to Mary, too. With the self-righteous purity of the ideologue who is dispensed from responsible description of someone else's work (particularly that of a priest), she felt no ethical restraints which might prevent her from distorting the book beyond all recognition. Her most telling critique was that Mary's reflection of the womanly beauty of God would have no appeal to a homosexual. In the ideological world in which Johnson lives, that is a decisive and unanswerable criticism. One murmurs mildly that the argument assumes that gay men do not find women attractive (albeit not as sexual partners). But then one gives up. To argue with those who are caught up in the miasma of ideological fashions is to waste one's time.

Neither the Academy nor the Church is all that generous. Social science at least praises the theory of the 'marginal man' but treats him as a pariah in practice, especially if he has the temerity to insist on new paradigms and ideas. The Church may praise the real marginal man but only after he is dead. As Mr Dooley remarked, 'histry always vindicates the Dimycrats, but only after they're dead. Nothing is ever officially true until the Raypublicans admit it and by that time all the Dimycrats are dead.'

The Church, or at least its elites like Beth Johnson, cannot tolerate someone who refuses to be subsumed under the label of 'conservative' or 'liberal', especially when he doesn't prate a party line or knuckle under to the currently fashionable ideological lines. God protect us from anyone who thinks for himself, especially if he has some success in writing fiction.

Sociologists, oddly enough, like my fiction and have, in substantial part, decided that I am, after all, a good, and perhaps a great, sociologist because of my fiction – though they still don't read my sociology. In the Church, however, intellectuals and quasi intellectuals of the left and the right take it as a matter of right and duty to lie about me.

I'm not complaining. I knew what I was getting into. Perhaps I am a born dissident, but even in my dissidence I can't resist the temptation to reject (and disprove if data are available) the various conventional wisdoms. That's part of the fun of the game.

After *The Mary Myth*, I began to think seriously about testing my theories of (the sociology of) religion by writing popular novels. Might not fiction be, I asked myself, the stained glass window of the modern world, a tool for handing on a religious heritage not by indoctrinating or educating but by illuminating, by asking the reader to enter the world of the story and then providing him with an enhanced view of the possibilities for his life as he returns to his own world?

My novels were and are theological novels, stories about God's love, as is patent to any fair reader and was and is patent to the thousands of people who write to me to tell me how the stories have changed their lives. I have often thought that I would have experienced no problem over them if they had been (very) modestly successful. However, much to my surprise they have been enormously successful and thus stirred up a firestorm of hostile reaction within the Catholic intellectual community. If I wanted to be taken seriously, even as a sociologist, by Catholic theologians and priests, I was told, I should never have written best-sellers. Sometimes I ask why this would be so and am answered with the shrug of the shoulders that suggests I have asked a stupid question.

Secular sociologists were more benign. Somehow I had become a distinguished sociologist without anyone realizing it. It did not follow that my theories in the sociology of religion or the empirical research I did to test the theories would be accepted or even noticed. But it did follow that I was not a pariah and indeed a person to be celebrated.

Charming. Or, as the Irish would say, half charming.

In the 1980s and the early 1990s I continued my research on American Catholics and, after I joined the International Social Survey Program in the late 1980s, became a student of religion around the world. I wrote the first paper based on survey data on religion in Russia. Again my observation that there was a religious revival of stunning proportions in Russia passed from the impossible to the commonplace, just as had my research on Catholic schools. What I learned from these experiences is that no one should ever be the first to write about a phenomenon. Never.

What are American Catholics like in the late 1990s? Socially and economically they have caught up with the American mainstream and indeed caught up 25 years ago. They are now half again as likely to graduate from college as the national average. They continue to be more liberal on most issues than the average American – including sexual issues (for instance, they have sex more often, are more playful in their sexual behavior, and even engage more frequently in oral sex). To the reader who says s/he does not and cannot believe such findings I say (to avoid obscenity), go collect your own data and prove me wrong.

Catholics are still a quarter of the American population, their defection rate (about 15 percent) has not changed since 1960. They like the changes of the Vatican Council and like being Catholics. However, and this is perhaps the most important effect of the ill-advised birth control encyclical, they are now Catholics very much on their own terms. It finally dawned on the media, if not on the Academy at the time of the Pope's 1995 visit to the United Nations, that Catholics see no contradiction between cheering for the Pope as the symbol of Catholicism *par excellence* and at the same time tuning out what he says on matters from birth control to immigration. Moreover, in research that Michael Hout and I did in 1996, we found that the vast majority of American Catholics want to return to the ancient practice of electing their own bishops, to have representative laity among the Pope's advisors; they favor the ordination of women, married priests, and the decentralization of power from the Vatican to the national hierarchies. Incidentally, though men and women do not differ significantly on the issue of the ordination of women, and never have (65 percent of both genders), women are more likely than men to advocate married priests.

The study is being replicated in many countries. Data available at this writing indicate that in Spain, a traditional Catholic country under the rule of the Falange for 40 years (and where the Opus Dei, a secret Catholic reactionary group, was founded and remains very strong), Catholics are even more radical on these issues of institutional reform than are Americans; Spanish women more strongly so than Spanish men.

In the middle 1990s I combined the work of a couple of decades into what, so far, is my *Summa: Religion as Poetry*. It is fair to say, I think, that it represents a history of my pilgrimage in the empirical study of religion. It is difficult for me to judge the impact of the book. Neither of the major sociological review journals have noticed it. It has been reviewed (favorably) by the *Journal for the Scientific Study of Religion, Cross Currents, The Furrow* (from the Maynooth Seminary in Ireland) and *Doctrine and Life*, a publication of the Irish Dominicans. On the other hand, the Jesuit magazine *America* turned it over to a graduate student at Yale Divinity School who patronized it. The reviewer in *The Christian Century* was incoherently angry, for reasons which escaped me. Though it did not receive much of a reaction in the academy, the book sold out two editions within a year and was converted to paperback at the end of its first year.

And they did seem to like it in Ireland!

My most serious mistake, I believe, was naively expecting scholars to take scholarly evidence seriously. Dogma is by no means limited to the Catholic hierarchy. I challenged a lot of dogmas. Truth to tell, I have rather enjoyed doing so. I propose to continue to do so as long as God gives me health and life.

Notes

1. By the time I arrived at the University in 1960, this group had dispersed. Only a few of them 'made it' in the intellectual world – for reasons that are not clear to me even today. There were many more Catholics in the University community by 1960, although we were still small in numbers and regarded with a mixture of curiosity and dismay by many of our faculty. However, we were not banded together in an intellectual community as were the 'Greenwood Avenue' group of a decade before and we did not have their ambition to remake the Church. None of us, for example, would have dreamed of writing to the Cardinal suggesting an evening Mass for the

'workers'. Cardinal Stritch had replied to them that 'since the time of Pliny the Younger' the Mass had been celebrated in the morning. Only a few years later the evening Mass had become commonplace, despite the words of 'Pliny the Younger'.

2. He once boasted that he had urinated against the wall of the Palace of the Holy Office in Rome.

3. An unsuccessful venture it was. The theologians on the board felt they wanted an American empiricist. But they thought Peter Berger was an empiricist and that the 'critical sociology' of the Frankfurt School was what sociology was supposed to be. I was quickly dismissed as a positivist who spoke bad English (Chicago accent) and was in addition a kind of wild Irishman.

4. See my memoir, *Confessions of a Parish Priest*.

5. To a certain kind of (clerical) mentality there is no such thing as a proven fact, only an 'opinion'. Thus my findings about Catholic schools were not treated as carefully documented empirical findings, but only personal opinions. Our birth control research is still ridiculed (though never refuted) by some Catholics of both the left and the right. Even as recently as 1993, a Catholic executive of the Lilly Endowment made fun of the research at a gathering of most of the priests of the Chicago Archdiocese. Under his direction the Endowment has invested heavily in a number of projects that are designed quite explicitly (according to some of the scholars who are doing the research) to refute me. They haven't succeeded in doing so and won't, but I'm astonished that the Endowment would bother.

6. This finding never did persuade the National Institutes of Mental Health to fund further research on mysticism and mental health. I suppose they would not have funded William James either.

7. Scholars Press published last year a collection of my refereed essays. It establishes that I did pay my dues to the profession.

8. The Lilly Endowment is an exception, but it has displayed consistent bad taste in the projects which it funds. The Knights of Columbus funded a study of young Catholics in 1980 but refused further research because it took umbrage at my best-selling novel, *The Cardinal Sins*.

9. Tracy is also the Andrew Thomas and Grace McNichols Greeley Professor of Catholic Studies at the University of Chicago, a title which Catholic publications routinely do not notice. Tracy is so much an academic that he actually thinks that there are such realities as modernity and post-modernity and even pre-modernity. I am not sure however that he thinks, as so many academic theologians do, that this quasi-Hegelian paradigm actually exists in the world beyond the corridors of theology and English departments.

10. The differences between Catholics and Protestants in this article did not decline either with youthfulness or education: hence there was no sign that they were going away. These findings ought to have had profound implications for Catholic thinkers and teachers, but they were so orthogonal to the ideological concerns of the Catholic elites at the time that they were ignored.

11. I dismiss the 'goddess worship' of small cliques of radical feminists as
     being numerically trivial and unlikely to ever become anything more
     than that.

11

Of Churches, Courts, and Moral Order

PHILLIP E. HAMMOND

The author who speaks about his own books is almost
as bad as a mother who talks about her own children.

Disraeli

Perforce, I discuss here my books but in such a way that what is highlighted is their substance as well as the circumstances surrounding their creation. Even Disraeli might have tolerated a mother's talking about her own children if she spoke chiefly about what she learned from them and how they were conceived. A certain amount of immodesty might still prevail, but it would likely be an instructive immodesty. To the degree I am successful in this task, therefore, I will link my scholarly products to at least three sets of influences, showing how they intermingled and became contexts for this aspect of my life as a student of religion.

The three sets of influences are: (1) My academic interests, including how they were formed and developed. (2) The more-or-less enduring impact of such things as my graduate training, colleagues, and job opportunities. And (3) the fortuitous events, conversations, and persons chancing onto paths that I, too, was on. These three influences did not, of course, operate separately, even though any discussion of them will make it appear that they did. The goal here is pedagogical, however – to show how the studies of religion that I undertook actually came about. This is a lesson that cannot be inferred from any book in the form in which it is published – given the conventions of scholarly writing – because, as any author will testify, nobody just sits down and writes a book, beginning with a first chapter and concluding with a last. Rather, the process is dialectical and disjointed, as well as deliberate, and it is several portraits of this process I seek to convey here. Moreover, what one learns by writing a book does not cease when the book is

213

published but continues to influence one's thoughts and subsequent research; and this process, too, I hope to describe.

ACADEMIC INTERESTS

My interest in religion is easy enough to explain, since, as the son, grandson, and great-grandson of Methodist clergymen, I was immersed in religion (though sprinkled in Baptism). My father aspired to the academic life, however, an aspiration thwarted by the Depression and the Second World War. Finally, in 1946 he moved his family from the Northwest to Massachusetts so that he could pursue a PhD in philosophy, a goal accomplished in 1949. My last two years of high school thus occurred not amidst the overwhelmingly waspish students of the Oregon, Washington, and Idaho towns that I had earlier known but with the ethnically rich mix of Greeks, Jews, Italians, Irish, and French Canadians I had never encountered before moving to Lynn, Massachusetts. This experience fascinated me and, as will be shown below, remained in my memory.

In 1948, I returned to Oregon to attend Willamette University, a school founded by the Methodist Church and still related to that denomination. With no clear occupational goal in mind, I declared first a major in Sociology (whatever that was!), then switched to Speech and Drama. By the time I woke up to the fact that I had no talent for the stage, I already had enough credits for the major, with three semesters yet to go. Briefly – a matter only of a few months – I entertained the idea of entering the ministry, but in rather sudden fashion I had the insight that probably I would be frustrated in that job and gave up that goal. My father's lack of success in finding an academic post had led him back to the parish ministry, and my awareness of his ambivalence about this turn of events may have influenced me more than I then realized. He had been pleased when I announced that I was contemplating the ministry, but he was even more pleased when, a year later, I indicated my interest in the professoriate. (And he fairly burst with pride when, as a newly minted PhD in Sociology, I took a first job at Yale.)

My father was extraordinarily liberal, both in theology and in politics, and this fact – it is clear to me now – played a huge role in the development of my scholarly interests. Very much the product of the social gospel movement, my father nonetheless continued in the assumption that liberal Protestant Christianity was the rightful religious custodian of American democratic culture. In the 1940s this assumption could still be entertained more readily in the American Northwest than in ethnically plural New England, but it led him to experience certain tensions in parish life, and it led me – as inchoate then as my understanding of such forces was – to the realization that a ministerial life was not for me. In retrospect, I can see that the question of how and why mainline Protestantism had lost its custodianship of American culture is a fairly constant theme in much of my research. A parallel question – What, then, does occupy that position? – is the other constant theme.

ENDURING INFLUENCES

Calling Charles Glock an enduring influence on my scholarly life is no exaggeration. As it happened, my first year as a sociology graduate student at Columbia was Glock's final year because he was then hired by UC Berkeley to direct its new Survey Research Center. I took his year-long Sociology of Religion class and found – especially in survey analysis – the major method I would use in my own work. It was through Glock, moreover, that I became involved in the Society for the Scientific Study of Religion and the Religious Research Association. Active in the latter organization was the Research Director for the Congregational Church (now United Church), Yoshio Fukuyama, who, in Spring 1959, made available to me a survey of 4000 members of a dozen, urban Congregational churches. He also gave me a small stipend that, together with the income from teaching three Introductory Sociology classes, allowed me to quit my research assistantship job and pursue my dissertation more or less full-time.

Glock was not just the link between me and Fukuyama's survey data, but he also invited me to spend the Summer of 1959 at his new Center in Berkeley, where I began my data analysis. The survey had been put together rather hurriedly, so, while it contained much information, especially about parishioner attitudes, discovering an analytic scheme was not easy. The 12 churches had been selected because all were in downtown transition areas and were thus threatened by loss of members. Presumably, the questionnaires were to reveal who among the congregants were remaining loyal and why. But since, by definition, all respondents were members and thus not defectors, the aggregate data were not very revealing. I developed a typology of theological orientations toward church involvement to see if such ideological differences influenced parishioners' level of involvement, their satisfaction, and their likelihood of defection. Ideological differences, I discovered, did influence those things but only a little. Mine was not going to be a dramatic dissertation if I relied on those feeble findings alone.

I spent a number of months, therefore, theorizing about possible roles that ideology *might* play in religious organizations, which necessarily led to thoughts about other forces that might also be influential. The first half of my thesis was thus a discussion of these abstract issues (including some speculation about how government institutions might replace churches as agencies that function 'religiously'), which the second half empirically illustrated in fairly pale fashion. I thought I deserved the PhD on the basis of my thesis, but it never occurred to me to seek its publication. I was therefore surprised when, 20 years later, it was selected to appear in the Arno Press Series of Sociology Dissertations.

Though I doubt if I could have articulated the issue very clearly in 1959, in retrospect I was puzzling out the question of just why people are involved in churches, and discovering that doctrinal considerations – the ostensible reasons – are not all that important. This was the period of extraordinary church growth, and many analysts were questioning the 'authenticity' of church-goers' motivations. I was not among the cynics, but that was because I was coming to see that 'authentic' motivation, at least in the sense these church critics meant it, had probably never been much of a factor in the life of religious organizations. Perhaps better, I was coming to appreciate that sociology of religion does not study the sacred but rather people's reports of their experiences of the sacred, which also led me to wonder about where else, if not exclusively in churches, the sacred might be found.

A FORTUITOUS CONVERSATION

About the time I was finishing the dissertation and getting ready to take the Yale job, I had a chance conversation with Yoshio Fukuyama, during which he described the request he – as Research Director for the Congregationalists – was getting to study their campus ministry. It seems that many in that occupation were complaining of 'role conflict', in the sense that they felt they were expected to engage in contradictory activities by their employer (the denomination) on the one hand and by their clients (college campuses and students) on the other hand. This complaint, moreover, was not peculiar to the Congregationalists but seemed to characterize most of the full-time Protestant campus ministers, who were at that time almost exclusively representing liberal, mainline denominations.

Fukuyama indicated that his agenda would not allow him to research this topic, but I saw it as a chance to practice my survey skills, this time not with data already collected but with data I could create. In addition, the topic allowed me to take another step into the sociology of religion, this time with a focus on the clergy. The presumption of job-related stress among my subjects meant that I could apply for a small grant from the National Institute for Mental Health, and with that money ($3,500) I bought a tape recorder (incredible as it seems now, it cost over $300 and weighed 40 pounds) and traveled during Summer 1962 to interview a variety of campus ministers from Massachusetts to Virginia. The grant also paid for transcribing those interviews, quotations from which were included in the eventual monograph, *The Campus Clergyman* (Basic Books, 1966).

The 'role conflict' campus ministers experienced presumably resulted from their being on the margins where the church and university meet. I imagined their situations analogous to that of factory foremen, who exist at the margins where labor and management meet. Nothing in the interviews caused me to doubt this picture, and I carefully developed a lengthy questionnaire designed to uncover both the sources of such conflict and its consequences. In April 1963, a very handsome booklet was sent to over 1500 persons, and, by September, 79 percent (997) were returned from those eligible to respond, a very respectable return rate.

Being confronted with 339 observations on each of 997 persons is daunting unless one has a planned strategy (a 'theory', if you will) to guide the analysis. My strategy, as I mentioned, revolved around the notion of role conflict, and the questionnaire contained many items to measure its character, intensity, and consequences. I quickly discovered a fundamental flaw in that strategy, however, an experience all too common in survey research. In an Appendix to *The Campus Clergyman*, I described that experience:

> One can imagine the horror of discovering that those scoring 'high' on measures of conflict were no more unhappy, dissatisfied, vague, or likely to quit than those scoring 'low'. Many other tables 'made sense'; I was developing great confidence in the data; but obviously conflict (at least as I had conceived it) was not the key to understanding the campus ministry occupation. At this point, the only solution was to think up alternative explanatory 'keys'. The one I eventually settled upon came in the spring of 1964 when I chanced upon a new book in a colleague's office. The book is William A. Rushing, *The Psychiatric Professions*, a theoretical analysis of structural devices used by paramedical professions that are trying to gain greater attention and deference, and be of greater service, in the mental hospital. The points of similarity between those occupations and the campus ministry struck me. My analysis techniques and concepts were going to be different from Rushing's, but I was now led to ask entirely new questions of my data. If conflict was 'absent', for example, might that indicate the fact that nobody 'cares'? And could not the perception that nobody cares generate in campus ministers the same responses I noted before but had assumed to be consequences of conflict? Such, of course, is the way things turned out many months later, but it is instructive to see that most of my study was not overhauled. I went ahead with measures of campus ministry values, of campus ministerial styles, of college campus characteristics. But until the guiding theme was identified, these were but interesting classifications.

Fortunately for me, I had asked respondents to indicate not only what they thought were their approval ratings from various church and campus quarters but also how much the people in those quarters even knew about their ministry. It turned out that it was not others' disapproval but their disinterest that campus clergymen had to overcome. My book analyzed where this handicap was great and small and suggested some compensatory remedies. Chief among these was the idea of professionalizing, inoculating themselves from both church and college administration by setting their own standards.

I learned something else from that research that did not appear in my book but was published as an article in the *American Journal of Sociology*, co-authored by Robert Mitchell. Mitchell had been a fellow graduate student at Columbia, and I knew that he had surveyed the *parish* ministers of the same denominations whose campus clergy I was to survey. I included a number of questions he asked, thus allowing us to test the notion that the campus ministry attracts the more liberal sector of the ministry. The evidence overwhelmingly supported that notion, which of course was no surprise. The organizational consequences of that systematic fact, however, were not so easy to foresee. These included:

(1) More persons are recruited and remain in the ministry because of the possibility of campus ministry positions.
(2) Liberals are removed from parishes, where their liberalism could be disruptive.
(3) Liberalism in the churches is sustained by the existence of campus ministries.
(4) Liberalism is returned to parishes through campus ministers who resume a parish ministry.
(5) Also through campus ministry liberalism enters parishes through student clients who become parish church members.
(6) Campus ministers have greater leadership potential in liberal causes because of their more flexible schedules.

We entitled the article 'The Segmentation of Radicalism' and showed how the church – via the campus ministry – is more likely to benefit from change-oriented clergy by having 'insulated' places to install them. By extension, this model might apply to, say, research and development divisions in industry, to war colleges in the military, and so forth, the key idea being organizations' ability to tolerate radicals in their midst with minimal disruption.

EDITORIAL LIFE

I have thus far described some of the sources of my academic or intellectual interests, and I have illustrated the role of both enduring influences and chance encounters. These episodes have thus been 'lifted out' of what in reality was a jumble of experiences that together formed the context of my scholarly life. That life has always been rewarding but it has not been as orderly as the illustrations would suggest. From 1960 until 1979, for example, I taught in Sociology Departments, and while religion remained my major focus, it represented only a small portion of my teaching duties. Correlatively, I was involved in researching topics other than religion, publishing papers, for example, on juvenile delinquency, higher education, methodology, selective perception, press coverage at sociology conventions, the history of ballet, and status inconsistency. Another editorial project illustrates once again the Glock influence. Charles Glock had been elected President of the Society for the Scientific Study of Religion and in 1969 asked me to serve as Program Chair. Because the Society was in dire financial straits, one of Glock's ideas was to commission some 'stock-taking' papers to be delivered at the 1969 meeting of the Society and then published by the SSSR as a fundraising book. Thus did *Beyond the Classics?* (Harper and Row, 1973) get born. While the essays, all by distinguished scholars, are variously successful in assessing the lasting impact of the classic works in the social scientific study of religion, all established clearly that the work published subsequent to those classics did not exhibit much of an accumulative character. Moreover, all the 'classics' were variations on the theme of secularization, and our essayists were telling us that we understood that process no better than had the 'founders' of the sociology of religion. The field obviously had not moved far beyond the classics, so Glock and I added the question mark to our title and wrote the Introduction and Epilogue accordingly.

Within a decade it was clear to all that 'secularization' needed rethinking, and I was asked by the 1981 Council of the SSSR to undertake that editorial task. I reflected back on the 1973 volume, which had added up to a general 'secularization' paradigm, but now, a decade later, we were observing spiritual forces not seriously imagined back in the 1960s. Fundamentalisms abounded, as did new religious movements, religious nationalisms, and unending religious conflicts. The new volume, with close to two dozen entries, thus tried to address the issue of 'the sacred in a secular age', which became the title of the book published by the University of California in 1985. I think the SSSR's goal was admirably reached in that while I don't think its sale has made the book a moneymaker for the Society, at the same time, it has been widely cited.

Starting in 1978 I spent four years as the Editor of the *Journal for the Scientific Study of Religion.* I had served on the editorial boards of several journals, and from 1970 to 1977, I was Advisory Editor in Sociology for D. C. Heath and Co. However, having responsibility for making provisional judgments about submitted manuscripts, seeking (and weighing) referees' comments, editing the manuscripts that are accepted, and ultimately receiving the rewards (and punishments) for the final product of a quarterly scholarly journal is a heady experience. At least it is heady for the first three years, after which the burdens begin to outweigh the rewards.

I had submitted enough of my own manuscripts to journals to know the difference between a well-run journal and a shoddy operation, and I took it as a challenge to make the *JSSR* a well-run journal. I instituted several changes from what I perceived to be the standard procedures of scholarly journals. For example, most referees' forms used by journals ask for an 'evaluation' of an anonymously authored article, a request all too often interpreted as meaning 'How would you, the referee, have written this article?' No two referees are likely to agree on this score, which explains why authors so frequently receive conflicting, and thus confusing, messages from editors. The form I devised asked first whether an article was good enough *as is* to be published in *JSSR* and second, if so, how might it be improved. This information enabled me to do two things: (1) accept a paper and leave to the author to decide whether to revise it, and (2) virtually eliminate the 'revise and resubmit' category. I believed (and still believe) that most authors submit what they regard are their best efforts; my primary job as editor was to render, with the help of referees, a judgment that such efforts were or were not good enough to be published.

A second change addressed the problem of turn-around time. As was the case when I put together the book, *The Sacred in a Secular Age*, I was not about to tolerate referees who accepted an assignment and then delayed carrying it out. I asked for responses within two weeks, therefore, and if they were not forthcoming I sought substitute referees. There were important exceptions, however, that further served to speed up the process, and those were the cases in which one referee's response came in on time and was strongly in accord with my own evaluation, either positive or negative. I reasoned that no third judgment would be sufficient to change the verdict, so I did not wait for it. Problems arose where both my evaluation and that of one or both referees were lukewarm, but such cases were rarer than might be supposed.

Considerable agreement on standards of excellence exists if evaluators are encouraged to judge, rather than rewrite, other people's
work.

I have discussed – and exemplified – three types of influences on
my scholarly study of religion: (1) the sources of my long-term
interests, (2) the enduring impact of certain people and organizations, and (3) the coincidental or chance event. I also have
shown how much of my scholarly life has involved editorial work
in one or another form. There remain two more tasks. The first is to
present some case studies, instances in my research where the
above three influences can be seen to meet, merge, even conflict.
If one of the goals of the present volume is to convey how studies
in religion are done, it will probably best be conveyed this way. By
looking at further case studies there is revealed, in my case, the two
distinct themes mentioned early in this essay: first, exploring how
and why Protestantism lost custodianship of American culture,
and, second, speculating on what institution, if any, now holds that
custodianship.

The second remaining task is less precise, calling as it does for
reflection on theoretical approaches, on what, beyond facts, might I
have learned, and, finally, on whether I see any 'larger' meaning in
what I have done.

SECULARIZATION, OR THE LOSS OF CUSTODIANSHIP

I have already indicated how my dissertation reflected an interest
in the secularization process, and how, though chosen fortuitously,
the topic of the campus ministry also showed a decline in Protestantism's involvement in higher education. In fact the general
subject of secularization appears and reappears in my work. For
example, in 1966, *The American Journal of Sociology* published a
revised version of my MA thesis entitled 'Secularization, Incorporation, and Social Relations'. Using secondary data (from a
survey of social science professors in the waning years of the
McCarthy period), I selected the 56 private colleges that ranged
from those still closely controlled by churches to those with no
religious control, plus a third group in the middle. This was the
measure of secularization. The authors of the original study (Paul
F. Lazarsfeld and Wagner Thielens, *The Academic Mind*) had
already developed a measure of quality for each campus. I

therefore investigated a very Durkheimian question drawn from his *Division of Labor*: Is it possible that with the loss of mechanical solidarity (that is, secularization) an alternative source of solidarity may emerge? The overwhelming evidence was positive. Faculty members at strongly religious schools, especially low quality religious schools, were likely to say that they felt supported by their administration, to look favorably upon their working conditions, characterize faculty relations as good, etc. These measures of solidarity declined in low quality schools with weak religious control, and declined further in low quality schools with no religious affiliation at all.

Significantly, just the reverse was the case with high quality schools. There the measures of solidarity *increased* with secularization, suggesting that an alternative moral code operated. As Durkheim would say: organic solidarity replaced mechanical solidarity.

I returned to the theme of secularization in a study of ballet history employing Weber's notion of rationalization, and in several papers on Tocqueville's relevance to contemporary society. However, it was in a paper, 'Religious Pluralism and Social Order' that I distinguished secularization as loss of sovereignty from secularization as loss of centrality. The first is reflected in Protestantism's loss of custodianship of American culture, while the second allows a way to understand continued (or renewed) involvement of Americans in the church in spite of the first kind of loss. These concepts helped me think through several more problems, such as the changing relationship between religion and power in this century, and the political vulnerability of the Christian right.

Something was still missing, however, something that became clearer in the mid-1980s, when I taught a graduate seminar on religion and ethnicity. Everybody knows the close ties between these two identities, but surprisingly little is known beyond mere description. For example, it is well established fact that Italian-Americans who strongly identify themselves as Italian are more likely to identify themselves as Roman Catholic also. But in the event these identities fade, which fades first? Would Polish-American Catholic parents rather their child marry a Polish Protestant or an Irish Catholic? Little is known in a systematic way about such issues.

While most of my research during the 1980s continued to focus on religion and politics, with the help of that seminar I began to muse about religion, ethnicity, and their role in identity formation. In actuality I did not advance far with that precise issue of the interplay of religion and ethnic identity. Instead, what proved productive was thinking about religious identity *as if* it were ethnic identity – which, in a way, it is in the case of Jews, Amish, and some others. People generally regard their ethnicity as inherited – a 'given' – but many also regard their religious identity as inherited, even as many others regard it as freely chosen.

Evidence was mounting during the 1980s that religious identity was undergoing a significant shift away from being seen as inherited and becoming instead freely chosen. Religions increasingly competed in a marketplace where people decreasingly exhibited brand loyalty. But the *degree* to which this was true was no doubt variable, and I wanted to know why. In the Fall of 1987 I delivered the Presidential Address to the Society for the Scientific Study of Religion, entitled 'Religion and the Persistence of Identity'. Though largely speculative, it served also as a research proposal to the Lilly Endowment, which awarded me (along with several others in a 'package' grant) a generous sum to explore my ideas.

My talk opened with an anecdote about the annual Greek Festival held each summer in Santa Barbara. The food booths were operated by the Greek Orthodox Parish in town, but the signs on the booths indicated that the sponsor was simply the 'Greek Church'. Anyone inheriting Greek ethnicity, it seems, also inherited the religion that goes with it. This was an example of the kind of inherited religion that seemed to be fading, and I wanted to see how ethnicity of all sorts 'carried' – or failed to 'carry' – religious identity.

I also imagined that the persistence, the 'inheritability', of religious identity varied by region. This, I thought, is true in at least two senses: first, some regions have much richer ethnic subcultures than other regions, and, second, some regions (especially the South) themselves act like ethnic groups and thus 'bequeath' their religion. I expected to find, among intense ethnic subcultures and in regions with strong regional identity, that religion would more likely be regarded as inherited.

Four states were selected with these considerations in mind: (1) Massachusetts because of its strong ethnic communities and its status as a 'Yankee' state, (2) North Carolina because of its near homogeneity ethnically but strong identity as a 'Southern' state with a conservative Protestant history, (3) California because of its mobile population, and (4) Ohio because of its reputation for being a microcosm of America. A commercial survey company was employed to conduct telephone interviews with about 650 adults in each state. This was done in Fall 1988 and my analysis began the next Spring.

As with all surveys I know about, some things worked as expected and others did not. In this case regional differences proved to be strong and in the direction expected, but ethnicity was not a factor. This was not because people no longer claimed strong ethnic identity but because whether they did or did not had no impact on whether they regarded religion as inherited or freely chosen. This last variable, incidentally, was shown to be related to ('explained by') the degree people exhibited 'personal autonomy', which in turn was inversely related to: (a) how attached people were to their local communities, and (b) how strongly they held to a conventional morality in the sphere of family and sexual matters. Since these things varied greatly by denomination within regions, my resulting analysis mapped out where religious practices were most and least stable, and why. The book, published in 1992 as *Religion and Personal Autonomy*, carried the subtitle, *The Third Disestablishment in America* because, I argued, the shift wherein religion loses its inheritability is as important as the Founders' decision in the First Amendment to the Constitution to outlaw any established church (the first disestablishment) or the realization by the time of World War I that America was no longer a Protestant nation (the second disestablishment). In the same year, my *The Protestant Presence in Twentieth-Century America* was also published. It is a collection of essays, most of which deal in some fashion with secularization. Together the two books help us understand what the loss of Protestant custodianship means in American culture.

What had led me to take up this line of research came in the mid-1980s when I was asked to contribute a chapter for a book, *Liberal Protestantism: Problems and Prospects*. In this essay I explored the notion of how the sacred, once thought to reside almost exclusively in Protestant churches in America, had seemingly 'seeped out' of those vessels. Searching the thesaurus for a way to express more elegantly the idea of seeping, I encountered the word 'extravasate', meaning 'to pass by infiltration or diffusion from a proper vessel or channel (as a blood vessel) into surrounding tissue'. I thus entitled my essay 'The Extravasation of the Sacred'. Extravasation does not describe wounds where blood is lost, however, because, in extra-vasating, blood is not lost but merely spreads elsewhere (thus, for example, a black-and-blue mark). This image fit well with my thinking about sacredness outside of churches and became yet another way in which I wrote about secularization and, in this case, where the sacred in society is to be found.

CIVIL RELIGION: SHARING IN THE SACRED

This loss of custodianship by Protestantism, as I have said, does not mean that it is devoid of the sacred but only that it has lost something of what it once had in greater amount. The question can be asked, then, where the 'lost' sacred has gone. Classic social thought would have it simply disappear ('Is *nothing* sacred anymore?'), but that always struck me as too simplistic. This question, of course, is more difficult to frame than is the question regarding the secularization of traditional religious institutions. It is also more difficult to imagine what evidence is appropriate should some answer be suggested.

Thinking about this second theme began during graduate school days. In the 1950s the Warren Court was rendering a number of decisions that changed significantly the socio-moral contours of American society. Covering the Court for *The NY Times* during the period was Anthony Lewis, a person who not only applauded most if not all the changes but who also had a scholar's appreciation for the symbolism attached to those changes. Lewis wrote often about the Supreme Court as the moral leader of the nation, much as Dean Eugene Rostow of the Yale Law School referred to the Court as conducting a 'vital national seminar'. Such ideas intrigued me and fed my curiosity about where, if not in churches, was moral suasion being exercised. I wrote an article, 'Religion and the 'Informing' of Culture' (1963), in which I explored the notion that government agencies were supplanting religious organizations in molding public morality and thus were in some sense being 'religious' themselves. I even referred to a possible 'civic religion' that might be found in America.

When in 1965 I moved to the University of Wisconsin I became a participant in a faculty seminar on 'law and society' that included lawyers and political scientists as well as sociologists. Not only were some of the seminar readings pertinent to my interests in legal matters but also I discovered a political scientist, Kenneth Dolbeare, whose interests in courts coincided with mine. Together we published a 1969 article ('The Political Party Basis of Attitudes Toward the U.S. Supreme Court') showing, with the help of poll data going back to the 1930s, that the public's approval rating of the Supreme Court rests importantly on which party occupies the White House. We also experimented with small-scale surveys in the state of Wisconsin of newspaper editors, clergy, chairs of county party organizations, and the public at large to determine their relative knowledge and evaluation of the Supreme Court. Not surprisingly, we found that all categories of leaders, compared with the public at large, were far more knowledgeable of what the Court had done, but unlike the public at large, whose political values were essentially unrelated to their approval of the Court's actions, leaders' evaluation of the Court was strongly influenced by whether they were conservative or liberal, the latter indicating much higher approval levels in the 1960s.

Dolbeare and I inferred from these data that the Court's moral suasion was certainly not automatic. We also reasoned that if we were to investigate the public's response to the Supreme Court – if we were indeed going to gauge its moral suasion in public affairs – we would have to focus on a contemporary issue visible enough to have reached the public's consciousness. That limited our choice at the time to two areas – the public school desegregation decision in 1954 or the school prayer (1962) and Bible-reading (1963) decisions – both of which were known to about three-quarters of the public. On all other issues knowledge of a decision was held by fewer than half and often fewer than a third of the population. It was unimportant to us that the decision we would study dealt substantively with religion; it was the Court's symbolic role as moral arbiter that interested us. But, reasoning that more than a decade had elapsed since the *Brown v. Topeka Board of Education* desegregation decision, we chose the more recent schoolhouse religion decisions to study.

We were aware of a national mail survey of elementary school districts conducted in 1960 by Professor R. B. Dierenfield of Macalester College, inquiring into their use of Bible-reading and morning prayer. Published in 1962 with the title *Religion in American Public Schools*, Dierenfield's results showed that both practices were widespread (80 percent and 87 percent) in the South, nearly as widespread in the East (62 percent and 83 percent), and rare in the West (14 percent and 14 percent). In the Midwest, the figures were 28 percent and 38 percent. We requested the 1960 names and addresses from Professor Dierenfield and resurveyed all of the districts in 1967 which had reported engaging in religious practices in 1960. Superintendents of those districts in the East reported general compliance with the Court's decisions (93 percent); in the South they reported general noncompliance (only 21 percent complying); and, in the Midwest, about half (54 percent) reported complying. (So few districts in the West were engaging in religious practices in 1960 that the 'compliance' rate – 62 percent – is based on too few cases to be meaningful.)

Since our interest lay chiefly in the social forces – including the Supreme Court's pronouncements themselves – that led to compliance or noncompliance, we sought out four small cities in a single midwest state to study carefully. All were county seats, all had daily newspapers, and each was small enough to have only one school district. Superintendents in two cities had reported compliance with the Court's order, while superintendents in the other two had reported continuing religious practices. Our plan called for a comparison of the two pairs.

The Walter E. Meyer Institute of Law had granted us funds to conduct field work. The first step was to send a graduate assistant to the four cities to explore the newspaper records dating from the 1962 *Engel v. Vitale* decision. To our surprise, he uncovered nothing; at least locally, these four cities seemed totally undisturbed by both that ruling and the 1963 *Schempp* ruling. The newspapers reported the decisions, of course, but their relevance locally went unremarked. The second step confirmed such quiescence. When Dolbeare and I interviewed the Superintendent in each city we were told that no controversy had been stirred by those decisions, but – more importantly for our study – neither was there cessation of religious practices in any of the public schools, even in the two cities whose Superintendents had indicated compliance in the mail survey! We had no choice than to change research strategies; instead of documenting the Supreme Court's moral suasion and how it filtered down to some localities, but not others, we switched to an investigation of how the Court can pronounce on a vital, publicized issue and have virtually no local effect whatsoever. Our book was published in 1971 with the title, *The School Prayer Decisions: From Court Policy to Local Practice*. I came away from that research project convinced that, if the Supreme Court was increasingly the moral arbiter in American culture – if it was the locus of a 'vital national seminar', its judges 'nine high priests', as they have been called – then research more subtle than we had conducted would be required.

But we did learn some things. First, it became clear that, while the Court had outlawed schoolhouse religion on the grounds that it violated the No Establishment Clause of the First Amendment, many persons – including reasonably cosmopolitan school officials – understood the Court's ruling to be instead a violation of the Free Exercise Clause. That is to say, compliance was not necessary because 'everybody' wanted schoolhouse religion. Second, compliance with the Court's ruling required a decisive 'trigger'; somebody had to complain and insist on compliance, and in these towns anyway, nobody did that. The school superintendents were the logical persons to enforce the new law, but they made it clear that for them to do so would cost them support they needed in achieving other, and, to them, more important goals. Third – and this lesson shows up in further work I have done on judicial decision-making – it became clear that if the Supreme Court exerts moral suasion it does not do so directly through public opinion. Too many filters exist between the Court and people-in-the-street for that to happen automatically; intermediate agents are necessary.

The experience with the schoolhouse religion research did nothing to dampen my interest in the culture and institutions of civic religion, however. I had read Robert Bellah's justly famous *Daedalus* essay on civil religion in 1967 and saw that he was attempting to identify the same phenomenon that fascinated me. During the next five years I produced three or four essays dealing with this topic, but it remained more of a sideline interest until the coincidental receipt of two quite unrelated letters. One was from the National Institutes of Health discouraging me from seeking its funds to pursue research on religion among retirees unless I joined up with gerontologists and medical doctors. The other was a letter from the Book Review Editor of *Sociological Analysis* (now *Sociology of Religion*), inviting me to write a bibliographic essay on civil religion to appear in the Summer 1976 issue devoted entirely to that subject.

Faced with a choice between modifying a research project to such an extent that it would no longer reflect my interests, or spending time reading on a topic of great interest, I had no hesitation; a renewed devotion to the topic of civil religion was the result. Soon after this decision was made, moreover, I visited Mexico City for the first time and was hosted by Guillermo Margadant, an engaging and brilliant professor of comparative law at the National University of Mexico. On previous visits in that country I had observed the visible and colorful signs of patriotic fervor, but it was in conversations with Margadant that I began to see differences in the complex relationship between religion and politics in our two countries. Unlike the US where the two feed off one another, and thus encourage a 'civil' religion, in Mexico religion and politics are antagonistic, with the consequence that any civil religion is inhibited.

Why that is the case is easier to say than to understand, however, so, with a one-semester sabbatical leave from the University of Arizona, I moved my family to Mexico City to study the situation more closely. I had done considerable reading about the history of Mexico, but the opportunities to interview people in politics and education, to note the frequent public displays of political ideology, and read the daily press enabled me to 'see' how religion and nationalism were (un)related in Mexico. From one standpoint this contrast with the US was odd, because both countries fought wars of independence and civil wars; both were greatly influenced by Enlightenment political philosophy; both are ethnically diverse while officially celebrating unity; and both honor national 'saints' who figured prominently in their establishment as autonomous nation-states.

But even though virtually every taxi driver carries a medal of the Virgin of Guadalupe on his dashboard, and even though Mexico is regarded by many as the most 'Catholic' country in Latin America, Mexico is secular in a way that the US could never be. For example, the government effectively controls church property and the deployment of priests. It is the state that registers births and deaths but also conducts all official marriages. Public office holders may not attend religious services. The church, though visible, and cultic practices, though widespread, have not been blended into Mexico's vibrant and colorful political life. The essay I wrote during that sabbatical was an effort to explain why by contrasting Mexico with the US.

The essay was about two or three times the size of an ordinary journal article, however, while not long enough for a book. In Summer 1977, after returning from Mexico, I wrote to Robert Bellah and suggested that we jointly publish as a book the various essays we had each written about civil religion.

I had known Bob Bellah for many years and, while not closely acquainted, I knew he felt considerable frustration, as did I, over the failure of many scholars to give sensible attention to the civil religion concept as he had analyzed it in several articles and a book. Many critics expressed doubt that such a thing existed, or that it existed as more than a value position. Though I had not experienced the same critical reception to my articles on civil religion, I shared Bellah's views on the subject. We thought that essays that included applications of the civil religion idea to Mexico, Japan, and Italy as well as the US might advance the scholarly conversation. Our essays were published in 1980 with the title, *Varieties of Civil Religion*. Alas, reviews of the book, while not unfavorable, suggested that continued confusion about the concept was still rampant. Independently of one another Bellah and I essentially dropped the term from our vocabularies. Although the *idea* of a civil religion remains fruitful for me, I have found using the term 'legitimating myth' is less likely to invite the question 'Do you believe it?' and more likely to be met with 'How do you understand it?' Real discussion might then follow. I confess, however, that since the publication of *Varieties* I have written about civil religion in a half dozen essays, and my book, currently in press, gives a prominent place to that phenomenon.

REFLECTIONS

The novelist Wallace Stegner wrote 'Ambition is a path, not a destination.' Had I been asked about my ambition at the time I entered graduate work in sociology, my answer would have been 'to return as a teacher at a small private college similar to my own undergraduate college'. Encounter with my Columbia University professors, however, and discovering how much excitement could be generated by committing ideas to paper, led my ambition down the path of scholarly research and the wish for a university setting and teaching load that permitted such research. By the time I was offered a first job at Yale, where publishing research was of course expected, I no longer worried that, if I did not publish, others would see that I perished; my own sense of self was all I needed as motivation.

And so it has been since 1960 as a faculty member at four universities – a blend of desire and opportunity that has allowed me a satisfying professional life with only the normal number of disappointments and frustrations. I remain interested primarily in the same issues that drew me to the sociology of religion in the first place: Why and how did religious institutions lose their moral authority in modern societies, and what if anything has replaced them? It seems clear that the great moral issues of our day, the issues that engage our consciences and appear insoluble at times, are perhaps no longer even framed as 'religious' issues, at least by all participants. Yet such matters as abortion, homosexuality, euthanasia, parental and child rights, the death penalty – even health care, social welfare, and immigration policy – touch American citizens profoundly. By any reasonable measure they *are* religious issues because they reflect worldviews, the deep-seated convictions by which people make sense of the world. How we develop positions on these questions, where we search for light on them, and by what authority we act on them, are to me questions just as vital now as they were in the 1950s.

I want, then, to reflect on my efforts over the years to understand these matters by addressing the three questions earlier identified: (1) How, if at all, have my theoretical approaches changed? (2) What, beyond some facts, have I learned? (3) Is there a 'larger meaning' to it?

1   Theoretical Approaches

If the issues that animate me today remain fundamentally the same issues that drew me into the sociology of religion four decades ago, certainly it is the case that my theoretical (and methodological) approaches have undergone change. Most important, I think, is my increased concern to situate the subject matter of my research in history. I remain a committed believer in the merits of survey research, but I have seen many survey researchers go off the deep end into infinite quantification (because technically it is easy to do now). It has always been true that surveys alone tend toward the ahistorical, rendering desiccated accounts of the human situation that may have only fleeting validity. Also unfortunate, in my view, is the opposite error: compensating by what is often called 'thick description' or simply 'narrative', which is to gamble on losing the theoretical storyline in rich but irrelevant detail. Historians themselves must contend with this danger too if they have no theoretical storyline. To keep some balance between 'evidence' and 'storyline' (or fact and theory, as these often are misleadingly labeled), scholars should locate their topics in some more abstract setting, and I have obviously found my more abstract settings in history.

Granted, I am not an historian, and my primary data generally come from surveys, not library archives. But someone who reads in chronological order my books will see – as I did not at the time but can now – that I relied increasingly on historical context not only to help me tell a convincing story but also to discern that story.

This, perhaps, was no accident. It happens that in my first year at Columbia I took a course on historical methods in sociological research – for which I wrote a paper on Norwegian immigration into America in the first half of the nineteenth century. Subsequently it was published as 'The Migrating Sect' – but never then did I think that I would turn repeatedly to historical settings for guidance in how to argue my case. The story I told about the Norwegians only incidentally dealt with their 'Norwegian-ness' because I was making a theoretical argument that migrants are especially vulnerable to internal bickering and schism if religious sentiment is among their motives for migrating. I 'used' history to help tell my sect story, where an historian might have 'used' a theory of sect formation and development to help tell a story about Norwegian immigration. I would like to think that the historian's product and the sociologist's product are equally valid, and – if done well – may even be indistinguishable, however divergent their orders of production.

Perhaps I can look back and see another development in my theoretical viewpoint. As was the case with virtually all sociologists of religion of my generation, 'secularization' was (and, for some, remains) the master model by which religion in society is to be understood. The applicability of certain elements of the model is undeniable, of course, but it is now clear that care must be taken in those applications. For example, as religious pluralism replaces religious homogeneity, religion 'changes', but it does not necessarily 'decline'. Or, to cite another example, the shift from a rural, agriculturally-based economy to an urban, industrialized economy diminishes the power of religious organizations in some ways, but that change can actually enhance the power of those bodies in other ways. Democratization has a similar effect, which was Tocqueville's great insight during his early nineteenth-century visit to America.

I think I was early sensitized to the inadequacy of the secularization model because of my interest in alternative institutions of moral authority. To inquire into the 'religious' functioning of judicial decision-making is to entertain the possibility that the sacred has not declined but merely relocated. In similar fashion, an interest in civil religion takes one away from churches as centers of the sacred and toward other arenas where religious beliefs and rituals might be observed.

In summary, my theoretical and methodological approaches, even as they have modified over time, have – I can now see in retrospect – been directed toward understanding a Durkheimian portrait of religion and society that Talcott Parsons conveyed most succinctly. Parsons said, speaking of the overall thrust of *The Elementary Forms*, that its great lesson is not that religion is a social phenomenon so much as society is a religious phenomenon. Sometimes, therefore, religion is found in unexpected places.

2   What I Have Learned

A few pages above I stated that I remain interested in the issues that drew me into the sociology of religion. One could go through the material I have published, especially the data-based articles, and discover many 'facts'; it might be said, therefore, that I 'learned' those facts. But I take the challenge here to be asking what new understandings or perspectives might those facts suggest. I offer two:

In both accepting and rejecting the secularization model, I felt the need to think about organized religion's 'importance' in society. Whether churches were declining or not, some kind of scheme was needed to 'see' what was happening and then develop empirical measures of what is being seen. I indicated at the beginning of this essay that the period from my great grandfather's lifespan through my grandfather's and then my father's – all Methodist clergymen – bequeathed to me the sense that certainly Methodism (and probably all mainline Protestantism, and maybe all churches) had declined in importance. But what did that mean? In an essay drafted initially in 1976 for oral presentation, I began developing a scheme that distinguished between religion's 'sovereignty' and 'centrality'. Sovereignty refers chiefly to importance along structural lines, whereas centrality refers chiefly to importance people are free to assign or not assign to religion. This distinction I elaborated somewhat in a paper for a another conference in 1982, and elaborated it somewhat more for use as a Preface in my 1992 book of essays, *The Protestant Presence in Twentieth-Century America*.

The distinction allowed me to 'learn' that churches could lose sovereignty without losing centrality, a point of no great profundity perhaps, but it also allowed me to see that loss of sovereignty indicates a change in the relationship of churches to culture, and *that* alteration inevitably changes the meaning of church involvement irrespective of its degree of centrality. Put another way, churches can still be important in the lives of their members, but churches cannot retain (or regain) the structural importance for their members that they once had. That key Tocquevillean insight – that churches are vital voluntary associations for conveying their members' social and political interests to centers of power – decreasingly holds. Churches have become *too* voluntary to do that; as discussed above, they have declined sharply in 'inheritability'. This much I think I have learned. I think also it flows out of and helps explain my grandfather's conversion from evangelical to liberal Protestantism, my father's frustration in the parish ministry, and my own youthful ambivalence toward a career in the church. Whatever the merits of these last assertions, I do know that *Religion and Personal Autonomy* was my effort to research and nail down these ideas about religion's sovereignty and centrality. In retrospect it is also possible to look upon my dissertation, and later *The Campus Clergyman* and a number of articles, as earlier efforts to struggle with these themes.

If that first lesson deals with why and how churches lost moral authority, the second (and vaguer) lesson deals with the issue of what, if anything, now exercises that moral authority. I have earlier in this essay discussed my first major foray into this issue in the book I co-authored with Dolbeare, *The School Prayer Decisions*. I certainly learned a lot from that experience, especially how ineffective the judicial system is in changing people's behavior unless it has enforcement mechanisms. Without such mechanisms, then only if citizens squawk about violations of their constitutional rights, and pay the cost to have themselves represented, will anything be done to get compliance with Supreme Court rulings. Compliance won't come about just because it is a 'sacred' Court issuing the ruling. On this score the judiciary seems not to have replaced the priesthood, nor the courts churches.

But I was expecting too much, no doubt; I was too literal in my expectations. Just as people do not jump through hoops because judges tell them to, neither did people do it at the priests' command. Durkheim is misread if it is thought that he says 'religion unifies' and *therefore* speaks with authority. Properly understood, Durkheim was saying that the experience of unity will be rendered in religious terms, and among the small-scale Arunta it was. Nothing like that is possible in large-scale America, and to expect it is therefore folly. What is not folly is to look at where conflict is resolved and where, therefore, unity may be experienced in large-scale societies.

I think I learned, consequently, that even if legal combatants do not exit the courtroom arm in arm, they are provided with a ritual, and, more importantly, a language by which they can communicate. Moreover, persons not involved in that case can make inferences about what might be 'right' in similar cases. Thus, the sum of judicial rulings takes on something of the qualities of a sacred text. This lesson is less clear than the first, but it may turn out to be profounder. As I wrote in one essay, I have long been in awe of jurisprudence as the place where sacred and profane meet, but that orientation has not thus far yielded me as much understanding as I might hope for. In any event, this issue is the major bone I chew on in my next book.

3   The Larger Meaning of It All

At the risk of appearing to have no modesty left, I am asked to respond to an even more abstract question: What does it all mean? If I rephrase the question – What implications does my research have for any of the major issues Americans face today? – then I think I can respond in two ways.

First, after a half-century of Supreme Court zigging and zagging on the church–state issue, current doctrines regarding 'free exercise' and 'no establishment' of religion seem reasonably fixed, both legally and – when not inflamed by yahoo populists – in the public's understanding. Applying those doctrines can be murky, but the principles underlying them are not.

As I write this essay, the Republicans have the majority in Congress, and Newt Gingrich is threatening a Constitutional Amendment to allow 'voluntary' individual and group prayer in the public schools (a measure on which even President Clinton has lent his support!). Inasmuch as such prayer is possible right now – subject only to regulation as to time, place, and manner – one has to wonder what the real objective is of the Religious Right for whom Gingrich is the mouthpiece. But as my studies, as well as those of numerous others, make clear, there is little or no likelihood of once again having *government-sponsored* religious exercise in public schools or anywhere else. The reason is really quite simple, though obviously many have yet to think it through. It is that government sponsorship of religion, however slight, can be a restriction of the religious liberty of others, however few; and Americans prize religious liberty. Thus pious-sounding demands directed toward state officials will almost certainly be met with equally pious demands that those officials stay out of 'our' religion. For all of the noise from the Religious Right that 'secular humanism' has replaced religion in public affairs, therefore, my studies lead me to conclude that it is not the *ideology* of secular humanism that is being promulgated by schools, courts, the welfare system, etc. Rather, what is labeled 'secular humanism' is merely the *language* that is required when negotiation occurs among people of differing religious perspectives – required, that is, if the religious language used by one portion of the population is not to be forced onto all. American history can be read, especially since the Civil War, as an ever increasing realization that Protestant Christianity had thoroughly infused American institutions and culture, and this fact unfairly burdens those not sharing that religious outlook. Custodianship declined.

In throwing out the Protestant Christian language 'baby', however, the 'bath water' of all value language seems also to have been tossed, leading some observers to claim that secular humanism, the language of adjudication, has been elevated to Secular Humanism, the denial of God. This brings up my second response. Americans generally find themselves devoid of any language with sufficient currency and universality to make compromise possible between profoundly held positions. The remarks elsewhere in this essay regarding civil religion bear most directly on this issue, but I am speaking now of a more general phenomenon in American society – the absence of a level of discourse whereby persons holding differing value positions can communicate knowingly with each other. The naive conception of a civil religion made it into simply the 'common values' held by all citizens regardless of their 'religions'. But if that situation ever obtained in America, it certainly does not now.

Take, for example, the oft-quoted statement of House Speaker Newt Gingrich that 'It is impossible to maintain civilization with 12-year-olds having babies, with 15-year-olds killing each other, with 17-year-olds dying of AIDS and 18-year-olds getting diplomas they can't even read.' That is a good line; as *Newsweek* says, even 'George McGovern himself would no doubt agree.' So would any sensible citizen. The issue, however, is what to do about such problems, and with what justification. Gingrich says:

> I do have a vision of an America in which a belief in the Creator is once again at the center of defining being an American, and that is a radically different version of America than the secular anti-religious view of the left.
> (from a speech to the Heritage Foundation, quoted in *The New Yorker* (No. 21, 1994:7))

We can be sure that some Americans will nod their heads in agreement, just as other Americans will shake their heads in amazement. Where is the language that allows us all to honor life, liberty, the pursuit of happiness, and 'justice for all'? Somewhere there must be a level of abstraction – above the concepts of bullets and illegitimate births but below such concepts as God, Allah, or the Creator – in which all can participate. The Founders very likely looked upon the language of natural law as just such a level of abstraction, but strangely that language now seems out of reach.

Should values be taught in the public schools? Sure, but how? Should students learn about religion in school? Yes, but again how is it to be taught? Can citizens be expected to 'believe' in the rightness, if not of the laws as now articulated, at least in the justice those laws are meant to reflect? No doubt, but how do we protect the right of citizens to protest laws they believe are unjust? How, to put it in summary form, does a just and moral society steer a course between coercive conformity in belief and behavior, on the one hand, and anarchic nihilism on the other?

Do such ruminations have a larger meaning? My answer is they do, vague as that meaning might remain. As my late friend, Kenneth Underwood, put it eloquently:

> Once historical events become the source of judgment, and their uniqueness an occasion for review of assumptions which do not quite fit reality, time loses its monotony, its quality of uniform

succession. History takes on excitement and hope; and events, mystery and depth. This is the context of a creative society. People no longer just endure time; they have problems to solve, issues to win, causes to espouse.

(*The Church, The University, and Social Policy* [vol. 1], Middletown, CT: Wesleyan University Press, 1969:497)

The study of religion in contemporary American society has, for me, been just such a context.

12

Religion as Life and Text: Postmodern Re-figurations

EDITH WYSCHOGROD

Childhood can be thought of as the overcoming of an oscillation between transgression and transcendence. Transgression injects negation, the not, into human existence: sheer facticity, the physical situation of body and world, introduces the not of materiality, 'Don't touch, it burns.' Desire elicits the not of lack, 'I want that toy', or more ineluctably, 'I want something, I don't know what.' Ignorance opens up the not of fear, 'What is that shadow-thing that appears to be hurling itself at me?' Finally aggression brings forth the not of moral interdiction, 'Don't hit him, hitting hurts.' With the not of 'Thou shalt not injure' the transcendence of alterity, the constraint of the other as the limit of the child's world is introduced.

The point of entry into the self-overcoming that is growth and, with it, the taking up of the not into existence differs among children. These interlaced constitutive nots of childhood receive varying emphases depending on how they are configured by the child's disposition and circumstances (conversely, the child's disposition is as it is by virtue of the particular negations she or he stresses). For me the surmounting of ignorance, the hope of dispelling the terror of what was not known through labors of intelligence and imagination, and the neutralization of violence were the possibilities that I chose half-knowingly and, as it were, that chose me in my earliest remembered acts of self-overcoming.

These negations do not constitute an origin, the cause for my study of religion, but become after the fact as it were, moments in an expanding chain of meanings. I have come to see them not only as affecting the texture of my life but as prompting a key methodological challenge within the study of religion. Like the nots of my childhood, questions that seem to direct an inquiry about religious beliefs and practices are not starting points but provocations that change their meaning because meaning is constituted *post hoc* after having been augmented by further experiences. If this is so, then assertions that are made about the origins of a religious belief or practice are destabilized. With no fixed starting point for inquiry, the tales we tell about religion double back upon other tales, no one more reliable than another. What is more, when the study of religion focuses upon transcendence or the sacred, the object to be understood is already indescribable so that the problem of ineffability is doubled (Wyschogrod 1992). I would come to think about my life and work as continuous, as exhibiting the same methodological dilemmas, at once troubling because certainty is precluded and exhilarating because the chain of meanings in both life and work continues to expand, or in postmodern idiom, can never be brought to closure.

The childhood negations I have pinpointed then are not moorings but passageways through which I would retrace questions about religious experience, epistemic reliability and moral conduct, questions that enter into my recent work about fact and fiction, history and memory as well as ethics. I shall turn to the way in which I think these issues figure both in my own work and in the study of religion generally after some brief autobiographical narration.

The anti-auteurism of some recent literary criticism has called into question an appeal to the author's life on the grounds that the meaning of her text is reduced to authorial intent, to the contents of consciousness of the text's progenetrix. Yet the growth of biography and of confessional literature shows that, apart from prurient curiosity, these genres are motivated by the need for anchoring interpretation in a milieu. The introduction of life into interpretation, of the question 'says who', is not an appeal to an isolated subject, but rather a piggy-backing of worlds, as it were, those of author and text which unfold as a chain of interpenetrating meanings. It is in this spirit that I shall say something about the a/theological and devotional sides of my early life. What is more, having argued for the *Nachtraglichkeit*, the deferred meaning of significant experience, such narration is not an excursus but an attempt to configure the back and forth moments of life and work in a single narrative.

AUTOBIOGRAPHICAL RUMINATIONS

That the overcoming of the twin nots of ignorance and injury to the other should be my points of entry into the study of religion is not surprising. I was a child of the Enlightenment in more ways than one. Social justice to be achieved through the progress of art and science was the watchword of my parents, living exemplars of what Hegel calls the philosophy of reflection, of its strengths and its weaknesses. The metaphor of light associated with the etymology of the word reflection as bending back upon itself governs this conception. For my parents this meant the illumination of a world that could be mastered through scientific knowledge, *Wissenschaft* in the sense of cultural erudition and knowledge of the human subject made transparent through the insights of literature and psychology. Such knowledge would be placed in the service of a higher politics that would mitigate natural catastrophe and the evils of humankind. This anthropocentric view was the fruit of my father's bitter disillusionment with the efficacy of prayer and with religion generally captured *in nuce* in his oft-told story of an uncle clutching a prayer book and reciting psalms in a gesture of perfect Abrahamic faith as he was stabbed to death by invading Cossacks during the period just prior to the Russian Revolution. No theodicy extolling the value of human freedom could shake my father's conviction that justice must be humanly contrived and implemented. This perspective was not foreign to the New York ambiance in which I grew up.

That the piety of my maternal grandparents remained unshaken although they had comparable experiences conferred a sense of bewildering ambiguity upon my conception of the transcendent. Later John Wisdom's by now classical essay about whether the order displayed in a garden with no visible gardener attests divine presence or chance and, in another philosophical tradition, Emmanuel Levinas's account of the invisible but inexpugnable trace or track of transcendence in the human face, would articulate this ambiguity. My earliest efforts at grasping dilemmas of a larger sort were governed by the conviction that solutions could be discovered in books – never, of course, in media which my parents thought rotted the brain and corrupted moral sensibility – specifically those I found in the small library left with my grandparents by my maternal uncles, neatly aligned leather bound volumes in glass fronted oak cases. They included sets of the works of Oliver Goldsmith and Edgar Allan Poe, all of Gibbon's *Decline and Fall of the Roman Empire*, Macaulay's *History of England*, Goethe's *Hermann und Dorothea* (in German) and Nietzsche's *Zarathustra* (forbidden to me because perceived as dangerously decadent), works by Dickens,

Longfellow, Balzac. I suspect that the more political fiction about which I heard them speak – Zola, Dreiser, and I think Richard Wright – went along with my uncles when they left home.

There was also the poetry of Tennyson whose lines in 'Locksley Hall' I was later compelled to memorize at school and still create for me an ineluctable nostalgia for a certain vision of progess that, despite my postmodern skepticism, I still cherish:

For I dipt into the future, far as human eye could see
Saw the vision of the world, and all the wonders that would be;

Saw the heavens fill with commerce, argosies of magic sails,
Pilots of the purple twilight, dropping down with costly bales;

Heard the heavens fill with shouting, and there rained
   a ghastly dew

From the nation's airy navies grappling in the central blue;

Far along the world-wide whisper of the south-wind rushing warm

With the standard of the peoples plunging through the
   thunder-storm

Till the war-drums throbbed no longer and the battle flags
   were furled

In the Parliament of man, the Federation of the world.

A general encyclopedia and Bunyan's *Pilgrim's Progress*, works that left indelible imprints, were included in this collection. An illustration in the encyclopedia's article on India showed a hideously emaciated child, an example of that country's recurrent famines, a photograph that I have come to see as an emissary that would lead me to an interest in comparative philosophy and towards an ethics whose primary concern is the indigence of the other. The walls of selfhood had been breached by a certain empathy for this child of the sub-continent but not yet surmounted in that empathy renders the self rather than the other the point of reference for ethics. Bunyan's Pilgrim seemed to me a European explorer in the age of adventure chaffing under a burden, not of sin, a term marginal to my family's lexicon, but of lack of knowledge about a certain terrain called the 'slough of despond', to my child's eye merely another exotic port of call. I have spent much time in the academic study of religion in the hope of avoiding such hermeneutical mistakes. Inspired as I have been by the beauty, the terror and the moral ambiguities of frontier myths, I hope that my recent resettlement in Texas will not result in misprisions of the same sort.

Despite the cognitive dissonances I have described, I discerned in the synagogue worship and home rituals of my grandparents a celebratory affirmation of God's covenant with Abraham surrounded by that penumbra of sadness built into Judaism because Israelite history's dark moments are included in its observances. This history would become darker still and its salvific compensations withheld. The incorporation of the past into the present – 'Not only then, but today we are freed from the bondage of Egypt' – would rule my accounts of a scission or split in time, of a present that can never be wholly present, and of a future that holds in front of itself an archaic past. At the same time, one of my several Protestant aunts, low church and of Huguenot descent, for whom the redemptive events of the Gospel presented opportunities for joyous celebration, brought a Christian presence to family life. Her annual Christmas gift of the Elsie Dinsmore novels about the little girl whom Jesus loves, a child who could be myself, opened for me the aporia of incommensurable faiths. I welcomed this manifestation of difference, would not tamper with it, but would try to articulate this fissuring in my work. In short, my path to the study of religion was neither direct nor indirect, neither intentional nor unintentional but rather, in this *post hoc* reconstitution of it, inevitable.

FACT AND ERRANCY IN THE STUDY OF RELIGION

My entry into the discipline of religious studies came by way of the history of philosophy. The trajectory of my undergraduate work was governed on the one hand by the promise of progress in human affairs that the Enlightenment ideal of getting at the facts still held out. On the other, I turned to the contemplative tradition from Plato to Augustine as a way of overcoming this narrowly construed rationality. Although these perspectives are in many ways incommensurable, they are linked by the common ideal of certainty. In my recent essays on fact and fiction (Wyschogrod 1994), on history and memory (Wyschogrod [in press a]), I try to show the problems the matter of certainty raises for the student of religion.

Facts had long been a seduction and a lure for me as well as for what is generally referred to as the scientific study of religion, especially in its sociological aspects, because of the security promised by facts. What makes a fact a fact, according to an unreconstructed realism, is its intimate relation to truth. True propositions describe facts, objects and events just as they are and description is transparent towards its referents. Facts are what settle matters. To be sure, I understood that facts are not isolated but bound together in assemblages, the atomic constituents that, taken together, constitute our beliefs about the world, beliefs that no reasonable person could dispute. The conditions of observation could be regimented even further by restricting the field of observation to conform to the conditions of the laboratory rendering certainty greater still. The entire edifice rested on fact so that even if truth broke down when propositions about some elementary bit, some relevant fact, were shown to be false, it could be rebuilt in the light of new facts.

I saw that one might come by the facts in yet another way, through a process of elimination governed by some stipulated end, a procedure that enters into the study of religion when archaeological remains or ancient manuscripts require identification. On this view, the facts are what is left over after the whole to be studied is pared down and only what is relevant remains. This is the strategy of the detective who eliminates a host of inapplicable clues until only those that solve the crime are isolated. On this reading, facts mean salient facts.

I did not yet see how the observer's presuppositions affected her observations. An early acquaintance with Kant's problem – how can the conceptual order of our minds, an order independent of experience, be applied to reality – left my proto-positivism intact. The phenomenal world, the one to which, according to Kant, I had access, had to be the only one that counted and the noumenal, the unknown world of the thing-in-itself, so vexing to philosophers from Hegel to Nietzsche could simply be cordoned off on pragmatic grounds. The world of poetry and literature which loomed large in my life were similarly cordoned off, a universe of discourse protected from contamination by fact.

Omitted from my then view of truth as fact, was the notion that facts might already be theory-laden and that the idea of factuality itself might be ruled by a deeper ontology that was hidden from view. Nor did I see that facts might be bound up with interests, that the way in which facts are narrated might reflect the concerns of the narrator. What I found attractive about my early account of realism was not merely its claim to truth and certainty but rather a half-conscious identification of objectivity with fairness. The seductiveness of the view of truth I held was parasitic upon a more primordial notion of justice as the elimination of partiality. Just as the objectivity militated by the quest for facts elicited facts, so too, I thought, a standpoint of neutrality could be trusted to judge the interests of disputants. Unless all parties were held to a common measure, justice could not be attained. I later examined the relation of fact and objectivity to fairness in *Saints and Postmodernism* (1990: 156–9).

There are still ways in which the academic study of religion is embedded in the empirical tradition and necessarily so. After all, can the investigation of religion, the linguistic and ritual articulation of a community's or an individual's encounter with the sacred, wholly circumvent the common sense view of facts without risking the charge of ignorance or of making false claims? Do not questions about chronology and provenance, about whether an action did or did not occur, demand straightforward answers? Either Augustine wrote in the fourth century or he did not; either the Dead Sea scrolls emanated from the Essene community or they did not; either a particular Saivite ritual involves immersion or it does not.

But can the *arcana* of religion, the artifactual, literary and oral archives of communities and the testimonies of individuals, be brought within the purview of observation by eliciting the facts about them? How, for example, would knowing the year of Dogen's birth help to understand the structure of temporalization exhibited in his teachings? On the other hand, if one departs from the factual, can the logic of a sacred text and the logic of the strategy used to inquire into its meaning be made homologous so that the object of inquiry is permeable to interpretation? Or is interpretation necessarily estranged from its object? For example, could the circumventions some medieval thinkers use to depict what cannot be described, what is known as apophatic discourse, be interpreted through comparable categories of negation in the manner of the original text itself? These questions would later hold my interest when they emerged in my work as issues for postmodern speculation.

In sum, these considerations opened a number of seemingly irresolvable dilemmas: first, if facts as the term is generally understood contribute to interpretation in only a trivial way, what criteria of truth are to be invoked in interpretation? Second, if interpretation is primary and the appeal to fact becomes marginal, how can a fit be attained between text and the terms in which it is to be analyzed? If truth in interpretation entails that text and interpretation be somehow homologous then how are they to be distinguished? There would be no exit from a single continuous text, as it were. Just as in childhood self-overcoming with respect to the not of ignorance had been achieved by turning to fact, I had now to interrogate both fact and interpretation by turning to the strategies of recent French and German thought as I and other students of religion with a taste for Continental philosophy had previously turned to Tillich, Bultmann, Marcel and Buber.

If the conflict between fact and interpretation in the study of religion is not to eventuate in the abandonment of fact but rather if inquiry is to benefit from fact, I came to see that factuality must become reflexive so that interpretation remains attentive to the ontological, cultural, social and political conditions of its production, or to borrow a Hegelian phrase, factuality must become self-reflectively aware of itself. Equally important, the object of inquiry, for example, a belief or doctrine, must be explored, not only by asking what it says but also by regarding it as what Michel Foucault thinks of as a discursive formation, an ordered group of statements that do not point to facts but rather to their conditions of emergence. Beliefs and doctrines become meaningful in the light not only of what is said, their content, but of what can be said because a certain intellectual space has been opened up at the time of their production. What is crucial is the entry of time into the construal of fact. This is not to say that, for example, the earth ceases to be flat only after it is discovered to be round, but rather that the question of how the earth is to be envisaged is asked differently before and after this discovery.

What is more, interpretation cannot appeal to the symmetry between the internal logic of the text and its interpretation in any straightforward way. Derrida, sometimes thought to hold this view because the line between text and interpretation is blurred in his work, offers interesting suggestions for the interpreter of the canonical texts of Western religion and perhaps of some Asian religious texts, strategies for revealing what is hidden in these texts. A system of conceptual opposites, antithetical terms like body and soul, appearance and reality, that depend on one another are the philosophical simples of Western philosophy and theology. By reversing the order of the terms, it is possible to see how the one that previously connoted a disvalue actually sustains the coherence of the text. Once the terms are reversed, fresh meanings can be inscribed in the new conceptual space opened by the act of trans-position itself. Thus, for example, the use of negation in contem-porary deconstructive interpretations may superficially resemble negative theology so that they appear to be structurally similar but, in actuality, each appeals to quite different suppositions. Negative theology depends upon a theological center about which nothing can be said because language is inadequate to this fullness of being. But when fullness is turned upside down, becomes empty, that center is construed as an absence, the logic of the text is altered and opens previously unthinkable configurations, an errancy, wan-dering or leaching of meaning that is irrecoverable as that which is fully present. This strategy was of considerable help to me in developing a notion of saintliness that would reconfigure saintly altruism so as to transcend the sometimes saccharine qualities attributed to saints by traditional hagiographic literature.

The logic of negation broadly construed has, I believe, served me well in engaging other philosophical issues that would ulimately enter into my thinking about issues in the philosphy of religion. The critiques of truth and certainty by Nietzsche, Heidegger, Lacan, Derrida, Deleuze and Lyotard for whom negation figures significantly, enabled me to engage the analytic philosophies of Quine, Davidson, Searle, and Parfit whose questions about truth, meaning and reference could no longer easily be ignored. I found myself writing about the logic of counterfactuals in Quine and Derrida (Wyschogrod 1983), about how not only words but tools and artifacts generate meaning in Dewey and Lévi-Strauss (Wyschogrod 1981) about issues in comparative philosophy where the logic of negation comes to the fore, such as in the Jain account of knowledge (Wyschogrod 1985a) or in Quine and the Buddhist logicians Dignaga and Dharmakirti. I saw this work at the time of writing as a part of my continuous overcoming of my childhood not of ignorance. I now see these absorbing technical questions as a pianist sees finger exercises, a prelude to the all-absorbing question I would put to an ethically construed post-philosophy: how was I to reconfigure the 'Thou shalt not injure' of my childhood into an ethic for my own dark times. All this technical work on epistemo-logical issues was, in my view, done against the incessant rumbling of a genocidal century in which bodies and not words were at issue. I might from now until doomsday try to refine my accounts of speech and writing, meaning and reference; still the problem of the other would be at the forefront of my thinking. I would never truly make the linguistic turn.

ETHICS AND THE WITHHOLDING OF POWER: THE INCARNATE GOOD

Just as the historian of religion and the comparativist are confronted with seemingly insoluble epistemological dilemmas, the scholar of religion who approaches religion from the standpoint of ethics is confronted with a collapse that appears to paralyze further thought. Philosophy in its analytic, existential, and post-structuralist versions takes for granted the death of metaphysics as, in Wittgenstein's phrase, a proposition that stands fast for us. And if metaphysics is dead, what possible grounding can there be for ethics? It would not do simply to consider specific moral questions piecemeal in the fashion of some analytic ethicists because, as their critics argued, without consensus about background claims, ethics would flounder and moral issues would remain unresolved. The hope for some fresh moral theory that would provide a way out of this *cul-de-sac* is equally futile because moral theories are modeled upon theories in science but moral questions are not like questions in science. Nor had a way around Heidegger's repudiation of neo-Kantian and phenomenological moral philosophy been devised. At the same time, the scholar of religion could not overlook the ever more pressing social problems bound up with violence, race and gender which generated emotive utterances or were left to be discussed empirically by the social sciences.

Before some of these challenges received their standard formulation in the works of Alasdair MacIntyre, Stanley Hauerwas, Bernard Williams and others, a number of these difficulties were made thematic for me earlier in a series of steps. Graduate study with an excellent philosophy faculty deepened my acquaintance with key figures in the history of Western thought. Paul Tillich paved my way to the German nineteenth century and to Heidegger. Jacob Taubes of Columbia's Religion Department who later accepted a professorship at Free University, Berlin, mesmerized the small coterie of students in his seminars which, whatever their title, regularly turned out be Kabbalistic disquisitions about Pauline eschatology, Plato's *Laws* and Hegel's *Phenomenology*.[1] But it was some notions put forward by Henry M. Rosenthal, one of my undergraduate philosophy teachers, who like Calhoun at Yale and Pollock at Fordham wrote little, that became flashpoints for further thought.[2] A brilliant and maverick thinker with a radical vision of a moral universe, Rosenthal, speaking of Hobbes, held that no social contract could be negotiated without a prior cessation of violence so that there must have been a social contract before the agreements of the actual social contract were reached. In the light of this contention, I could now interpret the 'Thou shalt not injure' of my childhood as my personal preliminary draft of a social contract, the kind of contract Rosenthal claimed had become in a larger context the *a priori* of history. This view opened the question that would continue to drive my work: what conditions need to be present in order to make a cessation of violence possible?

Rosenthal also introduced the astonishing notion of ethical corporeality: 'The durational human body is an ethical body. We put this in the Kantian metaphor: it is a good will made flesh and a born loser,' he would say. What is a philosopher of religion to make of this? For me the issue would become '*How* can the good will be made flesh, *how* can it be incarnationally inscribed?' With the discovery of the philosophy of French Jewish philosopher Emmanuel Levinas, whom I learned about from Paul Ricoeur, I found a corporeal locus for the proscription against violence in the vulnerable flesh of the Other. Gripped by his vision of alterity, I wrote *Emmanuel Levinas: The Problem of Ethical Metaphysics* (1974), a study of what happens when the roles of metaphysics and ethics are reversed so that ethics grounds metaphysics without at the same time becoming a foundation for metaphysics.[3] Ethics on this reading is a call to responsibility through the advent of the other person, the one who remains other because she cannot become a content of consciousness, an item of knowledge. The encounter with the Other as other is an encounter with the human face, with an epiphany that commands, 'Thou shalt not kill.' Through a consideration of alterity, I hoped to suggest a new context for ethics that would have a direct bearing upon seemingly insoluble social ills.

Levinas turned to the radical transcendence of the Other as the starting point (not the origin in any causal sense) of ethics. Not only does ethics begin with the Other but Levinas makes the bolder claim that philosophy begins with ethics: ethics is first philosophy.

The face of the Other has special significance. What is given in the datum of the face is neither a form nor a sign to be interpreted, but something experienced before thought or reflection as a solicitation, a claim. The bodily vulnerability of the Other who is in my vicinity, who is near (from the Latin *vicinus* or neighbor), disrupts my world with a demand: 'Thou shalt not harm me.' The command's force derives from the Other's defenselessness and exposure.

But the Other is not only perceived as near. The space between us is also assymetrical, curved so that no matter where the other is in physical space, the Other *qua* Other is perceived as at a height. The demand authorized by this elevation is such that I put myself in her place, substitute for her or him, give up all I am and have for the Other. It is clear that a starving child appeals in this way. I came to see the Other's command in its negative form, 'Thou shalt not injure this other', as constituting a pre-condition for ethics and the positive command, 'Thou shalt become hostage for the other', (departing on this point from Levinas) as weighing only upon the exceptional individual. Only the saint can command the resources for its fulfillment. For Levinas, who had appropriated modernity's critiques of religion but still wished to leave the question of transcendence open, the ethical is seen to derive its strength from elsewhere, the track or trace of an altogether Other, an archaic transcendence that once passed by and is now present as an absence.

What had I, in my efforts to think about religion, learned from Levinas about self and Other? I had discovered through the tradition of criticism from Hume and Nietzsche to Sartre, Bataille and Derrida that, if the phrase 'being a person' had any meaning, it could involve no substantive entity, no Cartesian *cogito*, no stable presentness, no moral core, that in fact all meaning had been evacuated from the term. But now I could say that to be a person means to be none of these but to be morally alterable by the proximity of the Other.

THE GENOCIDAL CENTURY

Through Levinas I had found an entering wedge into thinking the 'ought' in a genocidal century. But could a philosopher of religion so quickly dispense with Hegel or Heidegger? Phenomenological analysis and existential philosophy developed numerous ways to distinguish between the being of human being and the being of entities, insights of importance. Still, Heidegger's early philosophy (politics aside) conveyed the sense that the call of conscience (*Ruf des Gewissens*) was a call of the self (of being-in-the-world) to come to itself, that the self subsisted side by side, *partes extra partes*, with other selves but was never called into question by another. Being-in-the-world understood itself through anticipation of its own death but what of another's death? What requiem would be sung for the millions who had perished – perishing is after all Heidegger's word for the death of animals – in war and by means of racial and political extermination policies? The later Heidegger's stress upon getting behind the concrete conditions of existence toward what primordially makes these conditions possible had led to a certain meditative quietism. The quest for what is ever more primary loses contact with the experiential matrix so carefully articulated in *Being and Time*. What was left of my Enlightenment mindset protested against the passivity of this position with its increasing withdrawal from the world of others. I examined alternative philosophical approaches, the endless disquisitions about specific moral issues which could never be settled and current variants of Kantian ethics and found them wanting, my encounter with Levinas having left me resistant to both. Yet Levinas's ethical writings, although holocaust driven, do not speak directly of mass death. Does this reflect a wish to stress the universality of his ethics without, of course, returning to ethics as system, a desire to avoid a semblance of special pleading? I do not know.

Although Heidegger could not be ignored, the technical distinctions in Heidegger's writings – fundamental ontology and ontic clue, Being, *Ereignis* (Appropriation) and *Es gibt* (It gives) – were, in my view, unable to provide resources for thinking the twentieth-century annihilation condensed in the name Auschwitz. Is Auschwitz an ontic clue that leads to some more primordial level? If so, what primordium could subsume the mass death of our century? Or, to the contrary, if man-made mass death itself is this abyss and all else swallowed up in it, would not any humanly construed world descend into an all-consuming nihilism? Above all, there would be no faces, no responsibility for the Other, only an indifferent play of forces.

Spirit in Ashes: Hegel, Heidegger and Man-Made Mass Death (Wyschogrod 1985b) was my effort to think through the despair of nuclear, biological and chemical warfare, artificially created famine, death, concentration and slave labor camps. What is unprecedented in these manifestations of mass death is the effort to destroy the largest number of persons in the briefest possible time frame, a state of affairs I call the death event. How could a student of religion ignore the enclaves of death, death worlds, in which death is both process and product? How could philosophical inquiry disregard a world in which qualitative relations are reduced to connections of utility and computation and whose inhabitants are mythologized through criteria of race or politics as the demonic other? Heidegger does in fact explicate the reduction of persons to things in terms of calculation: persons have become numbers, the calculable. Yet by arguing that *all* persons are seen as calculable units, that calculation is an attribute of our age generally, he bypasses the question of responsibility for specific massacres, for the fact that some were *declared* items of calculation, disposable, refuse, while others were not. I argue further that the formal patterns and abstractions of the Western philosophical imagination are not just intellectual displays but have become historical actualizations. Here, for all its difficulties, Hegel's philosophy helps in that for him philosophical abstractions are integrally linked to concrete history.

I had hoped when I wrote *Spirit in Ashes* that the book would self-destruct, that if it remained interesting it would do so as an archaeological artifact, an account of what *had* occurred but exists no longer, that it would have no premonitory value. To my horror, the phenomena I had described and whose worst manifestations I believed had come to an end, are cloning themselves: Bosnia, Rwanda, the Sudan, Haiti and...

GETTING AROUND MORAL THEORIES: SAINTLY LIVES

In *Saints and Postmodernism: Revisioning Moral Philosophy* (1990), I take up another childhood not, the not of desire, of wanting what one lacked, that I had hitherto neglected in my work. How could desire be harnessed to ethics? There were clues in the work of Levinas but still, it seemed to me, desire as a conceptual resource for ethics had hardly been exhausted. Is it possible that overcoming the not of desire can perhaps be expressed as desire that remains desire, but becomes disinterested? Is disinterested desire not an oxymoron? If not, how does disinterested desire become manifest? If the relation of desire to ethics is to be brought to light, the scholar of religion must appeal not to moral theories but rather to narratives, the stories of lives that, in their excessiveness, exhibit extremes of generosity and compassion, attributes manifested in the lives of saints in traditional hagiographic literature. Here the religionist (even if a philosopher of religion) is at an advantage because even if her training did not focus on medieval studies or on an Asian or African religion, it is likely to have included a historical and comparative dimension that sensitizes her to the contexts of hagiography.

Still, today's world is not the world of classical Christianity nor that of the great ages of Buddhism. The response to suffering has been traduced, our compassion for the Other contested, by the endless repetition in televised likeness of human wretchedness. What is more, Nietzschean and psychoanalytic critiques of sympathy have created a suspicion of sympathy for the Other in that such emotion may conceal hostility. At best, sympathy may be lukewarm betokening the reflex response of an emotional system on overload.

With these criticisms in mind, if I chose to use saintly lives as models, the naiveté of traditional hagiography would have to undergo an acid-bath of ambiguation and anti-nomian fracturing. Some saints at least would need to be inspired not only by compassion but also by desire; they are what I call saints of depravity. Their self-sacrificing actions are driven, as Georges Bataille would have it, both by 'experience as a voyage to the end of the possible', and by altruism. I try to show how the fiction of such iconoclastic writers as Yukio Mishima and Jean Genet displays this broken saintly generosity.

In other recent work, I have begun to focus upon the corporeal dimensions of saintliness (Wyschogrod [in press b]), what I saw in childhood as the not of materiality, by turning to manifestations of ascetic practices. Can the body, that in the Platonic tradition and in many Asian religions is regarded as a vehicle for eros and as the casing for an inner more valuable self, become a conduit for justice? If so, is repression – a phenomenon so trenchantly analyzed by modern and postmodern thought – a sufficent explanation for ascetic practice? Can ascetic piety in its numerous cultural expressions be regarded as prefiguring a contemporary erotics as depicted by Foucault, Baudrillard, Kristeva, Deleuze and

Guattari? Or does the regimentation of eros through ascetic practices give birth to the etiolated shadow-men that Nietzsche describes?

I take up the not of desire again in an article that considers a text that continues to be a lure for theologians and logicians and never ceases to interest me since I first puzzled over its logical conundrums and strange architecture: Anselm's ontological argument (Wyschogrod 1989). Only by examining the argument's articulations and movements from level to level, can what I see as the erotics of the text, the dimension of desire that is intrinsic to it, be brought to light. It is not enough to explore faith as the precondition of Anselm's quest in the manner of Karl Barth. One must also become attentive to the yearnings expressed by the text, analyze the text as if it, not the man Anselm, exhibited unconscious dimensions. Guided by Lacan's post-Freudian apothegm, 'the unconscious is structured like a language', the text can be coaxed to display its wishes and resistances, the direction of its erotic intent. Anselm's name for God, a being such that a greater cannot be conceived, may seem transparent but resists interpretation. He seeks to bestow meaning upon objections to the name of God, objections dredged up from the text's unconscious, as it were, in order to restore the objects named in these objections to language. Only then will these limited objects posited in place of God, the heart's desire of Anselm, cease to present impediments to his love of God.

In my most recent thinking, I return to the theme of man-made mass death in a new context, that of the problem of historical truth. The questions (raised earlier in a formal way) are daunting. Can historical truth be reclaimed from the powerful philosophical critiques that have undermined any straightforward notion of truth, so that the histories of the dead others whom conventional history has abandoned may be told and believed? How can the historian or the scholar of religion trust the documents about the massive destruction of persons in this century if language can never represent events? Could re-membering – the word's etymology, the gathering again of a body's scattered members, is suggestive in an age of mass death – be relied upon? Does vagueness as a principle of interpretation not open the door to self-serving accounts of what actually happened? Do the claims of historians reflect nothing more than the *parti pris* of self-interested factions? And what of Nietzsche's analysis of memory as a drag upon the present?

My recent work about negation and counterfactuality that I earlier referred to as finger exercises may help to configure limits to this ambiguity without returning to an older view of fact. Perhaps eliminating what could not have been suggests a way of limiting what can and cannot be said about what actually happened.

No reflection upon the problem of history can, I think, evade a fundamental recasting of the meaning of past time. I want to show that the primacy of the past in our understanding of temporality has been covered up. Heidegger's stress upon the future leaps over an unsurpassable negation opened up by the materiality of the world, the past's sheer irrecoverability. The past cannot be brought back materially: no, not, never. Perhaps the contemporary historian must 'ground' history in ethics just as the philosopher influenced by Levinas 'grounds' metaphysics in ethics. Perhaps the contemporary historian's task is that of a calling in the sense that 'that old time religion' gave to this term. Perhaps she is summoned to consider the moral demand placed upon her by the dead others in the epoch of man-made mass death. How the historian is to decide the way in which suffering is to be allocated in narratives about the past, how factuality is to be reconfigured, how past and future are to be reinterpreted, I do not yet know. I can only report my sense of urgency with regard to these challenges.

Notes

1. In 1968, a historic year for universities around the world, I visited with Jacob Taubes in Berlin where we conversed in a seminar room made memorable by a plaster bust of Kant that had been blackened and inscribed with the legend: 'Mao has answered all question that I have left open' [translation mine].
2. Rosenthal's single published full-length work, *The Consolations of Philosophy: Hobbes's Secret, Spinoza's Way* (Temple University Press, 1989), was edited by his daughter, Abigail Rosenthal, and appeared posthumously.
3. As the first book written about Levinas in any language, it preceded what could perhaps be viewed as a cooptation of Levinas's work by those who believe it provides an ethics that is 'categorially' continuous with much Continental thought and thus able to compensate for that thought's deficiency. But such thinking may fail to gauge the extent to which Levinas's ethics is rooted in traditional Jewish sources.

References

Wyschogrod, Edith. 1974. *Emmanuel Levinas: The Problem of Ethical Metaphysics*. The Hague: Nijhoff.
—— 1981. 'The Logic of Artifactual Existents: John Dewey and Claude Lévi-Strauss'. *Man and World* 14:34–9.
—— 1983. 'Time and Non-Being in Derrida and Quine'. *Journal of the British Society for Phenomenology* 14 (May):112–26.
—— 1985a. 'Plato and Some Surrogates in a Jain Theory of Knowledge'. pp. 73–89 in *Civilizations East and West: A Memorial Volume for Benjamin Nelson*, edited by E. V. Walter, Vytautis Kavolis and Edmund Leites. Atlantic Highlands, NJ: Humanities Press.
—— 1985b. *Spirit in Ashes: Hegel, Heidegger, and Man-Made Mass Death*. New Haven: Yale University Press.
—— 1989. 'Recontextualizing the Ontological Argument'. pp. 97–118 in *Lacan and Theological Discourse*, edited by Edith Wyschogrod, David Crownfield and Carl Raschke. Albany: SUNY Press.
—— 1990. *Saints and Postmodernism*. Chicago: University of Chicago Press.
—— 1992. 'How to Say No in French: The Lineage of Negative Theology in Derrida'. pp. 39–55 in *Negation and Theology*, edited by Robert C. Scharlemann. Charlottesville: University of Virginia Press.
—— 1994. 'Facts, Fiction, Ficciones: Truth in the Study of Religion'. *Journal of the American Academy of Religion* 62, 1:1–16.
—— [in press a]. 'History, Memory, Revelation: Writing the Past'. Forthcoming in *The Uses and Misuses of Memory: Memory and History in Christianity and Judaism*, edited by Lawrence Cunningham and Michael Signer. South Bend, IN: University of Notre Dame Press.
—— [in press b]. 'The Howl of Oedipus, the Cry of Heloise: From Asceticism to Postmodern Ethics'. Forthcoming in *The Ascetic Dimension in Religion and Culture*, edited by Vincent Wimbush, Oxford University Press.

13

Retracings

MARK C. TAYLOR

It began, as it always begins, with a loss, lack, absence. A loss that occurred not long before I was and will continue long after I will have been. This loss was not, therefore, *my* loss and yet it is the loss that has, in no small measure, made me what I am. The loss was the loss of a nameless one – a nameless one who will remain nameless or who will be named only in the absence for which 'my' name has become the mark. The loss had something to do with binding and rebinding – a binding and rebinding that were her death as much as my life. Always bound to a double bind, 'my' presence has never been my own because it has always already been her absence. Have I betrayed her by telling you even this much? Perhaps. And so I shall say no more – at least not for now. But even this not-saying remains a saying, for I am always thinking about, talking about, teaching about, writing about what I am not saying. This not, which is almost nothing, is the not I cannot (not) think.

***

If *autos* is always at the same time *heteros*, then autobiography is impossible. The self cannot write itself without writing (of) an other it can never know. To write the narrative of the life that seems to be my own is, therefore, to betray myself by betraying the other without whom I am not. I realize, of course, that this all seems hopelessly abstract – even unreal. But I assure you that these matters, which are what truly matter to me, are as concrete as the unnameable one, who sometimes is named (improperly) 'the real'.

If I had a story to tell, it would not be my own but would be the story of an other. The story of an other, which I cannot tell and yet cannot help but telling. My telling is always less than telling because it is unavoidably a telling not. This not is the obsession that will not go away. The not that eternally returns is not anything and yet is not nothing. In all that I write, this not is what remains most telling and, thus, is always what must be told.

The not, which does not go away and yet is never present, is, for me, what religion is about. I do not know whether the thinkers, writers, and artists whose thinking I have rethought have led me to this not or this not has led me to them. What I do know is that even before the beginning, what has fascinated me is not the appearance of religion as such but the religious dimension of that which does not appear to be religious. Religion, I believe, is as unavoidable as the not to which it is inescapably bound. It is precisely when the so-called religious seems most absent that it draws near without ever becoming present. In the liminal domain about not, every approach is a withdrawal and every withdrawal an approach.

Over the years, the not that religion is about has approached under the guise of numerous pseudonyms – some familiar, some less familiar, but all of them in one way or another undeniably strange. Though I was raised a Presbyterian, institutional religion has never held much interest for me. Worlds beyond the church – every church – have always seemed more fraught with religion than the world within precincts once declared holy. It was, however, time as much as place that determined my intellectual trajectory. For young people coming of age during the extra-ordinary decade of the 1960s, moral and spiritual questions were unavoidable. The struggle for civil rights and against the war in Vietnam created sensibilities and concerns that brought streets and classrooms into an unavoidable proximity.

From 1964 to 1968, I was fortunate enough to study at Wesleyan University. During these years, Wesleyan was emerging as one of the centers of the student protest movement. This development was, in large measure, the result of the leadership of certain members of Wesleyan's distinguished department of religion. Throughout the early and mid 1960s, John Maguire joined Ralph Abernathy, Martin Luther King, Jr, and others in the struggle for civil rights. Each spring, Maguire would lead Wesleyan students south to help with voter registration drives. Though I was not able to participate in these trips, some of my most vivid memories from my Wesleyan years center around King and Abernathy. I shall never forget listening to King's powerful voice as he recited verses about justice from the book of Isaiah. For a brief moment, the possibility of effecting significant social change seemed more than an idle dream.

The first course in religion I took at Wesleyan was with John Maguire. In Maguire's classroom, intellectual rigor and social concern came together to create an atmosphere in which the issues we probed seemed both important and urgent. One of the enduring lessons Maguire taught me was that academic excellence and personal commitment should be mutually reinforcing. My intellectual interests did not begin to come into clear focus until my junior year in college when I took two seminars with Steve Crites: 'The Dialectic of Alienation and Reconciliation in Hegel, Feuerbach, and Marx', and 'Kierkegaard's Dialectic of Existence'. It is no exaggeration to say that these courses directly and indirectly established the coordinates for all of my subsequent thinking and writing. In Hegel and Kierkegaard I discovered more than two monumental thinkers; their writings came to represent for me two major philosophical and theological alternatives as well as two contrasting ways of being-in-the-world. But Crites taught me much more than how to read the texts of some of the most demanding writers in the western tradition; he also introduced me to the world of scholarship. As I listened to Crites, I began to imagine the demands and the pleasures of writing.

By the time of my senior year at Wesleyan, I had decided to pursue a career of teaching and writing. Actually, this decision probably had been made long before I realized it. Having come from a family of teachers – my mother, Thelma Kathryn Taylor, taught American literature, and my father, Noel Alexander Taylor, taught biology and physics – teaching was no doubt my destiny. But it was a destiny that was also a vocation. Though I was not sure who or what called me to be a teacher and writer, I was convinced that some kind of a call had been issued and I had no choice but to accept the demand it placed upon me.

These were tumultuous times on university campuses. The second semester of 1968 was marked by an escalation of the war in Vietnam, the revocation of most draft deferments, Russia's invasion of Czechoslovakia, the assassinations of Martin Luther King and Robert Kennedy, and the shooting of Andy Warhol. Overwhelmed by these events, the social, political, and ethical questions that led me to study religion assumed renewed urgency. While many students declared the necessity to leave the classroom and take to the streets, I was convinced that effective social engagement presupposes critical analysis and self-reflection. In the midst of social turmoil, my academic work became more rather than less important.

In the fall of 1968, I headed to Harvard to pursue a PhD in the study of religion. My early years at Harvard were marked by student unrest that reached unprecedented proportions. When students went on strike and took over University Hall shortly after noon on April 9th, 1969, the Harvard administration reacted quickly and violently. Though many faculty members condemned both students and the administration, some appreciated the serious moral concerns that had inspired the protest. For the most part, the faculty of Harvard Divinity School responded thoughtfully and creatively by transforming the strike into an occasion for critical reflection and constructive dialogue. Once again I saw how academic inquiry and social concern could complement each other.

While at Harvard, I studied primarily with Gordon Kaufman and Richard R. Niebuhr. I recall a conversation I had with Kaufman in the spring before I enrolled at Harvard. Explaining the motivation behind Harvard's doctoral program, Kaufman remarked: 'Our aim is to produce constructive theologians. Not just historians of theology but *constructive* theologians.' At the time, I was not quite sure what he meant by 'constructive theologians'; nor was I confident that my background had prepared me for such a daunting undertaking. After beginning my studies at Harvard, it did not take long for the distinction between historical and constructive theology to become obvious. It also became clear to me that one cannot do constructive theology without a thorough understanding of the western philosophical and theological traditions. Kaufman and Niebuhr instructed their students as much by *how* they taught as by *what* they taught. While their seminars concentrated on major historical figures, they devoted lectures to the development of their own theological positions. To study with Kaufman and Niebuhr was to undergo an apprenticeship in thinking. By issuing an open invitation to think with them, these master teachers initiated their students into the art of thinking constructively.

During my doctoral studies, I concentrated in modern Christian theology and did extensive work in the related fields of New Testament and the philosophy of religion. My training was not, however, limited to what took place in the classroom. When I arrived at Harvard, Erik Erikson was completing his career and some of the people who had worked with Robert Bellah were still in residence. A series of seminars initiated and conducted by graduate students introduced me to the writings of major psychological and social theorists. This was the context in which I first engaged in a serious reading of Freud and psychoanalysis. My work in the social sciences complemented my work in theology and philosophy of religion in ways that were mutually productive. The lines separating theology, philosophy, psychology, and sociology were far less clear to me than they seemed to be to many of the writers whose works I was reading. I was particularly intrigued by the ways in which theorists who claimed to be decoding or demystifying religion were unwittingly reinscribing many of its most important insights. Nowhere was this more evident than in the writings of Freud, who, contrary to conventional wisdom, seemed to me to be a theologian *malgré lui*.

Though my intellectual horizons expanded considerably at Harvard, I continued to be preoccupied with Hegel and Kierkegaard. Two of the most influential courses I took while at Harvard were on Hegel. In the fall of 1970, Kaufman offered a seminar on Hegel's *Science of Logic*. Kaufman was, without a doubt, the best seminar teacher I ever had. His openness with students and willingness to admit that he did not understand a text created a sense of dialogue and mutual exploration that is, unfortunately, all too rare. In the course of the semester, we read the entire *Logic*. Each week for three hours we wrestled with this extraordinary work as well as with Kaufman. This was one of the most exhilarating – and exhausting – intellectual experiences I have ever had. Kaufman taught me not only how to think *about* Hegel but, more important, how to think *with* him. I did not realize for many years that he was also teaching me how to teach.

Two years later, Dieter Henrich, from the University of Heidelberg, visited Harvard and offered a remarkable lecture course entitled: 'Between Kant and Hegel: Post-Kantian Idealism – An Analysis of its Origins, Systematic Structures and Problems'. While most surveys of nineteenth-century philosophy usually jump from Kant to Hegel, Henrich concentrated on a series of often-overlooked thinkers who elaborated the details of Kant's critical philosophy in ways that made Hegel's speculative system all but inevitable. In addition to these lectures, Henrich conducted a weekly seminar on Hegel's *Logic*. This reading of the *Logic* was the perfect complement to Kaufman's course. While we had worked through the whole book with Kaufman, Henrich spent the entire semester analyzing the first two chapters of 'The Doctrine of Essence'. As a matter of fact, we only made it through the second section of the second chapter, which is entitled 'Difference' (a total of merely 42 pages). Henrich claimed that the essential structure of Hegel's dialectic can be seen most clearly in the second chapter of 'The Doctrine of Essence'. As I watched Henrich patiently unfold Hegel's argument week after week, I gained a new appreciation for the importance of careful and rigorous reading. But I was not only impressed by Henrich's pedagogical method; I also became convinced that he was right about Hegel. I still think that the heart of Hegel's system is the dialectic of identity and difference as articulated in the *Logic*. In the spring of 1973, I could hardly have known where my exploration of the problematic of identity and difference would lead me.

The more I studied Hegel, the more I was drawn to Kierkegaard. My examination of modern philosophy and theology had persuaded me that Hegel and Kierkegaard represent something like what Tillich once described as 'Two Types of the Philosophy of Religion'. In the highly charged anti-Barthian atmosphere of Harvard, Kierkegaard was not taken seriously. In retrospect, I suspect this was one of the reasons I was attracted to him. But something else drew me to Kierkegaard's writings – something less articulate but more important. This something else or something other was what I have always felt compelled to think. And yet, it was precisely this something else or something other that Hegel seemed to overlook. Kierkegaard had, of course, been venerated by twentieth-century existentialist philosophers and writers for his defense of the individual in the face of philosophical processes of abstraction and modern mechanisms of massification. But most existentialists tended to ignore Kierkegaard's theological and religious writings. I was convinced that for Kierkegaard, God and self are mirror images of each other. Without its theological underpinnings, Kierkegaard's account of selfhood, which so intrigued existentialists, simply dissolves. Henrich's analysis of the Hegelian dialectic of identity and difference gave me a way to mediate Kierkegaard's theology and anthropology. The difference between Hegel and Kierkegaard, I concluded, is difference itself. While Hegel attempts to reconcile identity and difference by reducing the latter to the former, Kierkegaard asserts the irreducibility of difference in opposition to identity. This insight formed the basis of my dissertation, which eventually became my first book: *Kierkegaard's Pseudonymous Authorship: A Study of Time and the Self* (1975). In this work, I argue that in contrast to Hegel, who negates time and individual selfhood by interpreting them as fleeting moments in an eternal, universal process, Kierkegaard relentlessly probes subjectivity by tracing the development of the self from the dispersed ahistoricity of aesthetic existence to the decisive moment of religious existence in which the self becomes itself by constituting its difference from all other selves in and through its response to what is apprehended as the call of 'absolute difference'.

In the course of developing this argument, however, my thinking took an unexpected turn. Kierkegaard's moment of decision, I discovered, is every bit as ahistorical as the eternal becoming of Hegelian *Geist*. In the leap of faith, the individual gains eternal blessedness by responding to the absolutely paradoxical appearance of the eternal in time. Life in this world is significant only insofar as it prepares us for the life to come. With this insight, I could no longer deny that Kierkegaard is, in Hegel's terms, a poet of unhappy consciousness. The issue upon which my thinking turned was ethical or, more precisely, political. Kierkegaard's existential dialectic is a reinterpretation of Luther's doctrine of the two kingdoms, which tends to be gnostic or quasignostic. The secret inwardness of faith reflects 'the infinite and qualitative difference' of God. As God transcends the world of space and time, so the interiority of faith transcends the exteriority of everyday life. With the realization that God and faith might be a difference that make no difference, Hegel's philosophy began to attract me. I began *Kierkegaard's Pseudonymous Authorship* intending to present a Kierkegaardian critique of Hegelian philosophy and ended by discovering that Hegel is a necessary corrective to Kierkegaard.

Having been led to this unanticipated conclusion, I once again turned my attention to Hegel. Upon rereading, Hegel's argument seemed considerably more insightful and persuasive. Notwithstanding criticisms to the contrary, Hegel does not simply reduce difference to identity and, correlatively, time to eternity, individuality to universality, history to idea, body to mind, and so on. To the contrary, he seeks a reconciliation of opposites in which differences are maintained while at the same time transformed. In 1978, I returned to Denmark, where I had written my doctoral dissertation, to write *Journeys to Selfhood: Hegel and Kierkegaard* (1980). After presenting what I regarded as a balanced comparison of their respective analyses of selfhood, I concluded that Hegel's argument was less problematic than Kierkegaard's position. But I still was not fully satisfied with Hegel's point of view. While Kierkegaard ends with an other-worldliness, which undercuts the significance of worldly existence, Hegel ends with a this-world-liness, which negates the possibility of criticism and resistance. Neither of these alternatives was acceptable. I was too much of a Kierkegaardian to be an Hegelian and too much of an Hegelian to be a Kierkegaardian. What I was looking for was something *between* Hegel and Kierkegaard.

Stuck on the horns of this dilemma, I began reading Nietzsche seriously. I quickly discovered that his notion of the death of God is far more important and subtle than most commentators and critics realize. Indeed, I began to suspect that a rethinking of the death of God might make it possible to develop a different kind of theology. Reexamining the debate between Hegel and Kierkegaard in terms of the death of God, I discovered that God can die in at least two ways: God can become so transcendent that he is functionally nonexistent (Kierkegaard); or the divine can become so immanent that it becomes indistinguishable from worldly processes (Hegel). The theological implications of the death of God never obscured the social and ethical ramifications of this 'world historical' event. Social critique presupposes some kind of transcendence and yet transcendence always threatens to slip into an opposition that allows for negation but removes the justification for affirmation. In Nietzschean terms, my question became: How can one say not only 'Yes' to 'No' and 'No' to 'Yes' but also 'Yes' to 'Yes' and 'No' to 'No'? An affirmation that is a negation and a negation that is an affirmation would not necessarily reconcile opposites but would maintain a tension that would leave everything in suspense. Long conversations with Thomas Altizer led me to suspect that what I was looking for could be found in Nietzsche's analysis of power. My turn to Nietzsche was far from innocent. Searching for a difference that would make a difference, I read *The Will to Power* through Hegel's account of 'Force and Understanding' in the *Phenomenology*, and reread Hegel's dialectical analysis through Nietzsche's fragmentary investigation of the play of forces. Perhaps the ceaseless interplay of forces pointed to a non-oppositional notion of difference, which would open the space and create the time for critique and resistance that could affirm while negating and negate while affirming.

It was almost by accident that I began reading Derrida's writings at exactly this moment. I had known of his work but had not followed the controversies surrounding deconstruction and, thus, was unprepared for what I found in his texts. Though the intellectual climate in which Derrida was writing was very different from the one in which I was thinking, it was immediately evident to me that we were preoccupied with many of the same questions. From my first encounter with Derrida's work, I realized that in spite of repeated denials, he is actually obsessed with religious issues and theological questions. Moreover, Derrida seemed to be seeking precisely the non-oppositional difference, which I thought could be found between Hegel and Kierkegaard. The more I studied deconstruction or post-structuralism, the more plausible this reading of Derrida's texts became. The abiding influence of Alexandre Kojve's *Introduction à la lecture de Hegel*, makes it possible to interpret Lévi-Strauss's structuralism as latter-day Hegelianism and Hegelianism as proto-structuralism. From Derrida's perspective, the problem with both Hegelianism and structuralism is their tendency to totalize differences by reducing other to same. While not drawing directly on Kierkegaard, the post-structural critique of structuralism effectively extends Kierkegaard's criticism of Hegel without falling prey to the temptation to reinscribe differences as irreconcilable oppositions. Neither identity nor difference, *différance* is the non-dialectical third in and through which identity and difference are simultaneously constituted and deconstructed. Comprehensible neither in terms of Hegel's both/and nor Kierkegaard's either/or, Derrida's neither/nor implies something else, something other, something that is not something and yet is not nothing. Neither something nor nothing, *différance* is the not to which and by which everything is simultaneously bound and undone. This is the not I could not (not) think.

Derrida gave me a way to think my ceaseless oscillation between Hegel and Kierkegaard by rethinking certain aspects of Nietzsche's writings. The result of this thinking and rethinking was *Erring: A Postmodern A/Theology* (1984). Several years earlier, I had tried to introduce post-structural discourse into theology and the study of religion by publishing a collection of essays entitled *Deconstructing Theology* (1982). Having never forgotten the challenge that Kaufman had issued on the occasion of our first meeting, I realized that this book had not gone far enough. Though the careful analysis of the history of theology and philosophy is necessary, it was not sufficient for me; I continued to harbor the ambition to write something like what was once described as 'constructive theology'.

Some of the most interesting chapters in the history of theology have grown out of efforts to recast traditional theological issues in new philosophical frameworks. I decided to undertake the seemingly impossible task of appropriating deconstructive philosophy to write a 'constructive' a/theology. Needless to say, I realized that such a project would provoke criticism from every side. For people committed to the theological tradition, deconstruction seems to involve a nihilism that undercuts every foundation of meaning and purpose, and for devotees of deconstruction, any effort to return to theological issues and reclaim religious concerns is nostalgic at best and reactionary at worst. My anticipation of hostile responses proved to be well-founded. *Erring* unleashed a barrage of criticism, which often confused more than it clarified. While charging me with giving in to the latest Parisian fashions, commentators and critics overlooked the ways in which *Erring* supplements the debate between Hegel and Kierkegaard with which I had been preoccupied for many years.

As I pondered the responses to *Erring*, I realized that most people in the fields of theology and the study of religion were not familiar with many of the writers upon whom I was drawing. Though deconstruction often is accused of shattering the notion of canon, Derrida actually extends the Western canon by opening it to writers usually overlooked or deliberately excluded. In an effort to create greater familiarity with the counter-canon that was influencing my thinking, I conceived of two closely related books. The first would be a collection of readings selected from the works of major writers who have contributed directly and indirectly to the emergence of post-structuralism (*Deconstruction in Context: Literature and Philosophy* (1986)). The second book would be a series of carefully conceived essays devoted to the question of difference and otherness in the works of many of the writers included in the first volume (*Altarity* (1987)). While intended to serve particular pedagogical ends, I also envisioned *Altarity* with certain constructive interests in mind. *Altarity* retraces and recasts the trajectory charted in the movement from *Kierkegaard's Pseudonymous Authorship* through *Journeys to Selfhood* to *Erring*. Having begun with Kierkegaard and moved to Hegel, I concluded that the position for which I was searching was *l'entre-deux*. In *Altarity*, I reversed directions by beginning with Hegel, ending with Kierkegaard and suspending a series of writers who had helped me reconceive the questions of difference and otherness – Heidegger,

Merleau-Ponty, Lacan, Bataille, Kristeva, Levinas, Blanchot, and Derrida – between these two.

The publication of *Erring* and *Altarity* opened many new and unexpected conversations for me. Since deconstruction had been of interest primarily to literary studies, my work on Derrida drew me into ongoing debates with writers and critics. Most members of the academy tend to view religion in traditional terms; thus, insistence that there is a theological dimension to deconstruction and a deconstructive side to some theology aroused considerable interest. One of the most rewarding developments that emerged from these writings was my friendship with Derrida. Over the years, I have benefited greatly not only from his remarkable writings but from our many productive conversations and exchanges.

The most surprising response to *Erring* came from architects. Shortly after the appearance of this book, I started to receive invitations to lecture at schools of architecture. I initially resisted, pleading that I knew almost nothing about architecture. But the architects persisted, responding that they did not expect me to lecture about architecture but were interested in discussing philosophy and theology with me. Over the years, I have found my conversations with leading architects like Bernard Tschumi, Peter Eisenman, Stanley Tigerman, Daniel Libeskind, Arata Isozaki, Toyo Ito, Frank Gehry, Rem Koolhaas, and others remarkably profitable. As I learned more about contemporary architecture and gained an appreciation for the philosophical sophistication of many architects, I gradually began to write about architecture. The more I wrote, the wider the discussion became until I found myself lecturing more often in schools of architecture than in schools of religion.

About the same time that I was venturing into the world of architecture, my friend and colleague, Tom Krens, left Williams to assume the directorship of the Guggenheim Museum in New York City. I had long been interested in painting and over the years had learned quite a bit from Krens about modern art. Insisting that I could use my theological and philosophical background to develop a distinctive critical approach, he kept prodding me to write about art. My experience with architects eventually convinced me to take his urging seriously. In the late 1980s, I began an extended investigation of nineteenth- and twentieth-century art and architecture. As my research progressed, I was astonished to discover that, with the exception of Tillich's scattered essays, no one had attempted to develop a sustained interpretation of modern and postmodern art and architecture from a theological perspective.

In *Disfiguring: Art, Architecture, Religion* (1992), I attempt to demonstrate the way in which avant-garde artists and architects throughout this century have carried out the aesthetic program first defined by post-Kantian philosophers and theologians like Schiller, Schelling, Schleiermacher, and Hegel. In elaborating and defending this argument, I was less interested in art and architecture that are overtly religious than in religious dimensions of paintings and buildings that appear to be completely secular. I organized my analysis around three different meanings of 'disfiguring': (1) disfiguring as the removal or erasure of figure; (2) disfiguring as the introduction or creation of figure; and (3) disfiguring as the impossible effort to calculate the incalculable by figuring what cannot be figured. These three strategies of disfiguring represent three different epochs in the history of modern and postmodern painting and architecture. Abstract or nonobjective art and high modern architecture disfigure by removing figures, symbols, designs, and ornaments. The goal of such disfiguring is the presentation of pure form, which is often indistinguishable from pure formlessness. For many of the artists and architects working in this tradition, pure form or formlessness is, in effect, absolute reality. When figuration returns in pop art and postmodern architecture, artists and architects disfigure by deforming, defacing, or corrupting the purity of modernist canvases and buildings. If one's aesthetic is ascetic, figures can actually disfigure. Contrary to conventional wisdom, the critique of modernism in what is traditionally defined as postmodernism is less significant than it initially appears. As Kierkegaard once observed, to do the opposite is also a form of imitation. To disrupt and dislocate the shared presuppositions of modernism and modernist postmodernism, it is necessary to think what modernism leaves unthought by trying to figure a disfiguring that struggles to figure the unfigurable. To pursue this seemingly impossible task is to approach another postmodernism, a different postmodernism, a postmodernism that subverts rather than extends the dream as well as the nightmare of modernism.

Though not immediately apparent, these three strategies of disfiguring correspond to three major alternatives, which have characterized theological debate throughout this century. Twentieth-century theology begins with the publication of Karl Barth's *Letter to the Romans* in 1919. In the face of the devastation wrought by World War I, Barth rejects the immanent development of the Kingdom of God proclaimed by the cultural Protestantism that dominated late nineteenth- and early twentieth-century theology. Drawing extensively on Kierkegaard's work, Barth declares that God is 'infinitely and qualitatively different' from sinful human beings and their corrupt culture. Since God is 'Wholly Other', the only way to affirm the divine is by negating the fallen domain of time and history. Barth's insistence on the transcendence of God is strictly parallel to the movement of abstraction that governs much of the so-called 'advanced' art of this century. Whether conceived theologically or artistically, every 'real' that is otherworldly can only be affirmed by negating sensual traces of time and space.

Paradoxically, the very effort to affirm the divine or the real by securing its radical otherness can render the real irrelevant and immaterial. Expressed in theological terms, when God becomes so transcendent that He is functionally nonexistent, the way is prepared for the divine to enter time and space and, correspondingly, the real to become totally present here and now. This dialectical reversal is effected in Thomas Altizer's death of God theology. The God who dies in Altizer's theology is the God who is infinitely and qualitatively different or radically other. While Barth returns to Kierkegaard to reaffirm the transcendence of God, Altizer returns to Hegel and an Hegelianized Nietzsche to reaffirm the immanence of God. According to Altizer, the transcendent God dies through a process of kenotic self-negation, and is reborn as the totality of the historical and cultural process. Since there is absolutely nothing beyond this world, what is must be affirmed as what ought to be. This theological move implicitly repeats the (dis)figuration of the real in pop art and postmodern architecture. For modernist postmodernism the real empties itself in the image. The image, therefore, is always the image of an image (or the sign is always the sign of a sign) and, hence, there is nothing outside the image. In the postmodern culture of simulacra, the 'real' is immanent in the figures that constitute culture. Art reflects culture, which, in turn, embodies art. In this way, postindustrial consumer culture represents a parodic realization of the dream of the avant-garde in which the world is transformed into a work of art. When this development is translated from artistic into theological terms, postmodernism can be understood to be something like the actualization of the Kingdom of God on earth.

At this point, the inadequacies of modernist postmodernism begin to become obvious. As I have suggested, the problem with every realized eschatology is the loss of any critical perspective that would create the possibility of resistance. If what is is what ought to be, there seems neither reason nor justification for criticism and resistance. While radical transcendence leads to a 'No' that allows no 'Yes', radical immanence issues in a 'Yes' that cannot say 'No'. Again, the problem seems to be to find a middle way between Kierkegaard and Hegel as well as their modern and postmodern heirs.

The third strategy of disfiguring – disfiguring as the impossible effort to calculate the incalculable by figuring what cannot be figured – points to precisely such a middle way. By drawing on the insights of post-structuralism, I attempt to develop something like a non-negative negative theology, which nonetheless is not positive. If Barth's God vanishes in the clouds of transcendence and abstraction, and Altizer's God disappears in the immanence of history and culture, might it be possible to refigure God by thinking a 'reality' that is *neither* transcendent *nor* immanent? And might such a concept or, more precisely, 'nonconcept' of the real create the possibility of critical engagement instead of hopeless resignation?

Nots (1993) is an effort to answer these questions by thinking not in ways it has not been thought. To think not is to linger with a negative, which is not merely negative. The not is something like a non-negative negative that is not positive. It is virtually impossible to articulate this strange notion in terms that do not seem utterly paradoxical. As structuralists never tire of insisting, our minds tend to work by setting up binary opposites: something is either true or false, either right or wrong, either positive or negative, and so on. But what if such a conceptual grid always leaves something out? And what if what is left out is precisely what needs to be thought? Thinking not explores territory that is not only unmapped but is unmappable. The not does not exist; nor does the not not exist; neither something nor nothing, the not falls *between* being and nonbeing. This is the margin of difference I have been tracing ever since *Erring*. A/theology is neither theology nor non-theology but something else, something different, something other, something whose affirmation is always a negation and whose negation is always an affirmation. The essays collected in *Nots* return to questions raised in *Tears* (1989) to probe this strange *between* as it appears and disappears in theological, artistic, architectural, and bodily texts. By rethinking the problem of negation in writers as different as Anselm, Nishitani, and Derrida, I struggled to refigure the *not* in a manner that eludes traditional philosophical and theological classifications. Moreover, I sought to demonstrate concrete ways in which this *not* is deployed in specific works of art, buildings, cultural practices and even bodily processes. The last sentence of *Nots* summarizes the existential problematic that haunts all of my writings: 'The dilemma, the abiding dilemma to which we are forever destined is to live not.'

In the course of writing *Disfiguring*, I came to a deeper appreciation of the importance of popular culture. Debates about the relation between so-called high and low art as well as elite and popular culture have, of course, become familiar. All too often, however, historical shortsightedness leads critics to overlook the ways in which the breakdown of such distinctions is implicit in the program of the avant-garde. Furthermore, the failure to recognize the ways in which avant-garde artists express religious beliefs and spiritual convictions leads to one-sided readings of modern and contemporary culture. Once again, religion proves most interesting where it is least obvious. Warhol's Catholicism, for example, is no less important for his iconophilic art than Mondrian's and Kandinsky's theosophy is for their iconophobic art. If, as Schiller insists, the work of art is fully realized in the transformation of society and culture, then the postmodern world in which the image becomes real and reality becomes imaginary might be understood as the completion of the avant-garde project. In contemporary culture, art leaves the gallery and becomes a part of everyday life. In this way, art becomes as all-pervasive and inconspicuous as religion had previously become.

If the realization of the aesthetic is at the same time the aestheticization of the 'real', it is necessary to try to understand the actual processes by which art comes to life and life becomes a work of art. As I surveyed the contemporary scene, it seemed clear to me that we are in the midst of an extraordinarily important socio-cultural shift, which has yet to receive the attention it deserves. This change is being brought about by remarkable technological developments. With the advent of electronic compu-telecommunications technology, we are rapidly moving from an industrial to a postindustrial society. While industrialism is governed by mechanical means of production, postindustrialism is regulated by electronic means of reproduction.

The analytic and interpretive strategies appropriate for modernism and industrialism are not directly transferable to postmodernism and postindustrialism. In an effort to explore what by this time has come to be known as 'cyberspace', I proposed a novel experiment to Esa Saarinen, my colleague who teaches philosophy at the University of Helsinki. I suggested that we try to use the latest teleconferencing technology to mount a semester-long interactive seminar, which would bring together students in Helsinki and at Williams. The aim of this undertaking was to integrate theory and practice in a radically new global classroom. In the fall of 1992, our plans came to fruition in a seminar entitled 'Imagologies'. Throughout the term, we met with ten Williams students and ten Helsinki students to discuss the philosophical presuppositions and implications of the electronic and information revolutions. The seminar was an enormous success. Indeed, by the end of the term we all agreed that our experiment had resulted in the most remarkable educational experience we ever had. One of the most surprising discoveries of our teleseminar was the impact of electronic media on pedagogy. While our global classroom simulated a traditional seminar, the atmosphere and dynamics were quite different. The hierarchy between teacher and students began to dissolve and a more collegial relation emerged. This tendency was even more pronounced in email discussions. When online, students were much more willing to pose questions and formulate criticisms. Moreover, some students who were reluctant to speak in class found their voices in the electronic environment. In addition to our conversations with students, Saarinen and I engaged in a semester-long email exchange in which we recorded our reflections on the form and content of our inquiry. We eventually published this electronic dialogue in *Imagologies: Media Philosophy* (1994).

In addition to opening new territory for analysis, *Imagologies* represents a departure in writing style and design. From the time I first conceived *Erring*, it had been clear to me that I could not say what I wanted to say without making language performative. I was now beginning to realize that performative utterance is not simply a matter of words but also involves images. Aesthetic considerations are present even when they appear to be absent. If disfigured canvases and ornament-free glass boxes are every bit as stylized as colorful figures and ornate buildings, then the traditional printed page is no less aesthetic than creatively designed texts. Though *Imagologies* is a printed book, we sought to reflect the mediascapes of electronic culture by breaking with traditional academic styles of writing and design. Within the digital environment, word, image, and sound are different inscriptions of the same 'stuff'. To write effectively with bits is to think with images and sounds as much as with words. This is part of what Saarinen and I tried to do in *Imagologies*.

As my explorations of electronic media have become more involved, I have been forced to admit that in spite of its extraordinary contributions, post-structuralism has reached a closure. This impasse is not only a function of a particular critical strategy having run its course but also reflects changes in broader social and cultural conditions. Having emerged in France in the early 1960s, post-structuralism provided a necessary corrective to processes of totalization that were evident in influential political movements and intellectual tendencies. From the explicit coercion of fascism and Stalinism to the implicit repression of formalism and structuralism, the obsession with order, homogenization, and universalization led to the negation of difference and the incorporation or appropriation of otherness. In this situation, it was essential to deconstruct totalizing structures in a way that allowed the repressed to return. By the 1990s, however, the things had changed considerably. While totalizing processes and structures surely have not disappeared, our differences increasingly are tearing us apart. Faced with this situation, I asked: Are the only alternatives a unity that excludes differences or differences that exclude unity? Might there not be a third alternative that neither mediates nor synthesizes unity and difference and yet opens the space and provides the time for connections and associations that create and sustain differences?

In my current work, I am attempting to develop a notion of something like a non-totalizing structure that nonetheless acts as a whole. My point of departure is the analysis of the logic of the networks and webs that increasingly form our milieu. In order to appreciate the scope of this undertaking, it is necessary to realize that the constantly-shifting structures, which are the matrix of contemporary experience, extend from internet and world wide webs to media, financial, and even neural networks. Within these webs and networks, all reality is becoming virtual reality. As the real becomes image and images become real, something is simultaneously withdrawing and approaching. The virtualizing of reality or the realization of virtuality leaves traces of a spectral other that is neither present nor absent. The medium through which this strange new reality is mediated is information. Since everything is always already in-formation, information is not merely a subjective construct but is a distributed process, which thoroughly in-forms everything that once appeared to be both objective and natural.

In attempting to articulate the logic of information webs and networks, I remain indebted to Hegel's logic, which, as I have stressed, directly and indirectly has informed aesthetic theories and artistic practices throughout this century. This appropriation of Hegel does not, of course, simply repeat his system. By reading Hegel first through Kierkegaard and then through Derrida, Hegelian structures are deconstructed and thereby opened to the very difference and otherness they are constructed to incorporate. Non-totalizing structures that nonetheless act as a whole function as something like a non-logocentric logos. Such a structure maintains relations without repressing differences. The vision that emerges in this hypertextual web is neither Kierkegaardian, nor Hegelian, nor Derridean, but something else, something other – always something else, something other.

My wanderings through the worlds of nineteenth- and twentieth-century theology and philosophy appear to have carried me far from the social and political concerns that initially inspired me to pursue the study of religion. But this is not the case. I have always believed that the worlds of theory and practice are inseparable. As we move into the twenty-first century, the domain of social and political contestation will be the symbolic order. If every sign is the sign of a sign, the distinction between supra-structure and infra-structure becomes reversible and thus finally implodes. Everything is always already mediated through networks of reproduction that are constantly undergoing transformation. To refigure these networks is to reconstitute the 'real'. We cannot change the world without altering consciousness any more than we can alter consciousness without changing the world. Consciousness/world, self/other, nature/culture, subject/object, transcendence/immanence, identity/difference, same/other, material/immaterial, real/virtual...are not opposites but are elusive interfaces that simultaneously call forth and resist thinking. The task of thinking at the end of theology is to think what theology has left unthought by repeatedly refiguring interfaces that cannot be figured. Such thinking or not-thinking is a thinking-not, which is forever kept in motion by a desire that knows it is wanting but knows not what it wants.

***

It ends, as it always ends, with a loss, lack, absence. A loss that occurred not long before I was and will continue long after I will have been. This loss was not, therefore, *my* loss and yet it is the loss that has, in no small measure, made me what I am. This loss was the loss of a nameless one – a nameless one who will remain nameless or who will be named only in the absence for which 'my' name has become the mark. The loss had something to do with binding and rebinding – a binding and rebinding that were her death as much as my life. Always bound to a double bind, 'my' presence has never been my own because it has always already been her absence. Have I betrayed her by telling you even this much? Perhaps. And so I shall say no more – at least not for now. But even this not-saying remains a saying, for I am always thinking about, talking about, teaching about, writing about what I am not saying. This not, which is almost nothing, is the not I cannot (not) think.

14

Who Are You Really, and What Were You Before?: Reflections on a Thinking Life

GILES GUNN

When Humphrey Bogart turns to Ingrid Bergman in *Casablanca* and puts to her the question that forms the title of this essay – asking in addition, 'What did you do, and what did you think?' – she gently puts him off with the reminder, 'We said no questions.' Bergman's refusal to answer does not mean that for her the past has no place in their relationship; indeed, the past will eventually determine the limits on where their relationship can go and what it can become. While Bergman has something she prefers to keep private, even though she has no reason at the time to believe that it will make any difference to Bogart (her marriage to the Paul Henreid character whom she now assumes is dead), the real reason for her reticence is that she, like the movie, believes that the only past that is important for Bogart to know anything about is the one out of whose traces in the present she hopes they can build a life together in the future. This is pretty much how the past will be treated here. The only past that will matter is the one that has influenced the intellectual formation of the present, which is to say the only past that, in its efforts to define itself, the present needs for the sake of its own narrativization. We tell stories out of the present for the sake of finding in the past elements for the emplotment of what, in effect, is a potentially meaningful future.

But where does one's intellectual life begin? How does one in fact know when it has commenced? What sorts of changes mark its initiation? How dependent are such perceptions on one's conception of the shape it has taken since? What role does the sense of such a shape, and the evolution of such a sense, play in the direction one tries, consciously or unconsciously, to give it in the future? How much of one's intellectual life is, precisely, the sense of its shaping, and of what, beyond the conversion of experience into ideas and, less frequently and more arduously, the reconversion of ideas back into the terms of felt experience, does that shaping consist?

My own intellectual life seems to have begun on its own without my quite realizing it; or, at any rate, by the time I had become conscious of its existence, I was somewhat surprised to discover that it had already been under way for some time and that I had become much more dependent on it than I realized. It wasn't that I was a bookish kid – a love of reading and the almost palpable thrill of intellectual inquiry didn't come until much, much later – or that life gave me that much more to ponder than anyone else. As I look back on my early life, it is simply that the recourse to thinking, and the need, almost the hunger, to convert experience into ideas seems to have been established rather quickly as my way of preventing myself from being overwhelmed by life's various immediacies and puzzlements.

I was a 'love child', as it was once called in a more benign age, who could neither get the math straight and actually figure this out until his late forties nor keep a marriage from dissolving that was probably doomed from the start. Consequently, I spent a good deal of my early life negotiating the tensions, conflicts, and general assymetries between the worlds of a rather wild and unstable but adoring mother, a father who would have been a prince of decency, generous-heartedness, and fidelity even in a world of saints, and a stepmother who never let the inner divisions she could claim as her own from accepting me completely as her son and teaching me the difference between taking my mind seriously and taking myself seriously. Placed in my mother's custody after my parents' divorce when I was ten, I eventually went to live with my father and his new wife when it became obvious to both of them, three years later, that my mother's frustrated ambition to become the next Faye Emerson, a television star in the medium's early days whom my mother resembled chiefly because of her rich speaking voice and impressive cleavage, was distracting her from fulfilling her parental obligations. By the time I was 11, I had been obliged to learn how to drive a car, seated on two telephone books or a large pillow properly rolled, so that I could retrieve her from parties or clubs where she was likely to be found, when not simply looking for a good time, pushing a career that in all her years of effort never managed to win for her more than short-lived positions as anchor for a morning news show in Phoenix or as hostess of radio talk shows for women in towns as distant as Evanston, Illinois, and Palm Springs, California. My mother's attempts in the early years after her divorce to become a national, or at least a local, media celebrity, like her much more prolonged efforts in later years merely to find and hold any job at all for more than a few months, were constantly shadowed by an appetite for liquor and for men that was at times prodigious and that once aroused was not to be denied. Too numerous were the times – indeed more, no doubt, than actually occurred – when I can remember waking up in the middle of the night to discover her in the noisy embrace of some worthy who had 'just happened to drop by', as the saying usually was, after I went to sleep, or trying to pull her from the arms of some fawning drunk in a bar.

This kind of behavior, at least when exhibited in the presence of an impressionable pre-teenager, might well have been have expected to leave some deep emotional scars, especially when his other parent still bore traces, albeit faintly, or at least gracefully, of his own family's former Puritan background. But my father's sense of morality had far more of understanding and sympathy and forgiveness in it than of judgment, and it operated, for the most part, so unobtrusively that it confirmed in me a belief that the most important part of anyone's moral and religious makeup is probably the least obvious. And in addition, my mother's sins, if that is what they were to be called (at any rate, they were not to be discounted as mere indiscretions) were never committed 'cold', as one of the few women friends whose patience she didn't quite manage over the years to exhaust once said, but 'hot', and that seemed, both to me and to her friend, to make all the difference. Thus while my mother represented to some an example of genuine depravity, or constituted for others a model of unrelieved pathos or, less charitably, bathos, she as often struck me, notwithstanding her disappointments, and loneliness, and recurrent moments of panic, as a figure who was also in her way both Quixotic and, in a Chaplinesque sense, truly comic.

As a comedic and Quixotic as opposed to, say, a demented figure, my mother saw life, when she saw it at all clearly, as a kind of gamble in which the point of it all has virtually nothing to do with winning the game and everything to do with enjoying the play. To her frequent dismay and confusion, the stakes in this game were usually set at higher levels than she could afford to risk, but this mattered hardly at all since, like any real gambler, she was an absolute sucker, so to speak, for the bet. The wager is what counted, and losing was something which, until she lost her health, she could often carry off as though it, and not winning, were the real laurel. Condemned, nonetheless, to appearing the fool much of the time, my mother seemed to know instinctively with Kenneth Burke that the real trick is to keep from being the fool all of the time. A trick that, as it turned out, my mother never successfully mastered, in her best moments of self-knowledge she nonetheless managed to enjoy the joke even when it was on her.

At the time, of course, during my teenage years, none of this was fully clear to me, but it lent a certain urgency to, indeed necessity for, learning how to sort out for myself certain kinds of ethical tangles. While my heart told me that however exasperating and selfish and outrageous she was, my mother was not by any means, as the official institutional guardians of morality were sometimes wont to declare, 'all bad', my head nevertheless informed me that the only way I could cope with the minor cruelties and the major embarrassments that I suffered at her hands – and still find them sufficiently humorous and, in their defiance of every social propriety as well as her own self-interest, life-affirming to be worth the trouble – was by taking thought and, in effect, cultivating a sense of humor as well as of irony. Taking thought and cultivating a sense of ironic humor was not, as is obvious, my father's way of being in the world, but it is one that he eventually took considerable delight in seeing me pursue even when he couldn't fully comprehend it. On the other hand, relying on the intellect to develop a sense of the perspectives afforded by incongruity was my stepmother's way of being in the world, and it was she who put me in a position educationally to adopt it as my own. What my father gave me instead is the conviction, subsequently lent still more spirited realization by my wife Deborah, that life should aspire to what F. Scott Fitzgerald, thinking of an America we have yet to see, called 'a willingness of the heart'.

If, then, my own intellectual life seems to have begun, as perhaps most everyone's does, without my quite realizing it, it also appears to have developed whatever distinctive contour or profile it has managed to achieve long before I actually realized it. The only thing noticeably odd or unusual about that contour or profile for a person who has now spent more than three decades as a professor is its lack of conventional professional identification. Instead of resembling, in other words, the profile of someone in literary studies, or in religious studies, or in what is now called (even though it can mean many different things) cultural studies, or in what, back in the 1980s, was simply termed 'Theory', or what, even further back in the 1970s and 1960s, was traditionally referred to as 'humanistic studies', most of my own intellectual life has been spent on the borders between such 'fields' or 'disciplinary formations', the borders that simultaneously delimit, differentiate, and yet connect them – sometimes charting places where they overlap, sometimes investigating intersections that seem unusually productive, most often exploring the unmarked territory where they diverge. Still more curious to me is the fact that much of my work on those borders has also been devoted to figuring out more specifically how, in fact, those borders were created to begin with, who maintains and monitors them, what institutions and practices they serve (and frustrate), how they have been challenged and redrawn over the past several decades, what those changes have done to our notions of religion, literature, culture, and humanity, whether such borders constitute, in addition to lines of demarcation, places, regions, margins, peripheries, or zones with their own customs, protocols and laws, and, finally, what sorts of intellectual and professional credentials – the academic equivalent of birth certificates, passports, and visas – one needs to cross such borders without violating rules of trespass, much less risking professional humiliation, disgrace, or ostracism.

A good deal of my lifelong interest in surveying disciplinary borders was subsequently to originate from motives that were sometimes consciously and sometimes unconsciously interdisciplinary. These motives were activated at a fairly early age – I can actually date them from several courses I took in college on 'Modern War and Its Impact on Society', taught by the noted intellectual historian Donald C. McKay, for which I wrote a paper on the Italian playwright Luigi Pirandello, and on 'American Romanticism', taught by the literary and cultural critic Leo Marx, for which I wrote a still longer essay on 'Moby-Dick and Job' – and persuaded me, as did much of the rest of my education at Amherst, that intellectual disciplines are essentially heuristic and pedagogical conveniences valuable only when they further learning;

and when they don't, then not. In later years, and particularly as a result of my graduate work at the University of Chicago in an interdisciplinary program in literature and religion, this opinion was to be reinforced by the belief that disciplinary crossings can sometimes produce not only a new configuration of methodological practices but a new refiguration of the material on which they are directed. Change the paradigms by which one discipline makes sense of itself to itself by forcing it to look through the eyes of another and you can sometimes alter the way disciplines represent their own knowledge to themselves.

But this is to get ahead of my story, to introduce conceptions that, in this case, define a notion of interdisciplinarity that I only came to much later in my work and then not before numerous false starts, dead ends, and embarrassing mistakes. More influential in generating my interest in intellectual practices that seek to redraw disciplinary boundaries and explore 'bordered knowledges', particularly as they emerge at the interface of such practices as literary, cultural, and religious studies, was – thanks again to Amherst and Leo Marx, and then again later to the University of Chicago and several other teachers of mine, principally Nathan A. Scott, Jr, but also Preston T. Roberts and James E. Miller, Jr – my early introduction to a literary and intellectual tradition with which I have been continuously absorbed ever since. This is the tradition of reflection and expression, loosely philosophical, that goes back in America at least to Ralph Waldo Emerson, Margaret Fuller, and Frederick Douglass, and that has its sources in Europe in the thinking of everyone from Vico, Herder, and Madame de Staël to Edmund Burke and Samuel Taylor Coleridge. A tradition variously described by Raymond Williams and Richard Rorty, it possesses as its subject the meaning of culture itself when the chief business of culture can be said to be devoted to taking over and reshaping from theology and philosophy whatever is worth keeping in such various departments of experience as science, art, politics, social thought, literature, morality, humor, and religion.

If it was Leo Marx who first introduced me to the American version of this tradition and taught me how to follow its rich seams of reflection and revisioning in ways not unlike those more recently elaborated at greater length by the philosopher Stanley Cavell and the political theorist George Kateb, it was Nathan Scott who helped me grasp a sense of this tradition's immense significance in establishing and maintaining what might be described as a people's, as we called it in those days, 'sense of ultimacy'. In recent years, however, this tradition that has turned on the meaning of culture itself when culture becomes the repository of what is still deemed valuable and capable of repossession in all the other formalized precincts of life has now come under severe attack, where it has not been simply dismissed, as a reinscription of the old Arnoldian, or, if you prefer, Genteel American, idea of culture. Much of this attack has struck me as by turns glib and self-serving since it could be plausibly argued that instead of having thoroughly broken with such a conception of cultural work, much less having successfully superseded it, we have merely decided to reconceive what it is that culture actually seeks to repossess and reshape, who in fact may be said to participate in or contribute to this process, and why it is that this project is deemed important in the first place.

Consistent with our more democratic, or at least less elitist, sexist, or racist views of such matters, we now say that culture seeks to appropriate and redescribe what any given people have, if you will, learned from their experience, as reflected not only in the specialized forms of their science, philosophy, religion, and so forth, but also in their tales, songs, aphorisms, jokes, dances, riddles, oratory, and manners – in short, what strategies they have devised, to put this into a register reminiscent of Kenneth Burke, for answering, or at least for symbolically encompassing, the questions put to them by the problematics of their own existence. We assume that the people who deserve credit for contributing to and advancing this process are not only those who, in response to questions posed by the problematic forms of their existence, have produced the most sophisticated symbolic answers to them but also those, far more numerous, who have had a hand in turning those answers into modes of ritual re-enactment and ceremonial self-realization for other people and later times. And we now take such cultural work to be important not alone because it reveals, as was once assumed, an essential oneness of being underlying all its expressions but rather because it suggests – or can suggest – something of the greater diversity of life forms that can now be comprehended and accepted as not only recognizably human but also ethically significant.

Culture in this sense has developed in the interests of its own explication a kind of writing that from the time of Goethe, Carlyle, and George Eliot to that of Hannah Arendt, Ralph Ellison, Jacques Derrida, and Elizabeth Hardwick is neither, as Richard Rorty has put it, 'an evaluation of the relative merits of literary productions, nor intellectual history, nor moral philosophy, nor epistemology, nor social prophecy but all these things mingled together in a new genre' (Rorty 1982:66). While the idioms in which this kind of writing represents itself have clearly changed over the past several decades, thanks in no small measure to the importation of a variety of new discourses from the Continent, the kind of task that this 'new' genre of critical reflection has set for itself has remained surprisingly consistent. That task might be described as what to make of our customary ways of making sense when there is now no longer any universally authoritative vocabulary in which to describe them, much less any universal agreement within such a vocabulary about how to evaluate their comparative advantages and disadvantages?

In recent years my own thinking about this tradition – and particularly its distinctive job of work in an intellectual world as rapidly and radically globalized as our own – has been strongly influenced by the renaissance of an American tradition of pragmatic reflection that once contributed heavily to its development, then ceded the field, during and after World War II, to other discursive practices and programs like linguistic analysis in philosophy, the New Criticism in literary studies, and neoorthodox theology in religion, and is now undergoing a fairly important revival, due in no small measure to its strong contemporary commitment to what Salman Rushdie has called – thinking not only of the virtues he has tried to exemplify in his own life and writing, but also of those that seem to characterize the nature of contemporary experience itself – 'hybridity, impurity, intermingling...and mongrelization' (Rushdie 1990:3).

A pragmatism evident in the political theory of Jürgen Habermas as well as the literary criticism of Richard Poirier, in the reflexive sociology of Pierre Bourdieu as well as the moral critique of Cornel West, in the feminist philosophy of Nancy Frazer as well as the discourse theory of Michel de Certeau or some of the discursive analysis of Michel Foucault – this is an intellectual movement that ranges across a number of academic disciplines. Devoting much of its attention to the development of critical concepts and methods that cut across many of the categories of modern disciplinary specialization and that thus afford us some possibility of critically scrutinizing and potentially revising our methods for making sense of the senses we make, this newest, cosmopolitan strain of pragmatism is particularly concerned with the organization and conduct of thought. Deriving its credibility, as the cultural critic Morris Dickstein has put it, 'from the way it questions all forms of received opinion without succumbing to radical doubt, [it] seeks to provide a general approach to a firmer knowledge in many areas without developing into a rigid methodology' (unpublished). This is not, then, a pragmatism that any longer holds out the prospect of constructing some version of the metaphysical sublime which will explain how all of life hangs together. It is rather a pragmatism that is content from an ethical perspective to help us determine which among various options is the better way to live.

This cosmopolitan pragmatism, as I am calling it, is very different from the version of neopragmatism that has become most familiar in American academic literary circles and that is now associated with critics like Stanley Fish, Walter Benn Michaels, and, in a different way, Barbara Herrnstein Smith. Drawing predominantly on that side of Rorty's work that is anti-foundationalist, anti-essentialist, anti-mimetic, and emphatically constructivist, theirs is a neopragmatism that repudiates any possibility of radical cultural criticism on the grounds that culture affords no position from outside of itself from which to bring itself under scrutiny. In the absence of any stable or neutral epistemological standpoints, all criticism from this perspective takes place from within the shelter of a specific body of practice defined by some institutional or professional community and merely works to buttress its own values. Assuming that criticism offers no basis beyond its own prejudices for deciding between rival claims of interpretation, this version of pragmatism reduces all interpretive acts eventually to the attempt to state, and sometimes to get, what we want.

By contrast, the alternative and more international form of pragmatism variously expressed on this side of the Atlantic (in addition to figures already mentioned, one might cite philosophers like Richard J. Bernstein, John McDermott, and Charlene Haddock Siegfried, religious thinkers like Jeffrey Stout, Henry Samuel Levinson, and Gordon Kaufman, literary critics like Ross Posnock, Steven Mailloux, Jonathan Levin, and Peter Carafiol, social scientists like Clifford Geertz and Jerome Bruner, historians such as David Hollinger, James Kloppenberg, James Livingston, Joyce Appleby, and Lynn Hunt, legal thinkers such as Richard Posner and Thomas C. Gray, and such fellow travelers as Stanley Cavell, Martha Nussbaum, George Kateb, Charles Taylor, and, from an earlier generation, Nelson Goodman) follows out some of the implications of the other side of Rorty's work. Concerned with the problem bequeathed to us by the great modernist writers of America and Europe, this other side of Rorty's writing attempts to determine what it is like to live when 'the quest for certainty', as John Dewey termed it, has become permanently frustrated. Whatever its preferred idiom – aesthetics, sociology, philosophy, metaphysics, history, or law – the task that this alternative and less exceptionalist form of pragmatism has taken on for itself is how, through an assessment of the benefits and liabilities of those devices, disciplines, and discourses that human beings have designed precisely for the sake of compensating for this loss when they have resisted the temptation to seek safe haven in some surrogate form of metaphysical certitude, to acquire a renewed sense of human solidarity and community.

On the assumption that much of what I once called the contemporary 'culture of criticism' now concerns itself with just this issue, I have for some time been interested in exploring the way the pragmatic imagination, as I find it expressed both in American and in Continental thought, can be construed less as a polemical alternative to the poststructuralist revolution that has now overtaken us critically, at least within the university, than as a useful and often perhaps corrective intervention within it. In this sense I am prepared to believe that Rorty may well be right when he asserts somewhere that in this cultural moment we think of as postmodern it might be more helpful to reconceive of poststructuralism as fundamentally 'an attempt to think through a thorough-going pragmatism'.

Reconceptualizing contemporary intellectual culture as an effort to think through any frame of thought is nonetheless a far cry from what I first supposed I was doing at the beginning of the 1970s, when I found myself invited by the American religious historian Martin E. Marty to organize a small book for a series he was then editing on some of the more representative modern ways of discussing the relations between literature and religion. I had been drawn into this discussion by a set of experiences that had their origin in a year I spent in Japan on a fellowship. During this year abroad (it was the same year that John F. Kennedy was to assume the Presidency and America was to begin to pour military advisors into Vietnam to commence what, even then, appeared to high-ranking friends of one of my uncles a doomed and immoral policy of imperialism), my interest in the relations between the literary, really the aesthetic, and the religious, or at least the numinous, intensified rather decisively in two very distinct ways. On the one hand, I rather quickly came to appreciate from weekly visits in Kyoto to famous Japanese temples and gardens that the line between the aesthetic and the sacred is extremely thin in certain Asian artistic forms and frequently disappears altogether. To any other mentality but a Protestant one, this benign discovery might perhaps have come as no surprise at all, but to me it took on the character of something like a minor revelation which succeeded in wiping out in a flash virtually all that I had been taught to believe about the radical difference between the world of man, as neoorthodox theologians then liked to put it, and the world of God! On the other, my occasional associations with various American communities in Asia – diplomatic, commercial, and even ecclesiastical – aroused considerable doubts about the accuracy of their representations of the United States, and particularly about what I wouldn't have then probably called some of the deeper structures of American life and thought. This second episode in what might be described as my own narrative of 'Innocents Abroad' led to another startling epiphany of sorts, but an epiphany, let me hasten to add, bearing no resemblance whatsoever to that vastly more consequent illumination suffered by Perry Miller on the banks of the Matadi in the former Belgian Congo when the man destined to become our greatest intellectual historian in the postwar period suddenly felt called to return to graduate study in the United States and prepare himself to expound the true meaning of America, presumably both to the natives at home and to the natives abroad. The substance of my own, altogether less glamorous or fateful, revelation simply had to do with a suddenly awakened sense of the depth of the misinterpretations that were being disseminated about the United States by various of its so-called official cultural representatives around the world, and an as intensely aroused desire to try to dispel at least some of them in my future teaching and writing.

Whether intellectual deliverances such as these were momentous enough to justify my year in Japan and Southeast Asia, in any event they provided me with sufficient incentive to complete a course of graduate study at the University of Chicago that then left me, at the time Martin Marty's invitation arrived, just in the process of revising for publication my PhD dissertation on the American literary and cultural historian F. O. Matthiessen. Author of *American Renaissance: Art and Expression in the Age of Emerson and Whitman,* a study that gave a name to a whole era in the American mid-nineteenth century, Matthiessen had made such a strong impression on me in part because his own understanding of the commerce between the literary and the religious in American cultural history was anything but doctrinal or even theological. Endowed with a mind too historically empirical to retain much patience with or capacity for grand theory, Matthiessen furnished me with an excellent model of a scholar who was skeptical of all attempts, insofar as he could detect them, either to turn literature into an apologia for faith or to reduce religion to an higher form of eloquence. Neither assuming that the normative aspect of criticism is a cousin to theology nor that the spiritual factor in literature is always paramount, Matthiessen helped me understand how infinitely various and particular the relations between literature and religion can be, and thus confirmed in me a healthy suspicion of all constructions of their association that are conceptually overdetermined, ahistorical, or culturally unspecific.

Yet it is one thing to possess strong reservations about the ways that critical study of the relations between literature and religion was constructed back in the late 1960s and early 1970s; quite another to come up with a formulation that wasn't – as, say, T. S. Eliot's was – too apodictic and prescriptive, or – as W. H. Auden's – too dialectical and formulaic, or – as Soren Kierkegaard's – too typological and unhistoricized. While persuaded that some of the great historicist studies of the subject in the modern period, from Erich Auerbach's *Mimesis* and Perry Miller's *The New England Mind* to Josephine Miles's *Eras and Modes in English Poetry,* Walter Houghton's *The Victorian Frame of Mind,* and M. H. Abrams's *Natural Supernaturalism,* held out more possibilities for getting straight the relations between literature and religion without detriment to either, I was still at a loss to come up with an explanation for exactly why this was so. There was, to be sure, a loosely pragmatic orientation to such studies that, as I and several other generations of critics had learned from M. H. Abrams's *The Mirror and the Lamp,* descended from Sir Philip Sidney and other Renaissance critics. This orientation was reflected less in their predisposition to subordinate the element of pleasure to the element of instruction than in their concern to measure the interactions of the

literary and the religious in terms of the difference that their recon-
figuration makes to the kinds of activity and forms of life that are
represented within any given work. Their pragmatism was also
evidenced by their construction as forms of what Wayne Booth was
to call 'epideictic history'. By epideictic history Booth meant to
describe a kind of history intent on re-presenting the significance
and stature of the object it studies, 'by discovering what kind of
historical account you can give of it – both of what went into it and
what came out' (Booth 1979:163, 162). This is an historical genre that
possesses a heuristic ambition even when, as in forms of it with
which I was later to become acquainted – Walter Jackson Bate's *The
Burden of the Past and the English Poet*, Lawrence Levine's *Black
Culture and Black Consciousness* Irving Howe's *World of Our Fathers*,
Martha Nussbaum's *The Fragility of Goodness*, or Eric J. Sundquist's
To Wake the Nations – it is intensely analytic and discriminating.

Nevertheless the real breakthrough in my own thinking about how
to conceptualize the relationship of the literary and the religious
had to await my introduction to the social anthropology of Clifford
Geertz – the occasion was the publication of *The Interpretation of
Cultures* in 1973 – where I finally found what for me had been the
missing term in so many twentieth-century attempts to theorize
their affiliations. That term was the word *culture* which immediately offered itself to me as the missing link in my conception of the
relation between literature and religion. Culture in this formulation
was simply the genus of which literature and religion, respectively,
were individual species. Or, as I later recast it, if culture is to be
identified in the Weberian model with that continually expanding
web of symbolic meanings which human beings employ to seek
some interpretive control over their experience, then literature and
religion possess a relationship to meaning that might be thought of
as complementary. Literature employs meanings hypothetically, to
show where they lead and what they amount to, by adumbrating
the consequences they imply. Religion, on the other hand, employs
meanings paradigmatically, to show where they come from and
why they matter, by legitimating the order of significance they
entail. Viewed in this manner, literature and religion could be seen
not only as performing parallel cultural functions but also as
sharing a common hermeneutic purpose: to help human beings
understand and negotiate their relations with the world around
them by casting those relations in forms symbolically designed to

encompass them by delineating an appropriate set of attitudes to be taken toward them.

One possible objection to this functionalist formulation of their relationship was that while literature and religion might be said to share similar interpretive aims, they aren't - or at least weren't - usually held to interpret the same kinds of experience. But this objection seemed to recall what the philosopher Alfred North Whitehead had designated as 'the fallacy of misplaced concreteness'. If literature and religion often dealt with different contents of experience, they nonetheless both found themselves drawn to forms or kinds of experience which tend to present themselves as somehow decisively 'other'. The sense of 'otherness', I of course realized, can and often does express itself in an infinite number of ways - the alterity that in the 1920s the Swiss theologian Karl Barth taught his readers to associate with the absolute impassability of the divine was not the same sort of 'otherness' that in the 1980s we had learned to identify with expressions of racial, ethnic, sexual, and class difference - but I also believed that what makes 'otherness' or alterity 'religious' has less to do with the substance of which it was composed than with the kind of response it evokes in those who experience it. In other words, I tended to agree with phenomenologists and historians of religion like Gerardus Van der Leeuw and Charles H. Long (another teacher and later colleague of mine) that objects, acts, or individuals are denominated as religious not because of the form in which they present themselves - everything from stones, animals, storms, people, and events have been so regarded - but because of the power imputed to them and the distinctive way in which people perceive and relate themselves to that power as they experience it breaking into, and possibly transfiguring, the structures of their own world.

No doubt this helps explain why for a time I was strongly attracted to the comparative religious phenomenology of Mircea Eliade. Associating religion with the attempt to respond to those transmundane elements of experience that seem to disrupt the flow of profane existence and confront people with a sense of 'otherness' over which they have no control, Eliade's claim that religious forms seek through myth and ritual to repeat those acts *in illo tempore*, so to speak, by which their supposedly 'sacred' character was first made manifest - and thus bring people into spiritual conformity with them - seemed to have much to commend it. But my own pragmatist and historicist orientation eventually drew me more closely to Clifford Geertz's less morphological view of religious interpretive structures. Differentiating such structures by means of the particular kind of perspective they convey on experience, the specific way they 'read' it, Geertz distinguished religious interpretive structures from those associated with other cultural systems, such as ideology, art, law, or common sense, by maintaining that the former presuppose an 'unbreakable inner connection' between a metaphysic, or view of how the whole of reality coheres, and an ethic, or sense of how one should act in reaction to such a view. Yet as Geertz went on to insist, it is neither alone the metaphysics it presupposes nor the ethic it produces that makes this perspective religious but rather the way in which each implies and reinforces, as they might not, for example, in philosophy, say, or moral theory, the other.

By the time I came to pull together and refashion the essays that comprised *The Intepretation of Otherness: Literature, Religion, and the American Imagination* (1979), Geertz's functionalist definition of religion helped me more clearly reconceive the nature of the symbiotic relationship between literature and religion. If from a Geertzian perspective religious paradigms enable people to manage their experience of the otherness of their circumstances by correlating that experience with a metaphysical idea of order that symbolically represents it and an ethical code of behavior that contains an appropriate set of attitudes and actions to take in response to it, so works of literature, it seemed to me, could then be viewed as at least sometimes putting such paradigms to the test, whether for the purpose of strengthening, subverting, or displacing them, by registering some of their deeper, and sometimes more disturbing, effects on what William Butler Yeats called 'the fury and mire of human veins'.

As it happens, I was assisted in reaching these formulations and then, during the late 1970s and early 1980s, in extending them by a number of other thinkers and critics. E. H. Gombrich, the art historian, helped me see, in *Art and Illusion*, what kind of literary and cultural history might follow from this construction of the relationship between literature and religion, but not before hermeneutic philosophers like Hans-Georg Gadamer, in *Truth and Method*, and, more particularly, Paul Ricoeur, in a host of studies from *The Symbolism of Evil* to *The Conflict of Interpretations* and, eventually, his great trilogy on *Time and Narrative*, enabled me to grasp more clearly the extent to which works of literature shape themselves around questions to which they purport to provide the answer, or, as in the case of more contemporary texts, constitute themselves as answers to questions that have yet to be asked. No matter which the text is presumed to be – as Hayden White once remarked in an observation that brilliantly summarizes an entire tradition of reflection in the history of interpretation – 'either a question put to reality which demands an answer from the reader, or an answer to a question which the reader must himself provide', works of literature command our serious attention whenever they seem to be produced 'at the point where our apprehension of the world outstrips our capacities for comprehending it, or, conversely, where canonized modes of comprehension have closed off our capacities for new experience'. Either way, by appearing to breach 'the conventional hierarchies of significance in which experience is presently ordered and [to] produc[e] a new vision of things which previously existed only as a perceptual possibility', such works could be said to bear a critical relation to what Gombrich referred to as a culture's mental set and by this reckoning the moral history of art could be reconstrued as the history of, in Gombrich's pregnant phrase, 'violated mental sets' (White 1970:179–180).

In all this, as I can now see, I was trying to protect the idea that art, or at any rate some art, and particularly that art whose 'otherness', as Ricouer put it, is manifest in the power to disclose a world of potential meaning and significance beyond its own ostensive reference, provides at least one position from which a criticism of culture might be mounted. An idea that I had derived many years before from the writings of cultural critics like Matthiessen, Lionel Trilling, Alfred Kazin, Irving Howe, Henry Nash Smith, and, particularly, Leo Marx, this idea, and the notion of cultural criticism that derived from it, was to undergo, with the arrival of deconstruction in the late 1960s and early 1970s, a series of assaults from which it is still struggling to recover. Together with the wider range of critical projects lumped under the term *poststructuralism*, deconstruction created serious but often important problems for most of the more traditional forms of cultural critique by challenging not only their epistemological legitimacy but also their moral basis.

Deconstruction was especially effective, as I came to appreciate over the years, in pushing inquiry up against its own interrogatory limits and then in questioning the subject position of the interrogator and the methods of interrogation. It was less effective at, much less even capable of, submitting its own premises to the same kind of critique it directed at other discursive practices. In this sense, deconstruction, like various versions of poststructuralism, was not without moral problems of its own. Even where it resisted the temptation to deploy its intellectual armaments chiefly for the sake of confirming its own premises, those same premises nonetheless carried with them an enormous burden of intellectual presumption. By proposing to put everything in question all at once, deconstruction was in effect pretending to do what the American pragmatist philosopher Charles Sanders Peirce had already demonstrated to be impossible a century before. Hence despite deconstruction's candor in acknowledging that all critiques, like its own, remain partially confined within the system they are attempting to disassemble, even in the process of disassembling it, so long as they continue to make the subject of their own discourse the oppositional repressions on which that system of thought is based, deconstruction nonetheless possessed no way of getting off, as Kenneth Burke might have put it, 'before the end of the line'. If in moral terms this tended to leave the authority of the critic supremely intact, in political terms, as Frank Lentricchia noted of Paul De Man in *Criticism and Social Change*, it almost inevitably led to passivity and inaction (Lentricchia 1983:50).

For many at the time, Mikhail Bakhtin's critique of the politics of monologism seemed to provide a useful counter-statement to the totalism of deconstruction, but the Bakhtin who actually interested me more – and who incidentally constituted the strongest challenge to the irregular metaphysics of deconstruction – was not the political champion of dialogism, or the anatomist of polyphony, or the historian of heteroglossia, important as these Bakhtins were, but the theorist of exotopy. This is the Bakhtin who asserted that interpretation presupposes, and generates, a certain kind of epistemological distantiation; the Bakhtin who maintained that dialogical understanding presupposes and preserves a certain measure of exteriority. Predicated on the experience of 'finding oneself outside' that which one wants to know (including oneself), Bakhtin's notion of exotopy proved most helpful to me in rethinking some of the problems of cultural interpretation. Over against all those ethnographically-inspired thick describers in the human sciences of the late 1970s and early 1980s (or the ideologically-minded multiculturalists of the later 1980s and early 1990s), the epistemology as well as ethics of whom (Geertz excepted) was still based on a Romantic hermeneutics of sympathy ('seeing from the native's point of view'), Bakhtin held that a sense of alterity – 'theirs' from 'ours' and 'ours' from 'theirs' – remains an indispensable ingredient in, and result of, any interpretive transaction among cultures. Thus if 'difference', as this notion was then being valorized in almost every form of cultural inquiry under the sun, is that which is to be understood, 'difference', as Bakhtin conceived it, is also that from which, and only on the basis of which, understanding as such is even assumed to be possible. As Bakhtin wrote, 'The chief matter of understanding is the *exotopy* of the one who does the understanding – in time, space, and culture – in relation to that which [s]he wants to understand.' This conviction merely confirmed not only what anthropologists like Geertz and, in a different form, Victor Turner, were trying to say in books such as *Local Knowledge* and *Dramas, Fields, and Metaphors*, respectively, but also what a cultural critic like Tzvetan Todorov was up to in his extraordinary study *The Conquest of America*: 'It is only to the eyes of an *other* culture that the alien culture reveals itself more completely and more deeply (but never exhaustively), because there will come other cultures, that will see and understand even more' (quoted in Todorov 1984:109–110). Yet what gave Bakhtin still greater interest to me at a certain moment was his conviction that these insights into the exotopic nature of consciousness, and the centrality of alterity to interpretation, came not from theory alone or even theory primarily; as he understood them, they came from literature itself, from the actual history of the novel.

Here, then, was a critical thinker who, like Milan Kundera from a later generation, mounted a powerful challenge to that denigration of the imagination and all its works which seemed to accompany the contemporary poststructuralist critique of the Enlightenment. Finding that forms of the imagination furnished, in Kenneth Burke's phrase, 'equipment for living', Bakhtin, Kundera, and Todorov, to name only three critics, like anthropologists such as Geertz and Turner, or philosophers like Stanley Cavell and Martha Nussbaum, were all drafting in their own terms important elements of an argument aimed at recuperating the heuristic value of the literary or the aesthetic without by any means necessarily confining the literary or the aesthetic to the merely canonical or the culturally elitist (Burke 1973:293–304). Each of them shared a view not unlike John Dewey's. Works of art perform a function that is not only critical but also, at least in a proleptic sense, emanicipatory. Works of art emancipate even in the act of criticizing, so I tried to argue in *The Culture of Criticism and the Criticism of Culture* (1987), just insofar as they are able, within the tensions, resistances, and refractions of their forms, to submit actual conditions – social, political, psychological, economic, and so on – and their probable consequences to the contrasting prospect of the purely plausible outcomes of merely potential experiences. Descrying through such contrasts those horizons of possibility that border, as it were, our notion of the actual, works of art possess a capacity that is, in other words, potentially liberatory as well as revisionary since, as Dewey said in one of the most famous sentences of *Art as Experience*, 'it is by a sense of possibilities opening before us that we become aware of constrictions that hem us in and of burdens that oppress' (1934: 346).

But what sense did it make, in the heavily ideological climate of American intellectual culture in the early 1980s, to talk about the importance of criticizing the world, much less of changing it, if culture itself was conceived as a seamless semiotic whole dominated by a single system of meaning? If all of the terms by which a culture might be challenged and revised from within were simply provided by the hegemonic system by which it understands and performs itself, could cultural critique have any other effect but to legitimate the values of that in whose name it does its work? This was the question raised by the new forms of ideological criticism that came into play in the 1980s and that became the center of focus in my *Thinking Across the American Grain: Ideology, Intellect, and the New Pragmatism* (1992).

One group of neopragmatists 'against theory' had already answered this question negatively by arguing that while interpretation is, in effect, the only game around, it remains a game whose rules, and, for that matter, whose results, are determined in advance by the interpretive communities that govern its practice. Convinced that this view of interpretation, like this notion of culture, was contrary to the spirit of pragmatism itself, I went back to some of the sources themselves and found that James, Mead, and Dewey, not to say later figures like Rorty, Bernstein, McDermott, West, Posnock, and others, said something quite different. Consistent with all of them was a view of cultural formations as plural, provisional, and problematically experienced, and of interpretation as context-specific, open-ended, and potentially self-revising. More to the point, all of them shared a conviction that theory is integral to practice precisely because practices always imply theories needing to be tested against still other practices.

If it was Dewey who furnished me with the clearest model of how criticism tests theories by measuring them against the practices they imply, it was James who first managed to install the aesthetic at the very center of reflective life. Following Peirce but altering his intentions, James had insisted that if the meaning of ideas is to be associated with outcomes and consequences as well as origins and premises, these must necessarily include outcomes and consequences that can frequently only be envisaged or projected rather than verified, that can merely be inferred or divined rather than confirmed. Dewey then simply gave this pragmatist notion of the 'critical imaginary' an explicitly genealogical as well as ethical-political dimension by showing how understanding always involves a double historical movement – backward into the past to ferret out the conditions from which something putatively emerged and also forward into the future to try to fathom the results or effects to which it may, but not necessarily will, lead. Critical inquiry, in the pragmatist understanding of it, is therefore always directed in pursuit not of meaning in general but of meaning that expresses itself as difference – the difference meanings make and the meaning of difference; and pragmatism's interest in difference is always propelling consciousness toward comprehensions that it can neither completely subsume nor suppress, toward a horizon of experience which is always presenting itself as intellectually elusive and refractory, as puzzling and even 'other'.

But is 'otherness' or, as it is sometimes called, 'the problem of the other' an issue of any real consequence for the pragmatist tradition? The conventional intellectual verdict has too often been negative, but this requires a good deal of historical and critical amnesia. Not only does it fly in the face of Charles Sanders Peirce's notion of fallibilism, or the idea that all conclusions are susceptible to further correction and revision by experience, and William James's criticism of 'a certain blindness in human beings'; it also fails to acknowledge W. E. B. DuBois's lifelong study of 'the strange experience' of 'being a problem', George Herbert Mead's theory of the social construction of the self, and Dewey's commitments to pluralism, as well as, more recently, Cornel West's defense of, in Frantz Fanon's phrase, 'the wretched of the earth', or Richard Rorty's preoccupation with forms of social marginalization and personal humiliation, or Clifford Geertz's studies of the opacity of cultural formations different from our own. The continuing challenge for this more cosmopolitan pragmatism is simply to figure out how the self may be made more fully corrigible to the 'other', made genuinely responsive to 'otherness', without turning the 'other' simply into another surrogate of the self.

As it happens, this is the same problem that has for so long perplexed the great Jewish philosopher and Talmudic scholar Emmanuel Levinas: how to keep the alterity of the 'Other', in such transactions, from being reduced to the 'Same'. If the self, as Levinas believes, is constituted by its encounter with that which is different, how does this 'different' retain its alterity? A question posed most sharply in recent years by debates surrounding the issue of 'multiculturalism', it is a question which, according to Richard Bernstein, Jacques Derrida may have answered more cogently than Levinas himself. Derrida's contention, against Levinas, is that the 'Other' can only retain its alterity if, in fact, it remains part of the 'Same', which is to say, part of the 'Self'. In other words, only if the 'Other' is represented, as Levinas did not think it should be, as an alter ego – that is, as something which, because it possesses the form of an ego, I must address – can it remain that in relation to which I must understand myself. 'I' and 'other' thus constitute for Bernstein a relationship of reciprocity, even if that relation also contains within itself dimensions of estrangement, enmity, and violence, conceivably of abjection and horror. Without going quite as far as Mikhail Bakhtin, who believed that the exotopic nature of understanding necessitates that the 'other' always be comprehended in part, if it is to be comprehended at all, from the point of view of the self, Bernstein asserts that 'other' cannot, as certain multicultural and neopragmatist theorists maintain, be totally incommensurable with the self so long as the self feels an ethical obligation, if not to understand the 'other', then at least to understand itself in response to the 'other'.

But what if selves no longer feel this sense of ethical obligation? What if, along with the religious and social as well as epistemological transactions it once sponsored, this ethical sense has dissolved into thin air, or, more likely, has been reduced to ash by the furnace of hatred that has been set ablaze in this century by ideologies of race, ethnicity, class, nation, religion, and gender? What if, as the political theorist William E. Connolly has recently asserted, identity, whether personal or cultural, can only establish itself by defining itself paradoxically in relation to a set of differences that it is constantly tempted to view not simply as 'other' but also as inimical? In a world where questions of cultural identity seem locked so often in such destructive embrace with issues of cultural difference, a world where people not only seem to prefer their own values to the values of others but appear to be able to maintain their own values too often only at the expense of disparaging and frequently demonizing the values of others, is it possible to imagine that the forms of life that we traditionally encompass within the structure of 'self' and 'other' can any longer have what Geertz calls 'a genuine, and reciprocal, impact on one another'?

This is the question that for me can now no longer be begged, that, indeed, has now cast a dark shadow over our whole notion of the human. A question given fresh currency, perhaps, by the politics of multiculturalism, it should have already been burned into the mind during this most violent and cruel century in the history of the human race since it has seriously undercut the whole metaphysics of human solidarity. Premised as that metaphysics was (and for many still is) on the concept of a unitary humanity, the notion of human solidarity originally offered a way of symbolizing the nature of the human bond not only within cultures but potentially across them during a period, particularly in the West itself, when it was no longer possible to employ more theologically orthodox formulations to define our commonality as creatures. Not only in the master paradigms of some of those prominent nineteenth-century social thinkers who quickly became our secular theologians – Tocqueville, Marx, Weber, Tönnies, Durkheim – but also in the master narratives of many of those nineteenth-century writers who took upon themselves the task of supplying us with a new set of what Northrop Frye called 'secular scriptures' – Balzac, Tolstoy, Eliot, Melville, Conrad, Woolf – the appeal to human solidarity has for some time been the way we expressed, enacted, and critiqued our shared attributes as a species.

But now this notion of human solidarity – and the rites of social, moral, and metaphysical exchange which sustained it – is in deep eclipse, if not totally discredited. Initially censured by social and political historians who linked the notion of human solidarity to the history of Western imperialism, it has now been subjected to renewed attack by the very science that imperialism begat, the human science known as anthropology. Instead of sharing, as was once assumed, a common nature, human beings, we have now been told, merely share a common predisposition to define themselves by means of their practices, or, rather, by the connection, as Geertz puts it, between their generic capacities and their specific performances. Whichever the case, we are no longer understood to be creatures possessing a universal nature to whose collective ethical center one can appeal but are rather assumed to be members of a species given to defining itself recurrently, and sometimes relentlessly, in terms of a deprecation of whatever it assumes to be significantly different and 'other'. The question then becomes, to state it differently, when so many of our former constructions of human solidarity – frequently white, male, and Western – have been rendered innocuous or worse, is there any way out of this seemingly universal practice of scapegoating where, as Kenneth Burke long ago reminded us, we continuously transform others into sacrificial objects for the ritual unburdening of our own unwanted vices and phobias?

This is the question around which, I believe, a newly emergent and vital cosmopolitan pragmatism is currently shaping itself. More to the point, it is also the question that is likely to define the next phase of my own thinking life.

References

Booth, Wayne C. 1979. *Critical Understanding: The Power and Limits of Pluralism*. Chicago: The University of Chicago Press.

Burke, Kenneth. 1973. *The Philosophy of Literary Form*. Berkeley: University of California Press.

Dewey, John. 1934. *Art as Experience*. New York: Perigee Books [reprinted in 1980, New York: G. P. Putnam Sons].

Dickstein, Morris. Unpublished. 'Proposal for a Conference on "The Revival of Pragmatism"'.

Lentricchia, Frank. 1983. *Criticism and Social Change*. Chicago: The University of Chicago Press.

Rorty, Richard. 1982. *Consequences of Pragmatism*. Minneapolis: University of Minnesota Press.

Rushdie, Salman. 1990. *In Good Faith*. London: Viking.

Todorov, Tzvetan. 1984. *Mikhail Bakhtin: The Dialogical Principle* (Wlad Godzich, trans). Minneapolis: University of Minnesota Press.

White, Hayden. 1970. 'The Point of It All'. *New Literary History* 2 (Autumn):173–85.

15

The Rest is History

IVAN STRENSKI

I cannot remember a time when I was not interested in religion. More than anything else, growing up in a Polish-American home pushed me toward an intellectual life in religious studies. Largely at the behest of my mother, I was raised an enthusiastic Roman Catholic. Although I grew up on my physician father's dairy farm outside Philadelphia in Moorestown, New Jersey, my world was large and cosmopolitan, filled with books, music, records and art. It was also John XXIII's time to shine forth with brimming optimism and spiritual daring. I followed.

Active ahead of official changes from on high, thanks largely to my religiously radicalized Catholic high school teachers, I was experimenting in the liturgical movement as a Third Order Benedictine at Mount Savior monastery. On school holidays, I would hitchhike into Manhattan to work in Dorothy Day's Catholic Worker soup kitchens by day. By night, I turned 'beat,' and roamed the bohemian lofts and bars of the lower East Side with the 'Worker' staff already talking the talk of Liberation Theology *avant la lettre*. I read voraciously – or at least as much as the demanding school work of a chemistry major or mind-numbing summer factory jobs would allow. Ralph Ellison, Jimmy Baldwin, Richard Wright, Gabriel Marcel, Romano Guardini, Edward Schillebeeckx, George Orwell, Dorothy Day, Camus and Sartre, Michael Harrington and *Jubilee* magazine were favorites. This vital life gave me a sense that religion was alive, something creative, on the cutting edge of cultural life, and something which informed my deeply held political views. This romantic mix that was my early life – rural and urban, academic and proletarian, ethnic and worldly, intellectual and worker – laid a broad foundation of experience preparing me for a wide open approach to studying religion, even though at the time I was then more enthused by actively living it.

That I have always felt that religion was (or ought to be!) both rich and consequential is probably why I have always placed religion in cultural, political, esthetic and other human contexts.

My *Four Theories of Myth in Twentieth-Century History* (1987a) presupposed that theories are not simply propositions, ideas or
arguments to be applauded or dismissed. They are also cultural
creations or 'social facts' (see Strenski 1989). As such they can best
be understood by linking them to the actual situations in which
they emerged. Why does it, for instance, make sense that a particular theory of myth arises in the time and place that it did, and
from the pen of a particular author in question? In the case of
Mircea Eliade, is it only accidental that a certain antagonism to
history pairs with the fact that the catastrophes of war destroyed
his own 'historical' life in Romania? Was it further only accidental
that Eliade was drawn to contradictory or, if you will, mystical
notions like the 'coincidence of opposites', in speaking of the
essence of myth? Could this be accidental especially when we
know as a youth that Eliade adhered to the mystical, nativist and
irrationalist Romanian Legion of the Archangel Michael (see
Strenski 1987a, Chapter 4)? In short, was Eliade, in the way his
lifelong scholarly interests and orientations took shape in relation
to his life, like me? I concluded that it often made good sense – at
least at some point – to interpret an author's work in terms of the
context of the situation in which an author lived, that despite
the alienated and fragmented condition of much of modern life in
the West, things may hang together more than may at first seem the
case. The challenge, however, was to make this insight into more
than a license to meander impressionistically among the trivialities
of personal biography. The only way I knew how to avoid impres-
sionism was to keep to what was important in an author's thought
and to interpret that thought within a recognized historical context,
bearing in mind all the while how such a location might help us
understand the texts. It took me quite of number of attempts –
some of them amateurish – to hone the historical craft of locating
'letters' in 'life'.

While the generally happy and consequential nature of my
youthful engagement in religion may go some way to make sense
of my cultural and social interests in religion, the necessary
movement beyond my own personal Catholicism, and even Christianity, stemmed from other parts of that early life. While my
mother affected my original appetite for religion by sending me
to Catholic schools, she also inculcated in me her own adventurous
attitudes towards ideas and languages. I was bilingual until about
the age of 12 – a fact that considerably expanded my cultural and

especially linguistic horizons. Because I was already comfortable with a 'foreign' language like Polish, I took naturally to learning Latin, German, French, Spanish, Sanskrit and Pali. Being bilingual also made me practiced in a quality of my work in which I have always taken pride – a certain mental agility in maneuvering among different cultural codes. Shifting between Polish and English was for me a kind of sport. So, instead of getting frustrated trying to make myself understood to my Polish grandparents, I made of it a kind of game. Along with language, naturally enough came a love of all those things making up culture – religion, music, art, food, customs – as well as an abiding affection and curiosity about faraway peoples and places.

But being able to shift between linguistic codes was no guarantee that I could take on the peculiar problems of operating with specifically religious codes – something which I assume is essential to religious studies, since, as I have argued, comparative study of religion must ground all our efforts (see Strenski 1985 and 1996). Added to the milieu of diversity contributed by my mother were the ethnic and religious differences my father brought to what made up for me a 'normal' religious life. His family was Carpatho-Rus or Rusyn (Ruthenian in its Latinized form), a Slavic people occupying a territory roughly defined by the Carpathian mountains and its network of associated valleys, and, in terms of religion, was close to Ukrainian orthodoxy. Thus, I learned to take for granted that he would either ignore Christmas as a religious holiday entirely or in his own way 'have' *his* Christmas at about the same time we were dismantling our trees and creches in early January.

Despite his periodic religious observances, my father was basically a New Deal secular humanist. I always shall be proud of the way he lived his left-wing ideals of social justice by serving a mostly working class clientele of patients in his years of medical practice. Later in life I learned what made him the way he was – both tolerant of religious differences, yet intolerant of claims to exclusive religious truth by any party. He had grown up in a community of near 'Bosnian' religious diversity in Central City, Pennsylvania, a coal mining town of about 500 inhabitants, nestled in a perfect little valley near the highest ranges of the Allegheny mountains. Central City is neatly divided into four communities of equal size: Russian Orthodox, Rusyn Greek Catholics (part Uniate, the other part not), Polish Catholics, and Slovak Lutherans. There are Strenskis (or near Strenskis) in *each* of these communities. So, the roots of religious and ethnic diversity, of their crossings and confusions, fanned out in all directions. In living among different religious groupings, my father was party to their often acrimonious partisanship. As a result, he developed a certain impatience with inter-religious disputes, and resolved the clashes among them by transcending them in a lofty skepticism about religious truth. In place of traditional religion, he assumed for himself an agnostic humanism, realized in a career serving suffering humanity as a small town general practitioner.

In his own way, my father inadvertently taught me to distinguish between scientific and theological kinds of explanations – a distinction I have maintained in my writings to this day. One day at my Catholic elementary school, Sister Dulcia, I believe her name was, sent us first graders home to ponder a mystery: 'Why are there holes in bread?' At dinner, when I asked my dad, he gave me a picture of nature in action according to its own inherent laws, of the generation of carbon dioxide gas and the workings of yeast. In class, the next day several students volunteered answers, but none like the one my father had given me. So, I piped up accordingly with my dad's yeast/gas theory. After tolerating our (to her) feeble attempts to answer this question, with a wave of the hand, Sister Dulcia delivered her magisterial solution: 'Children, *God* put holes in bread so that you could fill them with butter!' I remember thinking that something was distinctly fishy about this answer, not merely because 'God' had not been part of the original question, but because Sister's answer headed off in another direction than the one my dad had given me. She was all keen to theologize – to give voice to a cosmic teleology encompassing a divine plan for the marriage of butter and bread; my dad was playing by ground rules governing our humble attempts at knowledge within the limits of human capacities. Even at six years of age, I reckoned that both explanations could be right in their own unique ways, and thus need not exclude one another. But I doubted that either Sister Dulcia or my dad would have agreed.

Years later, the lessons of that day in grade one still abide. First, I learned the difference between *being* a religious person and *thinking* systematically about it. My historical essays on Eliade, Max Müller, Albert Réville, Cornelis P. Tiele and other representatives of a theologized phenomenology of religion were doubtless informed by my sense of the differences between 'doing' theology and doing the *study* of religion. When Sister Dulcia gave voice to her sense of God in the mystic *coincidenta oppositorum* of butter and bread, as it were, she was *being* religious – no mistake about it; when at age six, I pondered what Sister Dulcia had done and said, I was beginning a primitive form of the *study* of religion, because I was reflecting on someone's religious action, trying to make sense of it. I also learned a second lesson about the difficulties in talking religiously where the status of religious discourse was itself in question. Did it 'trump' science? Or was my scientific offering to Sister Dulcia's question necessarily inferior to hers? I came down on the side of saying at least for the time being that religious answers now had to give some kind of an account of themselves, that they had to take account of the power of scientific knowledge. The incident with Sister Dulcia merged with the experiences of the religious diversity of my family to produce a third and final conviction. So many viewpoints populated the world, and each felt it provided the proper starting point for such conversations. Given the deep and perhaps incorrigible differences among religious groupings, not to mention the profound gulf between the different communities of non-religious folk, to insist on pressing a particular religious position would only bring ruin to all. So, providentially, the somewhat haphazard tolerance of religious and ethnic differences of my own family plus my father's naturalistic worldview uncannily prepared me for the real world in ways I could scarcely have anticipated. While 'science' is often opposed to 'religion' as if it were an alternate faith, it is not really so. 'Science' provides at least a modicum of a neutral venue for discussion – and certainly more than that provided by the religions. This, I take it, is at least provisionally what the scientific ideal of public knowledge offers. In this, I am truly my father's son.

Despite the variety of my own family's various and dissident religious traditions, I remained a contentedly pious, although not a scrupulously observant, Roman Catholic. I saw no particular reason to breach the Catholic, much less Christian, frontier into the wider religious world. Until my twenties, I knew relatively little about Judaism, Buddhism, Hinduism and such, even if I had done my fair share of recreational yoga and meditation, or used a Hebrew-English psalter for my evening prayers, bought specially for that purpose on one of my city adventures in Philadelphia. It was as a result of my affection for the Eastern liturgy, especially for

Russian sacred music, which opened me to the bigger religious world in a most unlikely and comic way.

I shall recount this incident because it first raised the issue of the relation of religious commitment to academic study of religion. In my case, 'relaxing' my commitment to Roman Catholicism probably made my entry into religious studies possible. I say 'relaxing' and not 'abandonment', because I find the issue of my own status as a Catholic still puzzling even though I have not taken sacraments or regularly attended mass in 25 years. It, second, also showed how my religious sensibilities once established in youth remained a constant part of my outlook uninterrupted by the relaxing of my own religious performance. Although I no longer 'perform religion' in my present life, I have always felt comfortable talking and writing about religion because I had had the invaluable opportunity of having deeply 'performed and learned religion' in my youth. In the same way, although I now cannot say that I 'perform music' any longer, I still feel at ease discussing music, because I had early in life 'performed and learned music'. Third, this incident also taught that religions are real things, in the sense that they constitute communities of people, with their sociological reality, history and memory. This further means that 'being one' differs from 'understanding one'. Just because one feels that one understands a religious tradition, does not qualify one as a member. Methodologically, this along with other things, led me toward my conviction of the importance of the social dimension of a religion, emerging in my Durkheimian studies, which I will discuss later. So, how did I come to be convinced of so much about the nature of religion, just because I so loved the Eastern liturgy and its music?

Mostly out of 'roots'-driven curiosity, I had for some years attended both Uniate and Orthodox liturgies on occasional Sundays and feast days. After a while, I began to draw nearer to 'conversion'. Of course, I could have changed 'rites' to the Uniate observance at any time. But, going all the way over to Russian orthodoxy would have marked a decisive break with my Roman affiliations. The Russian orthodox church which I frequented was a sublime thing, a real dream palace of the sacred. A perfect little Greek temple, all gleaming white and flanked with clean Doric columns, it stood out amidst the grime and urban decay of North Philadelphia. When its full male choir gave forth, the whole structure hummed in sympathy. One Sunday, I decided to break with Rome and to pledge myself to the Russian Orthodox community by taking communion. I am not sure whether the occasion for this was the disappointment and frustration I was then feeling with Roman retrenchment after Vatican II, whether it was the recent death of my paternal (Rusyn) grandmother, the near death of my father and thus a desire to claim something close to their tradition, or whether it was the religious surge of the sublime music filling the air of that resplendent sacred place. Whatever it was, it made no difference: I had decided that the moment had come to step forward and change the direction of my religious life. According to custom, the priest dispensed communion from a position at the top of a short flight of three or four steps leading to the high altar. Behind him, the massive marble iconostasis rose up, with all the patriarchs, archangels, and saints of the Slavic lands looking down at the people and at me. As the choir roared out its alleluias, my heart filled in sympathetic joy at finding my spiritual home. Lining up with the Russian faithful, I marched quietly ahead to take communion in pious silence, head bowed, arms crossed over my chest until I had mounted the steps to the top where the priest, Father Borichevsky, awaited me. Preparing to receive communion, I opened my mouth wide, and looked straight into the eyes of the priest. He waited for me at the top of those now seemingly towering stairs, with something I did not expect: '*You* haven't been to confession!' Borichevsky sternly declared. 'Quite true', I managed feebly in response, and shamefacedly retreated whence I had come.

On the way out of church, after this dismal (and doubtless self-important) bit of attempted religious engagement, Borichevsky greeted me in a sporting manner. 'Why not come for a little chat in the rectory, young man?' I agreed, hoping at least to recoup a shred of my tattered dignity. Our cordial meeting gave us all the chance to laugh at my show of religious derring-do. Still, the moment had passed, and I felt as spiritually unsure as I had felt firmly convinced only a short while before. Our conversation moved away from my aborted attempt at conversion, and I silently thought about things which have been in the back of my mind ever since. This encounter between the difference between 'being one' and understanding, between religion as an idea and religion as a social reality, jarred my consciousness into some new space. In making my commitment to the Russians, I had pretty much forsaken Rome. But my rebuff by the Russians left me out in the cold, so to speak. Was this position 'betwixt and between' just the right place for receiving the 'good news' of the kind of religious studies worked out by Ninian Smart at Birmingham? Providence works in uncanny ways, for now it seemed that as a considerably 'relaxed' Roman Catholic-cum-rejected Russian Orthodox, I was ready for Ninian's openness to the diversity of religious truth.

While Borichevsky and I finished munching on marinated mushrooms, I told him that I was setting out for England in a few months to do my doctorate with Ninian Smart, perhaps to concentrate on Buddhism – probably at that time with a lingering Roman Catholic agenda in the back of my mind. 'How very interesting,' Borichevsky noted. 'You know, of course, that the Buddha is honored by us as a saint?' (I didn't). Borichevsky then proceeded to relate the story of saints Barlaam and Josaphat, and how their legend was actually a Christianized form of a bodhisattva myth. The name 'Josaphat' turns out to be a Syriac rendering of 'bosat,' an elision of 'bodhisattva'. At the time I did not know where to place this notion. But, oddly enough, this anecdote from a Russian Orthodox priest attempting to soothe my feelings of religious rejection worked in some strange way to open me up even further to the religious world beyond Christianity, which I had not yet breached, but which I shortly would after arriving to study with Ninian Smart. Not longer after, I would sit in Ninian Smart's office at the University of Birmingham, discussing strategies for my doctoral research, thus beginning my professional career in religious studies, even as I was still in disarray about my own religious identity from that Sunday with Borichevsky. I have essentially remained in that state to this day.

My attraction to Ninian's work went back to my undergraduate days at Toronto. I cheered his scathing attacks on the obscurantism of the fashionable Christian theologies of the time, for example, Ian Ramsey, Tillich, or the 'Death of God' crowd. They charged me with confidence in the way my father's elegant account of the reasons for holes in bread had done long ago. But when I reached England, I discovered a Ninian who, while no less the analytic and critical thinker, was moving in new directions. This was less the Ninian Smart, B.Phil., The Queen's College, Oxford and John Austin, but more the Ninian revolutionized by his encounters with racism and colonialism from his service in the British army's Intelligence Corps stationed in then Ceylon, the Ninian in league with K. N. Jayatilleke, the Ninian who surrounded himself with a veritable mini-Sangha of Sri Lankan Buddhist doctoral students. Dharmasiri, Panabokke, Marasinghe and I made quite a gang, cooking up those radioactive curry suppers in the dank murk of an English winter evening. This was also the Ninian on the verge of leaving Birmingham to launch the new Department of Religious Studies at the University of Lancaster, where the historical studies later to become important to me would have been somewhat more at home.

I did not however immediately join Ninian's new effort, since I was still under the sway of philosophy and the philosophical Ninian I had read as an undergraduate. I had yet to be convinced that 'phenomenology' or 'history' of religions had much of a future. That would come later. Doing 'history' was something I, as a philosopher of the analytic sort, then held in contempt. What was this 'history' anyway? Was it not little more than a grubbing around in minor details promoted to some level of importance because of their brute facticity? Historians, to my mind, were good at the 'what', but miserable failures at the 'so what?' The 'so whats?' mattered most to me. At the same time, however, the environment of positive studies of religion which Ninian promoted in Lancaster gradually seduced me away from philosophy of religion eventually to the history of religions. True, I had yet to work myself completely out of philosophy, but I was making a start.

Early on in my graduate studies, I came to a crossroads. I had begun by first following my heart to read the critical scholarship on the Jewish Bible. A short spell of this convinced me, however, that I was not ready to slog my way through the language training needed to pursue this interest. I was still at heart a philosopher. I cared most about biblical scholarship because it raised such delicious fundamental religious issues, such as the debates about the offbeat religiosity of Proverbs, puzzles over the variety of biblical words for time (subsequently to appear in different form in Eliade's work), James Barr's demolition of the methodological assumptions of Kittel's *Wörterbuch* and, not least of all, the question of myth. 'Myth' offered me a splendid invitation to think about such fascinating questions as the relation of so-called 'myth' and 'history' or 'myth' and 'revelation'. How do we tell the difference, if there is one? Does the difference between 'us' – Jews and Christians – and 'them' – Babylonians, Sumerians, Egyptians, Greeks, and thus subsequently, Buddhists, Hindus, and so on –

really boil down to the difference between folks who live religion historically and enjoy the fruits of 'revelation' over against those benighted others lost in 'myth' and left to the feeble religious resources of human reason?

It wasn't long before I saw through the hidden apologetics of this sort of biblical scholarship, and began – but just barely – to see the cryptic polemical uses which, as I have argued in *Four Theories of Myth in Twentieth-Century History* (1987a), characterized the discourse of 'myth'. These and other scholars simply cut the 'cloth' of myth to fit their particular 'suits'. If they felt Christian scriptural 'revelation' was essentially 'history', then non-Jewish or non-Christian sacred literature was by definition not historical, that is to say, 'myth'. If Christian 'revelation' spoke of 'linear' time, then 'myth' was characterized by 'circular' time, and so on. Sister Dulcia had returned, bread and butter in hand, in a most unanticipated place.

In methodological terms, this crypto-theologizing discourse about myth in biblical scholarship taught me that 'myth' was a loaded term, that it was basically a polemical device for achieving certain purposes. In the case of the biblical theologians, they used 'myth' to practice a sleight of hand over biblical literature, the way Sister Dulcia's declaration of God's agency in the mystic marriage of butter and bread in effect dispatched scientific accounts to the realms of irrelevance. Religious literature, which thus embodied cyclical notions of time, ranked low on the scale of truth, and thus was 'myth', because Christian scripture, that is, 'revelation', taught that God created heaven and earth in linear time. My sense of intellectual chivalry was offended by what I took to be less than honorable attempts to score theological points against even the long-dead Babylonians by labeling their creation narrative a 'myth', so that one could contrast it with the 'historical' (and thus superior) Jewish or Christian biblical narrative. I could not quite grasp why the cyclic nature of time presumed in the Babylonian narrative (as I recall) should require that we term such a narrative 'myth'? Why, conversely, did the (supposed) lack of such a cyclic notion of history in Genesis free it from having the same label apply? Why did not a talking serpent, a man formed from mud, and a woman fashioned from a man's rib qualify Genesis as equally 'mythical'? I distinctly recall feeling that the biblical scholars had failed a kind of moral test of authenticity and integrity in using their scholarship to score theological points. They were diminished in my eyes forever.

How then to make further progress on 'myth', if my erstwhile inspirations proved corrupt beyond rehabilitation? The answer both Ninian and I concluded was to end my dalliance with biblical studies. In effect, I was to revert, in a way, to my Toronto training in linguistic philosophy – with the signal exception that the 'ordinary language' I would now analyze would be 'myth' and the theoretical writings about 'myth' by such figures as Eliade and Lévi-Strauss, then all the rage. The task of my PhD dissertation would be to get to the bottom of the logic of the most influential concepts of myth in our time. What were the major theories of myth informing contemporary thinking about the subject? How did they hang together conceptually? On these conceptual bases alone, which concept or theory seemed most promising for use in the study of religion? Perhaps by getting to the fundamental conceptual assumptions and structures informing theories of myth, we could get at what was really going on in the discourse of myth as it appeared in biblical scholarship and elsewhere. Thus, I began the basic work on my PhD dissertation as an analytic and critical exercise which I called by the ungainly but candid title of 'Methodology and Myth, with Special Reference to Cassirer, Eliade, Lévi-Strauss and Malinowski'.

It was not long before I realized that in doing this dissertation I would be utterly on my own. In the late 1960s, when I researched and wrote it, no one had yet systematically analyzed the work of Eliade or Lévi-Strauss. We were all too much in their thrall to have done that. Certainly critical readings of Eliade were totally out of the question among religious studies types. Moreover, theorists of an earlier generation, Cassirer and Malinowski, had been passed over in the rush to more fashionable thinkers. Some years later, I moved on from this strictly analytic approach of 'Methodology and Myth' and became an historian by totally reconceiving and greatly amplifying the dissertation as *Four Theories of Myth in Twentieth-Century History*.

The crucial moment in sparking the historical method of *Four Theories* came one day in my second semester of teaching in my first job in an introductory course on religious experience at Connecticut College. That day the class was unusually restless, doubtless because I was trying to elaborate the intricacies of Lévi-Strauss's structural approach to myth, and not doing a particularly good job of convincing the students how wonderful it all was. Then, one brave and somewhat perturbed young woman raised her hand in the middle of my lecture, stood up, and asked, 'Why would *anyone* think about myth like that?!' I don't remember offering a particularly brilliant reply. But I do remember being both utterly stunned and insatiably curious at the same time. We – I and my closest colleagues of the time – Hans Penner, Don Wiebe, Ninian Smart, Robert Segal, Tom Lawson, Karen McCarthy Brown – found no such problem with Lévi-Strauss. Why should my students? We just took Lévi-Strauss for granted as making total sense; yet all attempted rationales for his method left my students dumbfounded.

The genuine germ of wisdom and good sense contained in my student's question was to ask why otherwise equally intelligent, hardworking myth theorists had come up with such different methods of approaching myths, and more fundamentally different conceptions of what 'myth' was. The more I looked and read, the more this puzzle gripped me. For one thing, some of the great thinkers of our field, for instance, E. B. Tylor, never thought much about myth at all. For others (too numerous to list), 'myth' was everything. Then, I found it most disconcerting that those for whom myth mattered often talked right past each other. Apparently the subject, 'myth', was an odd one, since very few of the great myth theorists were willing or interested in building upon the work of others – as at least the biblical scholars I had been reading earlier did. 'Myth' was then not like some vast unexplored continent about which travelers and geographers accumulated knowledge from generations of 'discovery'; it was rather as if each putative voyage of 'discovery' was in fact a project of 'inventing' the continent which they then said they wished naively to explore. If this were true, then to understand theories of myth, we needed to understand the conditions shaping the way 'myth' was 'invented', conceived and so on. Understanding theories in this way meant that I had to become an historian. How and why a theory was formed in a particular way was a question of seeing theories as actions, as embodying various strategies and interests – some of which might well lie outside the normal academic sphere and take in politics, the arts and indeed religion itself. Theories of myth, like the word itself, are highly charged and bristling with value commitments. Theories of myth, at least in a certain time and place, I argued, were not just methodological handbooks for making sense of stories; the theories typically determined what would be counted as a 'myth' in the first place and were often vehicles for promoting certain larger ideological, moral, or religious commitments. Lévi-Strauss's detached anti-anthropocentrism, his appeals to a perspective grounded in the indifference of nature, all serve to give support and impetus to his own latter-day quietism in politics and a certain equally abstract and humanly decentered way of conceiving of human nature itself. Lévi-Strauss's refusal to engage myth in its ideological capacities helped me understand why Lévi-Strauss's theory left us all so empty after a while. Lévi-Strauss's retreat into the mysteries of neurological structures only reinforced a sense of the aridity and lack of consequence of structural mythology. Who today reads Lévi-Strauss's multi-volume *Mythologiques* for his analyses of Brazilian myths? Who indeed reads *Mythologiques* at all? But until I started to see Lévi-Strauss's theory of myth in a larger intellectual and (anti)political context, I really did not understand how to read him, how to pick out what seemed trivial or stray remarks about brain structures, say, as more than just scientistic bravado.

Thus, the process of writing *Four Theories* was one in which I set out self-consciously 'reinventing' myself as an historian, as someone who could write *narrative*. I wanted to feel confident about working with *data* – with literature, correspondence, newspapers, diary entries, scribbled notes in the margins of books, sermons, and obituaries. Instead of being satisfied with having solved the 'logic' of an argument, I wanted better to understand texts by locating them in concrete *contexts* of time and place – in the flow of various academic, national political, religious and esthetic histories totally unknown to me up to that time. My goal became not proving that someone was wrong, but understanding why they thought that they were right!

Those who think of my work only as 'methodology' have also failed to see how my historical writings have engaged fundamental first-order religious issues. My interests have been drawn to the way the materials of traditional or exotic cultures have been 'recycled' into ideologies, moral paradigms, theologies and religious materials by the classic theorists of the study of religion (Strenski 1995). In our religious rush to find meaning for ourselves, we have exploited the cultural property of others unable to resist our efforts. Thus the hymns of the Vedas are exploited as evidence of the greatness of the Germans; the so-called Venus of Willendorf is pressed into ideological *corveé* in behalf of the precedence of mother goddesses over father gods; the ritual masks of West

African folk are enslaved in the interests of confirming our belief in the profound spirituality of 'primitive' society. Our 'colonies' have thus not only extended over the face of the earth, but to master the minds of people past and present.

Four Theories was my first major effort showing how *religious materials* such as myth have been *represented and theorized* for political purposes. In my studies of the rhetoric of late nineteenth- and early twentieth-century anti-Semitic uses of myth, for example, I have shown how these campaigns against Jews were informed and given scholarly legitimacy by appeals to the myths of Vedic India of two to three millennia before (see Strenski 1997). In my study of French nationalism and racial science, I investigated how the mythologies of Celtic, Germanic or Latin origins func- tioned to set apart ideological opponents fighting for a particular view of what it was to be French (see Strenski 1987b). Traditional and exotic societies have always been there, and for a good deal of time, we have also known about their existence. But it is only when we decide to engage in the risky process of *representing* them or *theorizing* about them for our purposes that they take on importance – even if in doing so this importance may be governed more by our needs than by 'theirs' (see Strenski 1993b). Malinowski knew this when he presented his studies of traditional cultures, cynically in part, in terms of being valuable to colonial adminis- tration in harnessing colonized folk for employment as cheap labor. When the romantics cast traditional folk as survivals of ante- diluvian religious harmony, they also 'made' the folk into something of their own. I have accordingly tried to bring out how the study of *our* colonization of the primitive and traditional mind for modern ideological, moral, political or religious purposes has been a persistent feature of how we have behaved to the past and far afield. In doing so, I think I have shown how the *representation and theorizing* of myths, rituals, and such really make a kind of difference which those cultural materials themselves could never make on their own.

In speaking here of the radical hermeneutic enterprise of making 'religion' out of the documents of traditional peoples, I invariably think of the works of Eliade and of the challenge it was for me fully to understand and explicate. From the time of my undergraduate days and continuing right through to my dissertation, I was deeply intrigued by Eliade's writing. But as a doctoral student, I was too preoccupied trying to make sense of Eliade's meandering and alluring thought to push further. Yet, I was sure Eliade was more than a mere 'historian' of religion, and that he was subtly pressing his own particular brand of religiousness as well through his scholarship. I just couldn't pull it all together – at least until I got a whiff of Heidegger's Nazism.

In the late 1970s, in one of two separate papers given at a special seminar hosted by the University of California, Santa Barbara, I argued the then scandalous thesis that Heidegger had been a sincere Nazi and that his political commitments made a difference to his ontology. After numerous rejections from 'respectable' journals of religious studies and philosophy, *The Christian Century* rose to the occasion and published my part of the seminar, the little *feuilleton*, 'Heidegger Is No Hero' (1982). Since then, and since the major studies of the deep Nazism of Heidegger's thought, the thesis which was argued at that seminar has been quietly assumed (see Farias 1987). With the help of the ground-breaking work of Karsten Harries, I pointed out how, for example, Heidegger's public addresses, while officially serving the Nazi regime, were mirrored in his philosophical writings. Thus, in his infamous address of 1933 as Nazi-appointed Rector of Marburg University, he proclaimed ' "The Führer himself and he alone *is* the German reality of today and for the future, and its law" ' (see Harries 1976:658). As late as 1953 (!), Heidegger argued a familiar enough Nazi theme – namely that political leaders must be ready to use violence in pursuit of power without regard for the normal constraints of law or limit (Harries 1976:657). Especially distasteful about Heidegger's performance when finally confronted with requests to account for his Nazi politics was the way he wrapped himself in the pious mantle of victimhood. 'Nur noch ein Gott kann uns retten,' said Heidegger sanctimoniously in 1976 to *Der Spiegel*. My God, I thought, the man has no shame!

Once completed, the project on Heidegger called forth all sorts of analogies with Eliade. Their Romanticism, their 'volkishness', their *Blut und Boden* nationalism, their 'crisis' existentialism, the religious aura of their writings, their anti-liberalism, their vaulting ambition to transcend the traditions, their pagan appeal to 'the earth' and the 'gods', their self-styled mystagoguery, their underlying authoritarianism, their intimate connection with Italian fascist politics and principles, Heidegger's anti-Semitism and the possibility of Eliade's – all pointed to some deep affinity I simply had to fathom. In trying to make sense of Eliade's thought, I experienced again how trying to understand Eliade in his social and historical context would more richly inform me than only in trying to understand the logic of his arguments, as I had done in my doctoral dissertation. I believe that I thus had discovered how Eliade's 'life' and his 'letters', so to speak, interacted. What Eliade thought in his so-called 'history' of religions bore analogies to the political inclinations he shared with the Legion of the Archangel Michael, also known as the Iron Guard. This was at least partly so because the Legion was itself a profoundly religious movement as well as being a paradigm of bully-boy fascism. Eliade freely admits in various autobiographical writings that during the 1920s and 1930s he was sympathetic to the 'European right' (Eliade 1977:197), and, amazingly, even continued to his last days defending the Legion as treading the 'path of non-violence' (Eliade 1988:65) and as being 'ethical' (Eliade 1988:65). We also know that a section of this Romanian right-wing, the Legion of the Archangel Michael, was dominated intellectually by Nae Ionescu, one of Eliade's closest personal friends as well as his esteemed mentor in philosophy at Bucharest University. Eliade and his peers in the young Romanian generation were in full revolt against parliamentary democracy, separation of church and state, economic and political liberalism. In Eliade's words, he and his friends were 'obsessed' by rebellion against the 'old ones' (Eliade 1981:261), by what Eliade himself saw as 'anti-democratism' (Eliade:1937).

Given that these things were true of the most formative period of the life of Eliade and his peers, I concluded that we might look for continuities or significant transformations of these values in his later thought. I felt that perhaps Eliade's style of doing history of religions and specifically his 'creative hermeneutics' carried on the commission of the radical political program of the Legion in the form of the worldview assumed by his approach to studying culture and society. Without trying to rehearse the entire argument of *Four Theories* here in this essay, one of the keys to my interpretation was the very anti-liberalism of the Romanian political commitments of which Eliade has been vocal. Now if the Legion sought the overthrow of the bourgeois liberal democratic world, perhaps this explained why Eliade spoke of his style of history of religions as seeking to 'promote the destruction of the official cultural world' (Eliade 1969:4). Another clue was Eliade's rejection of empirical falsification of his claims as an historian of religions. No historical fact, no words of disavowal from the folk we studied could ultimately upset the conclusions Eliade declared in his work. This style of interpretation, I reasoned, matched well with the epistemological style of groups and movements admired by Eliade – depth psychology, yogic gurus, and also the dictatorial or author- itarian epistemological mode of operation of the Iron Guard fascists themselves (for further discussion, see Strenski 1993c:17–27). In each case, the 'leader', whether doctor, guru, or dictator always knows best, and is above criticism arising from a consideration of facts or from the persons in their care. This is why Eliade can say that hermeneuts such as he 'considered that their approach was legitimate in that it enabled them to find those deeper mean- ings ... that can be apprehended only from the viewpoint afforded by a certain level of speculation' (Eliade 1972:236), or remarkably that he aims 'to seek meanings, even if they aren't there' (Eliade 1977:85). What else are we to conclude when Eliade tells us such things? I concluded that it meant that Eliade imagined himself specially endowed to know the absolute truth of things about religion. For me this absolutism echoed the equally absolutist men- tality of the religio-political movement to which Eliade was so passionately devoted in his youth, and which he never disavowed in his life.

Because this story dealt with the checkered and murky formative past of perhaps the world's most eminent student of religion, telling it involved risks. Some colleagues have not forgiven me to this day for the audacity of having even dared to raise the question of the nature of Eliade's right-wing Romanian politics, and for arguing that his revolutionary political and religious vision had some part to play in his approach to the history of religions. Never- theless, I plugged away as best I could trying to read Eliade's thought about religion and myth against the backdrop of what could be gathered from the literature on his times in the major European languages. But all along the way, when I probed the matter of Eliade's religion and politics in Romania, I met the stone wall of an apparent code of silence. Many whom I questioned about Eliade's life deliberately misled me. But the more they tried to put me off, the more I was sure I was on the right track. The great breakthrough came one day in the form of an airmail letter from a Bucharest scholar of impeccable credentials, typed carefully on half-sheets of onion paper, laying out detailed answers to questions about Eliade's politics that I had posted to him months earlier. The rest, as they say, is history. Today, I believe it is clear, *mutatis mutandis*, that I was fundamentally correct in locating Eliade and his thought in the right-wing politico-religious revolutionary context of Romania, even if many questions remain unanswered. But I am satisfied to rest on the Eliade matter, since as a thinker, I have never wanted to make a career of my interests in Eliade. Furthermore, I always felt it my talent to 'plow the field', to make the perhaps somewhat crude breaks with what has gone before, while perhaps surrendering the 'fine-grained' analysis to others more talented than I.

For the sake of religious studies, I hope that more and more will become known about Eliade, his times and his like. We ought to know how Eliade's adoption of the stance of guru in matters of interpreting religious data bears on his love of the Indian religious traditions, but also on the – equally authoritarian and religious – rightist Romanian political movement with which he was intimately connected. I have tried then to see beyond arguments, and thus surpass philosophy or 'methodology'. Instead, as an historian, I have sought to grasp the larger social and cultural contexts in which the methods inhere, and which give them their salience and meaning. When we take this route, I think we will be well placed to discover much more about the religious nature of certain modern so-called purely 'political' movements like the one of which Eliade was part. The radical romantic fascism of Eliade's Romania, like the fascisms of Franco's Spain, Salazar's Portugal and Mussolini's Italy, all traded in religious imagery, structure and purpose. Besides Eliade, we now know that creative religious types such as Joseph Campbell, Carl Jung and lately even T. S. Eliot were men of the 'right wing'. Why? Further research into Eliade's political religiosity and that of 'his like' will enable us in religious studies to make our proper contribution to an understanding of the radical events of our century by bringing to the fore the details of the religious dimension of those events.

In my latest work – that on Durkheim and the Durkheimians – I have tried even harder to show how well some of the most potent political notions of our time are encapsulated in religious thinking, institutions and history. I had always been drawn to the contrarian and unfailingly refreshing qualities of Durkheimian societism, to the enlightening way Durkheim's sociological apperception puts familiar things into sharper relief. Accordingly, I have turned to the Durkheimian theory of sacrifice as a companion effort to my book on myth, aiming here at trying to bring to light the underlying culturally and socially determined discourse of ideological, moral or religious concerns in which this theory of sacrifice is embedded. Most of all, I believe that these concerns can be seen to shape and govern the theoretical moves made within theories of sacrifice – at least of a certain period and place. In fact, these theories actually constitute a kind of societal polemic with implications going far beyond what they indicate on the surface. I have tried to show how, while people may seem superficially to be speaking about ritual sacrifice in exotic cultures, they are at the same time saying something, often primarily, about their own culture. They therefore spoke and thought *about* sacrifice by speaking or thinking *with* it.

This new investigation into the discourse on sacrifice uses the same methodology of historical understanding as *Four Theories of Myth in Twentieth-Century History*. In the new book, as in *Four Theories*, I attempt to understand theoretical thinking by situating it in both 'internal' professional and intellectual as well as in 'external' political, cultural and social contexts. But instead of looking at four theories in four historical contexts, I focus instead on a *single* theory and *single* book, Hubert and Mauss's *Sacrifice: Its Nature and Functions*, and within the single national and temporal context of *fin-de-siècle* France, articulated in terms of the four academic, political and religious contexts of the day: the Roman Catholic, Jewish, Protestant and Free thinker.

Hubert and Mauss's book became the object of my interest not only because it is by far the most influential book ever written on sacrifice, but because it was written at a time and place where the idea of *civic* sacrifice was a matter of public debate resonant with religious overtones, much like the topics of violence, gender role, gender identity or sexual preference are with us today. What does the individual owe the nation and what can the nation demand of the individual? Curiously enough both these discussions – the one about ritual and the other about civic morality – occur within the same book, and seem, in the minds of the writers, to depend in some deep way upon each other.

Thus, in sacrifice, I seemed to have happened again upon one of those especially charged subjects, like the earlier one of myth, where my appetite to understand the way we convert the materials of traditional societies into political or civic ideology promised to be richly satisfied. The Durkheimians believed that we, in societies threatened by instability, moral mediocrity, a dearth of collective passions to do great things, could draw policy lessons about how individual and collectivity might be made to articulate with one another. To learn these lessons, the Durkheimians felt that we should meditate on the lessons provided by the way the long religious history of humanity dealt with such matters. In studying the institution of ritual sacrifice in traditional and ancient societies, they felt that we could learn the secret of the stability and vitality of our forbears. My challenge was to try to show how they articulated this vision in their time and place sufficiently so that they could have been heard and heeded.

This book marks the most recent stage of my research of about ten years running, a period in my thinking concerned with the Durkheimians and the study of religion launched by them (see, for example, the massive list of Durkheimian students of religion and their work in Honigsheim 1960). The influence of the Durkheimians in religious studies remains generally unacknowledged or underappreciated by our peers. I suspect this is because prevailing liberal Protestant assumptions in our field favor the individual over the group, a position that results in the 'reduction' of the Durkheimians to being seen as simple 'reductionists' (sic). Yet, when I began taking account of what the Durkheimians actually wrote in their own time, I was amazed to find them up to their eyeballs in the study of religion. Not only were Durkheim's interests in religion well known and solidly established, but Henri Hubert and Marcel Mauss, Durkheim's closest confederates, were even more devoted to the study of religion. They had written about magic, sacrifice, prayer, myth, the sacred and many other topics central to the study of religion, and had occupied chairs in history of religions at Paris's prestigious institute of the study of religion, the École Pratique des Hautes Études, Fifth Section. I also learned that at the turn of the century, Marcel Mauss trained first in the history of religions under the great Indologist, Sylvain Lévi; Henri Hubert, his virtual intellectual twin, did likewise. They, in turn, stimulated the work of Granet on Chinese religion, Guignebert on Christianity, Lods on Judaism, Pryzluski and Mus on Buddhism, Bouglé on India, Lévy-Bruhl on the 'primitives' and so on. Moreover, their approach to religion informed generations of students of religion. Devoted to the Durkheimians are Robert Bellah, Lévi-Strauss, Georges Bataille, Germaine Dieterlin, Louis Dumont, Mary Douglas, Evans-Pritchard, Victor Turner, and such. I felt that it was time for a clear and unapologetic embrace of this intellectual tradition as a tradition of *religious studies*. In this effort, I have been extremely fortunate to share my interests in French and Durkheimian studies with a series of wonderful colleagues, Philippe Besnard, Michel Despland, Louis Dumont, Antoine Faivre, Marcel Fournier, Robert Alun Jones, Hans Kippenberg, Sam Preus and Bill Pickering. I could not have accomplished even a small part of what I have been able to do in connection with the Durkheimians without their aid in negotiating the Parisian intellectual scene, without their patient and candid scrutiny of often bulky manuscripts, without their example of polished intellectual work in an area to which I came as a novice in early mid-career.

Thus, after discovering that so many of the great figures in the study of religion owed their interests in religious studies to the evil 'reductionist' Durkheimians, I reasoned further that using the idea of reductionism to screen out 'bad' approaches to religion was quite useless. Instead, reductionist or not, I had to find out why the Durkheimians were so devoted to the study of religion, and what their approach to religion really amounted to. From there it was a matter of taking up seriously the substance of what the Durkheimians meant to religious studies. And so my recent scholarship on the Durkheimians began. As before, the rest is history.

In the course of putting together a picture of the Durkheimians, religion, and the study of religion, I have lately completed a book which explores the question of the 'Jewishness' of Durkheimian thought. Published under the title of *Durkheim and the Jews of France*, I decided to take up one by one the major attempts to show that Durkheim's thought is determined in some way by his Jewish birth and upbringing. To wit, are Durkheim's societism, his use of symbolic analysis, his ritualism, his apparent nostalgia for ancient Israel, signs of a secret Jewishness which he only expressed in cryptic form in his apparently deracinated sociology? Without going into the details of this intricate and detailed discussion, let me say that in it I try to understand Durkheim's thought by locating it in the historical context of the Jewish life of his time. This departs from the usual approaches from both anti-Semites and philo-Semites alike which ascribe certain 'essential' Jewish traits to Durkheim's thinking and thus argue about the Jewishness of Durkheim's thought on this – ahistorical – basis. When we look into the historical Jewish context of Durkheim's time, we instead see a plurality of contexts, a plurality of Judaisms – much as Jack Neusner and Jonathan Z. Smith have urged us to do more broadly. It is in relation to this historical plurality and complexity that

Durkheim's relation to Jewishness and Judaism is to be understood, and thus that the relation of his Jewishness (or lack of it) to his thought is to be understood. To say more than this at this time would not only be to give away the surprises of this book, but to oversimplify what should be left complex.

For me, one of the attractions of now being something of an historian of French Jewry is how this has allowed me to deepen my knowledge of the Jewish past, which I had explored in some depth in *Four Theories of Myth in Twentieth-Century History* and perhaps before that in my dalliance with studies of the Jewish Bible as a graduate student. For a Polish-American Catholic with a fairly acute sense of historical moment, reinforced by several intense visits to Krakow, the home city of my mother's family, it is hard for me adequately to convey what my affiliation with Jewish studies has meant personally. Besides being encouraged by such generous colleagues as Bill Green, Richard Hecht, Jack Neusner and Charles Vernoff, I was simply drawn to it by what I can only describe as some kind of sympathy rooted in my family's philo-Semitism. My mother nearly married Jewish, and always retained an affection for things Jewish. As the daughter of an inner-city shopkeeper, she grew up in a world where business brought people of all sorts into the life of the family. With a name as alien to American ears as 'Ivan Strenski' I often looked for my own kind in public life. This is (or at least was) not found easily in a world where everyone seemed named Campbell or Hamilton. But one day I thought that I had really struck it rich. As a child I can remember telling my mother how proud I was to have discovered so many Polish names on the rolling credits of my favorite TV programs. These 'Polish' names were of course 'Jewish' ones, as I was later to learn from her. But by that time it made no difference, since I reckoned with names like that, we were on the same side.

Even before I had made the transition to Durkheimian intellectual history, curiosity about 'reductionism' provided me an early rationale for what would later be my embrace of the Durkheimians. Although many talked against reduction and reductionism in religious studies, this talk seemed shallow. So, I decided that I needed first to teach myself what 'reduction' was. (In fact, many of my articles are the result of feeling ignorant about a certain topic, and then deciding that I simply needed to learn about it by teaching myself as I wrote.) What I found in researching the history and philosophy of science literature in preparation for writing these pieces was that the anti-reductionists typically knew nothing about what reduction meant; they merely used it as a 'boo-word' to smear their opponents. Instead, I found (and argued) that 'reduction' in the sciences happens all the time, and that it is basically an everyday tactic for achieving conceptual change. By this logic, even Eliade was a reductionist in that he wished students of religion to shift their conceptual frameworks into line with his revolutionary proposals about the nature of the sacred and its archetypes. So, despite his railing against reductionism, Eliade was just as reductionist as anybody (see Strenski 1976). I preferred to let competing explanations of religion fight it out in the open. For me, calling some account of a religious phenomenon 'reductive' is not necessarily a criticism: it is simply a fact (if indeed the charge be true). Now, whether or not a specific 'reductive' explanation gets us nearer the truth is what ultimately should matter – not whether in every case it is 'religious' or not. It is not ruled out from the start. It is thus on the basis of an explanation's being true or interesting that we should applaud it – not on the basis of whether or not it affronts the particular theory of religion we happen to cherish. Our theories must always be open to revision and refutation. We must be open to change. So, I think again not about 'who' put the 'holes in bread', but why are there holes in bread at all. Reduction always presses the possibility of conceptual change, and therefore is to be welcomed. I have tried to make this 'come hell or high water' openness to difference and change a guiding principle in leading the North American editorial board of *Religion*. Our overriding concern has been that articles – whether reductive or not – engage *religion*, period.

Now, this is not to abandon non-reductive or autonomous explanations of religious phenomena. In fact, I myself want to do much more of that because it has not, I believe, been lately convincingly done – except for Ninian Smart's various creative efforts in this regard. Here I shall try to make those outside the field of religious studies in particular informed about the religious nature of things usually seen under other aspects alone. I want to carve out what the 'religious' components of aspects of contemporary life might be. There seems to be a real need for this, since not enough of our appreciation of our world takes into account that people actually do things for religious purposes – not disguised purposes of other kinds. And having done things for religious purposes, we do not necessarily know very well what to make of these events, or how to predict what will follow next. For instance, my recent interventions into the debates about Waco reflect my puzzlement about what assuming a certain conception of the religious nature of Branch Davidian leader David Koresh's behavior entails (see Strenski 1993a and 1994b). In the case of Waco, the claim that Koresh's behavior could be anticipated because he adhered to an Eliadean millennial mythic pattern is stretching credibility of government agents rather far – especially when this pattern supposedly dictates that the 'cult almost never initiates violence, but defends itself from threat to its continued existence' (Rosenfeld 1993). Where is the referee who stands in the midst of opposed forces to decide whether someone who 'feels' he or she is under attack really is? Similarly, just to say that the government agents only needed to 'understand' Koresh better likewise flies in the face of the months of real efforts government agents exerted to make sense of Koresh and his plans. I believe that other conceptions of religion, and other explanations of religion than those recommended by my opponents, could have been more credible to government forces. For one, 'religion' is not necessarily good, and thus explanations which either glamorize the Koreshes of the world by casting them as characters in a noble myth, or which plead for more patience where more than enough may have been expended, are unlikely to be helpful. Perhaps the tragedy of needless death at Waco could have been averted if we had had notions and explanations of religion which did not flat out fly in the face of good sense.

If the frequency and enthusiasm with which colleagues in other departments raid our field are any indication, religious studies commands the best material in the humanities and social sciences. That is why I am optimistic about our future. Most of the time I feel that we are just beginning.

References

Eliade, Mircea. 1937. 'Postface' to Nae Ionescu, *Roza Vanturilor*. Bucharest.
—— 1969. *The Quest*. New York: Harper & Row.
—— 1972. *Zalmoxis*. Chicago: The University of Chicago Press.
—— 1977. *No Souvenirs*. New York: Harper & Row.
——. 1981. *Autobiography, Volume I: (1907-1937)*. New York: Harper & Row.
——. 1988. *Autobiography, Volume II: (1937-1960)*. Chicago: The University of Chicago Press.
Farias, Victor. 1987. *Heidegger et le Nazisme*. Paris: Editions Verdier.

Harries, Karsten. 1976. 'Heidegger as Political Thinker'. *Review of Metaphysics* 29.

Honigsheim, Paul. 1960. 'The Influence of Durkheim and His School on the Study of Religion'. pp. 233–46 in *Essays on Sociology and Philosophy by Emile Durkheim, et al.*, edited by Kurt H. Wolff. New York: Harper.

Rosenfeld, Jean. 1993. 'Fight Mythology with Words, not Tanks.' *The Los Angeles Times* (April 21):B7.

Strenski, Ivan. 1976. 'Reductionism and Structural Anthropology'. *Inquiry* 19:73–89.

—— 1982. 'Heidegger is No Hero'. *The Christian Century* (May 19):598–601.

—— 1985. 'Comparative Study of Religion: A Theological Necessity', *The Christian Century* 101/5 (6–13 February 1985):126–8.

—— 1987a. *Four Theories of Myth in Twentieth-Century History*. London: Macmillan; Iowa City: University of Iowa Press.

—— 1987b. 'Henri Hubert, Racial Science and Political Myth'. *Journal of the History of the Behavioral Sciences* 23:353–67.

—— 1989. 'Theories and Social Facts: A Reply to My Critics'. *Method and Theory in the Study of Religion* 1:196–212.

—— 1993a. 'Lessons for Religious Studies in Waco?' *JAAR* 61:567–74

—— 1993b. 'Mircea Eliade, Some Theoretical Problems'. *Religion in Relation*. London: Macmillan; Columbia: University of South Carolina Press.

—— 1993c. 'Political Culture, Religious Culture and Sacrifice'. pp. 293–322 in *Religious Transformations and Socio-Political Change: Eastern Europe and Latin America*, edited by L. Martin. Berlin: Mouton.

—— 1994a. 'Reduction without Tears'. pp. 95–107 in *Religion and Reductionism*, edited by T. Indinopulos and E. Yonan. Leiden: E. J. Brill.

—— 1994b. ' "Understanding Waco": Rejoinder to Stange and Rosenfeld'. *JAAR* 62:938–46.

—— 1995. 'Morality and Myth'. *International Journal of Comparative Religion and Philosophy* 1:1–12.

—— 1996. 'Between Theory and Speciality: Sacrifice in the 90s' *Religious Studies Review* 22:13–5.

—— 1997. *Durkheim and the Jews of France*. Chicago: The University of Chicago Press.

Index

Printed in the United States
94768LV00002B/169-198/A